AF746310

Aerodrome Governance in Asia

Sandeepa Bhat B.
Editor

Aerodrome Governance in Asia

Legal and Managerial Perspectives

Springer

Editor
Sandeepa Bhat B.
The West Bengal National University
of Juridical Sciences
Kolkata, West Bengal, India

ISBN 978-981-96-7567-8 ISBN 978-981-96-7568-5 (eBook)
https://doi.org/10.1007/978-981-96-7568-5

© The Editor(s) (if applicable) and The Author(s), under exclusive license to Springer Nature Singapore Pte Ltd. 2025

This work is subject to copyright. All rights are solely and exclusively licensed by the Publisher, whether the whole or part of the material is concerned, specifically the rights of translation, reprinting, reuse of illustrations, recitation, broadcasting, reproduction on microfilms or in any other physical way, and transmission or information storage and retrieval, electronic adaptation, computer software, or by similar or dissimilar methodology now known or hereafter developed.
The use of general descriptive names, registered names, trademarks, service marks, etc. in this publication does not imply, even in the absence of a specific statement, that such names are exempt from the relevant protective laws and regulations and therefore free for general use.
The publisher, the authors and the editors are safe to assume that the advice and information in this book are believed to be true and accurate at the date of publication. Neither the publisher nor the authors or the editors give a warranty, expressed or implied, with respect to the material contained herein or for any errors or omissions that may have been made. The publisher remains neutral with regard to jurisdictional claims in published maps and institutional affiliations.

This Springer imprint is published by the registered company Springer Nature Singapore Pte Ltd.
The registered company address is: 152 Beach Road, #21-01/04 Gateway East, Singapore 189721, Singapore

If disposing of this product, please recycle the paper.

Contents

Chapter 1
Chicago Convention and Airport Governance

Sandeepa Bhat B.

Abstract Airports play a pivotal role in the safe and orderly development of international civil aviation. Although the airports belong to individual States, leaving their governance entirely to the respective State results in chaos and confusion due to the absence of uniformity. Hence, the Chicago Convention 1944 incorporates some significant provisions relating to airport governance. In addition, the International Civil Aviation Organisation (ICAO) is entrusted with the responsibility to develop international standards and recommended practices (SARPs) relating to aerodromes. SARPs are developed over the years by ICAO in the form of Annexes to the Chicago Convention, and they are frequently updated especially due to the changing dimensions of civil aviation. The departure from these international standards and recommended practices is not permissible unless there are compelling reasons for States. Hence, understanding the SARPs and implementing them in their true spirit are most significant for safe and efficient air transportation. In this introductory chapter, the author first discusses relevant provisions of the Chicago Convention. Subsequent parts are devoted to evaluating different SARPs relating to airport governance. The major focus of discussions here is on aerodrome requirements under Annex 14, aeronautical information service under Annex 15, safety standards under Annex 19, and facilitation requirements under Annex 9. The procedural aspects to supplement SARPs provided under ICAO Procedures for Air Navigation Services (PANS) are discussed in the last part of this chapter.

Keywords Airport Council International (ACI) · Aviation security · Chicago Convention · Customs and clearance · ICAO Council · International Civil Aviation Organisation (ICAO) · Procedures for Air Navigation Services (PANS) · Safety management system (SMS) · Standards and Recommended Practices (SARPs) · State Safety Programme (SSP)

S. Bhat B. (✉)
Centre for Aviation and Space Laws, The WB National University of Juridical Sciences, Kolkata, India
e-mail: sandeep@nujs.edu

© The Author(s), under exclusive license to Springer Nature Singapore Pte Ltd. 2025

S. Bhat B. (ed.), *Aerodrome Governance in Asia*,
https://doi.org/10.1007/978-981-96-7568-5_1

1 Introduction

Soon after understanding the military advantages of aircraft, the States started to produce more and more aircraft for military uses. The First and the Second World Wars witnessed a huge increase in the production of aircraft.[1] After these wars, the aircraft and pilots became available for civilian services. In addition, the second half of the twentieth century saw tremendous developments in technology. All these factors resulted in the development of civil aviation as a popular and most efficient means of transportation especially after the Second World War.[2] Such a boom in civil aviation necessitated the construction of airports with the necessary facilities for air traffic across the globe. Systematic administration of airports also gained significance for maintaining air travel safe and efficient.

The need for the unification of rules regulating international air travel was first highlighted by an eminent French lawyer, Paul Fauchille.[3] His efforts in collaboration with the French Government for drafting a treaty in 1903 are hailed as the first attempt to draft a comprehensive international regime on aviation. Unfortunately, it failed due to the reluctance of States.[4] While the Paris Convention 1919 emerged as the first major multilateral norm to govern civil aviation after the First World War, the Chicago Convention 1944 substituted the former as a new international norm.[5] The Chicago Convention stands as the grund norm of international aviation law, and over the years, it has been supplemented by other instruments to deal with different issues concerning civil aviation.[6] The International Civil Aviation Organization (ICAO) was established under the Chicago Convention as a nodal agency, which started its functioning as a specialised agency of the United Nations in 1947.[7]

Airport governance, being an integral part of civil aviation, is subject to the norms of the Chicago Convention and its related instruments. The ICAO plays a definitive role in systematically updating Chicago Convention norms. Hence, it is pertinent to understand the foundational norms of the Chicago Convention applicable to airport governance before probing into different scenarios prevailing in Asian countries.

---

[1] 'History of Aviation', *Spartan College of Aeronautics and Technology*, available at <https://www.spartan.edu/news/history-of-aviation/> Last visited, 29 October 2024.

[2] *Id.*

[3] Peter H. Sand, Jorge de Sousa Freitas & Geoffrey N. Pratt, 'An Historical Survey of International Air Law before the Second World War,' *McGill Law Journal*, Vol. 7, No. 1, 1960, pp. 24–42 at p. 27.

[4] Paul Fauchille, *Trait é de Droit International Public,* Part 1, (Paris: Rousseau & Co., 1923) pp. 586–588.

[5] Arthur K. Kuhn, 'The Beginnings of Aerial Law', *American Journal of International Law,* Vol. 4, No.1, 1910, pp. 109–132 at pp. 111 & 115.

[6] See Michel Bourbonniere & Louis Haeck, 'Military Aircraft and International Law: Chicago Opus 3', *Journal of Air Law and Commerce*, Vol. 66, Issue 3, 2001, pp. 885–978.

[7] Karen Mingst, 'International Civil Aviation Organization', *Encyclopedia Britannica,* 18 November 2023, available at <https://www.britannica.com/topic/International-Civil-Aviation-Organization> Last visited, 29 October 2024.

2 The Chicago Convention Provisions Relating to Airport Governance

The Chicago Convention has 96 Articles and 19 Annexes that contain various legal obligations, standards, rules, procedures and guidelines. All the signatories of the Chicago Convention are bound to formulate their own national legislation as per the Chicago framework. While there were differences of opinion at the Chicago Conference regarding transit and traffic rights for international air transport, the matters of aviation safety, efficiency and orderly development were completely free from any controversy.[8] Hence, access to airports as well as types of access, which were parts of transit or traffic rights, were subject to two separate agreements; the International Air Services Transit Agreement 1944 and the International Air Transport Agreement 1944. However, the remaining aspects of airport governance are dealt with under the Chicago Convention.

To start with, the contracting States are empowered to designate routes and airports for international air service within their territories as per Article 68 of the Chicago Convention. Under Article 10, the States are entitled to conduct customs and other examinations of aircraft entering their territories. The aircraft of other States must land and depart only from designated customs airports. Every State is obligated to publish the particulars of all its designated customs airports. Also, those particulars must be furnished to ICAO for circulation to contracting States.

Article 25 of the Chicago Convention, though not directly on airport governance, is related to it. It outlines the obligation of States in case of distress or emergencies. While the States have a concrete mandate to assist aircraft in distress, they should also allow the owners of aircraft and the State of registration of aircraft to take necessary measures to provide assistance. Since in a majority of cases emergency situations arise during the takeoff or landing of aircraft,[9] necessary facilities in airports to provide assistance have become essential for ensuring safety in civil aviation. Recent developments in India stand as one of the examples of States realising the significance of airports in emergency assistance.[10]

Similar to Article 25, Articles 14 and 16 of the Chicago Convention have a connection with airport governance. The States are obligated to take measures to prevent the spread of communicable diseases under Article 14. Though this provision covers all aspects of civil aviation, the measures at airports become very significant in preventing communicable diseases crossing borders via infected air passengers. The

---

[8] 'Building on a Strong Foundation: ICAO's Precursors,' *ICAO History*, available at <https://www.icao.int/about-icao/History/Pages/civil-aviation-pre-icao.aspx> Last visited, 29 October 2024.

[9] 'Accidents by Flight Phase', *Airbus*, available at <https://accidentstats.airbus.com/accidents-by-flight-phase/> Last visited, 29 October 2024.

[10] See Murali Krishnan, 'Indian Air Safety in Focus after Series of Technical Faults,' *Made for Minds*, 25 July 2022, available at <https://www.dw.com/en/indian-airline-safety-in-focus-after-series-of-technical-glitches/a-62587289> Last visited, 29 October 2024; see also Arijit Garg, 'Aviation Update: Three international flights made emergency landing in India last week', *Zee news*, 18 July 2022.

world has already faced the COVID-19 pandemic and the regulators have clearly understood the importance of this provision as well as the need for adequate infrastructure at airports. Recently, the Airport Council International (ACI) has started a health accreditation system for airports to ensure passenger safety.[11]

Article 16 deals with the search of aircraft as well as the inspection of certificates and other documents of carriage. This has to be performed by the airport authorities and it is very significant since it has a direct connection with aviation security. All requisite facilities in this regard should be in place at international airports as the provision also mandates the prevention of unreasonable delay.

Article 15 is an important provision for establishing uniformity in airport charges. It says that the public airports must be open for the aircraft of other contracting States under uniform conditions, and all charges and fees for the use of air navigation facilities must be imposed by the contracting States in a uniform manner. The well-established principles of most favoured nation treatment and national treatment as envisaged under the GATT-WTO regime are also applicable here for the use of airports and facilities at airports.[12] The provision also requires the publication of charges and its communication to ICAO. The ICAO has the right to review the charges and make recommendations to the State levying the charges upon a representation by any contracting State.

The significance of airport charges has been highlighted by the ACI.[13] If we look from a practical perspective, airport charges have a very small impact on consumers and form a negligible portion of the total airline operational costs. However, these charges are a good source of revenue for airport authorities and governments.[14] The revenue generated from airport charges is the backbone of airports whenever they need to recover costs and have to finance infrastructural development for the benefit of the customers of civil aviation.[15] However, such revenue generation should not result in arbitrary imposition of airport charges on foreign aircraft.

Articles 22 to 24, which deal with the aspects of immigration, customs and clearance, have a direct connection with airport governance. Article 22 is a general provision on preventing administrative delays in connection with immigration, quarantine, customs and clearance. Every contracting State is obligated to take necessary steps to expedite aviation operations. Article 23 asks the contracting States to ensure that the customs and immigration procedures are set in accordance with established practices or recommendations, and Article 24 provides for customs duty exemption in

---

[11] 'Three Indian Airports Gets ACI Airport Health Accreditation for Safe Travel', available at <https://travelobiz.com/three-indian-airports-get-aci-health-accreditation-for-safe-travel/> Last visited, 2 January 2023.

[12] Chicago Convention, Art. 15.

[13] Patrick Lucas, 'Airport Charges: Challenging the Conventional Wisdom,' *ACI World Insights*, 16 December 2021, available at <https://blog.aci.aero/airport-charges-challenging-the-conventional-wisdom/> Last visited, 29 October 2024.

[14] *Id*.

[15] 'Airport Charges: turning the page on the regulatory relics of the past-ACI Insight', available at <https://blog.aci.aero/airport-charges-challenging-the-conventional-wisdom/> Last visited, 29 October 2024.

connection with foreign aircraft or their parts. Although every country has a separate set of legal rules to deal with the aspects connected with immigration, customs and clearance, how airports facilitate the immigration, customs and clearance authorities within their area falls under the scope of airport governance. Such facilitation to prevent unnecessary delay also requires adequate infrastructure at airports.

The contracting States are also mandated by Article 28 to provide requisite facilities for air navigation, which include airports, meteorological services, radio services and other navigational aid. They should put into operation different standard systems and publish aeronautical maps and charts to assist in improving civil aviation. The Council of ICAO, under Article 69, is empowered to test the adequacy of air navigation facilities and recommend the requisite improvement to the concerned contracting State. The ICAO Council is empowered to provide financial assistance to States in this regard.[16] Even the administration of airports and air navigation facilities may be undertaken by the ICAO Council upon the request of a contracting State.[17]

Articles 37 and 38 of the Chicago Convention are the two most significant provisions in connection with all aspects of civil aviation. Article 37 recognises the need for international standards and recommended practices and procedures to avoid confusion arising out of differential standards across the globe. While each contracting State has an obligation to strive towards the highest practicable degree of uniformity that facilitates and improves air navigation, the ICAO has been entrusted with the responsibility to develop and update international standards and recommended practices and procedures to be followed by the member States. This mandate is reiterated under Article 54 of the Chicago Convention, which stipulates the mandatory functions of the ICAO Council. Consequently, ICAO has developed nineteen annexes to the Chicago Convention over a period of time. These provisions of the Chicago Convention keep it as a living code since the Annexes of the Convention are amended and updated regularly by the ICAO to improve the existing standards and practices.[18]

A meticulous probe into Article 37 indicates that the open-ended list of areas provided therein for ICAO's work deals with several aspects of airport governance and related areas. A reading into Article 38 indicates that the standards and procedures set or amended by the ICAO are not always mandatory for the contracting States to follow. If it is impracticable for a State to implement any international standard or procedure, the difference between the practice of that State and the international standard has to be notified by the concerned State to the ICAO. This has been hailed as the strength of the Chicago Convention as it aims at uniformity while permitting a certain amount of flexibility to the States, which indicates the respect for sovereignty.[19]

The flexibility provided to the States is not unbridled. It has to be sparingly used only when there is any good reason for showcasing the impracticability. This

---

[16] Chicago Convention, Art. 70.

[17] *Id.*, Art. 71.

[18] See *id.*, Art. 90 for adoption and amendment of annexes.

[19] Assad Kotaite, 'Sovereignty under Great Pressure to Accommodate the Growing Need for Global Cooperation,' *ICAO Journal*, Vol. 50, No.10, 1995, p. 20.

strict standard has been reflected in the resolution of the ICAO Council, dated 13 April 1948, which asked the contracting States to keep the deviation to an absolute minimum.[20] Moreover, a reading into Article 12 of the Chicago Convention also unveils the obligation undertaken by the contracting States to adhere to the standards established from time to time under the Chicago Convention. Accordingly, the standards and procedures set by the ICAO are of utmost significance.

The annexes developed by the ICAO in the form of Standards and Recommended Practices (SARPs) emanate from different provisions of the Chicago Convention. A single set of SARPs solely designated for various factors related to the governance of Aerodromes was first developed as Annex 14 by the ICAO Council on 29 May 1951. With the developments in aviation-related technologies, this Annex has the credit of being one of the most frequently updated Annex.[21] Annex 14 has been divided into two parts. While Volume 1 deals with aerodrome design and operations, Volume 2 covers heliports. For this chapter, only Volume 1 is relevant, and the current applicable Annex in this regard is the ninth edition of July 2022.[22]

Annex 15 of the Chicago Convention is on Aeronautical Information Service and it imposes an obligation on the Contracting States to publish the differences between the practice at their national level and the SARPs prescribed by the ICAO through the Aeronautical Information Service. It is an additional obligation of Member States apart from Article 38 of the Convention. Upgradation or discontinuation of any facility, service or procedure that may have an adverse impact on aircraft operations should also be notified in accordance with the provisions of Annex 15.[23]

Even though air transportation is considered as one of the safest modes of travel,[24] with the growth in air transport, safety concerns have increased in air travel. Airports, being starting points of air travel, need proper safety mechanisms in place. As State practices in addressing aviation safety differed significantly, the necessity of harmonisation was felt by the international community.[25] This resulted in the adoption of Annex 19 by the ICAO Council on 25 February 2013, which came into force on 14 November 2013. The first edition of Annex 19 unified the then existing domestic

[20] Eugene Pepin, 'ICAO and other Agencies Dealing with Air Regulation', *Journal of Air Law and Commerce*, Vol. 19, Issue 2, 1952, pp. 152–165 at pp. 153 & 154.

[21] See Suzanne K. Kearns, *Fundamentals of International Aviation*, (Oxon: Routledge, 2018) p. 150; see also 'ACI welcomes ground-breaking amendments to ICAO Standards,' *International Airport Review*, 8 November 2018, available at <https://www.internationalairportreview.com/news/77607/aci-amendment-icao-standard/> Last visited, 30 October 2024.

[22] See Annexes to the Convention on International Civil Aviation (ICAO)' *Federal Office of Civil Aviation*, available at <https://www.bazl.admin.ch/bazl/en/home/themen/legislation/anhaenge-icao.html> Last visited, 30 October 2024.

[23] Michael Milde, *Essential Air and Space Law: International Air Law and ICAO*, (The Netherlands: Eleven International Publishing, 2016) p. 175.

[24] 'Report of Accidents Investigation and Prevention,' AIG Divisional Meeting (ICAO, 1999), pp. ii-4. The accident rate (measured in passengers facilities per 100 million passenger-kilometre) was approximately 0.025 in 2000 and 0.2 in 2006. *ICAO News Release*, PIO 5/02, 9 April 2002 and ICAO Doc. 9876, *Annual Report of the Council* (2006) p. 27.

[25] Jiefang Huang, *Aviation Safety through the Rule of Law-ICAO Mechanism and Practices*, (The Netherlands: Kluwer Law International, 2009) p. 9.

safety management provisions that were considered key in strengthening aviation safety.[26] This was further improved upon when the second edition was adopted in 2016.

Apart from the above aspects of airport governance, another significant element in the administration of airports is ensuring convenience to the users. Since international airports witness heavy traffic, having unnecessary obstacles in the entry or exit of aircraft, passengers or cargo goes against the objectives of the Chicago Convention. Accordingly, Annex 9 is developed for facilitating international air transport. It provides for the requirement of different facilities as well as procedures to be followed in different circumstances to ensure smooth air transportation. An overview of these annexes is provided in the subsequent sections of this chapter.

3 SARPs Under Annex 14

Volume 1 of Annex 14 has detailed provisions related to the aerodromes under ten chapters, five Appendices and two Attachments. While the first chapter provides general information with all definitions and other general aspects, the remaining nine chapters contain extensive information connected with various aspects of aerodrome operations, design, planning and governance.

3.1 Aerodrome Data

The second Chapter of Annex 14 contains the factors related to aeronautical data. There are 13 heads under which various recommendations and standards have been prescribed for the Contracting States. This Chapter deals with the process of determination and reporting of aeronautical data. These data are divided under three categories: critical data, essential data and routine data. This Chapter aims to ensure that there is uniformity in the process of collecting and reporting of aeronautical data among the Contracting States. The main criterion for the integration of aeronautical data shall be based upon the probability of risk that may result from the manipulation of data and upon the use to which the data item is put. Recommendations have been given for the protection of electronic data and routine electronic data.

This Chapter also deals with the establishment of an aerodrome reference point, which shall be located near the initial or planned geometric centre of the aerodrome. It further says that it shall normally remain where it was initially established. Another requirement is about the measurement and reporting of the exact location of the aerodrome reference point to the aeronautical information services authority in degrees, minutes and seconds. Other than this, the Chapter also deals with some very important issues like aerodrome and runway elevation, aerodrome reference temperature,

---

[26] *Supra* note 23, at 176.

aerodrome dimensions and related information, strength of pavements, pre-flight altimeter check location, declared distances etc. But the most significant part of this Chapter is the provisions on the condition of the movement area and related facilities which covers issues like the removal of snow and water from the runway and the recommendations related to rescue and firefighting.[27] It also includes the issue of the removal of disabled aircraft from the runway.[28]

The remaining portion of the Chapter includes various technical information regarding the visual approach slope indicator systems. It also has provisions for coordination between aeronautical information services and aerodrome authorities. It suggests an infrastructure under which such arrangements are available that are necessary for enabling the aeronautical information service units to obtain information so that they can provide up-to-date pre-flight information as well as to fulfil the requirement of in-flight information. Finally, the need for coordination between the aeronautical information services unit and aerodrome authorities is highlighted in this chapter. The significance of it is reflected in the coordination policies developed by several countries across the world.[29]

3.2 *Physical Characteristics*

The third Chapter of this Annex deals with extremely important issues like runways, taxiways, stop-ways, clearways, safety areas, radio altimeter operation areas, parking position of isolated aircraft, and de-icing and anti-icing facilities. It deals with some very significant environmental concerns as well. This Chapter contains all technical specifications for the above-mentioned aspects along with numerous recommendations to be followed by the Contracting States for good governance. There are several factors affecting the determination of orientation, siting and number of runways. Usability, being one of the most important factors, is determined with the help of wind distribution. Specific recommendations regarding this can be found in this Chapter.

Another important factor is the alignment of runways, which is essential for facilitating the provision of approaches and the fulfilment of the approach surface specifications. Chapter 4 as well as Attachment A (Section 1) of this Annex provide detailed information in this connection. It is also mentioned that in cases of re-location of any instrument runway, extra caution has to be taken regarding the areas over which

---

27 For example, the Airport Authority of India has established a specialised agency in this regard. See 'Rescue and Fire Service,' available at <https://www.aai.aero/en/content/fire-services/> Last visited, 30 October 2024.

28 Annex 14 to the Convention on Civil Aviation- Aerodromes, Vol. I, 9th Edition, 2022, Clause 2.10.

29 See, for example, <https://www.scaa.sc/files/Coordination%20policy%20and%20procedures%20establishing%20coordination%20between%20Aerodromes%20and%20Aeronautical%20Information%20Services.pdf> Last visited, 2 November 2024; see also <https://www.faa.gov/air_traffic/publications/media/aip.pdf> Last visited, 2 November 2024.

aeroplanes will be flying by using instrument approach and missed approach procedures. The authorities have to make sure that obstacles in these areas or other factors which may have an adverse impact on the flying of an aircraft are removed properly. Special attention should be given to noise-sensitive and residential areas to minimise interference via noise pollution.[30]

The runways are classified as primary runways, secondary runways, runways with stop-ways and clear-ways. Recommendations are given regarding their length and breadth, the choice of maximum permissible crosswind components, the distance between two parallel runways, requisite strength, slopes on runways and their various kinds, technical specifications for runway shoulder, runway stripes, runway turn pads etc. The need for a runway end safety area at the end of the runway strip has been highlighted in this Chapter. General as well as specific recommendations related to the dimensions of the runway end safety area and clearance of objects in this area are discussed. Recommendations on the location, length, width and slope of clear ways and stop ways and objects that can obstruct the aircraft therein are part of this Chapter. Just like runways, the Chapter contains detailed provisions regarding the design and physical characteristics of the taxiways along with necessary technical details. Finally, it covers de-icing and anti-icing facilities and related environmental concerns, such as groundwater contamination.

Thus, the main objective of this Chapter under Annex 14 is to address all aspects of the physical features of an aerodrome and to provide all Contracting States with technical details through detailed recommendations. All these recommendations are of paramount importance especially because several aviation accidents happen every year due to technical problems associated with these physical features. The Mangalore Air Crash is one of the major tragedies to remember in this connection.[31] Considering the importance of this issue, the ICAO has developed a draft of Runway Surface Condition Assessment, Measurement and Reporting (Cir 329 AN/191) in the year 2017.[32]

3.3 Restrictions Caused by Obstacles and Their Removal

Chapter 4 of Annex 14 deals with the management of obstacles which can cause danger to aviation operations. The key objectives of contents and recommendations of this chapter are first, to define the airspace which is in close vicinity of aerodromes and secondly, to ensure the maintenance of surrounding areas free from obstacles so that aeroplane operations at the aerodromes can be conducted safely. It seeks

[30] Annex 14, Clause 3.1.2.

[31] 'India jet crash leaves more than 150 dead in Mangalore', *The Guardian*, available at <https://www.theguardian.com/world/2010/may/22/india-budget-airline-jet-deaths> Last visited, 2 November 2024.

[32] 'Runway Surface Condition Assessment, Measurement and Reporting', available at <https://skybrary.aero/sites/default/files/bookshelf/3841.pdf> Last visited, 2 November 2024.

to prevent the possibility of aerodromes becoming inoperative due to the rapid and unplanned growth of obstacles around aerodromes. This can be made effective by the formation of several obstacle limitation surfaces, which include outer horizontal surface, conical surface, inner horizontal surface, approach surface, inner approach surface, transitional surface, inner transitional surface, balked landing surface and take-off climb surface. Depending on the type of runways, several of the above-mentioned obstacle limitation surfaces need to be kept in place.

In areas outside obstacle limitation surfaces, constructions or objects above a designated height should be regulated. Under certain special circumstances, there can be an increase in the obstacle clearance altitude/height of the objects infiltrating the obstacle limitation surfaces to prevent adverse impact on flight operation as well as the flight procedure design. Basic requirements for flight procedure design are further discussed in the Procedures for Air Navigation Services Aircraft Operations (PANS-OPS, Doc 8168).[33] The process of foundation and other necessary requirements of an obstacle-free surface for visual approach slope indicator systems are specified subsequently in this Annex. It is also recognised that certain objects that do not project above any of the surfaces mentioned in this Chapter may constitute a hazard to aviation. Accordingly, the need for appropriate measures to remove those objects is also highlighted in this Chapter.

3.4 Visual Aids

Chapters 5 to 7 of Annex 14 deal with three different types of visual aids: (i) Visual aids for navigation, (ii) Visual aids for denoting obstacles, and (iii) Visual aids for denoting restricted use areas. The key role of an airport's Visual and Navigational Aids (NAVAIDS) is to help pilots fly aircraft in a safe and efficient manner during the process of landing and take-off. It is the prime responsibility of every airport administration to have all visual and navigational aids in functional condition, which necessitates continuous maintenance.[34] Chapter 5 has detailed provisions on these aspects. Indicators like wind direction indicators and landing direction indicators, and different signalling devices such as signalling lamps, signal panels and areas are covered first in this Chapter.

The next aspect addressed here is the various types of markings on the runways and other operational areas. This Chapter recommends that in the case of intersectional runways, the more important runways should be marked (except for the runway side stripe) and such marks should be properly displayed. Separate guidelines for runway side stripe marking, which may either be continued across the intersection or interrupted, are also provided. Recommendations on runway designation marking,

---

[33] See <https://store.icao.int/en/procedures-for-air-navigation-services-pans-aircraft-operations-volume-i-flight-procedures-doc-8168> Last visited, 4 November 2024.

[34] 'Airport Navigational Aids', Louisiana Airport Managers Handbook, Chapter 8, April 2007, pp. 1–2.

runway centre line marking, threshold marking, aiming point marking, touchdown zone marking, runway side stripe marking, taxiway centre line marking, runway turn pad marking, runway-holding position marking, intermediate holding position marking, VOR aerodrome checkpoint marking, aircraft stand marking, apron safety lines, road-holding position marking, mandatory instruction marking and information marking are also provided in this Chapter.[35]

The use of different kinds of lights to assist the process of navigation is provided in the next part. While several types of lights are essential for air traffic management, lights that may affect the safety of civil aviation need to be eliminated. In this regard, the Chapter calls for elimination, screening or in suitable situations, alteration of non-aeronautical ground lights near an aerodrome which might threaten the safety of an aircraft operation. Laser emissions that may cause danger to aviation operations are also dealt with under this part. This Chapter also talks about emergency lighting, aeronautical beacons, approach lighting systems, visual approach slope indicator systems, circling guidance lights, runway lead-in lighting systems, runway threshold identification lights, runway edge lights, runway threshold and wing bar lights, runway end lights, runway centre line lights, runway touchdown zone lights, simple touchdown zone lights, rapid exit taxiway indicator lights, stop-way lights, taxiway centre line lights, taxiway edge lights, runway turn pad lights, stop bars, intermediate holding position lights, de-icing/anti-icing facility exit lights, runway guard lights, apron floodlighting, visual docking guidance system, advanced visual docking guidance system, aircraft stand manoeuvring guidance lights, road-holding position light, no-entry bar and runway status lights.[36]

The other two important aspects of navigational safety discussed in Chapter 5 are signs and markers used as visual aids. Two types of signs are recommended; fixed message signs and variable message signs. Guidance on signs is further contained in the Aerodrome Design Manual (Doc 9157),[37] Part 4. The purposes of signs are to designate an obligatory direction and provide information about a particular location or destination on a movement area or to furnish other information that are essential to comply with criteria of Chapter 9 of Annex 14. Different types of signs, such as, mandatory instruction sign, information sign, VOR aerodrome checkpoint sign, aerodrome identification sign, aircraft stand identification sign and road-holding position sign are discussed in detail.

About the markers, it is recommended that they must be brittle, and when located near a runway or taxiway, they must be kept sufficiently low. The frangibility of markers is subject to the guidance provided under Part 6 of the Aerodrome Design Manual (Doc 9157). The different types of markers that have been discussed are

---

[35] Ketan Pattekar, 'Types of Runway Configurations, Marking and Safety', available at <https://www.kpstructures.in/2021/08/types-of-runway-configurations-marking-and-safety.html> Last visited, 4 November 2024.

[36] Safwa Ashraf, 'Runway Lights Explained', available at <https://aviationforaviators.com/2022/02/09/runway-lights-explained/> Last visited, 28 December 2022.

[37] See <https://store.icao.int/en/aerodrome-design-manual-runways-doc-9157-part-1> Last visited, 4 November 2024.

unpaved runway edge markers, stopway edge markers, edge markers for snow-covered runways, taxiway edge markers, taxiway centre line markers, unpaved taxiway edge markers and boundary markers.[38] Recommendations are also made in this Chapter about different kind of markers as well as their minimum size.

The next category of visual aids is those used for denoting obstacles, which are dealt with under Chapter 6 of Annex 14. The importance of marking and lighting obstacles is discussed in detail in this Chapter. The markings are designated for minimising dangers to aircraft by manifesting the existence of the obstacles, though they do not necessarily reduce the operating hurdles created by an obstacle. The Chapter first stipulates the objects to be marked or lighted and then goes on to stipulate the ways of marking or lighting. Objects to be marked or lighted are categorised into those within and those outside the lateral boundaries of obstacle limitation surfaces. The former may include vehicles and other moving objects, excluding aircraft, on the area of an aerodrome designated for the movement of an aircraft. All of them must be marked properly, and if vehicles and aerodromes are used at night or in low visibility conditions, they have to be lighted.

The elevated aeronautical ground lights situated in the movement area should be marked to make them noticeable by day, and obstacle lights must not be installed on elevated ground lights or signs in the movement area. All obstacles need to be demarcated within the distance specified in this Chapter from the centre line of a taxiway, an apron taxiway or an aircraft stand taxi lane. Recommendations are provided for the use of taxiway, apron taxiway or an aircraft stand taxi lane at night, which need to be lighted properly. To prevent any hazard to aircraft from objects outside the lateral boundaries of obstacle limitation surfaces, similar requirements of marking and lighting are provided in this Chapter.

The technical requirements for marking and lighting mobile objects, fixed objects, overhead wires, cables, supporting towers and wind turbines are stipulated in the next part. The issue of installation setting angles for high-intensity obstacle lights is covered in this chapter. Objects to be lighted and marked as per the specifications of this Chapter shall be indicated by low, medium or high intensity obstacle lights, or by a combination of such lights. The types of lights to be used under low, medium or high intensity obstacle lights are also mentioned specifically. The number and arrangement of low, medium or high-intensity obstacle lights at each level to be marked shall be in such a manner that the object is denoted from every angle properly. Whenever there is any obstruction to a light in any direction by some other part of the object, or by a nearby object, additional lights have to be installed on that adjacent object or the part of the object that is obstructing the light. The use of specific colours and flags for marking different obstacles is also recommended.

Visual aids required for indicating the areas restricted for use are dealt with under Chapter 7. It has separate provisions for closed runways, taxiways, non-loadbearing surfaces, pre-threshold areas and unserviceable areas. There shall be markers indicating any portion of a taxiway, apron or holding bay that is not fit for the movement of an aircraft. A movement area that is used at night shall be marked properly with

[38] Annex 14, Clauses 5.5.2 to 5.5.8.

unserviceability lights. These visual aids are essential for aviation safety as they provide necessary warning to pilots if there is a hole in a taxiway or apron pavement or any unserviceable area.

3.5 Electrical System for Safety Operations

The quality of power supplied is a significant factor in determining the operational safety at an airport. Both external sources of electric power supply and local power generating facilities along with transformers and switchgear for distribution of electricity may be part of the electrical power supply system of an aerodrome. While stressing the adequate power supply at all points in time, this Chapter recommends that any equipment failure should not result in paralysing the pilots with insufficient visual and non-visual guidance or misleading information. Part 5 of the Aerodrome Design Manual provides additional guidance to avoid different types of malfunctions in the electrical systems. In case of failure of the primary power supply, the secondary source of supply should become active without wasting time. Recommendations for system designs and monitoring mechanism are also provided in this Chapter.[39]

3.6 Aerodrome Operational Services, Equipment and Installations

The first issue that has been covered in this penultimate Chapter is aerodrome emergency planning. This is one of the most significant aspects to minimise damage during any emergency. These emergencies, among others, may include technical problems, sabotage, unlawful seizure, natural disasters and public health emergencies. Every airport administration must develop an emergency plan to deal with such a variety of situations. Procedures for coordination among different aerodrome agencies and also other agencies in the vicinity, which may be of assistance in dealing with an emergency, are mentioned as the most significant elements of emergency planning. Those agencies may include air traffic control units, rescue and firefighting units, aerodrome administration, medical and ambulance services, police, health authorities, military, coast guard and others. Guidance material to assist the appropriate authority in establishing aerodrome emergency planning is given under Part 7 of the Airport Services Manual. Specific recommendations for the emergency operations centre and command post, communication system, dealing with emergencies in difficult environments and aerodrome emergency exercise are also provided in this part.

The next significant issue under this Chapter is rescue operations and fire-fighting. Saving life in case of an aircraft accident or incident is the prime function of rescue

[39] Annex 14, Clauses 8.1 to 8.3.

and fire-fighting services. The rescue and fire-fighting services provide routes of escape to the occupants and also make necessary arrangements for rescuing those occupants who are unable to make arrangements on their own. Some of the most important factors that may make the rescue process more effective in an incident or accident are how well the personnel are trained, the efficiency of the equipment and how rapidly the entire process of rescue can start. The Chapter contains provisions on the level of protection to be provided, the extinguishing agents, rescue equipment, response time etc. It also contains many recommendations regarding various infrastructural requirements; for example, emergency access road, location of the fire stations, communication and alerting systems, number of rescue and fire-fighting vehicles to be available at the time of rescue operations etc.[40]

Detailed recommendations for disabled aircraft removal, reducing wildlife strike hazard, apron management service, servicing of aircraft at the ground, aerodrome vehicle operations, surface movement guidance and control systems, siting of equipment and installations on operational areas, fencing, security lighting and autonomous runway incursion warning system are also found here.[41] Since the operational safety of air transportation is heavily dependent on the above-mentioned factors, airport authorities need to pay special attention to all these factors.

3.7 Aerodrome Maintenance

The last Chapter of Annex 14 is on the maintenance of various facilities in airports. It contemplates the need for a proper maintenance programme by respecting the need for safety, regularity and efficiency of air navigation. Recommendations are provided to member States on issues like maintenance of pavements, removal of contaminants, specifications of runway pavement overlays and visual aids. The purpose of such a maintenance programme is to have all facilities in a serviceable condition so that the aviation safety is not impaired by the disablement of navigational or other important facilities available at an aerodrome. The maintenance programme is also preventive in nature to avoid any kind of future danger to operational safety. It is recommended that the design and application of the maintenance programme should observe human factors principles that can be found in the Human Factors Training Manual (Doc 9683)[42] and in part 8 of the Airport Services Manual.[43]

[40] 'Rescue and Fire Fighting Services', *Sky Brary*, available at <https://skybrary.aero/articles/rescue-and-fire-fighting-services/> Last visited, 5 November 2024.

[41] Annex 14, Clauses 9.3 to 9.12.

[42] See <https://store.icao.int/en/human-factors-training-manual-doc-9683> Last visited, 5 November 2024.

[43] Annex 14, Clause 10.1.

4 SARPs on Airport Safety Management

Unharmed operation of aircraft is the need of the hour to ensure the optimal functioning of the global air transportation system. In this regard, the ICAO supports the continuous growth of revolutionary policies and the strategic development of improved safety norms. The main idea of the ICAO is to execute a State Safety Programme (SSP) that systematically takes care of the factors that may cause safety risks and assists the Member States in the proper implementation of better measures at the national level.[44] As an outcome of ICAO's High-level Safety Conference 2010, the Air Navigation Commission suggested having a new annex on aviation safety by following a two-phased development process.[45] While the focus of the first phase was to construct the safety management annex by unification and reconstruction of SARPs that are already in existence, the second phase was more in terms of the State responsibility for safety management at the municipal level.[46] This resulted in the development of Annex 19 to the Chicago Convention. Even though the ambit of coverage of safety mechanism is huge and all safety aspects are not connected with airports, airport governance forms a major part of it.

Annex 19 to the Chicago Convention contains five chapters and three appendixes to deal with safety management issues. Chapter 3 of Annex 19 points out the safety management duties that are directly imposed upon the State parties. Starting with a primary aviation legislation, States are obligated to put in place a proper system of licensing, certification, authorisation and approval. States must ensure the implementation of the safety management system (SMS) requirements by various service providers. The list of service providers includes the air traffic service providers and the operators of certified aerodromes. Safety risk assessment and management, proper surveillance, safety performance, and safety promotion through the dissemination of information are also given due importance. Thus, the focus of this Chapter is on the establishment and maintenance of SSP as well as ensuring appropriate State safety oversight standards.

The ICAO has established the SSP as an integral part of the SMS for better implementation of the safety norms at the national level. The Chicago Convention under Annexes 1, 6, 8, 11, 13, 14, and 19 contain the requisites for the establishment of an SSP by the member States so that a sustainable level of safety can be achieved in regular aviation operations. The main objective of the SSP is to synchronise and broaden the safety provisions for better management of all categories of aviation service providers. The regulatory setup for the execution and maintenance of a State's

---

[44] 'Safety Management,' *ICAO - Safety,* available at <https://www.icao.int/safety/safetymanagement/Pages/default.aspx> Last visited, 5 November 2024.

[45] See High-Level Safety Conference 2010, ICAO Doc. 9935, HLSC 2010.

[46] 'ICAO Annex 19, Safety Management', *Sky Brary*, available at < https://skybrary.aero/articles/icao-annex-19-safety-management > Last visited, 5 November 2024.

safety programme is provided under Chapter 11 of the ICAO Safety Management Manual (SMM).[47]

Chapter 4 deals with SMS and it emphasises the need for establishing SMS by different service providers. The SMS established by the service providers needs to be subject to the approval of the State/s concerned. Chapter 5 deals with the collection, analysis and sharing of safety data and safety information. States are obligated to establish and maintain proper systems in this regard. Collected data and information are also to be protected to prevent any misuse. Information sharing and exchange networks among the users of the aviation system are also to be promoted as per this Chapter.[48]

Even though the scope of SMS is very vast, it is one of the basic criteria for the aerodrome certification process. The process of aerodrome certification is governed by Volume I of Annex 14 to the Chicago Convention, which says that in order to certify the aerodromes used for international air transport, the member States are required to fulfil all specifications of Annex 14 as well as other relevant specifications mentioned under the appropriate regulatory framework of the ICAO.[49] In addition, the certification process must be in accordance with the aerodrome manual, which would contain information on many aspects among which the safety management system is one of the most significant one. Such an aerodrome manual has to be approved properly prior to the certification process of the aerodrome,[50] and it stands as the basic requisite for the aerodrome certification process.[51] The other equally significant document is the Aerodrome Design Manual.[52] Factors like runway, taxiways, aprons, pavements and holding bays safety, visual aids, electrical systems, frangibility etc. are significant while obtaining certificates and the specifications for these are detailed in Annex 14, Volume I, which is already discussed.

The ICAO has a specialised monitoring mechanism for the better functioning of the SMS and SSP. It has developed a State Safety Programme Implementation Assessment (SSPIA), which is a performance-based activity that falls under the framework of Continuous Monitoring Approach (CMA) within the scope of the Universal Safety Oversight Audit Programme (USOAP). Through this programme, an assessment process is undertaken by the ICAO to objectively review the level of maturity of SSPs by assessing the mechanism of the implementation and maintenance of SSPs by different member States. The ICAO is also working in the direction of improving its methodology, processes and tools so that the SSPIAs can be conducted

47 'ICAO State Safety Programme', *Sky Brary*, available at <https://skybrary.aero/articles/state-safety-programme-ssp> Last visited, 5 November 2024.

48 Pratik Suresh Purswani, 'Annex 19- Safety Management', *Academia*, available at <https://www.academia.edu/30595690/ICAO_Annex_19_Safety_Managemnt> Last visited, 5 November 2024.

49 See Annex 14, Clause 1.4.

50 *Id.*, Clause 1.4.4.

51 Doc 9774-AN/969, First Edition, 2001.

52 Doc 9157-AN/901, Third Edition, 2006.

in a more efficient manner.[53] Under the CMA, audits are performed regularly with a continuing process of gathering safety information. There are eight vital areas covered under these audits, including Air Navigation Services (ANS) and Aerodrome and Ground Aids (AGA), which are directly connected with the issue of airport governance.[54]

5 SARPs Related to Facilitation

Annex 9 of the Chicago Convention is developed to ensure smooth and efficient performance of aircraft operations. It attempts to address such issues that may cause unnecessary delay in aircraft operations. Obligations under this Annex are dual in nature with a combination of positive and negative lists. The positive obligations are directed towards having facilities that ease passenger and cargo traffic. The restraint on the imposition of stringent rules on entry and exit, cumbersome border control measures, delay in clearing cargo, unnecessary paperwork etc. are examples of obligations that are negative in nature. The basic principle of this Annex, as mentioned in the first Chapter, is to strike a balance between the smooth functioning of aircraft operations and the safety and security of civil aviation.

Annex 9, under nine distinct Chapters, mainly deals with three subject matters-aircraft, passenger and cargo. It contains specific provisions for providing certain facilities to all three subject matters. The first Chapter contains important definitions and general principles for expediting the completion of different formalities of air transport without compromising the law. The next three chapters contain detailed procedures of different formalities to be complied with upon entry or departure of the aircraft, passengers and cargo. Just like the first Chapter, all three Chapters begin with the general principles on expediting different processes upon entry or during departure of aircraft, passengers and cargo; however, without disrupting the application of laws relating to narcotics control, immigration control, aviation security etc. As per the requirements under Chapter 2, every State party is under an obligation to make such arrangements for aircraft that cover factors affecting public health, some global emergencies related to public health, disinfection of aircraft, documents that need to be produced upon entry or departure of an aircraft, electronic forms if any and other factors connected with international general aviation or other non-scheduled flights.[55]

---

[53] Ariel Wiess, 'What are ICAO State Safety Implementation Assessments', *Uniting Aviation*, 12 July 2021, available at <https://unitingaviation.com/news/safety/what-are-icao-state-safety-programme-implementation-assessments/> Last visited, 5 November 2024.

[54] See 'Guidelines for National Continuous Monitoring Coordinators of the Universal Safety Oversight Audit Programme', *ICAO*, Second edition, June 2021, p. 2, available at <https://www.icao.int/training/USOAP_iPack/ORD/NCMC_EN_Jun%202021_2Ed.pdf> Last visited, 5 November 2024.

[55] Erik Slavenas, 'Introduction to Annex 9: ICAO SARPs on Traveller Identification and Border Controls, available at <https://www.icao.int/Meetings/mrtd-madrid-2014/documents/7_Slavenas-Annex-9.pdf> Last visited, 6 November 2024.

Chapter 3 deals with the entry and exit of persons with their baggage and the formalities associated with it, which is extremely significant for ensuring aviation as the most efficient means of transportation. The main portion of this Chapter contains SARPs for travel documents and their inspection and review for the safe and orderly operation of civil aviation. It talks about Machine Readable Travel Documents (MRTDs) being used for the ease of transport. The specifications of Doc. 9303, part 1 must be followed by States in the issue of MRTDs. All State parties must periodically update the processes and security features of their travel documents to avoid any kind of falsification of data. Additionally, States must have full control over the process of issuance of travel documents to maintain the legality of the process. States are recommended to join the ICAO Public Key Directory (PKD) whenever they intend to issue electronic MRTDs. After discussions on entry formalities, this Chapter deals with departure procedures, and addresses aspects like advance passenger information, passenger name record, transit processes, handling of baggage, crew member certificates and facilities required in case of an emergency.

The next Chapter of Annex 9 deals with the entry and departure of cargo and other articles. The States are obligated to adopt and apply regulations and procedures on air cargo operations with a view to avoiding unnecessary delay. In the clearance of imported goods or goods intended for exportation, only relevant information, document or data shall be sought by the authorities concerned. Specific SARPs are found on materials imported or exported by aircraft operators, containers and pallets, mail documents and radioactive materials. Chapter 5 of this Annex contains standards and recommendations regarding the handling of inadmissible persons and deportees. State assistance in the acquisition of the replacement travel document, whenever required, is also stipulated under this Chapter.

Since airports are entry and exit points of air travel, the airport administration needs to discharge the majority of obligations stipulated above under Annex 9. In addition, Chapter 6 enumerates specific facilities and services to be in place at international airports. Recommendations on customs and immigration facilities, border clearance services, health and quarantine services etc. are provided. The compliance with Annex 9 requirements is mandatory even in the case of the privatisation of airports. Detailed recommendations are provided on airport traffic flow arrangements, clearance controls, dealing with unruly passengers and providing different amenities for passengers. Other important factors, such as, landing at an alternative airport, facilitation of search, rescue, investigation of accidents, salvage, transportation of persons with disabilities, assistance to victims of aviation accidents in special circumstances, and combating human trafficking are covered under Chapters 7 and 8. The last two chapters of this Annex deal with passenger data exchange systems and health-related aspects of civil aviation to reduce unnecessary barriers to air transport.

6 ICAO PANS Relating to Airport Governance

ICAO Procedures for Air Navigation Services (PANS) and SARPs are interdependent. While SARPs are substantive in nature and contain detailed specifications for facilitating smooth air transport services, PANS are procedural in nature. They deal with comprehensive procedures for continuous monitoring, and thus, ensure the successful implementation of standards laid down under different annexes. So, together they establish a framework under which the Member States are obligated to conform to similar standards and harmonised procedures.[56] Although PANS are very important for the development of the civil aviation sector, they have a different status than that of SARPs. While SARPs are formulated by the ICAO Council in pursuance of Article 37 and the process of application is mentioned under Article 90 of the Chicago Convention, PANS are mere recommendations to the State Parties. The PANS may in due course become SARPs based on their relevance, substantive nature and immutability, and thus, attain binding force. It is also significant to note here that though PANs do not fall under the purview of Article 38 of the Chicago Convention, a trend of publishing differences between State procedure and ICAO procedure in the Aeronautical Information Publications (AIPs) can be seen very often.[57]

The aspect of aerodrome governance has been discussed in detail under ICAO Doc. 9981, which is known as PANS-Aerodromes. The current version of this document is the third edition of 2020. It was developed by the Air Navigation Commission after realising the limitations of SARPs contained in Annex 14, Volume I. Since Annex 14 is more like a design manual, it was found useful in designing a new airport; however, its application to existing airports posed practical difficulties. Hence, the Air Navigation Commission came up with PANS-Aerodromes as a complementary document to Annex 14. It comprises PANS that are classified under two parts namely "Aerodrome Certification, Safety Assessments and Aerodrome Compatibility" and "Aerodrome Operational Management." These two parts are further classified into 4 and 9 chapters respectively. At the end of each part, they contain appendices that explain various procedures in detail along with some additional technicalities.

6.1 The Procedures for Aerodrome Certification, Safety Assessments and Aerodrome Compatibility

The first Chapter of Part-I of PANS-Aerodromes, being introductory in nature, describes various terms and procedures. The remaining three chapters contain

---

[56] ICAO Doc 9981, Procedures for Air Navigation Services: Aerodromes, 3rd edn., 2020, p. ix, available at <https://www.scribd.com/document/565932928/Icao-Doc-9981-Pans-Aerodromes-3rd-Edition-Yr2020> Last visited, 7 November 2024.

[57] *Id*, at x.

elaborate procedures connected with the certification, safety assessment and aerodrome compatibility. Chapter 2 delineates the fundamentals to be followed by the contracting States while providing certificates to aerodrome operators.[58] It includes every component starting from the meeting between the State and the aerodrome operator to the technical inspections of aerodromes[59] and after all verifications, the final approval and issuance of the certificate.[60] The entire verification process is comprehensive, and corroboration is done at every stage. The verification process starts with the approval or acceptance of all or relevant portions of the aerodrome manual and along with that on-site verification of aerodrome operational aspects including the safety management system (SMS) of the operator. In the subsequent stages, analysis of deviations from regulatory requirements is also done.

After the issuance of certificates, there is a requirement for continuous monitoring.[61] Appendix 1 to Part I of this Chapter further embodies a list of key technical and operational aspects that have to be checked during inspections and verifications. Appendix 2 contains provisions on data connected with safety occurrences. The attachments to this Part I provide for a checklist of potential issues for developing an aerodrome manual, guidelines on the initial certification process and a checklist that is useful to the State while forming an opinion on an aerodrome manual and initial certification process. These attachments play a definitive role in establishing uniformity by providing guiding principles for every State.

Chapter 3 focuses on key aspects of the safety assessment system. The utility of safety assessment as an integral part of the aerodrome SMS as a whole is described in this Chapter for appreciating its significance. The fundamental aspect of this Chapter is the assessment of risk arising out of any alteration of the design or deviation from any international safety standard in the existing set-up. Such safety hazards may often involve multiple stakeholders, and thus, the entire assessment must be conducted in such a manner that every organisation can become a subject of it. Therefore, the identification of various stakeholders before conducting a safety assessment is necessary.[62]

The last Chapter of this Part deals with techniques of evaluation of compatibility between aeroplane operations and the existing aerodrome infrastructure. Additionally, it also includes operational details under exceptional circumstances, such as, an aerodrome accommodating an aeroplane that is beyond the certified components of that aerodrome.[63] Alternatives to be used in exceptional cases where it is either impractical or physically impossible to comply with the design criteria of Annex 14, Volume I are also provided in this chapter.[64] There is a requirement for continuous monitoring by conducting periodic review under this Chapter whenever such

---

[58] *Id.*, Clause 2.1.2.

[59] *Id.*, Clause 2.3.2.

[60] *Id.*, Clause 2.3.6.

[61] *Id.*, Clause 2.5.

[62] *Id.*, Clause 3.4.1.2.

[63] *Id.*, Clause 4.1.1.

[64] *Id.*, at xii.

alternative measures, operational procedures and operating restrictions are in place. The attachments to Chapter 4 consist of data related to specific aeroplane characteristics.[65] The main purpose of providing these data is that it gives an opportunity to the aerodrome operator to draw comparisons between the distinct characteristics of commonly operated aeroplanes. Such data must be gathered from the documents prepared by aircraft manufacturers before any official assessment of the compatibility of aerodromes for different types of aircraft.

6.2 Aerodrome Operational Management

There are nine chapters under Part II, and each chapter has three specific segments. While the first segment of each chapter introduces the background and general principles, the second and third segments outline the objectives and operational practices respectively. The first Chapter of Part II along with the appendix and attachment contains the principles, obligations, and provisions that shall apply to the training of aerodrome personnel who are responsible for daily aerodrome operations, and includes within its scope, the training programmes and checklists for assessing their competence.[66]

The second Chapter addresses the issue of assessment and reporting data related to runway conditions. A list containing different methods and techniques in this connection is also provided in the Attachment to this Chapter. The next Chapter provides guidelines and procedures for the proper inspection of all types of aerodrome movement areas. It covers inspection of runways, taxiways, aprons, and their associated aeronautical lighting systems, markings and signs. The frequency of inspections needs to be decided on the basis of the magnitude of risk identified in SMS.

The next five chapters (Chapters 4 to 8) list all remaining safety concerns, especially in connection with safety on the ground. Chapter 4 talks about the precautionary methods to be observed during an ongoing work on the movement area of an aerodrome. The primary objective of this Chapter is to ensure effective execution of the work, and at the same time, protection of the worksite and workers along with ensuring smooth functioning of aircraft operations. The appendices and attachment to this chapter address aspects such as reduced runway length operations, procedures for worksite control and worksite checklist.

Chapter 5 deals with the issue of control and management of foreign object debris (FOD). The presence of FOD on the movement areas poses a serious threat to the safety of aircraft operations. This Chapter has detailed guidelines for having an efficient FOD control programme. It covers the aspects of prevention, identification, removal and evaluation of FOD. An equal importance is also given with respect to

[65] *Id.*, Attachment A to Chapter 4.

[66] *Id.*, Appendix to Chapter 1.

creating awareness as well as training and educating staff regarding the same.[67] Each of these aspects is detailed in three appendices to Chapter 5.

The methods for reducing aviation safety risks caused by wildlife hazards are discussed in Chapter 6. Active assessments of wildlife risks, expulsion or deterrence of hazardous wildlife, reporting and listing of incidents caused by wildlife,[68] habitat and management of land use[69] etc. are the aspects found in this Chapter. All these components together form part of a wildlife hazard management programme (WHMP), which needs to be developed by aerodrome operators.[70]

Chapter 7 contains provisions related to the identification of threats and minimisation of risks to apron safety through personnel awareness. It ensures better coordination among different agents who are associated with apron safety by defining their responsibilities. The appendix and attachment to Chapter 7 provide for airside vehicle rules and the circulation of information to apron users. Chapter 8 provides for a strategic framework under which the incidents of runway incursions,[71] excursions[72] and confusion can be prevented, and risks can be mitigated by identifying the potential danger. It focuses on the need for better cooperation and coordination among different stakeholders for the smooth functioning of safety programmes. The establishment of runway safety teams (RST)[73] and the formulation of runway safety plans are also stressed in this Chapter. In addition to these, the appendix and the attachment to this Chapter further provide for composition and terms of reference for the runway safety teams and also detailed guidelines on "hot spot",[74] common causes of runway safety events, and suspension or closure of runway operations.

The last Chapter of part II has specialised provisions for having an airside driver permit (ADP) scheme and a setup under which safety requirements for vehicles and equipment operating at an aerodrome can be achieved. The prime objective of Chapter 9 is the reduction in the number of accidents resulting from the use of vehicles in the airside areas that cause injury to persons and damage aircraft and property.[75] The appendices to this Chapter further contain complementary provisions on the framework for an airside vehicle driver training programme, radiotelephony and record keeping.

---

67 *Id.*, Clauses 5.3.1 to 5.3.4.

68 *Id.*, Clauses 6.3.1–6.3.4.

69 *Id.*, Clause 6.3.5.

70 *Id.*, Clause 6.3.1.1.

71 *Id.*, Clause 8.3.2.

72 *Id.*, Clause 8.3.3.

73 *Id.*, Clause 8.3.1.

74 Hot spot is "A location on an aerodrome movement area with a history or potential risk of collision or runway incursion, and where heightened attention by pilots/drivers is necessary."

75 ICAO Doc. 9981, Clause 9.1.2.

7 Conclusion

In the past, airports were simply terminus, just like bus terminuses, but at present, airports are very complex industrial enterprises. Considering the rapid growth in the aviation sector, airport governance has emerged as one of the most serious concerns of every State. Apart from the landing and departure of aircraft, every airport is involved in several types of technical and commercial activities on a regular basis, which need to be guided and monitored properly to ensure the highest level of safety.

It is already a settled principle that the States and their respective civil aviation authorities are primarily responsible for the governance of their airports. However, in the modern globalised world, the influence of the international legal framework at the domestic level is the undisputed reality. The Chicago Convention, being the *grund norm* of civil aviation, has a strong influence on the governance of airports across the globe. Apart from some direct provisions on airports, the Chicago Convention also provides for annexes developed by the ICAO to ensure uniform standards and practices relating to airport administration. Though deviation from annexes is possible, such deviations should only be on a justifiable basis and can be resorted to only by reporting to the ICAO Council. The substantive provisions of the ICAO annexes on standards and recommended practices are supplemented by the procedures provided under PANS.

Despite the Chicago Convention's norms to ensure proper administration of airports, implementation of them at the domestic level heavily depends on the awareness and willingness of administrative authorities. In the era of privatisation of airports, keeping a vigil on the compliance of norms by private agencies has also become an added difficulty for States. The ICAO, as a nodal agency, is attempting to unearth inadequacies and standard deviations through regular audits and monitoring. Cooperation of States in ensuring better administration of airports by implementing Chicago Convention standards and recommended practices is essential for preventing disarray in civil aviation.

Chapter 2
Airport Governance in Asia: Role of IATA

Kanchan Yadav

Abstract The International Air Transport Association (IATA), established in 1945, is a non-governmental and non-political organization, comprising more than three hundred airlines across the world. This commercial and voluntary multinational body operates with the goal of regulating and enhancing civil air transport throughout the world. Other than regulations and guidelines for the airlines, the IATA also provides tools, suggestions, and best practices for airports, to be implemented by the airport operators, governments, and other relevant entities. It has been widely recognised that without ensuring that the airports comply with certain minimum requirements regarding infrastructure, governance, and sustainability, safe and sustainable international air travel will simply not be possible. However, considering that the IATA membership is limited to airlines only and does not include any representatives of relevant airports or nations, implementation of IATA recommendations in aerodromes is abysmally low. The problem is also compounded by the fact that the IATA is a body with voluntary membership and lacks enforcement mechanisms, so it cannot ensure compliance across the different airports. Against this backdrop, this Chapter analyses the implementation of IATA's airport- related guidelines in the Asian continent, particularly in the context of three nations of different levels—Japan as a developed nation, India as a developing nation, and Bangladesh as a least developed nation. After analysing how these nations are faring regarding IATA's aerodrome-related guidelines, the author provides recommendations as to how to balance the need for better compliance of IATA's airport-related standards with the nation-specific challenges.

Keywords Airport Consultative Committee (ACC) · Airport Development Reference Manual (ADRM) · Airport Governance Toolkit · Delhi Airport · Dhaka Airport · International Air Transport Association (IATA) · Narita Airport

K. Yadav (✉)
West Bengal National University of Juridical Sciences, Kolkata, India
e-mail: kanchanyadav@nujs.edu

National Law School of India University, Bengaluru, India

© The Author(s), under exclusive license to Springer Nature Singapore Pte Ltd. 2025

S. Bhat B. (ed.), *Aerodrome Governance in Asia*,
https://doi.org/10.1007/978-981-96-7568-5_2

1 Background

In the last few decades, civil aviation as an industry has undergone tremendous growth. As per data shared by the International Civil Aviation Organization, there has been a steady and rapid growth in the annual number of passengers carried since the 1970s, with it being at an all-time high of 3.5 billion in 2015.[1] While the pandemic and subsequent restrictions greatly hindered the civil aviation industry, things are now almost back to normal.

Considering that civil aviation is not solely a domestic venture but requires collaborative international effort for ease and safety of flights, the Convention on International Civil Aviation (Chicago Convention) was enacted in 1944. The Convention provided certain basic guidelines regarding air travel requirements, aircraft registration, aerodrome requirements, and in general, the safety and sustainability of civil aviation. The Convention came into force with fifty two nations signing the same, and currently, it enjoys almost a global membership, with one hundred and ninety three signatory states.[2] The Convention also provides for the establishment of the International Civil Aviation Organization (ICAO) as a part of the United Nations, which is the primary authority regarding international air travel regulation.

Along with the ICAO as a UN counterpart, another international organisation, the International Air Transport Association (IATA), was established in 1945, but with distinct membership criteria. While the Chicago Convention had the other nations as their signatories whose civil aviation-related actions were governed by the ICAO, the IATA was a non-governmental association, with memberships from major airlines worldwide. It describes itself as a trade association, with membership from three hundred and thirty airlines from over one hundred and twenty countries, which accounts for more than 80% of global air traffic.[3] Considering how national compliance with Chicago Convention standards would ultimately be dependent upon the actions taken by the airlines, the IATA is an effort to represent, lead, and serve the airline industry and hold the airlines accountable for their actions. The mission of the IATA is described as "working together to shape the future growth of a safe, secure and sustainable air transport industry that connects and enriches our world".[4]

To ensure the element of safety, security, and sustainability of the industry, the IATA regularly publishes various guidelines and other such documents to be complied with by its members. However, besides aircraft standards, the Association also provides guidelines for aerodrome standards, as that is a crucial element of safety and sustainability in civil aviation as well. It regularly publishes an Airport Development Reference Manual (ADRM), which enables the national governments to optimise the infrastructural capabilities of their airports during building and maintenance.[5]

---

[1] 'Air Transport, Passengers Carried' (*The World Bank*), available at <https://data.worldbank.org/indicator/IS.AIR.PSGR> Last visited, 10 October 2022.

[2] Convention on International Civil Aviation, 7 December 1944, (Doc 7300/9).

[3] 'IATA - About Us', available at <https://www.iata.org/en/about/> Last visited, 25 March 2024.

[4] *Id.*

[5] IATA, *Airport Development Reference Manual (ADRM)* (12th edn., 2022).

On the other hand, there is also an Airport Governance Toolkit, which primarily deals with the soft governance requirements for an optimised airport.[6] The IATA also engages in consultative activities through its Airport Consultative Committee and has described one of its goals as "influencing airport planning and development worldwide in order to achieve safe and efficient, capacity balance, cost-effective, functional and user-friendly airports".[7]

2 Airport Building and Governance: IATA Requirements

The Airport Development Reference Manual has provided several guidelines for airport development and maintenance across various areas. These can be majorly divided into airport planning, economic aspects, environmental aspects, passenger convenience, and security and contingency.[8] On the other hand, the Airport Governance Toolkit discusses recommendations on areas such as accountability, regulatory framework, safety, and sustainability. However, it primarily focuses on the different stakeholders and their interactions to facilitate these goals.[9] The basic tenets of these two guiding documents for airports are discussed here.

2.1 Airport Planning

Regarding the overall planning of the Airport, the ADRM emphasises that as the 'primary users' of an airport, the airlines should be a part of the consultation process during the development of an airport. To facilitate the same, the IATA provides for the establishment of an Airport Consultative Committee (ACC). The function of the ACC is to facilitate communication between the airlines and the airport developing authority when a new airport is being built, or a major expansion on an existing airport is happening. The plans proposed and agreed upon by the ACC and the development authority would then be reviewed and confirmed by the IATA.[10] Apart from the ACC, the IATA also establishes Regional Airports Steering Groups (RASG), which are multi-disciplinary and multi-national bodies overseeing airport development in their designated regions.

These bodies, along with other key stakeholders, take care of several essential planning items during the airport planning procedure—including access to the airport, design of the terminal, signage, security, baggage handling, gate management, etc. The primary objective behind the planning procedure is to ensure convenience and

[6] IATA, 'Airport Governance Toolkit', (2020).

[7] *Supra* note 5.

[8] *Id.*

[9] *Supra* note 6.

[10] *Supra* note 5.

safety for airlines as well as passengers.[11] From the perspective of the passengers, they should have easy access to the airport, short and convenient walking distances, an efficient baggage delivery system, appropriate signage, and a variety of quality retail establishments and eateries around the airport.[12] For the airline, the focus is on an appropriate runway layout with low aircraft taxing distances, appropriate working spaces for the staff, and an airport management mechanism that does not create conflict between passenger flow and airline operations.[13]

2.2 Economic Aspects

The ADRM highlights that for airports and airport development, management of its economy plays a pivotal role. On the one hand, modern-day airports must be commercially profitable entities to maintain their operations and obtain the necessary financing for further development. On the other, particularly in the context of privatised airports, there is also the requirement of economic regulation so as to keep air travel affordable for the people.[14] This is all the more important in the context that there is low competition in the airport industry and most of them enjoy a nearly monopolistic business position. Thus, the scope for abuse of this position to demand unreasonable fares from the users remains high.

The IATA has recognised that currently, the capital cost associated with establishing or expanding an airport is rather high. Suitable land that is environmentally viable for an airport is no longer readily available near the city regions. Conversely, if the airports are built far away from the cities in question, it increases the burden of creating new roads, railways, and other such public transport options.[15] Other than these capital costs, operation, maintenance and staff costs are also associated with running an airport. To fulfil these requirements, airports rely upon their aeronautical and non-aeronautical revenue sources. To keep costs for airlines low and still maintain viability for the airport, the IATA recommends that non-aeronautical sources such as renting of space, duty fee, lease, etc., should be explored to the fullest extent.[16] This would ensure that the aeronautical charges, which are passed off to the airlines and then ultimately to the consumers, are reasonable, equitable, and non-discriminatory—an aspect which is overseen by the User Charges Panel under the

[11] *Id.*

[12] 'Overview of Airport Planning and Programming' (*Federal Aviation Administration*), available at <https://www.faa.gov/airports/central/planning_capacity/overview> Last visited, 27 June 2024.

[13] IATA, 'Airport Master Planning', (ICAO, 2022).

[14] *Supra* note 5.

[15] 'Airport Economics Manual', (ICAO, 2020) Doc 9562.

[16] Belford Brown, 'Economics and Finance in Airport Planning', (1964), 90, *Journal of the Aero-Space Transport Division*, 197.

IATA.[17] Moreover, while incentives and rebates to increase air traffic in an airport are welcome, this should also be done in a fair and non-discriminatory manner.

2.3 *Environmental Aspects*

While dealing with efficiency-related concerns and convenience for both airlines and passengers, the IATA does not ignore the broader concerns arising out of the operation of airports, particularly, environmental concerns. It mentions that while meeting the demands of the increasing air traffic, the airports must progress in a sustainable manner, ensuring an 'optimal balance' on social, economic, and environmental fronts.[18] The primary areas of environmental impact, as categorised by the ADRM, can be described as emissions, noise, and land use. The idea is to cut down on both carbon dioxide (CO_2) and nitrogen oxide (NOx) emissions significantly, ensure noise reduction from airplanes and other operations, and enhance sustainable land use.[19]

The most crucial step, as highlighted by the IATA, to combat the harmful environmental impacts of airports and air traffic in general, is to formulate an environmental management plan. The ARM highlights that it is the first step to identify the concerns before any environmental improvements can take place. It would also ensure that initiatives are taken with regard to their long-term impacts instead of blindly implementing actions in a gimmicky manner. The plan would take into account the access to the airport, how well the airport integrates with its ecology and natural habitat, as well as managing emissions, energy consumption, land use, water use, and waste management in a way that minimises negative impacts of the airport's operation on the surrounding environment. It takes into account the associated social and political impacts and considerations influencing such decisions as well, so as to integrate the airport fully with its surrounding community.[20]

In particular, for noise reduction, the IATA relies upon the Balanced Approach, as explored by the ICAO. Under the Balanced Approach, noise management relies upon the major steps of reducing noise at the source, land use and management to facilitate noise reduction, operational steps to restrict noise and operational restrictions on air traffic.[21] These steps encompass aspects such as technological developments to reduce noise, modernisation of aircrafts, noise insulation in airports and surrounding

[17] *Supra* note 5.

[18] *Id.*

[19] Fiona Greer, Jasenka Rakas & Arpad Horvath, 'Airports and Environmental Sustainability: A Comprehensive Review', (2020), 15, *Environmental Research Letters*, 103007; *Supra* note 5.

[20] *Supra* note 5.

[21] ICAO, 'Guidance on the Balanced Approach to Aircraft Noise Management', (2008), Doc 9829.

areas, in-flight and on the ground operational noise abatement procedures, and restrictions on night traffic or particular noise-inducing movements.[22]

For emissions, due to the efforts of the ICAO, IATA, and the different national governments, there has been a great deal of success. Since the 1960s, there has been a reduction of more than 90% in harmful carbon dioxide and nitrogen oxide emissions. However, considering the increasing nature of airports and air traffic, efforts are crucial for further reduction in emissions.[23] In this regard, the IATA highlights the second main culprit for emissions in airports, other than aircrafts, which would include airside vehicles, ground support equipment, landside vehicles, and power generation plants—all of which operate within or immediately surrounding the airport. To reduce emissions at these levels, suggested steps would include optimising airport design to reduce ground transport and waiting, maintaining of equipment and introducing more efficient vehicles and technology, alternate energy methods and conservation systems, and so on.[24]

2.4 Passenger Convenience

Passenger facilitation or convenience in an airport is a highly multifaceted area. Anything and everything from access to the airport and parking areas to the check-in experience, convenience to and from terminals, baggage claim, waiting times, safety and comfort within the airport, retail and food options etc. are all parts of passenger convenience.[25] Thus, it requires a much more extensive approach than the others, and often, requires the interventions of other authorities and the local or national government. Many of these aspects are also impacted by the size of the airport and the amount of air traffic and passengers that it serves.

To facilitate this, the guidelines provide that there should be ample road, rail, and other public transport access to the airport with appropriate signage to guide travellers. The terminal should be protected from weather, well-lit, and should have adequate space for passengers to board or deboard their vehicles. The check-in area should be equipped with flat screen computers, baggage scanners, passport readers, boarding pass printers, etc. Moreover, the distance that the passengers would need to travel to their gates or the baggage handling areas, should be as short and hassle-free as possible.[26]

---

[22] *Supra* note 5.; Nesimi Ozkurt, Samet Feyyaz Hamamci& Deniz Sari, 'Estimation of Airport Noise Impacts on Public Health. A Case Study of İzmir Adnan Menderes Airport', (2015), 36, *Transportation Research Part D: Transport and Environment*, 152.

[23] Annex 16 to the Convention on International Civil Aviation - Environmental Protection 1944; Andrew Monsalud, Denny Ho & Jasenka Rakas, 'Greenhouse Gas Emissions Mitigation Strategies within the Airport Sustainability Evaluation Process', (2015), 14, *Sustainable Cities and Society*, 414.

[24] *Supra* note 5.

[25] *Id.*

[26] *Id.*

Signage also plays a significant role in passenger convenience. Thus, the document mentions that appropriate signage to guide the passengers to the different counters and checkpoints should be available through fixed and dynamic signage, and the signs should be uniform and continuous to guide the passengers through the whole process.[27] Similarly, the baggage handling system should be swift and efficient, with there being as few number of stages as possible to minimise delays. In the baggage claim area, a system must be there which would allow the passengers to stay in their place while the baggage is delivered to them, similar to the luggage delivery belt utilised in most airports.[28]

However, other than these few primary recommendations, the IATA also provides several other guidelines regarding passenger arrivals and departures, flow of passengers, optimal temperature, lighting, signage, and advertising levels within the airport, and passenger comfort in general.

2.5 Security and Contingency

While evaluating the functional aspects of an airport operation, the IATA does not overlook perhaps the most important aspect, security. Considering how a security threat at the airport that bypasses the relevant checks has the potential to cause devastating impacts, security regulations for air travel are much stricter than any other form of travel.[29]

The IATA provides a great deal of discretion to the concerned national authorities while developing security measures, as the individual security threats in a particular nation are more likely to be visible to the government itself. However, it suggests that the requirements should also be realistic and economically viable to ensure that they are actually implemented instead of remaining only a theory. The overarching ideas provided by the IATA to ensure security include prohibiting weapons, explosives, and dangerous devices within the airport premises, ensuring implementation of an airport emergency plan during a crisis, and minimizing the impacts of an explosion or other similar event through design features. This can be done by implementing steps such as simple and evident passenger and baggage transit, separate passenger and cargo flows, multiple security checkpoints, implementation of security-restricted areas without access to pedestrians, separate screening areas and baggage handling for VIPs under high threat, etc.[30]

In case of a crisis, the IATA recommends the three elements of risk analysis, contingency planning, and consequence management. Emergency response planning, traditionally the domain of airlines to mitigate accidents or incidents, is now gradually

[27] *Id.*

[28] *Id.*

[29] Douglas H Harris, 'How to Really Improve Airport Security', (2002), 10, *Ergonomics in Design*, 17.

[30] *Supra* note 5.

being implemented by airports as well, as they are best situated to develop stationary crisis centres and other such facilities. These contingency plans should be consistent and easy to follow, so as to not further confuse the staff during a chaotic situation.[31]

2.6 Governance

While the previous sections explore individual guidelines regarding different areas of airport management under the IATA ADRM, the Airport Governance Toolkit by the IATA focuses on optimising governance and stakeholder participation to achieve those goals. The idea here is to facilitate interactions among governments and other stakeholders to ensure reduced risk and maximised value to all parties.[32]

The document highlights that the governance of an airport is highly different than that of any other organisation, considering the role an airport plays in the public life, and its socio-economic impacts on the community. The five primary areas of governance, as identified by the Toolkit, are (a) policy, regulation and government affairs, (b) community and environment, (c) safety and security, (d) operations, and (e) capital projects.[33] Moreover, there are several spheres of operation under airport governance, which include international, national, and regional governance, international and national regulatory framework, the airport operating environment, its ownership model, and prospects for development. Good governance for airports is, thus, dependent upon the few guiding principles of fairness, participation, decency, transparency, accountability, and efficiency.[34]

To facilitate the five primary governance sectors, the Toolkit recommends that there should be adequate participation from the most neglected stakeholder group when it comes to airport development, the customers. Allowing the customers and the community to voice their concerns without fear of political interference or repercussions would be the first stepping stone to establishing good governance in this sector. Moreover, knowledge sharing should be ensured across the different groups and bodies, and consultation and collaboration should be encouraged.

The IATA, in the Toolkit, provides several specific guidance and tools to ensure that the concerned authorities can gauze their progress towards good governance. The simplest and most effective of these tools is the Governance Self-Assessment Checklist, which provides a bird's eye view of the existence or non-existence of certain governance mechanisms and shortcomings. For decision making, it provides a Responsible-Accountable-Consulted-Informed (RACI) matrix, which identifies the key stakeholders and their roles and responsibilities in the decision-making process for airports.[35] The Recommended Airport Governance Mechanisms take the best

---

[31] *Id.*

[32] *Supra* note 6.

[33] *Id.*

[34] *Id.*

[35] *Id.*

practices and bodies regarding airport governance that are recommended for an airport to establish. Finally, it also provides Implementation Guidance, as in practical steps on how to implement the good governance model.[36]

As is evident from the IATA's side, there is no dearth of recommendations and suggestions on how to build and maintain an efficient, convenient, and sustainable airport. However, considering the non-enforceable nature of the ADRM and the Toolkit, implementation of the same depends upon the discretion of the concerned authorities. At this juncture, it becomes crucial to analyse the reality of the same in the context of different airports.

3 Implementing the ADRM and the Toolkit in Airports

3.1 Narita International Airport (Japan)

The Narita International Airport in Japan, located close to the capital city of Tokyo, serves as an essential transport and communication hub for not only Japan but also Asia in general. It transports more than 30 million international passengers and more than 2 million tonnes of international cargo each year.[37] In general, the airport can be deemed as well planned and accessible as per IATA standards, with existing requirements for economic and environmental sustainability, passenger convenience, security, and governance. However, when examined closely, certain discrepancies can be found.

The ADRM mentions that the planning phase of a new airport should be done in consultation with the various stakeholders, including but not limited to the airlines, and would need to be overseen by the ACC and IATA.[38] However, in the 1960s, when talks began to shift the existing Tokyo International Airport from Haneda, no such consultation process came into play, which resulted in a lengthy period of discontentment and violent protests from the local community. It is true that the proposed alternate site, which combined the erstwhile Sanrizuka and Shibayama villages, would be in tune with many accessibility-related guidelines of the IATA—it allowed for easy expansion and creation of roads, rails, and other public vehicle access mechanisms.[39] However, the villages in question were already populated by

---

[36] *Id.*

[37] 'Passengers at Narita Airport Soar 72% in Fiscal 2023',*The Japan Times*, (25 April 2024), available at <https://www.japantimes.co.jp/news/2024/04/25/japan/narita-airport-passengers-surge/> Last visited, 31 August 2024.

[38] *Supra* note 5.

[39] Philip Brasor, 'Fight or Flight: Narita's History of Conflict', *The Japan Times*, (13 December 2014), available at <https://www.japantimes.co.jp/news/2014/12/13/national/media-national/fight-flight-naritas-history-conflict/> Last visited, 31 August 2024.

locals, who had their residences and farmlands in the area and were not consulted or even notified before beginning the process.[40]

As the residents learnt about the proposed new airport site through the news in 1966, public protests erupted throughout the country. Many students and other activist groups supported the local farmers, who did not want to relocate from their homesteads. During construction, roadblocks and riots became common in the area, and policemen and riot vehicle patrols were regular activities. The opening of the airport in March 1978 had to be delayed when the protestors broke into the control tower and destroyed some of the equipment.[41] Ultimately, it opened in May 1978 under high security. The conflicts and protests continued till as late as the 1980s.

After a few consecutive years of loss, the Narita Airport has reported a net profit of 10 billion yen in 2023. This is a marked improvement from the previous year, when a loss of 50.2 billion yen was reported.[42] In terms of sustainability and environmental aspects, due to being located close to residential areas and even one house with farmland situated in between the runways, there are several restrictions that the Narita Airport goes through. The Airport remains non-operational between 12 mid-night and 6 am to appease the several noise complaints received from the nearby residents.[43] However, the Airport has set a lofty goal of net zero carbon emissions by 2050 and for that purpose, aims to strengthen relationships with various stakeholders. To facilitate the same, it has established the Eco-Airport Development and Planning Council, which has members from all major stakeholder groups, including airlines and air freight forwarders.[44]

Passenger access and convenience are strong points of the Narita Airport, with the Airport being easily accessible through public transport such as rail and bus as well as by private cars and taxis. In case passengers are disabled or require special assistance, there are dedicated parking lots and support staff available for them. For travelling between terminals and within the airport, there are access corridors and transit passenger shuttle buses that operate between all terminals with a maximum gap of ten minutes between buses.[45] Even though flights do not operate in the Airport between 12 mid-night and 6 am, basic services such as transport, convenience stores, and capsule hotels are accessible at any time.[46]

---

[40] David E Apter & Nagayo Sawa, *Against the State: Politics and Social Protest in Japan*, (Reprint edition, Harvard University Press, 1986).

[41] *Id.*

[42] 'Narita International Airport: Net Income 2023', (*Statista*), available at <https://www.statista.com/statistics/1242414/narita-international-airport-net-income/> Last visited, 31 August 2024.

[43] Saburo Ogata & Naoaki Shinohara, 'Relaxations of Operating Restrictions on Noise and Resident's Reaction at Narita International Airport', (2014).

[44] 'Sustainable NRT 2050 | Narita International Airport Corporation', (*Narita International Airport Corporation*), available at <https://www.naa.jp/en/environment/ea_vision.html> Last visited, 31 August 2024.

[45] 'Access Top | Narita International Airport', (*Narita International Airport Official Website*), available at <https://www.narita-airport.jp/> Last visited, 31 August 2024.

[46] 'Terminal Use at Night and Early Mornings | Narita International Airport', (*Narita International Airport Official Website*), available at <https://www.narita-airport.jp/> Last visited, 31 August 2024.

From 1978 to 2015, any visitor to the Narita Airport was required to show their ID during entry to prevent incidences of protesters entering and causing disturbance. However, the ID checks have now been stopped, being replaced with modern security mechanisms such as cameras, explosive detectors, and millimetre wave scanners.[47] Considering how there have been no major security incidents in the Airport since its inception, it can be determined that the security and contingency requirements have been performing adequately. However, the Airport has not published any information regarding its risk management plan or contingency planning, so it is unclear how prepared it is, should an event occur.

In 2003, the governance of the Airport was privatised through the Narita International Airport Corporation Act, placing the governance of the Airport in the hands of the newly established Narita International Airport Corporation (NAA).[48] Through the years, the NAA has tried to rebuild its tumultuous relationship with the community by facilitating efforts such as those of the Community Consultation Centre. However, given that the anti-airport struggles happened not too long ago, public perception is still divided regarding the Narita Airport.

3.2 *Indira Gandhi International Airport (India)*

The Indira Gandhi International Airport in India, known more commonly as the Delhi Airport, is situated in Palam, New Delhi, the capital city of India. The Airport handles more than 70 million passengers each year, and it is considered the tenth business Airport in the world and the busiest Airport in Asia.[49]

The current Airport was constructed by replacing the erstwhile Palam Airport, which gradually became unable to handle the increased traffic and facilitate international flights. It currently has three terminals, with domestic and international flights entirely segregated, and four runways. Currently, discussions are in place to increase its runway capacity by 30% and passenger handling capacity by 40–50%, and the Airport Authority of India is consulting with international experts on how to facilitate the same.[50] However, no plans are yet noticed to discuss the expansion activities with other stakeholders, such as the airlines or the community.

[47] 'Narita Airport Ends ID Security Checks for Non-Passengers', *Japan Today*, (30 March 2015), available at <https://japantoday.com/category/national/narita-airport-abolishes-id-security-checks-for-non-passengers> Last visited, 31 August 2024.

[48] 'Directory of Strategic Partners', available at <https://www.iata.org/en/about/sp/partners-directory/> Last visited, 31 August 2024.

[49] 'Delhi's IGI Airport Is the 10th Busiest Airport in the World: Report | World News', *The Indian Express*, (18 April 2024), available at <https://indianexpress.com/article/world/world-busiest-airport-ranking-delhi-igi-airport-9277020/> Last visited, 31 August 2024; 'Busiest Airports in the World 2023 | OAG', available at <https://www.oag.com/busiest-airports-world-2023> Last visited, 31 August 2024.

[50] Deepak Patel, 'Delhi Airport to Increase Peak Runway Capacity by 30% in 3 Years: DIAL CEO', *Business Standard*, (7 June 2024).

Regarding economic sustainability, the Delhi Airport is currently at a loss-making stage, even after considerable net worth and total income, due to high depreciation costs.[51] However, the Airport authorities have recognised the importance of non-aero revenue channels, as the IATA has also suggested. Currently, more than half of the total income of the Airport comes from non-aero revenue sources such as rentals, convenience stores, food and beverages, advertising, and parking.[52]

The Airport has a dedicated Environmental Sustainability Policy, highlighting its efforts towards environmental compliance, establishing adequate bodies, risk management, employee awareness, monitoring and reporting, and actions towards reducing waste and emissions. It has established aircraft noise level standards that the airlines must maintain.[53] There is also an Environmental Management System (EMS) in the Airport to oversee the implementation all pollution reduction and prevention mechanisms. It is evident that the Delhi Airport's sustainability efforts are yielding at least some results, as it is the first Airport in Asia to reach the Level 3 standard in the Airport Carbon Accreditation program of the ACI. Dedicated measures are in place in and around the Airport to maintain air quality as well as water and waste management. The biodiversity in the region is also maintained to some extent by landscaping, tree plantation, and relocation of endangered wildlife.[54]

Regarding accessibility, the Delhi Airport enjoys exemplary connectivity through various modes of public and private transport. It is connected by metro to the rest of the city via the Airport Express Line, and is well connected by public buses and local trains as well. Due to great roadway connectivity, one can easily reach the Airport through taxis or private vehicles. It also offers a 'park n fly' option, where visitors can park their cars inside the Airport for the duration of the travel. For travelling between terminals, there are Airport Shuttle buses and DMRC Feeder bus services available.[55]

The Airport regularly announces advisories to its passengers regarding restricted and prohibited items.[56] However, any notification or similar instrument regarding risk management or contingency procedures could not be found. The security measures are often ramped up in the Airport before important events by subjecting passengers to additional checks. But the flip side is that it tends to result in significantly lengthy

[51] Ameya Joshi, 'Delhi Airport Is Making Money, but Not in the Way You Would Imagine', *Hindustan Times*, (2 February 2024), available at <https://www.hindustantimes.com/business/delhiinternationalairportmakesmoney-101706855570221.html> Last visited, 31 August 2024; 'India: Net Worth of Delhi Airport 2023', (*Statista*), available at <https://www.statista.com/statistics/1411902/india-net-worth-delhi-airport/> Last visited, 31 August 2024.

[52] *Supra* note 51.

[53] 'Environment Sustainability Management at Delhi Airport', available at <https://www.newdelhiairport.in/corporate/our-company/sustainability> Last visited, 31 August 2024.

[54] *Id.*

[55] 'Travel To & From Delhi Airport with Ease', available at <https://www.newdelhiairport.in/to-and-from-airport> Last visited, 31 August 2024.

[56] 'Security and Baggage Advice | New Delhi Airport', available at <https://www.newdelhiairport.in/passenger-guide/security-and-baggage-advice> Last visited, 31 August 2024.

wait times and additional hassle for the passengers.[57] Moreover, the unpreparedness of the Airport for any contingency became apparent in the recent incident when, in Terminal 1, a portion of the roof collapsed, killing one person and injuring six others. Not only were the authorities unaware of the potential risks associated with the heavy rainfall and did not take adequate steps to prevent them, but the accident resulted in a complete and abrupt stop of all flights from the terminal, stranding thousands of passengers.[58]

The management of the Delhi Airport is a joint venture between the Airports Authority of India and GMR Airports Limited, with GMR holding the majority portion. GMR advertises their objective for the Airport to be 'passenger delight'[59]; however, does not provide any concrete information regarding collaborative efforts with the various levels of stakeholders.

3.3 *Hazrat Shahjalal International Airport (Bangladesh)*

The Hazrat Shahjalal International Airport, located in the capital city of Bangladesh, Dhaka, is the largest Airport in Bangladesh, with a passenger carrying capacity of 18 million. Compared to other international airports, it has a low volume of passenger and cargo, with the annual passenger count remaining at around 9 million.[60]

The planning and initial construction activities on the Airport started under the Pakistan Government in 1966. However, the timeline was disrupted by several years during the Bangladesh Liberation War in 1971, as the work was halted and many already constructed portions were also damaged. Efforts only resumed after independence under the newly constructed Government of Bangladesh. Work on the same finally finished and the Airport opened its doors to the public in 1983.[61] Since then, there have been regular expansion activities at the airport, one of the most notable being the construction of a third terminal and a second runway, which is

---

[57] '"Average Wait Time at Security… 256 Minutes": Videos of Long Queues at Delhi Airport Viral - CNBC TV18',*CNBCTV18*, (14 August 2024), available at <https://www.cnbctv18.com/travel/average-wait-time-at-security-256-minutes-videos-of-long-queues-at-delhi-airport-viral-19459721.htm> Last visited, 31 August 2024; 'India: Authorities Increase Security Measures at New Delhi's Indira Gandhi International Airport through July 30' (*India: Authorities increase security measures at New Delhi's Indira Gandhi International Airport through July 30 | Crisis24*), available at <https://crisis24.garda.com/alerts/2024/06/india-authorities-increase-security-measures-at-new-delhis-indira-gandhi-international-airport-through-july-30> Last visited, 31 August 2024.

[58] 'Indira Gandhi International Airport: Roof Collapse Smashes Cars in Delhi', *BBC*, available at <https://www.bbc.com/news/articles/c725ny6p960o> Last visited, 31 August 2024.

[59] 'Delhi International Airport Limited', available at <https://www.gmrgroup.in/delhi-international-airport/> Last visited, 31 August 2024.

[60] Rejaul Karim Byron, 'New Int'l Airport to Cost Tk 50,000cr', *The Daily Star*, (28 August 2010), available at <https://www.thedailystar.net/news-detail-152589> Last visted, 31 August 2024.

[61] Staff Correspondent, 'ZIA Made Shahjalal International Airport',*The Daily Star*, (16 February 2010), available at <https://www.thedailystar.net/news-detail-126503> Last visited, 31 August 2024.

still ongoing.[62] However, the information is missing on whether the interests and concerns of other stakeholders were taken into account during the planning stage, both during the construction and for further expansions.

Regarding the economics of the airport, no information can be found with respect to the financial status of it at the current stage. The economic analyses in question take into account the under construction third terminal and its profitability potential. As of yet, BDT 21,300 crore has been spent towards the new terminal, with a target financial internal rate of return at 1.98%.[63] Initially targeted for a May 2024 opening, the terminal was supposed to be fully functional by October 2024.[64] However, considering the recent fall of the government in Bangladesh, such efforts are likely to be delayed.

No specific efforts undertaken for the functioning terminals of the Dhaka Airport could be found. However, an environmental clearance has been issued for the expansion efforts of the new terminal, with specific sustainability guidelines. These guidelines mention that there needs to be mitigation activities to minimise biodiversity loss, noise pollution should be controlled, and solid and liquid waste must be appropriately disposed of.[65]

The Airport is connected to the public transport system through the Airport Railway Station. It is accessible by private cars and various taxi services as well. It has the usual security guidelines in place concerning prohibited and restricted items. The Airport is managed by the Bangladesh government.

4 Concluding Remarks

There remains no doubt that for the global community overall, civil aviation is emerging as one of the key development areas, no matter the economic prowess of a nation. The IATA plays a key role in facilitating this by providing important guidelines regarding the building, maintenance, and expansion of airports in a way that the conflicting interests of the airlines and the community could be balanced. The existing guidelines are detailed and comprehensive in nature, covering everything starting from airport planning to passenger convenience and security. However, given the non-enforceable nature of these guidelines, it is up to the individual nations and governing bodies how much they want to implement the same. In this regard, irrespective of the economic and development status of a nation and the constraints associated with them, some common trends emerge regarding problem areas.

---

[62] Byron (n 60).

[63] SajjadHossan, 'Economic Impact of Third Terminal in Dhaka Airport', (*Business Inspection BD*, 23 November 2022), available at <https://businessinspection.com.bd/economic-impact-of-third-terminal-in-dhaka-airport/> Last visited, 31 August 2024.

[64] 'Construction of Dhaka Airport's 3rd Terminal to Be Fully Completed by April 5', (*Dhaka Tribune*).

[65] 'Environmental Clearance for HazratShahjalal International Airport Expansion Project (Phase-1)', (Department of Environment, Government of the People's Republic of Bangladesh, 2017).

To begin with, there seems to be a lax attitude among the airport authorities regarding the need for stakeholder opinion and consultation. The IATA emphasises upon the importance of the same at almost every stage, from building and expansion to environmental initiatives. Yet, in the case of the Narita Airport, the construction itself started with vehement opposition from one of the most important stakeholders, the community. While such apparent stakeholder dissatisfaction was not visible for Delhi and Dhaka airports, they do not highlight any efforts towards stakeholder connection and consultation either.

The risk management and contingency seem to be problem areas as well. None of the three airports in question had any such plan available to the public, even if one exists at all. As the recent roof collapse incident at the Delhi Airport showed, the absence of a proper risk management plan was severely felt by the people involved in the accident, as well as the other passengers.[66]

However, the most prominent issue, perhaps, is the airports' lack of transparency regarding their IATA compliance. Operating in a profit-making business-like manner, it seems that airports across all nations are quick to publicise their positive efforts as a means of advertisement but are silent in the areas they are found lacking. For example, both Narita and Delhi airports publicized their environmental efforts but were silent about any risk management efforts or stakeholder consultation activities. For the Dhaka Airport, the authorities have published environmental guidelines regarding the construction of the new terminal but are conveniently silent about similar efforts towards the existing terminals.[67] While it is true that financial and administrative constraints might be higher in some countries compared to others, what is sorely needed for all airports is an accurate assessment of the areas in which they are lacking.

Even though the IATA cannot mandate all global airports comply with their guidelines, it might be useful to mandate an annual compliance report to be submitted by them, highlighting the problem areas needing improvement. After all, the first step towards curing any problem starts through acknowledgement and if the concerned authorities are forced to face the glaring gaps regularly, it would encourage them to try and devise appropriate solutions.

[66] *Supra* note 58.

[67] *Supra* note 65.

Chapter 3
Governance and Law of Aerodromes in China

Dejian Kong and Rong Jiang

Abstract Chinese aerodromes play an important role in promoting China as the world's second-largest aviation services market. This chapter will first introduce a general pattern of aerodromes in China, clarifying the number, location, and development plan of Chinese aerodromes. Secondly, it will address the governance structure of construction, where the Civil Aviation Administration of China (CAAC) plays a crucial role. Meanwhile, this chapter will present the aerodrome management reform promoted by CAAC, particularly in transferring the management of more than 140 aerodromes to provincial governments and the commercialisation of aerodrome operations. Certain large aerodrome holding groups will be selected as examples to demonstrate the modern model of aerodrome corporate governance in China. Thirdly, this chapter will list the legal system of aerodromes in China, including (i) congress legislation that is the Civil Aviation Law of China, (ii) administrative regulations such as the Regulation on the Administration of Civil Airports, (iii) the rules at the ministerial level such as the Provisions on the Permission for the Use of Transport Airports, and (iv) regulations & policies made by CAAC. Lastly, this chapter will look into the future of the governance structure and legal system of aerodromes in China, considering a vital background of promoting the development of a low altitude economy in the next decade.

Keywords Airports Council International (ACI) · Airport Layout Plan (ALP) · Civil Aviation Administration of China (CAAC) · Civil Aviation Law of China · Corporate structure · Guangdong Airport Authority (GAA) · Shanghai Airport Group

---

D. Kong (✉)
Aerospace Law, China University of Political Science and Law, Beijing, China
e-mail: kong.dejian@hotmail.com

R. Jiang
Foreign-Related Rule of Law, China University of Political Science and Law, Beijing, China
e-mail: 202120190033@bfsu.edu.cn

© The Author(s), under exclusive license to Springer Nature Singapore Pte Ltd. 2025
S. Bhat B. (ed.), *Aerodrome Governance in Asia*,
https://doi.org/10.1007/978-981-96-7568-5_3

1 Introduction

As the Airports Council International (ACI) notes, "Airports are economic engines of growth for the communities they serve, providing critical social and economic impacts beyond the runway."[1] Data shows that aviation transports close to 2 billion passengers annually and 50% of international exports of goods (by value), generating a total of 29 million jobs globally, which includes 4.3 million directly employed by the airline and aerodrome industry and approximately 6.7 million direct tourism jobs supported by the spending of international visitors arriving by air, and through either direct, indirect, induced and catalytic impacts stimulates global economic impact at US$2960 billion, which equivalent to 8% of world's Gross Domestic Product (GDP).[2] Despite three years of the pandemic, the air service market is experiencing new growth momentum and is expected to achieve positive growth in 2024 as global air capacity gradually returns to pre-pandemic levels. On 12 December 2023, Airbus released the latest "Global Market Forecast" report in Beijing, predicting that China is expected to become the largest air service market, surpassing Europe and the United States when the global aviation market value reaches US$255 billion in 2042, which also shows the world's confidence in the recovery and development of China's aviation and aerodrome industry.[3]

China also attaches great importance to the development of the aviation industry. When President Xi Jinping visited and inspected the new Beijing Airport on 23 February, 2017, he made an important conclusion that "the new Beijing Airport is a new power source for our country's development",[4] fully affirming the important driving role of the aerodrome in the country's social and economic development. On 26 October 2020, the Fifth Plenary Session of the 19th Central Committee of the Communist Party of China adopted "The Outline of the 14th Five-Year Plan for Economic and Social Development and Long-Range Objectives through the Year 2035 of the People's Republic of China", which also put forward new requirements and deployments for accelerating the construction of a transportation power.[5] Since air transportation is the fastest and widest coverage of the lowest unit of energy

---

[1] ACI World, 'Economics', available at <https://aci.aero/airport-advocacy/economics/> Last visited, 17 July 2024.

[2] See ATAG, 'Air Transport Drives Economic and Social Progress', The Economic and Social Benefits of Air Transport, Air Transport Action Group (ATAG), September 2005, available at <https://atag.org/media/mjhpjhxp/atag_socialbenefitsairtransport.pdf> Last visited, on 17 July 2024.

[3] Airbus, '2024 Global Market Forecast', available at <https://www.airbus.com/en/products-services/commercial-aircraft/market/global-market-forecast.> Last visited, 17 July 2024.

[4] Lan Cheng, "Xi Jinping's Inspection in Beijing: Strengthen urban planning and construction, and ensure the successful organization of the WinterOlympic Games". *Xinhua Net*, available at <http://www.xinhuanet.com/politics/2017-02/24/c_129495572.htm> Last visited, 17 July 2024.

[5] National Development and Reform Commission, 'The 14th Five-Year Plan for Economic and Social Development and Long-Range Objectives Through the Year 2035 of the People's Republic of China', available at <https://en.ndrc.gov.cn/policies/202203/P020220315511326748336.pdf> Last visited, 18 July 2024.

consumption, the construction of a comprehensive transportation system with aerodromes as the core is bound to become a new backbone for the construction of a modern comprehensive transportation system and a new driving force for the construction of a robust transportation country.

However, it takes a good blacksmith to make good steel. Compared to world aviation powers, the gaps between China and those countries in safety management, security capability, operation efficiency, quality of service and management level remain. Problems caused by resources and environment constraints and unbalanced and inadequate development have become more prominent,[6] which has posed new challenges to the modern governance capacity and governance level of Chinese aerodromes. To construct a modernised national aerodrome system which can meet the needs of its people for safer, greener, smarter and more people-oriented aerodromes and to spur the vitality of the Chinese aerodromes industry, a systematic, scientific and complete legal governance system adapting to the condition of China's aerodrome and leading its future direction is indispensable. Further discussion and the call for taking a new look at the current governance and legal system of Chinese aerodromes triggered. Since Article 53 of the Civil Aviation Law of China provides that military aerodromes or military-civilian common-use aerodromes are not subject to the Civil Aviation Law of China, they will be left out for the purpose of this paper.

2 Overview of Chinese Aerodromes

Chinese aerodromes, a vital component of the nation's transportation infrastructure, have undergone remarkable growth and modernisation, mirroring the country's swift economic progress and strategic goals. In addition, since opening up in January 2023, China's domestic market has seen phenomenal growth at 7.1% compared to 2019 and reached a staggering 138.8% in 2022, demonstrating its immense market potential and resilience as one of the world's three largest domestic passenger markets who drove most of the industry performance in 2023.[7] What is more, while construction activities at aerodromes took a back seat and investment levels in aerodrome projects have shrunk over years globally, from US$800 billion to US$330 billion during the pandemic, China's aerodromes are still striving for recovery from its past prosperity and new development has been seen.[8] At a time when the grand total of existing or new aerodromes remained less than the pre-pandemic, a thrive has been

[6] National Development and Reform Commission, 'China Civil Aviation Four-Type Airport Construction Action Outline (2020-2035)', *China Government Network*, 25 March 2020, available at < https://www.gov.cn/zhengce/zhengceku/2020-03/25/content_5495472.htm> Last visited, 24 July 2024.

[7] CAPA - Centre for Aviation. (2024). 'Global Airport Construction and Investment Report MId-2024 – Part 1 – Intro, Asia Pacific & Europe'. available at <https://centreforaviation.com/analysis/reports/global-airport-construction-investment-report-mId-2024-part-1-intro-asia-pacific-europe-689705> Last visited, 24 July 2024.

[8] *Id.*

seen in the Asia Pacific. Six of the top 10 aerodrome construction projects in the Asia-Pacific region are from Chinese mainland and the largest project which has an investment of US$1930 billion is from Hong Kong.[9] These developments have indicated that China is still progressively striving for its modernisation in aerodrome construction which aims to serve its development of low-altitude economy in the next decade. The following section offers a comprehensive overview of the current landscape of Chinese aerodromes, encompassing their number, strategic distribution, and development outlook.

2.1 Data of Chinese Aerodromes

The number of Chinese aerodromes has increased magnificently ever since the Chinese reform and opening-up policy and the construction and development of Chinese aerodromes had entered an unprecedented stage. Before 1978, there were only 78 civil transport aerodromes of which 36 were also for military use. And the passenger throughput at that time was merely 75. After 46-years-construction, by the end of 2023, there were 259 transport aerodromes (excluding Hong Kong, Macau and Taiwan) and 449 general-purpose aerodromes in China. In addition to that, 6 airstrips, 193 parking stands and 59 ha terminal were newly built, which adds up to 289 airstrips, 7508 parking stands and 1857.9 ha terminals as a whole. In 2023, the passenger throughput and cargo and mail throughput of aerodromes in China are reported to grow by 142.2% and 15.8%, respectively, in comparison to the previous year.[10] Furthermore, in addition to the 1260 billion passengers and 16.83 million tons of cargo and mail, 38 aerodromes are handling more than 10 million passengers and 63 aerodromes are handling more than 10,000 tons of cargo and mail per year.[11] In comparison to 1978, the growth in these two indicators is 5477 times and 1180 times, respectively.[12] The construction of Chinese aerodromes has played a significant role in supporting this growth.

2.2 Strategic Distribution of Chinese Aerodromes

Firstly, in terms of geographic location, the general feature of distribution tends to be dense in the east and sparse in the west. Secondly, the throughput of passenger

---

[9] *Id.*

[10] See CAAC, '2023 Statistical Report on the Development of Civil Aviation Industry', available at <https://www.mot.gov.cn/tongjishuju/minhang/202406/P020240621367394142022.pdf> Last visited, 24 July 2024.

[11] *Id.*

[12] See CAAC, 'Reform and Opening-up 40 Years of Civil Aviation Airport Construction', November 2018, available at <http://www.caacnews.com.cn/special/4260/4992/ggkf40nlm6/201811/t20181120_1261128.html> Last visited, 24 July 2024.

and cargo also align with its distribution, though in recent years, a tendency to tilt towards the west has been shown. Finally, China's aerodrome construction focuses on building an aerodrome system with a clear hierarchy, reasonable layout and perfect functions at the level of aerodrome positioning and scale.

The geographical layout of China's transport aerodromes is more eastern than western. Of China's 259 transport aerodromes, 56 are located in the eastern region, 44 in the central region, 132 in the western region and 27 in the northeastern region, accounting for 21.6%, 17.0%, 51.0% and 10.4% of the country's licensed transport aerodromes, respectively.[13] The number of aerodromes in the eastern region accounts for only 21.6% of the country, while that in the western region is 51.0%.[14] However, the density of aerodromes in the west is lower than in the east due to its vastness and lower population density. For example, in Xinjiang, which has the largest number of aerodromes in the country with 22, the average aerodrome density is only 0.13 per 10,000 sq km. In Inner Mongolia, which has the second largest number with 19, the density is only about 0.16 per 10,000 sq km. In contrast, some typical high value areas in eastern China, such as Shanghai and Beijing, respectively, have a value of 3.17 and 1.22, while other eastern cities have an average density of 0.5 or more.[15] The theoretical coverage of aerodromes obtained by the Tyson polygon method shows that the eastern region is usually smaller than the western region.[16] For the western region, especially Tibet and Xinjiang, is full of high mountains and deserts and has a low population density, so the coverage is larger so as the per capita density. In addition, the construction of aerodromes has tilted towards the west in recent years, driven by a trend of balanced development between east and west, which is conducive to better service for the country. There were 50 of the 31 new, 8 expanded and 34 reconstructed small hub and fly-hub aerodromes built during the 13th Five-Year Plan period. They were located in China's western, border and less-developed regions. This trend will help to meet the strategic needs of its Western development.[17]

The distribution of passenger, cargo, and mail throughput at Chinese transport aerodromes is more concentrated in the eastern region than in the west. Despite its relatively limited number, the densely populated and economically developed eastern region accounts for a significant proportion of the passenger and cargo throughput of all civil aviation aerodromes in China. In particular, it accounts for 50.6% of passenger throughput and 71.7% of cargo and mail throughput, contributing to the majority of the country's passenger and cargo throughput. It is typical for the aerodromes in the three major cities of Beijing, Shanghai and Guangzhou to account for

---

[13] *Supra* note 9.

[14] *Id.*

[15] Density is calculated as the number of airports divide by the area of that province through the end of 2023.

[16] Zhang Yi-Han, Liu Wan-Hua, Xu Xiao-Cong, *et al.*, 'Spatial Distribution and Accessibility Analysis of Airports in Mainland China', *Acta Scientia rum Naturalism Universitatis Sunyatseni*, Vol. 58, No. 6, November 2019, pp. 56–63 at p. 56.

[17] CAAC, 'China's airports may reach 241 by the end of the 13th Five-Year Plan with a total capacity of 1.4 billion Passengers', *China News*, October 22 2020, available at <http://news.china.com.cn/txt/2020-10/22/content_76833438.htm> Last visited, 25 July 2024.

20% of the passenger throughput in China and 60.8% of the international passenger throughput. Furthermore, the cargo and mail throughput of the aerodromes in these three cities constituted 42.7% of the total. In particular, the throughput of Shanghai and Guangdong reached 3803 kt and 3712 kt, respectively, last year, accounting for 22.69% and 22.05% of the national total.[18] It is apparent that the aerodromes situated in the eastern region are accountable for the majority of the nation's passenger and cargo transportation, exhibiting a significantly higher number and scale than those in other regions and fulfilling an essential role as a hub.

The Chinese transport aerodromes sector is characterised by the construction of a system comprising clearly defined tiers, a discernible positioning and optimal functionality, which is planned and laid out in accordance with a three-tier, three-dimensional structure comprising world-class aerodrome clusters, international hubs and regional hubs. World-class aerodrome clusters are found in Beijing-Tianjin-Hebei, the Yangtze River Delta and Zhu River Delta regions of China. International hubs are in the cities of Beijing, Shanghai, Guangzhou, Chengdu, Kunming, Shenzhen, Chongqing, Xi'an and Urumqi, while the country's 29 regional hubs are situated in Taiyuan, Hohhot, Dalian, Shenyang, Changchun, etc. International aviation hubs assume the primary role of transhipment for international passengers and cargo, facilitating the transfer of these resources to regional hubs and fostering the growth of surrounding areas. These hubs play a pivotal part in the Chinese aerodrome system. In 2023, international aviation hubs handled 554,042,000 passengers, representing 43.97% of the national total, and additionally, they managed more than 10.86 million tons of cargo and mail, accounting for 64.57% of the country.[19] It offers vital infrastructure and technological support for China's import and export trade and cultural exchange with the world. It has become an important representation of China's external profile.

2.3 *Outlook of Chinese Aerodromes Industry Development*

Nevertheless, there are still some irrationalities in the current aerodrome layout in China. In order to establish a more rational layout, new plans must be formulated and implemented. Following the approval of the National Civil Airport Layout Plan (exclusive of general aviation aerodromes) by the State Council in 2008, the number of aerodromes has increased significantly, as has their density, the extent of their coverage and the encryption of their locations. However, in light of the ongoing economic and social development several problems exist. The total number is still insufficient, the layout is not yet entirely reasonable, and the imbalance and insufficiency of aerodromes coverage between regions persists. These problems present challenges in adapting to the implementation of major national strategies and meeting

[18] *Supra* note 9.

[19] *Supra* note 9.

the requirements of the general public for convenient travel.[20] Consequently, the National Development and Reform Commission (NDRC) and CAAC undertook the requisite amendments to the plan on 15 May 2017 and issued a new version. This plan, together with the 14th Five-Year Plan for Civil Aviation Development and the Outline of Action for the Construction of Four Types of Civil Aviation Airports and other normative documents, offers guidance for the construction of civil aerodromes in China.

According to the original plan of the National Civil Aviation Airport Layout Plan (ALP), China planned to build 260 aerodromes by 2020, and a modern aerodrome system consisting of three world-class aerodrome clusters, 10 international hubs, 29 regional hubs and a modern aerodrome system with wide coverage, rational allocation, perfect operation, intensive and eco-friendly operation by 2025.[21] Although we are now halfway to 2024, and there are concerns that the ALP's projected construction targets will be challenging to achieve within the original timeframe, the ALP's understanding of China's level of local economic development, the distribution and their relationship with the development of neighbouring regions is profound and insightful. Therefore, it is still of great strategic importance for formulating the "Fifteenth Five-Year Plan" after 2025 and guiding the future layout of national aerodrome construction.

The ALP divides China's aerodromes into six major clusters: North China, Northeast China, East China, Central and South China, Southwest China and Northwest China,[22] with different positioning and development expectations. Overall, 139 new civil aerodromes are projected to be added, bringing the total to 370 (of which 320 will be completed). The planned numbers of new aerodromes for the six aerodrome clusters are 16, 23, 16, 24, 29 and 28, respectively, and the overall target of 48, 50, 61, 60, 78 and 73 for each region is planned, aiming to balance the development between the eastern and western regions and to increase the aerodrome density of the western region, with the higher number of planned constructions in the western region accounting for 41% of the total target.[23]

In addition to this, the ALP forms a step-by-step, hierarchical development plan, which calls for the formation and rapid development of world-class aerodrome clusters in Beijing-Tianjin-Hebei, the Yangtze River Delta and the Zhu River Delta,

---

[20] CAAC, '14th Five-Year Plan for Civil Aviation Development', *State Council of the People's Republic of China*, January 7 2022, available at <https://www.gov.cn/zhengce/zhengceku/2022-01/07/5667003/files/d12ea75169374a15a742116f7082df85.pdf.> Last visited, 17 July 2024.

[21] CAAC, National Civil Aviation Airport Layout Plan (ALP), available at <https://www.gov.cn/xinwen/2017-03/15/5177519/files/f3d9d7a20f984f4d8d153432b07b3f0e.pdf> Last visited, 17 July 2024.

[22] The North China Airport Cluster in the ALP refers to aerodromes in Beijing, Tianjin, Hebei, Shanxi and Inner Mongolia; the Northeast refers to Liaoning, Jilin and Heilongjiang; the East China refers to Shanghai, Jiangsu, Zhejiang, Anhui, Fujian, Jiangxi and Shandong; the Central and South China refers to Henan, Hubei, Hunan, Guangdong, Guangxi and Hainan; and the Southwest refers to Chongqing, Sichuan, Guizhou, Yunnan and Tibet; the Northwest refers to Shaanxi, Gansu, Qinghai, Ningxia, and Xinjiang.

[23] *Supra* note 20.

which have a high-level of the economy, favourable geographic location—which is most important to serve the international market. Apart from that, the ALP also puts forward several directions that needs further perfection and adoption. For instance, the coordination of transport aerodromes and general aviation aerodromes in terms of policies and measures, policies on financing the aerodrome industry and the capacity of air traffic management, which should emphasis more on the integration of various modes of transport such as urban railways, rail transit, high-speed railways and highways. Besides, the design, construction and operation of aerodromes should adhere to the initiative of green and intensive development and its construction, operation and management should meet with requirements of scientific and technological innovation capability.

Although the Chinese civil aviation industry and aerodrome industry in 2024 did not reach the targets planned in 2017 due to the pandemic, there has been a strong recovery drive and huge market demand shown by the Chinese aerodromes industry in 2023. The amazing growth trend of more than 140% allows us to believe in China's development potential. Although delayed in time, China's development goals have maintained continuity and consistency in general. Its goal of building a perfect and multi-level aerodromes network has not changed, and science and technology, green, coordinated and integrated coordinated development is still the goal of Chinese aerodromes construction. China should now adjust and rationalise its detailed plans in conjunction with the socio-economic changes caused by the epidemic, giving more consideration to the response to sudden public accidents in the layout of its construction, which will turn the past three years from stagnation into a lesson that we should learn from.

3 The Revolution of Aerodrome Governance in China

3.1 Date Back to the 1910s: The Initial Status

A review of historical records reveals that China was among the first countries in the world to commence aerodrome construction, a process that has been ongoing for over a century, which can be traced back to August 1910, when the first aerodrome, Nanyuan Airport, established in Fengtai, Beijing, during the late Qing Dynasty.[24] This was also the first military aerodrome in Asia, opening one year after the establishment of that in the United States in 1909. In the following century, particularly in the decades following the establishment of the People's Republic of China, despite several changes in leadership, the CAAC spearheaded the construction of numerous aerodromes and implemented significant reforms to the management system and organisational structure. The construction and management of Chinese aerodromes have been constantly adjusting itself in accordance with the objective situation of

[24] Chen Chen, 'The First Airport in China: Nanyuan Airport', in *Fengtai History*, (Beijing edn.), 20 March 2024, p. 7.

economic development and summation of experiences, endeavouring to identify its unique mode and road with Chinese characteristics.

3.2 *From the 1950s to 1960s: Recovery and Adjustment*

The establishment of China's civil aviation industry occurred concurrently with the formation of the People's Republic of China. One month after its founding, the Political Bureau of the Central People's Government established the CAAC under the People's Revolutionary Military Commission. This meeting, held on 2 November 1949, marked the inception of China's civil aviation development.[25] In its infancy, the Civil Aviation Administration of the Military Commission was subordinated to the Air Force Command and operationally was led by the Central Finance Commission. Subsequently, despite the CAAC's leadership structure undergoing several reforms, so as the ownership of China's aerodromes, it persists as the primary entity for governing China's civil aviation sector, advocating for reforms through the formulation of regulations and other normative documents.

During the early 1950s, while China was still in a period of national economic recovery and the demand for air transport was relatively limited, the principle of "organising limited flights" was adopted along with the steady progress of the civil aviation business in China.[26]

On 7 May 1952, the Chinese Central Military Commission and the State Council decided to reorganise civil aviation. Therefore, a major reorganisation of the CAAC began.[27] The reorganisation included the transformation of the former Civil Aviation Administration of the Military Commission into an Air Force department, the separation of administration and business operations, the transfer of repair stations, schools and assets to the relevant departments, and the transfer of materials needed for civil aviation to the Air Force. This reform intended to unify civil aviation management and improve the efficiency of personnel and resources, but excessive downsizing hampered its development. Two months later, the People's Airline of China was established in Tianjin in accordance with the decision to separate government from enterprise and centralise operations and vertical management.[28] However, due to overlapping organisations and inefficient management, a second structural reform initiated in June 1953 and the company was abolished and incorporated into CAAC. In 1958, another change was made to CAAC, which was placed under the leadership of the Ministry of Transport, while most of the operational work was still guided

---

[25] Liu Li & Wang Yong, 'A Brief History of Civil Aviation in China', *China Civil Aviation Press*, 2011, p. 41.

[26] *Id.*, at p. 45.

[27] Li Yong, 'A Concise Course on the History of Civil Aviation Development', *China Civil Aviation Press*, July 2011, p. 47.

[28] *Supra* note 24, at p. 47.

by the Air Force. Later, the principle of dual leadership and partial decentralisation of civil aviation was established, however, due to the barely satisfactory results, authority soon returned to the CAAC. In 1962, the CAAC was adjusted and directly subordinated to the State Council, and two years later, a strategic plan of exploiting international routes was set. However, between 1966 and 1976, the development of civil aviation was severely hampered by the decade of social change and in 1969 the CAAC was, again, returned to the Air Force with a quasi-military management system.[29]

3.3 *During the 1970s: Ready to Take-Off*

After the 1970s, the People's Republic of China regained its legal seat in the UN and the seat later in the ICAO, which greatly encouraged the development of Chinese civil aviation. In 1973, China made great efforts to open up international routes and successively signed navigation agreements with Albania, Romania, Italy, Japan and other countries to prepare for China's recognition of the Convention on International Civil Aviation and the development of international routes. On 15 February 1974, the Chinese Government decided to recognize the Convention on International Civil Aviation (the Chicago Convention), signed in 1944 by the former Nationalist Government. Later, China was elected to the ICAO at the 21st General Assembly in Montreal, Canada, in September. Since then, China's civil aviation industry has made breakthroughs, and China's aerodrome construction has also flourished. Beijing Capital Airport, Zhejiang Hangzhou Jianqiao Airport, Xinjiang Urumqi Diwopu Airport, Hefei Luogang Airport, Tianjin Zhangguizhuang Airport and Harbin Airport have all expanded.[30] At the same time, after 1974, civil aviation enterprises resumed the economic accounting system, and finally turned losses into profits in the second year, reversing the long-term loss-making situation. What's more, the indicators of China's civil aviation industry have been developing for the better, with steady growth year by year.

3.4 *From 1978 to 2004: Reform in Progress*

The milestone for China's civil aviation industry to truly take off was the implementation of reforming and opening. Since then, China's civil aviation system has undergone four major reforms, including three system reforms and one operation model reform. China's economic system began to change from a planned economy to a market economy under the guidance of the government. A modern enterprise

---

[29] *Id.*, pp. 64–66.

[30] See Li Xiaojin, 'A Century of Archives: Observing the Development of China's Transportation - Civil Aviation Chapter', *Economic Science Press*, 2021, pp. 95–98.

system has also been established in the field of public utilities, a series of incentive mechanisms have been introduced, and the government has played a role in macroeconomic regulation and control in the market. The operation of the market has made the resources in the society flow freely, and various sources of wealth creation such as talents, science and technology, capital, and management have also flowed into the field of China's civil aviation, stimulating the construction and development of the aerodrome industry.

The initial institutional reform occurred on 5 March 1980, with the publication of "Civil Aviation Must Follow the Path of Enterprise" in the "People's Daily".[31] This marked the beginning of the enterprise reform in the civil aviation sector. Ten days later, the State Council and the Central Military Commission officially issued a document to notify the reclassification of CAAC under the direct leadership of the State Council for enterprise management. A dual management system led by CAAC was implemented, with regional management bureaus under CAAC and provincial management bureaus being jointly managed by both CAAC and local governments. Local governments began to develop their own civil aviation industries, operating independently, managing their finances autonomously, bearing their own profits and losses, and paying taxes to the state. At this time, local aerodromes also saw significant development, with construction led by local management bureaus and governments, such as the constructions in Xiamen and Dalian. Although the management included local governments as new entities, the civil aviation sector still operated under a system where government and enterprise functions were combined, with CAAC handling specific aviation transportation business activities. Apart from service inputs such as aircraft landing fees and terminal site rentals, other service inputs constituted a small proportion of the overall revenue. This was due to the system where government and enterprise roles were not clearly separated, making it difficult to enhance vitality and efficiency.

The main content of the second structural reform was to promote the separation of government and enterprises. In 1985, the State Council issued a notice on the CAAC "Report on the Reform of the Civil Aviation System Management System" to implement the reform in accordance with the principle of separating government from enterprises, and CAAC no longer carried out the direct operation of civil aviation transport business, but only exercised administrative functions.[32] In addition, all kinds of subsidiaries of the civil aviation industry were independent from the executive branch and carried out independent business activities. At the same time, the central government should also support and encourage local governments to set up local aviation enterprises. In January 1987, the State Council approved the CAAC "Report on the Reform Plan and Implementation Steps of the Civil Aviation Management System", marking its promotion throughout the country.[33] According to the principle of separation of government and enterprises, the regional

[31] Wang Jingxia & Dai Shaoyong, 'Airport Strategic Planning and Control: A Value-Oriented Approach', *China Civil Aviation Press*, 2015, p. 35.

[32] *Id*., at p. 36.

[33] *Id*.

administration, aviation enterprises and aerodromes were separated. The latter one also became an independent enterprise rather than the logistics support department of aviation, and the three parts were independent. China's six backbone airlines and corresponding regional administrations, as well as Chengdu Shuangliu Airport, Shanghai Hongqiao Airport, Beijing Capital International Airport, Xi'an Xiguan Airport, Shenyang Xiantao International Airport and Guangzhou Baiyun International Airport have been established one after another. With the economic development opportunities brought about by China's reform and opening up, China has opened up international routes with the Philippines, Thailand, Singapore, Japan, United Kingdom, France and other countries, and the demand for air transport has grown rapidly, such as in 1987, the passenger traffic increased by 281% compared with 1980, of which the international route increased by 284%, the central and local governments have continued to expand their investment in aerodromes, financing channels have been gradually liberalised, and local construction had ushered its spring.[34]

On the one hand, the Circular on Policies Relating to Domestic Investment in the Operation of the Civil Aviation Industry was issued by CAAC in June 1993 with the approval of the State Council. The circular explicitly stated that the establishment of joint ventures or wholly-owned air transport enterprises by the central government or local governments, or economic organisations was permitted. China Cargo Airlines Ltd. was established as a joint venture between China Eastern Airlines, China Ocean Shipping Company and Taiwan's China Airlines, with respective equity stakes of 65%, 10% and 25%. Subsequently, there was a notable increase in the number of market-oriented air transport enterprises, which underwent a series of mergers, acquisitions and joint ventures. For instance, China Eastern Airlines invested 240 million yuan in equity participation in Wuhan Airlines, leading to the formation of the Orient Airlines Wuhan Limited Liability Company. Additionally, China Southern also engaged in a joint venture with Wuhan Airlines. Airlines, including Shanghai Airlines, Shandong Airlines and Sichuan Airlines, collectively established the Sichuan Airlines Co Ltd with a proportionate shareholding of 39%, 10%, 10% and 40% of the equity in Sichuan Airlines.[35] Conversely, in May 1994, the CAAC and the Ministry of Foreign Trade and Economic Cooperation (MOFTEC) jointly issued the "Circular on Relevant Policies on Foreign Investment in Civil Aviation Industry", which designated foreign capital as a principal source of capital for air transport enterprises.[36] In order to facilitate China's accession to the World Trade Organisation (WTO), CAAC, MOFTEC, and the National Development and Planning Commission (NDPC) jointly formulated new "Regulations on Foreign Investment in Civil Aviation Industry" in 2001, which expanded the scope of foreign investment in the civil aviation industry. The Regulations on Civil Aviation Industry serve to expand the scope and mode of foreign investment, liberalise investment ratios and increase

[34] *Supra* note 26, at p. 109.

[35] *Supra* note 30, pp. 132–133.

[36] *Id.*, at p. 135.

foreign management powers. They thus constitute an institutional guarantee for the full utilisation of foreign capital in China's civil aviation industry.

The third stage was the comprehensive reform of the civil aviation system in 2002.[37] This was initiated by the CPC Central Committee and the State Council, who approved the Civil Aviation System Reform Programme. This was designed to establish a management system and operation mechanism that would meet the needs of the socialist market economy and the development of modern civil aviation. The State Council also approved the Reform Programme of the Provincial (Regional and Municipal) Civil Aviation Airport Management System and Administration System, which was submitted by CAAC in September 2003. This marked the beginning of the localisation reform of the 129 civil aerodromes and the reform of aviation enterprise systems. The reform of the localisation of the 129 civil aerodromes and the reform of the aviation enterprise system commenced.[38] The fundamental tenets of the reform were as follows:

1. Separation of government management of aerodromes from their production and operation, with aerodromes running their own business.
2. Separation of the government's industry supervision function over aerodromes from its asset management function, with the former being the responsibility of government-industry authorities and the latter being the responsibility of local governments.

In 2004, the transfer of management of the last four aerodromes marked the completion of localisation reform, except for Beijing Capital Airport and Tibet Airport. Most aerodromes were transformed into enterprises, some became listed companies or Chinese-foreign joint ventures, and a small number of companies were positioned as local institutions.[39]

The fourth is the reform of the mode of operation. Originally as a public infrastructure, civil aerodromes still bore most of the social responsibility, and in the process of marketisation, there was also a public risk. On 1 July 2009, the Regulations on the Administration of Civil Airports were formally implemented. It clarifies the positioning of civil aerodromes as public infrastructure in China and takes into account the dual characteristics of public welfare and profitability of civil aerodromes. At the same time, aerodromes were encouraged to change from operators to managers, entrusting companies with aerodrome business to professional companies by way of concessions or franchises and transforming themselves into managers, overseeing the safety, services, charges and business practices of these companies. Review and supervision while improving efficiency. China's aerodromes still maintain state ownership, but the corporate nature is also gradually increasing and gradually began to transition to a purely economic entity. Local governments are actively involved in the construction of aerodromes to promote local socio-economic development.

---

[37] *Supra* note 30, at p. 37

[38] *Supra* note 30, pp. 37–38.

[39] *Id.*, at p. 38.

3.5 Current Modern Corporate Structure

After the reform of localisation, China's aerodromes began to show diversification of management systems, complexity of affiliation, and the emergence of aerodrome holding groups of different sizes across the country. A modern corporate structure of civil aerodromes supervised by the Department of Airport under CAAC was fixed, formulating a state where the business operation of civil aerodromes is conducted by enterprises while the administration is conducted by the department. The department carries these 11 main responsibilities:

1. Draft laws, regulations, policies, standards, and quotas governing the construction, safety and operational management of civil airports (including the civil portions of military and civilian combined airports, the same as below), and oversee the implementation.
2. Review the site of new civil airports to be built and the name of the airports; review the master plans for civil airports and oversee the implementation.
3. Manage the licensing of civil airports; issue and revoke the license for civil airports and conduct oversight.
4. Review the initial design for engineering and construction projects in civil aviation and conduct industry acceptance affairs.
5. Manage project bidding in civil aviation (excluding international bidding for mechanical and electrical products and bidding for government procurement) and supervise and manage engineering quality in civil aviation.
6. Manage qualification of organisations responsible for engineering design, construction and supervision as well as intermediary organisations.
7. Oversee and inspect the operational safety at civil airports.
8. Manage emergency rescue, environmental protection, land use, and clearance protection for civil airports.
9. Authorize the use of special equipment at civil airports.
10. Oversee and manage the operational safety of fuel suppliers at civil airports.
11. Undertake other tasks assigned by CAAC executives.[40]

There are mainly three management modes, which are; (i) management by the state, (ii) management by the local government, and (iii) mixed shareholding management.

Firstly, the state-controlled aerodromes are directly under the CAAC, and only two remained after the reformation in 2004. One of them is the Xizang Airport Group and the other is the Capital Airport Holdings Co Ltd (CAH), which is also the largest airport holding in China. Take the CAH for an example, it was established in 2002 and completed its restructuring in 2021, with a registered capital of 55.7 billion yuan, and is a wholly-owned legal entity of the CAAC. It is a management group of over 50 trunk and branch aerodromes in Beijing, Tianjin, Jiangxi, Jilin, Inner Mongolia and Heilongjiang provinces. In 2023, the annual throughput of passengers, cargo and mail and the number of transport sorties reached 202.6 million, 1.908

[40] See CAAC, 'Department of Airport', March 30 2023, available at <http://www.caac.gov.cn/English/AboutCAAC/Departments/202303/t20230330_217774.html> Last visited, 17 July 2024.

million tons and 0.174 million, respectively.[41] Its organisational structure contains one office and 11 departments dealing with business management, safety and quality control, capital operation, international science and technology, etc. Besides that, 34 economic entities, including Beijing Capital Airport Tourism Industry Co Ltd, Beijing Capital Airport Food Management Co Ltd and Capital Finance Co Ltd and so on, are affiliated to the CAH and together formulated a systematic operational structure that runs the Titan.[42]

Secondly, there are aerodromes controlled by local governments, such as Shanghai Airport Group, which is 100% owned by the State-owned Assets Supervision and Administration Commission of Shanghai. It owns two aerodromes, Shanghai Pudong Airport and Hongqiao Airport. Under the management of Shanghai Airport Group, the shareholding structure of aerodromes operated under marketisation is more affluent, for example, in 2023 Shanghai International Airport Co Ltd, in addition to Shanghai Airports Group's 58.38% shareholding, the shareholding composition of the rest of the company includes a variety of state-owned legal persons and domestic natural persons, etc., and the use of the issuance of listed shares, equity transfer, financing of operating assets and operating projects, the issuance of ultra-short term.[43] It has also used instruments of operation under the market economy such as issuance of listed stocks, equity transfer, financing of operating assets and operating projects and issuance of ultra-short-term financing bonds to expand its sources of funds. It also has made full use of the joint-stock company as the financing platform of the Airport Group in order to guarantee the sustainable development of the aviation homepage.[44]

Thirdly, a typical example of a large holding aerodrome group managed under a mixed shareholding system is the Guangdong Airport Authority (GAA) affiliated with the Guangdong Provincial Government. In 2013, it underwent a transition from ownership by the whole people to a corporate system. This restructuring resulted in the formation of six aerodrome companies, which fall under the GAA's leadership, namely Baiyun, Chaoshan, Zhanjiang, Meizhou, Huizhou, and Shaoguan airports. In addition to the daily management and operation of aerodromes, GAA has wholly-owned and holding subsidiaries, including Baiyun International Airport Co Ltd, Guangdong Airport Group Logistics Co Ltd, and Airport Property Co Ltd. It should be noted that Guangzhou Baiyun International Airport is 57.2% owned by Guangzhou Airport Group. Furthermore, Guangzhou Airport Group plays an active role in the development of business aviation. It has constructed a business aviation base (FBO) at

[41] China National Aviation Holding Company, 'About Us: Overview', available at<https://www.cah.com.cn/en/AboutUs/overview/> Last visited, 19 July 2024.

[42] China National Aviation Holding Company, 'About Us: Structure', available at <https://www.cah.com.cn/en/AboutUs/Structure/> Last visited, 19 July 2024.

[43] Shanghai International Airport Co. Ltd., 2023, Annual Report, 28 March 2024, pp. 55–56.

[44] Liu Wujun, 'The Chinese Airport Group Financing Model and Corporate Governance', *Shanghai Science and Technology Press*, February 2018, p. 37.

Baiyun Airport and established Baiyun Airport Company, a joint venture of Wingtone Business Aviation Services Co Ltd. and Guangzhou Xinke Aerospace G2 Aircraft Maintenance Depot, which aims to facilitate the growth of the aviation maintenance industry.[45]

4 Legal Framework of Aerodrome in China

China has consistently maintained a stance of actively promoting the rule of law in international civil aviation. This has entailed active participation in international civil aviation legislation, including the ratification of or accession to international conventions and bilateral or multilateral agreements. Additionally, there has been a continuous process of improvement in domestic legislation, accompanied by a commitment to the rule of law in aerodrome governance and management.

4.1 International Treaties

Firstly, in terms of accession to international treaties, as of the end of 2023, China has joined or ratified a series of international conventions, including Convention on International Civil Aviation (1944), The Convention for the Suppression of Unlawful Seizure of Aircraft (1970), the Convention for the Unification of Certain Rules for International Carriage by Air (1999), Protocol for the Suppression of Unlawful Acts of Violence at Airports Serving International Civil Aviation (1988), and Convention for the Suppression of Unlawful Acts Relating to International Civil Aviation (2010), and so on. By incorporating international rules into its domestic law, China has been striving to fulfil its conventional obligations by improving its domestic legal framework.

4.2 Domestic Legal Framework

With regard to domestic legislation, China, as a member of the International Civil Aviation Organization (ICAO), has fully adopted the safety standards and recommended measures set forth in the Chicago Convention. Furthermore, it strives to establish a comprehensive safety management system encompassing a range of critical areas, including flight standards, aircraft airworthiness, air traffic services, aerodrome management, the transportation of dangerous goods, and investigating

[45] Guangdong Airport Authority, 'Official Website of Guangdong Airport Management Group Co. Ltd.', available at <https://www.gdairport.com/portal/site/site/portal/gdjc/lsyg.portal> Last visited, 24 July 2024.

accidents. A system of regulations and standards has been established, comprising the Civil Aviation Law as the core, dozens of administrative regulations, over a hundred departmental rules and regulations, supplied with a quite amount of industry standards. This system encompasses both administrative and technical regulations pertaining to the management and operation of aerodromes. A relatively more scientific and comprehensive set of hierarchical and systematic aerodrome governance laws and regulations has been established, which aims to adapt to the actual situation and unexpected problems of its governance. Furthermore, efforts have been made to implement China's obligations under international conventions and the ICAO into China's domestic legislation, with the aim of creating a legal system of aerodrome governance with Chinese characteristics.

The Civil Aviation Law represents a foundational and central legal framework within China's civil aviation domain. The legislation was adopted by the Standing Committee of the National People's Congress in 1995 and came into force on 1 March 1996. It has been amended six times, with its most recent iteration currently in force in the 2021 edition. Chapter VI of this legislation provides a separate set of regulations for civil aerodromes. A total of 17 articles regulate the concept of civil aerodromes, the principles and main body of layout and construction planning, the scope of the aerodromes themselves and the airspace protection zone, the licensing requirements for civil aerodromes, the establishment of international aerodromes and the obligations of civil aerodrome management agencies. This chapter establishes a framework for standardising and unifying the management system for civil aerodromes, as well as for the administrative control of civil transport aerodromes by the CAAC, the local people's governments, and the civil aerodrome. Furthermore, it provides legal safeguards to protect the authority of CAAC, local people's governments, and civil aerodrome management agencies to carry out administrative management of civil transport aerodromes.

Administrative regulations are legal documents adopted by the State Council, which represent the second tier of the Chinese law system. With respect to regulatory frameworks, six documents pertain to the management and operation of aerodromes, while five address matters related to express logistics, radio installations, and the transportation of dangerous chemicals. Of particular note are the Regulations on Civil Airport Management and the Regulations on Civil Aviation Safety and Security, representing the most central legal norms on civil aerodrome management.

The Regulations on the Administration of Civil Airports, which came into effect on 1 July 2009, is enacted with the objective of regulating the construction and management of civil aerodromes, ensuring the safe and orderly operation of civil aerodromes, and safeguarding the legitimate rights and interests of the parties concerned. The principal topics addressed are the construction and operation of civil aerodromes, safety and operational management, safety and environmental protection, and administrative penalties. The regulation constitutes a refinement of seventeen legal provisions contained within the Civil Airports chapter of the Civil Aviation Law. It serves to clarify the status of civil aerodromes as a form of public infrastructure while simultaneously requiring the relevant local governments to implement measures designed to encourage and support the development of civil aerodromes. Furthermore, it defines the specific behaviours that are in violation of the management of civil aerodromes and sets out clear criteria for penalties and the basis for penalties for civil aviation authorities, thus making them legally enforceable and enabling their practical implementation.

The Regulations on the Safety and Security of Civil Aviation were initially issued on 6 July 1996 and subsequently amended on 8 January 2011. The Regulations were enacted with the objective of preventing any form of unlawful interference with civil aviation activities, maintaining the integrity of the civil aviation order and safeguarding civil aviation safety. It stipulates the security conditions that civil aerodromes are required to meet and the responsibilities of civil aerodrome operators with regard to safety and security. It also establishes the requirements for safety inspections at aerodromes and sets forth the obligations of passengers to accept safety inspections. In addition, it enumerates illegal acts that contravene the safety and security of civil aerodromes and specifies the corresponding penalties. The implementation of security checks represents a crucial preventive measure for the safeguarding navigation safety, reducing the number of human-caused accidents and preventing hijacking and kidnapping of aircraft, as well as other offences. Such measures can significantly reduce the likelihood of such accidents or crimes occurring, safeguard the personal and property safety of travellers and flight crews, and significantly reduce irreparable damage.

The Departmental Regulations, otherwise known as Civil Aviation Regulations of China (CCAR), are legally binding standards established by the Ministry of Transport under the auspices of the State Council and are thus situated at the third level of administrative law. Several regulations pertaining to aerodromes that have been issued by the Ministry of Transport directly regulate the use and operation of aerodromes. By way of illustration, one may cite the Regulations on Permission for the Use of Transport Airports and the Rules on Emergency Response and Rescue Management for Civilian Transport Airports.

Formerly, Provisions on Permission for Use of Transport Airports set forth the supervision of the CAAC and regional administrations of civil aviation in obtaining aerodrome use permits for transport aerodromes within their jurisdictions. It also required local administrations to conduct annual applicability inspections and compliance evaluations of transport aerodromes within their jurisdictions once every five years, thus establishing a long-term and effective system for aerodrome use and operation. Furthermore, the Regulations require local authorities to conduct annual applicability inspections and five-year compliance evaluations of transport aerodromes under their jurisdiction. This establishes a long-term and effective regular supervision system through which operational and business conditions at the aerodromes may be continuously monitored following the grant of licenses. It aims to ensure the long-term effective and stable operation of the aerodromes.

Furthermore, the civil aviation policies and China Civil Aviation Industry Standard, as issued by CAAC, effectively supplement existing laws and regulations. The formulation of civil aviation policies represents a crucial means for CAAC to fulfil its supervisory and managerial functions over the national civil aerodrome industry, as stipulated by legislation, and to facilitate the implementation of national policies and development plans within the civil aviation sector. For instance, to implement the requirements of energy conservation, emission reduction and green development as set out in the 14th Five-Year Plan, CAAC formulated a Green Development Plan for Civil Aviation for implementation in the 14th Five-Year Plan. While the standard is recommended for implementation, it is legally binding if a company publicly states that it implements the recommended standard or agrees to adopt the standard in a contract. Furthermore, any violation of the standard may result in administrative penalties. However, in the field of aerodrome security, a violation of the standard "Safety and Security Facilities at Civil Transport Airports" (MH/T 7003-2017), which sets out specific requirements for safety and security facilities, such as aerodrome perimeters, intrusion alarm systems, road gates and patrol lanes, to ensure the safe operation of aerodromes, may result in the imposition of appropriate penalties.

5 Outlook for Chinese Aerodromes Development

With 2025 looming on the horizon, China's next five-year plan is again on the line. Under the impact of the resurgence of the epidemic, we have seen the rapid recovery of China's aviation market in 2023, with the figures of 235 million passengers and 2,858,200 tons of cargo and mail transported in 2023. But China is still a long way from achieving the targets of 930 million passengers and 9.5 million tons of cargo and mail transported in 2025 as set out in the 14th Five-Year Plan meaning that China's air transport industry is still under great pressure to reach the target. However, the growth rate of Chinese aerodromes in the world is predicted to become the world's largest air service market by 2042, and the growth rate of the aviation industry is also ranked first in the world, proving that the aftermath of the epidemic has brought new challenges as well as new opportunities to the global aerodrome industry.[46] If Chinese aerodromes are to live up to the world's high expectations, meet domestic demand while gaining competitiveness in the global market, and promote the development of a low-altitude economy in the next decade, they have to reform and improve the legal and governance structure of the aerodrome industry. To this end, the author has the following ideas.

Firstly, the market system should be enhanced in order to facilitate the full realisation of the economic benefits associated with aerodromes. Considering the corporatisation of aerodromes in China, it is imperative to ensure that they are fully utilised as financial entities, thereby enabling them to become a significant contributor to social wealth creation. China's "Civil Airport Regulations" have established the aerodrome as a fundamental public facility, categorising it as both a public welfare and revenue-generating entity.[47] Despite this, the ownership of aerodromes in China remains

[46] *Supra* note 2.

[47] See CAAC, Civil Airport Regulations 2009, Ch.1, Art.3: Civil airports are public infrastructure facilities. People's governments at all levels shall take necessary measures to encourage and support the development of civil airports and enhance their management standards.

with the state, which means aerodromes have a significant social responsibility to provide public products and services that meet the needs of the travelling public and facilitate the movement of goods. However, they must also focus on developing their economic value to generate financial benefits. As previously stated, Shanghai Airport has employed the utilisation of the projects and assets of Shanghai International Airport as a means of financing. This has effectively transformed the already fixed state-owned assets into a source of funding for the continued operation of the enterprise, thereby revitalising fixed assets and projects while reducing the waste of resources. However, it is important to note, that the aerodrome remains an integral component of the state-owned asset landscape. The infrastructure and facilities associated with aerodromes are of significant social importance and possess a distinctive character. To reduce the potential risk of asset loss, it is essential to implement a comprehensive market system that safeguards the interests of the aerodrome industry.

Secondly, it would be beneficial to examine the various forms of ownership of aerodromes and consider ways to increase their accessibility to external entities. As is the case with the WTO system on the topic of whether a country should open the aviation market, the question of whether a country should open its aviation market is a controversial one.[48] It is clear that each country should be aware of the benefits that opening up the aviation market can bring to a country, as well as the importance of the market itself. Even though China does not allow foreign capital to invest directly in the construction of aerodromes in China, it does not prohibit its participation in the aerodrome industry through the acquisition of equity, project investment and other means of market investment. The market is gradually becoming more open to foreign capital, with restrictions on its entry being reduced. Consequently, a more comprehensive and rational legal structure has been devised to oversee foreign investment, thereby enabling foreign capital to assume an active role in the construction and operation of China's aerodromes. Concurrently, it is crucial to enhance the capital structure of Chinese aerodrome enterprises, thereby augmenting their capacity to withstand risks and enhancing their market resilience.

Thirdly, it is essential to consider the impact of emerging domains and technologies on the governance of aerodromes. Considering the advancements in technology, it is imperative that aerodrome management evolves to become increasingly intelligent. The application of big data and the optimisation of algorithms can enhance the efficiency of flight scheduling, facilitate the integration of constrained flight resources, prevent and minimise wastage, and facilitate the efficient operation and rational scheduling of aerodromes, thereby creating economies of scale and reducing aerodrome operating costs. Concurrently, deploying innovative technologies is instrumental in bolstering aerodrome security protocols and augmenting emergency response capabilities while also advancing passenger safety and cargo protection.

Fourthly, it is imperative to prioritise the environmentally sustainable development of aerodromes. As previously stated in the 14th Five-Year Plan, China's commitment

[48] See Zhang Shiliang, 'WTO Aviation Legislation Research', *China Civil Aviation Press*, October 2006, pp. 249–258.

to achieving the carbon peak deadline by 2030 is a key objective of its green development strategy.[49] To attain this goal, a comprehensive set of low-carbon and green standards must be established and implemented across various stages of aerodrome operations, including design, construction, management, and even the transformation of waste aerodromes into sustainable reuse processes.[50] At the same time, a set of green supervisory and management mechanisms should be established throughout the entire life cycle of aerodromes, of which should be designed to dynamically supervise the development process of airports by regulating and precisely calculating the changes in data related to day-to-day operations, noise detection, recycling, and the use of alternative energy sources.

Fifthly, it is necessary to uphold the legislation process in the governance of civil aerodromes guided by the 14th Five-Year Plan. Though challenges have come along with the everlasting effect in the post-pandemic era, impeding the realisation of the plan, legislation of the governance of civil aerodromes admits no delay. In accordance with the Department of Airports under the CAAC, it shall continually play its role in drafting legal documents, which means further amending and refining legal regulations such as Regulations on the Administration of Civil Airports and Provisions on the Operation Safety Administration of Transport Airports to promote the development of general aviation.[51] Concurrently, given that Chinese aerodromes are still predominantly oriented towards the management of transport airports, it is also imperative to accelerate the formulation of the Regulations on the Management of General-Purpose Airports, with the objective of fostering the growth of the general aviation industry. Furthermore, while the low-altitude economy is experiencing significant growth, it also presents certain challenges to China's civil aviation legal system. In that case, investigations and analyses on how to classify and manage the low-altitude economy regulation objects more scientifically and implement comprehensive reforms, which can enhance the role of the market in the low-altitude economy and adjust to its features and needs remain a field uncultivated.

6 Conclusion

The chapter provides a comprehensive analysis of the governance and legal structure of aerodromes in China, highlighting the pivotal role these facilities play in the nation's economic growth and strategic development. With CAAC at the helm, the

[49] See CAAC, 'The 14th Five-Year Plan for Green Development of Civil Aviation', 27 December 2021, available at <https://www.gov.cn/zhengce/zhengceku/2022-01/28/5670938/files/c22e012963ce458782eb9cb7fea7e3e3.pdf> Last visited, 10 August 2024.

[50] See China Civil Aviation Environment and Sustainable Development Research Center & Air Transport Environmental Protection Committee of China Aviation Transport Association, eds., China Civil Aviation Green Development Policy and Practice, 2020, pp. 180–183.

[51] See CAAC, 'The 14th Five-Year Special Plan for Civil Aviation Legislation', 26 January 2022, available at <http://www.caac.gov.cn/XXGK/XXGK/FZGH/202201/t20220126_211320.html> Last visited, 17 October 2024.

governance structure has evolved significantly from a government-enterprise system to a more modern and market-oriented approach. The reforms have aimed to corporatise aerodromes, enhancing their operational efficiency and economic viability while ensuring safety and security standards are met.

The legal framework, with the Civil Aviation Law of China at its core, is complemented by a hierarchy of regulations and policies that address aerodrome management, safety, security, and environmental considerations. China's commitment to international conventions and the transformation of these global standards into domestic legislation demonstrates a proactive approach to aligning with international practices while tailoring them to the country's unique conditions.

Looking ahead, the development of Chinese aerodromes is poised to capitalise on new opportunities presented by technological advancements and the burgeoning low-altitude economy. The integration of intelligent systems, big data, and sustainable practices is set to revolutionise aerodrome operations, making them more efficient, secure, and environmentally friendly. The chapter also underscores the need for a diversified ownership structure that could attract external investments, thus bolstering the financial resilience and market competitiveness of Chinese aerodromes.

Despite the challenges posed by the global pandemic, the Chinese aviation market has shown remarkable recovery and growth momentum, reflecting the robustness of its aviation policies and the strategic importance placed on aerodrome development. As China moves towards its goals for the next decade, the continuous modernisation of its aerodrome system, underpinned by a robust legal and governance framework, is set to cement its position as a global aviation powerhouse.

In summary, the governance and legal structure of Chinese aerodromes reflect a dynamic and adaptive system that is responsive to both domestic needs and international standards. With a clear vision for the future, China's aerodromes are well-positioned and ready to contribute significantly to the nation's economic prosperity and its role as one of the leaders in the global aviation industry.

Chapter 4
Regulation of Airport Noise in China: Application of the ICAO Balanced Approach

Yuran Shi

Abstract Airport noise pollution poses a complex challenge, intensified by the growth in global air traffic and advancements in aircraft technology. Despite significant reductions in noise from individual aircraft, the overall noise footprint has expanded due to increased air traffic and the introduction of larger aircraft. This issue has become particularly contentious for communities living near airports, resulting in increased public opposition and complaints. To address these challenges, the International Civil Aviation Organization (ICAO) has promoted the Balanced Approach to airport noise management. This approach emphasises a comprehensive strategy comprising four key elements: noise reduction at the source, land-use planning and management, noise abatement operational procedures, and operating restrictions. In China, the regulatory framework has evolved from basic airworthiness standards to more detailed noise regulations, though gaps and inconsistencies persist. This chapter examines the historical evolution of airport noise regulations in China, evaluates the current regulatory framework, and suggests how integrating the ICAO Balanced Approach into domestic laws and regulations could improve airport noise management in China. Aligning domestic regulations with international standards could establish a more effective, self-standing framework for mitigating airport noise pollution, benefiting the environment, affected communities, and the civil aviation market.

Keywords Aircraft noise · Airport noise standards · Air services agreements (ASAs) · Airworthiness standards · Annex 16 · Balanced approach · Standards and recommended practices (SARPs)

Y. Shi (✉)
School of Law, Institute of International Law, Wuhan University, Wuhan, China
e-mail: yuran.shi@outlook.com; yuran.shi@whu.edu.cn

© The Author(s), under exclusive license to Springer Nature Singapore Pte Ltd. 2025
S. Bhat B. (ed.), *Aerodrome Governance in Asia*,
https://doi.org/10.1007/978-981-96-7568-5_4

1 Introduction

1.1 The Challenge of Airport Noise Pollution

Noiseis defined as any unwanted sound, and various factors influence people's perception of noise.[1] As an aircraft flies, the air is consistently compressed and rarefied, causing movement of air molecules and pressure waves.[2] Although the level of annoyance varies from person to person, these waves can be strong enough to create a sensation of noise. The aircraft engine is the most widely recognised source of aviation noise.[3] Most noise generated by aircraft engines typically originates from the high-velocity exhaust gases and airflow in the fan system.[4]Similar to various ground operations at airports, airframes also produce significant noise. While engine noise is primarily high-frequency, jet and airframe noise is low-frequency. People living near airports often notice low-frequency noise, which can travel long distances from the aircraft.[5]

Aviation operations generate significant noise, posing particular challenges for those living near airports or under flight paths.[6] Over the past few decades, advances in aircraft technology have significantly reduced the noise footprint of individual aircraft movements. However, global increases in air traffic and the introduction of larger aircraft often offset this progress in reducing aircraft noise at the source.[7] According to reports, new aircraft's noise footprint is at least 15 percent smaller than that of the models they replace, and modern aircraft are 75 percent quieter than those from 50 years ago due to technological improvements.[8] Despite the development of quieter, more modern aircraft, the simultaneous global growth in air transport operations means that technological advancements alone cannot address aviation noise.[9] Additionally, identifying new methods for significantly enhancing

---

[1] Yaw Nyampong, 'Aircraft and Airport Noise: Local Issues with Global Implications' in Paul Stephen Dempsey & Ram S. Jakhu (eds.), *Routledge Handbook of Public Aviation Law*(Oxon: Routledge, 2017) pp. 180–194 at p. 181.

[2] *Id.*

[3] Anuja Mahashabde, et al. 'Assessing the Environmental Impacts of Aircraft Noise and Emissions', *Progress in Aerospace Sciences*, Vol. 47, No.1, 2011, pp.15–52 at p. 20.

[4] Noisequest, 'Sources of Aviation Noise', available at < https://noisequest.psu.edu/sourcesofnoise-overview.html > Last visited, 23 August 2024; *see also supra* note 1.

[5] Benedicte A. Claes, 'Aircraft Noise Regulation in the European Union: The Hushkit Problem', *Journal of Air Law and Commerce*, Vol. 65, 1999, pp. 329–382.

[6] *Supra* note 1, at p. 183.

[7] Eoin A. King, 'A Balanced Approach to Aircraft Noise Management: The Curious Case ofDublin Airport's New Runway', *INTER-NOISE and NOISE-CON Congress and Conference Proceedings*, Vol. 259, No. 3, 2019, pp. 1–9 at p. 2.

[8] *Supra* note 1, at p. 180.

[9] *Id.*

the technical noise performance of aircraft has become increasingly challenging Consequently,[10] cumulative noise levels around some airports have increased.[11]

Due to concerns about aviation noise, airport expansion has become a significant global issue, particularly for those living near airports who experience diminished property values due to noise pollution from aircraft. In various ways, noise from aircraft and airport operations directly impacts the daily lives of those exposed to it.[12] Increasing numbers of individuals and communities are expressing negative attitudes towards airports and aviation activities.[13] This often manifests through extensive use of social media against airline expansion, leading to a significant rise in noise complaints and public opposition to aircraft noise at certain airports, potentially hindering the aviation industry's ability to meet increasing demand.[14]

Aircraft noise remains one of the main reasons for objections to airport construction or expansion projects.[15] Consequently, noise is both an environmental and political issue, with numerous efforts to regulate it at both domestic and international levels.[16] Research and social surveys indicate that acoustic factors account for only about 30% of noise-related community annoyance.[17] Individual States and industrial stakeholders must fully understand the remaining on-acoustic factors so that regulatory authorities can develop appropriate policies and actions. While maintaining a necessary focus on noise reduction, a broader perspective is required. It is crucial to base the design of noise management strategies and policy development on a comprehensive understanding of the factors influencing community response to airport noise, as well as the potential for modification of these factors.

1.2 State Responsibilities for Environmental Protection

Considering legal efforts to mitigate civil aviation's environmental impacts through international and transnational law, as well as multi-level governance,[18] the intersection of globalisation, climate change, global aviation, and sovereignty is highly complex. In civil aviation, the diminishing distinction between global and local is

---

[10] Aviation Benefits Beyond Borders, 'Reducing Noise', available at < https://aviationbenefits.org/environmental-efficiency/reducing-noise/ > Last visited, 23 August 2024.

[11] ICAO, 'Global Trends in Aircraft Noise', available at < https://www.icao.int/environmental-protection/Pages/Noise_Trends.aspx > Last visited, 23 August 2024.

[12] *Supra* note 1.

[13] International Civil Aviation Organisation (ICAO), *Environmental Protection—General provisions, Aircraft Noise and Local Air Quality–Policy and Standardization* (40th ICAO Assembly Session, A40-WP/260).

[14] *Id.*

[15] *Supra* note 1.

[16] *Supra* note 3.

[17] *Supra* note 11.

[18] Steven Truxal, *Economic and Environmental Regulation of International Aviation: From International to Global Governance* (Oxon: Routledge, 2017) at p. 175.

most evident in noise pollution from aircraft engines, which also negatively impacts the environment.[19]

On the one hand, climate change is a global phenomenon with causes distributed worldwide, necessitating a global response.[20] The complexity of aircraft noise-related annoyance, along with challenges from new technological developments and the potential impact on a broader range of stakeholders, demands a practical solution rooted in transnational cooperation.[21] Therefore, in the realm of environmental protection and civil aviation, multi-scalar and multi-jurisdictional responses may be more effective in mitigating negative environmental impacts than solely international or national approaches.

On the other hand, aircraft noise is recognised as one of the most significant local environmental impacts associated with airport operations.[22] Noise pollution primarily occurs in and around congested airports, where airport expansion proposals are often politically sensitive. Environmental problems arise in specific locations within particular jurisdictions, with the impacts of climate change varying from place to place, necessitating diverse adaptation measures.[23] Individual States bear the ultimate responsibility for implementing the Balanced Approach. Since the International Civil Aviation Organization (ICAO) lacks genuine enforcement powers, its contracting States must enforce regulations through their national legislation and Air Services Agreements (ASAs).[24]

1.3 The Structure of the Chapter

Environmental noise is a clear example of the undesirable technological and social outcomes of continuous human development, with evident negative health and behavioural impacts on the exposed population. According to various sources, aircraft noise is a significant cause of annoyance,[25]and remains the most significant adverse factor in airport operation and expansion. This is expected to continue globally for

---

[19] *Id.*

[20] *Id.*

[21] Thijs F.M. Etty et al., 'Transnational Dimensions of Climate Governance', *Transnational Environmental Law*, Vol. 1, No. 2, pp. 235–243 at p. 237. *See also* ICAO, *supra* note 7.

[22] K. I. Hume & A. Watson, 'The Human Health Impacts of Aviation' in P. Upham et al. (eds.), *Towards Sustainable Aviation* (London: Earthscan, 2003) pp. 48–76 at p. 52;*see also* Murray May & Stuart B. Hill,'Questioning Airport Expansion: A Case Study of Canberra International Airport', *Journal of Transport Geography*, Vol. 14, No. 6, pp. 437–450 at p. 440.

[23] The Orientalist Express, 'The Global & Local Impacts of Climate Change', available at <https://orientalistexpress.com/blog/climateimpacts>Last visited, 23 August 2024.

[24] Ludwig Weber, *International Civil Aviation Organization (ICAO)*, (Alphen aan den Rijn: Kluwer, 2017) at p. 185.

[25] T.N. (Niall) Buissing, "Challenging the 'Balanced Approach to Aircraft Noise Management' Principle: Will the Dutch Approach Stand or Will the Principle Prevail?", *Air and Space Law*, Vol. 49, No. 1, pp. 1–34 at p. 4.

the foreseeable and even distant future.[26]Any new technological developments in the aviation sector could contribute to increased noise annoyance, especially with the introduction of a new generation of supersonic aircraft. Even the introduction of electric aircraft, which is expected to be considerably quieter than today's aircraft with similar flight performances, should be carefully examined due to their likely close operation near residential areas. In line with its key role, ICAO is aware of and continues to address the adverse environmental impacts, including aircraft noise, striving to limit or reduce the number of people significantly affected.[27] Therefore, ICAO's top priority is to limit or reduce the number of people exposed to and affected by aircraft noise.[28]

Currently, the challenge of airport noise pollution in China is becoming increasingly serious. Several factors contribute to this, including the late start of relevant legislation, insufficient progress in implementing concrete solutions, and the slow development of the national regulatory framework.[29] There is a lack of effective and comprehensive rules to limit and reduce the impact of aircraft noise on people.[30] To address the challenge of airport noise pollution, it is essential to integrate international law into domestic regulation, update existing legislation, and draw on successful practices from other States.[31]

This chapter seeks to discuss the application of the ICAO Balanced Approach in China to address the issue of airport noise pollution. Firstly, Part I begins by providing context, examining the issues of airport noise, and discussing State responsibilities for regulation. Following this, Part II examines policy developments under the auspices of ICAO and the main elements of the Balanced Approach. This analysis demonstrates how the Balanced Approach is defined in international law. Part III highlights current practices for regulating airport noise pollution in China, enabling the identification and understanding of relevant laws and their effects. Finally, Part IV explores the potential for integrating the ICAO Balanced Approach into the Chinese regulatory framework, offering suggestions for the way forward. The Chapter concludes with a summary of the answers to the research question.

---

[26] Oleksandr Zaporozhets, 'Balanced Approach to Aircraft Noise Management', in Laurent Leylekian, Alexandra Covrig& AlenaMaximova (eds.) *AviationNoise ImpactManagement: Technologies, Regulations, and Societal Well-being in Europe*, (Cham: Springer, 2022) pp. 29–56 at 30.

[27] ICAO, *Resolution A39-1: Consolidated Statement of Continuing ICAO Policies and Practices Related to Environmental Protection—General Provisions, Noise and Local Air Quality*, (2016).

[28] *Id.*

[29] Ziyao Xia &Xisheng Huang, 'A Study on the Legislation Issues of Airport Noise Abatement in China', *Journal of Beijing University of Aeronautics and Astronautics*, (Social Sciences edn.), Vol. 24, No. 4, 2011, pp. 38–44 atp. 42.

[30] *Supra* note 1.

[31] *Id.*

2 The ICAO Balanced Approach

2.1 Policy Developments Under the Auspices of ICAO

In the mid-to-late 1960s, concerns about aircraft noise escalated due to the rapid expansion of air traffic, the introduction of jet aircraft and turbofans, and the near completion of the first jumbo jets.[32] For instance, in September 1968, the ICAO Assembly adopted Resolution 16–3, acknowledging that noise levels around many major airports had become so severe that public reaction was escalating, necessitating an urgent solution.[33] The Resolution also highlighted that the introduction of new aircraft types could exacerbate noise levels unless measures were taken to address the issue.[34]

Several meetings and conferences followed the adoption of Resolution 16–3, ultimately leading to the adoption of Annex 16—Aircraft Noise—to the Chicago Convention (1944) in April 1971.[35]

The evolution of international aviation owes much to the provisions of the Chicago Convention (1944), often referred to by scholars as the *Magna Carta* of international aviation.[36] The Convention aims to achieve global harmonisation of standards and procedures in air navigation, with a specific emphasis on aviation safety.[37] However, the Convention does not provide a comprehensive global framework for environmental regulation in air transport.[38] The only reference to regulating the environmental impacts of civil aviation is found in Article 37 of the Chicago Convention (1944), which urges contracting States to "collaborate in securing the highest practicable degree of uniformity in regulations, standards, procedures, and organisation about aircraft, personnel, airways and auxiliary services in all matters in which such uniformity will facilitate and improve air navigation."[39] The Convention also grants ICAO the authority to adopt and amend internationally applicable Standards and Recommended Practices (SARPs), which are outlined in the Annexes to the

---

32 *Supra* note 1, at p. 187.

33 ICAO, *Resolution A16-3: Aircraft Noise in the Vicinity of Airports*, (1968). *See* also *supra* note 1.

34 *Id.*

35 Convention on International Civil Aviation, 7 December 1944, 15 UNTS 295 [Chicago Convention], Annex 16.

36 Pablo Mendes de Leon & Benjamyn I. Scott, 'An Analysis of Unmanned Aircraft Systems under Air Law', in AlešZavršnik (ed.), *Drones and Unmanned Aerial Systems: Legal and Social Implications for Security and Surveillance*, (Cham: Springer, 2016), pp. 185–213 at p.187.

37 Gilbert Guillaume, 'ICAO at the Beginning of the 21st Century', *Air & Space Law*, Vol. 33, No. 4&5, 2008, pp. 313–317 at p. 313.

38 Fernando Fiallos, 'LACAC and Current Challenges of Civil Aviation in Latin America', in Pablo Mendes de Leon and Niall Buissing (eds.), *Behind and Beyond the Chicago Convention*, (Alphen aan den: Kluwer Law International BV, 2019), pp.83–97 at p. 89.

39 Convention on International Civil Aviation, 7 December 1944, 15 UNTS 295 [Chicago Convention], Article 37.

Chicago Convention (1944). These SARPs cover a wide range of topics, including personnel licensing, rules of the air, meteorological services, aeronautical charts, units of measurement for air and ground operations, aircraft operation, aircraft nationality and registration marks, airworthiness, facilitation of passengers, baggage, and cargo processes, environmental protection, and safety management.[40] Specifically, Standards are specifications whose uniform application is deemed necessary for the safety or regularity of international air navigation,[41] while Recommended Practices are not mandatory but are considered desirable.[42]

SARPs related to aircraft noise were first adopted in 1971 under the provisions of Article 37 of the Chicago Convention (1944).[43] ICAO developed these SARPs considering the subsonic aircraft fleet in service, aiming to reduce their environmental impact and enhance the public acceptability of air transport.[44] The initial SARPs set maximum noise levels that corresponded to the aircraft technology under development at that time. Since then, standard development has progressed with technological improvements, as the international community has gradually imposed stricter limits on newly designed aircraft. As a result, the public implicitly aligns these new limits with acceptable aircraft noise levels.

Annex 16 Volume I establishes a noise certification regime for aircraft, stipulating that noise certification must be granted or validated by the State of Registry based

---

[40] Pablo Mendes de Leon, *Introduction to Air Law* (11th edn.), (Kluwer Law International BV, 2022) at p. 26.

[41] As per the definitions sections of Annexes to the Chicago Convention (7 December 1944), a Standard is defined as any specification for physical characteristics, configuration, matériel, performance, personnel or procedure, the uniform application of which is recognized as necessary for the safety or regularity of international air navigation and to which Contracting States will conform in accordance with the Convention; in the event of impossibility of compliance, notification to the Council is compulsory under Article 38 [of the Chicago Convention, (7 December 1944)].

[42] As per the definitions sections of Annexes to the Chicago Convention (7 December 1944), a Recommended Practice is any specification for physical characteristics, configuration, matériel, performance, personnel or procedure, the uniform application of which is recognized as desirable in the interests of safety, regularity or efficiency of international air navigation, and to which Contracting States will endeavour to conform in accordance with the Convention.

[43] In its original form, Annex16 only addressed aircraft noise. In 1981, the scope of the Annex was broadened to cover all environmental issues relating to aviation. Thus, it was split into two volumes. Volume I addresses 'Aircraft Noise', whereas, Volume II addresses 'Aircraft Emissions'. In 2017, the 36-State ICAO Council has adopted a new aircraft CO2 emissions standard which will reduce the impact of aviation greenhouse gas emissions on the global climate. Contained in a new Volume III to Annex 16 to the Chicago Convention (7 December 1944), the aircraft CO2 emissions measure represents the world's first global design certification standard governing CO2 emissions for any industry sector. During its 214th Session in June 2018, the ICAO Council made important headway on adopting Volume IV supporting the new Carbon Offsetting and Reduction Scheme for International Aviation, (CORSIA).*See* ICAO, 'Annex 16—Environmental Protection', available at <https://applications.icao.int/postalhistory/annex_16_environmental_protection.htm> Last visited,23 August 2024.

[44] ICAO, *Emissions from Supersonic Aeroplanes* (AN-Conf/13-WP/211, 2018).

on the aircraft's compliance with requirements at least equal to the applicable standards in the Annex.[45] It also stipulates that documents attesting to an aircraft's noise certification must be carried on board, as required by the State.

In 2010, ICAO published the "Environmental Technical Manual on the Use of Procedures in the Noise Certification of Aircraft".[46] It provides guidance to ensure that all certificating authorities apply the same level of stringency and criteria when accepting and approving applications for equivalent procedures.

In order to improve the technical basis for the ICAO SARPs, guidelines, and policies pertaining to aircraft noise reduction, the ICAO has been working continuously.[47] The development of technical standards for upcoming supersonic aircraft, the effects of novel aircraft concepts on noise, and research into cutting-edge noise reduction technologies are all included in this project.[48] In particular, ICAO is concentrating on best practices for airport community engagement and the environmental aspects of land-use planning at airports. The ICAO Balanced Approach should remain the cornerstone of global aircraft noise management, according to the Airports Council International (ACI) and the Civil Air Navigation Services Organisation (CANSO), who have stated that it "provides for a globally harmonised framework, suitable for aviation as an international industry, while also recognising the varying local situations of airports and offering the necessary flexibility to address them".[49]

ICAO-sponsored international regulatory initiatives to lessen the adverse effects of aviation noise have so far mostly concentrated on lowering aircraft noise at its source, especially by creating quieter aircraft.[50]All of the Chicago Convention's (1944) contracting States are required to either implement the ICAO's noise standards domestically or report to the ICAO Council any differences between their domestic laws and customs and the international standards outlined in the Annex.[51]

---

[45] Convention on International Civil Aviation, 7 December 1944, 15 UNTS 295 [Chicago Convention], Volume I of Annex 16, paragraph 1.2. *See also supra* note 1.

[46] ICAO, *Environmental Technical Manual: Volume I—Procedures for the Noise Certification of Aircraft*, (Doc9501-1, 2018).

[47] ICAO, 'Aircraft Noise', available at < https://www.icao.int/environmental-protection/Pages/noise.aspx > Last visited, 23 August 2024.

[48] *Id.*

[49] *See* ICAO, *supra* note 7.

[50] In 2001, ICAO adopted a balanced approach to aircraft noise management and thereby recommendedthree other approaches for the management of aircraft noise (i.e. in addition to reduction at source—quieter aircraft).These are: land-use planning and management, noise abatement operational procedures and operating restrictions. The balanced approach is discussed in detail below.

[51] Article 38 of the Chicago Convention, obliges Contracting States to notify the ICAO Council of any differences between their national regulations and practices and the international standards contained in the Annexes. Under Annex 15, States are encouraged to publish such differences through the Aeronautical Information Service.

2.2 *Defining the Balanced Approach*

In response to fragmented aviation regulations concerning aircraft noise, the ICAO Assembly adopted the Balanced Approach to Aircraft Noise Management during its 33rd Session (2001).[52] Since then, all subsequent Assembly Sessions have reaffirmed this approach as the primary ICAO policy on aircraft noise.[53]

The SARPs outlined in Annex 16 to the Chicago Convention (1944) define the Balanced Approach, stipulating that:

> The balanced approach to noise management consists of identifying the noise problem at an airport and then analysing the various measures available to reduce noise through the exploration of four principal elements, namely reduction at source (addressed in Part II of this Annex), land-use planning and management, noise abatement operational procedures and operating restrictions, with the goal of addressing the noise problem in the most cost-effective manner. All the elements of the balanced approach are addressed in the Guidance on the Balanced Approach to Aircraft Noise Management (Doc 9829).[54]

This Standard identifies two key steps in enforcing the Balanced Approach: first, identifying the noise problem at an airport, and second, implementing various measures, in line with the four elements defined in Annex 16 to the Chicago Convention (1944), to reduce aircraft noise and mitigate its negative impacts.

On the one hand, a fundamental aspect of the Balanced Approach is to determine whether a noise problem exists at an airport. A noise problem is identified when there is a discrepancy between the assessed current noise situation and the defined noise objective.[55] Although noise annoyance is subjective, the balanced approach to assessing noise levels on and around the airport should be based on objective and measurable criteria.[56] Different States may have varying standards and policies regarding what constitutes a noise problem, how the legal effects of these rules are assessed, and the objectives pursued in airport-related noise programmes.[57] Under ICAO's Balanced Approach, a noise objective should be identified and defined to assess whether the progression of the baseline noise scenario meets the objective.[58]

---

[52] *Id.*

[53] ICAO, *Resolution A33-7: Consolidated Statement of Continuing ICAO Policies and Practices Related to Environmental Protection,* (2001).

[54] Convention on International Civil Aviation, 7 December 1944, 15 UNTS 295 [Chicago Convention], Volume I of Annex 16, Part V.

[55] Magdalena Habdas, 'Airport Noise as Public Bads: Comparative Remarks on Legal Challenges in Resolving the Neighbor Conflict Between the Airport and Landowners', *Journal of Air Law and Commerce*, Vol. 87, No. 1, pp. 91–130 at p. 103.

[56] ICAO, *ICAO Guidance Material on the Balanced Approach to Aircraft Noise Management*, (Doc 9829, 2004).

[57] *Supra* note 26, at p. 5.

[58] Joanna Langlade, "Noise Restriction Measures and the 'Balanced Approach': The Situation at Brussels-National Airport", *Air and Space Law*, Vol. 42, No.3, 2017, pp. 313–327 at p. 320.

On the other hand, the Balanced Approach includes four types of measures to address the negative impacts of airport noise, highlighting a flexible method to identify and transparently resolve specific noise problems.[59]

Firstly, reducing noise at the source encourages the use of quieter aircraft. Annex 16 to the Chicago Convention (1944) provides the SARPs that establish noise limits for aircraft. The aerospace manufacturing sector primarily drives airline demand and delivers this through improvements in engine and airframe technology.[60] Airports can influence noise reduction at source through noise-related operational changes or operating restrictions, which may incentivise airlines to use quieter aircraft.[61]

Secondly, land-use planning and management aim to prevent noise-sensitive developments near the airport and flight path.[62] Specifically, these measures can be categorised as either anticipatory or mitigation instruments. Anticipatory measures seek to prevent the need for mitigation by avoiding incompatible development in noise-affected areas. These measures include designating noise zoning, imposing restrictions, and implementing policies on new property developments. In contrast, mitigation measures involve identifying areas for inclusion in sound insulation schemes or compulsory home purchase and relocation programmes. Airports often provide financial instruments, such as noise-related airport charges, to fund noise mitigation and compensation schemes.

Thirdly, thrust settings and related aircraft noise can be decreased or aircraft can be isolated from noise-sensitive areas through alternative operating procedures.[63] In contrast to other traditional descents, a continuous descent approach, for instance, involves an aircraft approaching the runway prior to landing and is intended to minimise noise and fuel consumption.

Fourthly, operating restrictions at airports can be applied during night-time or limit the total number of movements. Night flight restrictions typically apply between 22:00 h or 23:00 h and 04:00 h or 07:00 h.[64] Night restrictions focus on noise and are based on a variety of criteria, including noise certification, quota systems, and movement limits. Airports like Amsterdam, Charles de Gaulle, Madrid, Heathrow,

---

[59] ICAO, 'The Balanced Approach', available at < https://anima-project.eu/noise-platform/the-balanced-approach > Last visited, 23 August 2024.

[60] William Richard Graham, Cesare Alan Hall, & M. Vera Morales, 'The Potential of Future Aircraft Technology for Noise and Pollutant Emissions Reduction', *Transport Policy*, Vol. 34, 2014, pp. 36–51 at p. 40.

[61] ICAO, 'Noise Reduction at Source', available at < https://anima-project.eu/noise-platform/noise-reduction-at-source > Last visited, 23 August 2024.

[62] ICAO, *Airport Planning Manual: Part II—Land Use and Environmental Management*, (Doc 9184, 2018).

[63] Several ICAO documents include recommendations on operational procedures, such as ICAO, *Aircraft Operations: Volume I—Flight Procedures*, (Doc 8168, 2018); ICAO, Continuous Descent Operations (CDO) Manual, (Doc 9931, 2010); ICAO, *Continuous Climb Operations (CCO) Manual*, (Doc 9993, 2013); ICAO, *Review of Noise Abatement Procedure Research and Development and Implementation Results*, (Doc 9888, 2007); and ICAO, *Guidance on Environmental Assessment of Proposed Air Traffic Management Operational Changes*, (Doc 10,031, 2014).

[64] ICAO, 'Operating Restrictions', available at < https://anima-project.eu/noise-platform/operating-restrictions > Last visited, 23 August 2024.

and Gatwick apply higher charges for aircraft operating during night periods or impose a night noise surcharge.[65]

2.3 State Responsibilities Under the Balanced Approach

The ICAO's Balanced Approach to aircraft noise management in airports should be reassessed, considering historical and technological challenges.[66] All four basic elements of the Balanced Approach are focused on controlling noise exposure, with particular emphasis on reducing noise at the source and ensuring compatible land usage within noise zones around airports.

Noise solutions must be tailored to the specific circumstances of each airport, necessitating airport-by-airport analysis as States adopt varying policies on noise management.[67] In this context, ICAO's Balanced Approach identifies the principal elements of the Approach and the relationship between them.[68] It represents an internationally agreed-upon concept for managing noise issues at individual airports but does not provide detailed guidance. Thus, individual States have considerable discretion in applying these key elements, considering their responsibilities for implementing the Balanced Approach. The premise is that they should do so with proper regard for ICAO rules and policies, fully considering ICAO guidance, relevant international air law treaties, and existing air services agreements.[69]

Given that Annex 16 to the Chicago Convention (1944) defines the Balanced Approach, State parties to the Convention are bound by the Standards set out therein unless they have notified ICAO of the impracticality of complying with a particular international standard or procedure.[70] Specifically, the ICAO Guidance on the Balanced Approach to Aircraft Noise Management provides building blocks for contracting States considering the implementation of the Balanced Approach to noise management.[71] The Balanced Approach seeks to implement noise measures that achieve maximum environmental benefit most cost-effectively. The responsibility for implementing the Balanced Approach and making decisions between its elements lies with the contracting States to the Chicago Convention (1944). States may assign authority to a qualified body to carry out noise assessments and pertinent cost–benefit analyses at different stages of the procedure.[72]

---

[65] Steer Davies Gleave, *Evaluation of Directive 2009/12/ECon Airport Charges: Final Report*, (2013).

[66] *Supra* note 26, at 29.

[67] *Supra* note 56, Appendix C.

[68] *Supra* note 25, at p. 6. *See also* ICAO, *supra* note 7.

[69] *Supra* note 56, Appendix C.

[70] Convention on International Civil Aviation, 7 December 1944, 15 UNTS 295 [Chicago Convention], Article 38.

[71] *See also* ICAO, *supra* note 7.

[72] *Supra* note 59.

3 Regulation of Airport Noise in China: Current Practices

3.1 *Airport Noise Problems in China*

Before the COVID-19 pandemic, the Chinese civil aviation market experienced significant and rapid development. In 2019, Chinese airports recorded 660 million passenger kilometres, marking a 7.9% increase from the 2018 baseline.[73] In the same year, these airports handled12.9 billion tonne-kilometres of freight, a 7.2% increase from 2018 levels.[74] The rapid development of the Chinese civil aviation industry has brought convenience and prosperity to cities with airports, but it has also led to various environmental issues, particularly severe aviation noise pollution. For example, Hangzhou Xiaoshan Airport, a key domestic hub in Southern China, faced severe protests within its first year of operation, as nearby residents, unable to tolerate the aviation noise, stormed the airport to halt flights.[75] Since 2000, residents around Beijing Capital International Airport have repeatedly petitioned the Civil Aviation Administration of China (CAAC) to address aviation noise pollution. In response, CAAC and the National Development and Reform Commission jointly issued the Energy Conservation and Emission Reduction Plan in the Civil Aviation Industry in December 2008, highlighting the urgent need to deal with airport noise pollution.[76]

3.2 *Historical Development of Regulation*

3.2.1 Laws

In China, laws enacted by the National People's Congress of the People's Republic of China hold the highest level of regulatory authority within the national legal system and are of crucial importance.[77] These laws establish principles addressing key issues in economic and social activities. Consequently, these principles are often fundamental and somewhat abstract, lacking specific rules and standards. Implementing these laws necessitates supplementary low-level regulations, with the former legislation serving as the foundation for the latter's legislation.

In 1995, the Standing Committee of the National People's Congress (NPC) adopted the Civil Aviation Law of the People's Republic of China (Chinese Civil

---

[73] The CAAC, *Development of the Chinese Civil Aviation Industry: The 2023 Statistical Bulletin*, (《2023年民航行业发展统计公报》, 2024).

[74] *Id.*

[75] *Supra* note 29, at p. 40.

[76] Energy Conservation and Emission Reduction Plan in Civil Aviation Industry, (《民航行业节能减排规划》, No. 120), issued in December 2008.

[77] Legislation Law of the People's Republic of China, (《中华人民共和国立法法》), adopted on 15 March 2000 and revised on 13 March 2023.

Aviation Law (1995)).[78] Although the Chinese Civil Aviation Law (1995) serves as a fundamental law in civil aviation, it does not address airport noise pollution, creating challenges for the civil aviation industry.

Additionally, Article 52 of the Law of the People's Republic of China on Prevention and Control of Noise Pollution (Prevention and Control of Noise Pollution (2021)) mandates that the local authorities where a civil airport is located must, based on the environmental impact assessments and monitoring results, determine the range and extent of aircraft noise impacts on the surrounding environment, designate areas where noise-sensitive buildings are prohibited or restricted, and enforce control measures.[79] This provision is relevant to the prevention and control of aviation noise. Local municipalities must delineate areas around the paths of aircraft taking off and landing where the construction of noise-sensitive buildings, including residential buildings, is restricted.[80] Construction companies are also required to take measures to mitigate or avoid noise impacts from aircraft operations.[81] Regulatory authorities of civil aviation should implement effective measures to address the negative impacts of environmental noise pollution resulting from air transport operations.[82]

3.2.2 The CAAC Regulations and Standards

Air industry standards, established by aeronautical authorities, play a crucial role in both air law and environmental law. Notably, standards related to aircraft noise form the foundation for preventing and controlling airport noise pollution, including the measurement of noise levels around airports and airworthiness standards concerning aircraft noise. Historically, the CAAC has developed noise-related regulations without a clear legislative foundation rooted in laws enacted by the National Congress.

Domestic regulation of airport noise pollution in China began in the 1980swhen the CAAC started issuing rules to set limits on aircraft noise as part of airworthiness

---

[78] The Civil Aviation Law of the People's Republic of China, (《中华人民共和国民用航空法》), adopted on 30 October 1995.

[79] Article 52 of the Law of the People's Republic of China on Prevention and Control of Noise Pollution: Thelocal government of the civil airport shall, based on the environmental impact assessment and monitoring results that determine the scope and extent of the impact of civil aircraft noise on the surrounding living environment of the airport, delineate areas where the construction of noise-sensitive buildings is prohibited and areas where it is restricted, and implement control measures.

In the areas where construction is prohibited, the construction of noise-sensitive buildings unrelated to aviation is forbidden.

In the areas where construction is restricted, if it is necessary to build noise-sensitive buildings, the construction unit shall carry out sound insulation design for the noise-sensitive buildings, in accordance with the relevant standards for sound insulation design of civil buildings.

[80] *Id.*

[81] *Id.*

[82] *Id.*

certification.[83]The first legislation introduced to address airport noise pollution was the Airworthiness Standards for Transport Aircraft (1985) (1985 Airworthiness Standards), including aircraft noise limitations. Airworthiness refers to the conformity of an aircraft's components, structure, and performance to the standards necessary for safe flight.[84] An aircraft must pass an airworthiness review before being allowed to fly. Incorporating noise-related requirements into airworthiness assessment is an effective way to reduce noise emissions at the source. However, the language was ambiguous, only stating in Sect. 25.771(e) that "vibration and noise characteristics of cockpit equipment must not affect safe operation" without specifying the technical standards for noise characteristics that could impact aircraft safety.[85]

In 1988, the CAAC issued the Environmental Standards for Aircraft Noise around Airports (1988) (1988 Airport Noise Standards).[86] This administrative document is legally binding on airports and other industrial stakeholders, setting environmental quality objectives for preventing and controlling airport noise pollution in China.The 1988 Airport Noise Standards established stringent targets for airport noise management. However, the implementation and enforcement of standards have been unsatisfactory. One major issue is that the classification of noise standards into two levels, 70 dB and 75 dB, is overly simplistic and does not support the sustainable development of airports.[87]Moreover, the Standards only apply to residential areas, as well as cultural and educational zones, but not to offices, factories, or other types of spaces. This narrow scope of application hinders the effective resolution of airport noise pollution issues.

In 2002, the CAAC issued the Noise Regulation of Aircraft Airworthiness (2002), outlining the technical requirements for noise factors to be considered in the type certification and approval of aircraft airworthiness.[88] In 2007, the CAAC revised this Regulation to align with the latest international standards on aircraft noise issued by ICAO. All noise-related regulations concerning aircraft airworthiness culminated in Article 59 of the Regulation of Civil Airport Management (2009).[89] This provision stipulates that civil aircraft must comply with national airworthiness standards for aircraft noise; otherwise, aircraft are not permitted to take off or land at Chinese airports.[90]

---

[83] Fengyun Wang &Qijun Xie, 'Noise Governance in Foreign Airports and the Enlightenment for China', *Urban Insight*, No. 3, 2015, pp. 147–153 at p. 147.

[84] Filippo De Florio, *Airworthiness: An Introduction to Aircraft Certification: A Guide to Understanding JAA, EASA and FAA Standards*, (Oxford: Butterworth-Heinemann, 2006).

[85] The CAAC, *The Airworthiness Standards for Transport Aircraft*, (《运输类飞机适航标准》, 1985).

[86] The CAAC, *The Environmental Standards for Aircraft Noise around Airports*, (《机场周围飞机噪声环境标准》, GB9660—88, 1988).

[87] *Id.*

[88] The CAAC, *The Noise Regulation of Aircraft Airworthiness*, (《航空器型号和适航合格审定噪声规定》, 2002).

[89] State Council of the People's Republic of China, *The Regulation of Civil Airport Management*, (《民用机场管理条例》, 2009).

[90] Article 59 of the Regulation of Civil Airport Management, (13 April 2009).

Another set of legislation related to airport noise management can be found in the regulations governing airport construction. In 2004, the CAAC issued the Regulation of Airport Construction (2004),[91] with Article 15 requiring that the airport plans include a compatibility plan. This plan must address issues such as the composition of different aircraft types, runway usage, take-off and landing frequency, and flight procedures.[92] Additionally, Article 52 of the Prevention and Control of Noise Pollution (2021) and Article 15 of the Regulation of Airport Construction (2004), as mentioned above, are pertinent when addressing aircraft noise in the context of airport construction planning.

3.2.3 General Observations

Over the past 30 years, from the 1980s to the present, Chinese legislation on preventing airport noise pollution has evolved from non-existent to an established yet incomplete system. Consequently, there are now some legislative foundations for regulating airport noise pollution. However, Chinese legislation in this area has been characterised by a late start and slow progress in updates. For example, it took 17 years for the regulatory framework on noise-related aircraft airworthiness to progress from the introduction of the Airworthiness Standards for Transport Aircraft (1985) to the effective implementation of Noise Regulation of Aircraft Airworthiness (2002), and 24 years until the establishment of Regulation of Civil Airport Management (2009). The choice of applicable legislation and the determination of regulatory authorities raise significant issues. Regulatory gaps and inconsistencies in the Chinese regulatory framework create fragmentation and exacerbate the problem, leading to serious challenges of airport noise and disturbance in surrounding communities. To mitigate these negative impacts, improvements in legislation and enforcement can draw heavily from the ICAO SARPs related to the Balanced Approach.

4 Applying the Balanced Approach in China: The Way Forward

The prevention and control of airport noise pollution should focus on integrating existing relevant regulations, drawing on international practices, and considering China's specific circumstances. Measures should be built on three pillars: "principal provisions, basic systems, and supporting rules" to establish a comprehensive legal framework for preventing airport noise pollution. Specifically, laws should establish the principal provisions for preventing airport noise pollution, administrative regulations should establish the basic systems based on these legal principles, and relevant departments should issue rules to enforce and operationalise these principles and

[91] The CAAC, *The Regulation of Airport Construction*, (《机场建设管理规定》, 2004).

[92] Article 16 of the Regulation of Airport Construction, (12 October 2004).

systems. Enhancing the Chinese regulatory framework for airport noise pollution should particularly focus on incorporating SARPs into domestic aviation and environmental legislation. A three-pillar domestic framework—comprising fundamental principles, concrete rules, and supplementary measures –can effectively integrate and apply SARPs associated with the ICAO Balanced Approach.

Firstly, fundamental principles established in laws enacted by the NPC can serve as the foundation for developing specific laws and regulations. Currently, the Chinese Civil Aviation Law (1995) lacks any provisions addressing airport noise pollution. Article 52of the Prevention and Control of Noise Pollution (2021) addresses the flightpaths of aircraft during take-off and landing but does not offer guiding principles for implementing the ICAO Balanced Approach in China. Amendments to both laws could include principal provisions aimed at addressing airport noise pollution. Specifically, these laws should acknowledge the principle that cooperation among civil aviation regulatory authorities, environmental protection agencies, planners of urban areas, airport management, and local municipalities is essential for effectively mitigating the negative impacts of airport noise.

Secondly, concrete rules should address the four key elements outlined in the ICAO Balanced Approach. Reducing noise at the source requires strict enforcement of Article 59 of the Regulation of Civil Airport Management (2009), which mandates that aircraft must meet national airworthiness standards for aircraft noise; otherwise, they are not allowed to take off or land at Chinese airports.[93] The Noise Regulation of Aircraft Airworthiness (2002) is also vital in this connection.[94] Gradually phasing out high-noise aircraft, such as Stage-2 aircraft, as defined in the 2002 Airworthiness Regulation, and promoting the development of low-noise aircraft can significantly contribute to reducing airport noise. Additionally, land use planning should ensure that noise-sensitive areas, such as residential zones and schools, are located away from airports while encouraging compatible land uses, such as industrial and commercial developments, near airports. Mitigating measures could include comprehensive land planning, zoning based on varying levels of aircraft noise, implementing soundproofing measures for nearby buildings, and imposing restrictions on construction projects around airports. Noise abatement measures could involve using preferential runways and routes to divert aircraft away from noise-sensitive areas; implementing noise reduction procedures during taking-off and landing to optimise ground noise distribution; and adopting continuous descent approaches, allowing aircraft to remain at higher altitudes for longer to reduce noise levels on the ground. The CAAC has initiated research projects in this area in collaboration with the United States (US) Environmental Protection Agency and Boeing.[95] Current and future manufacturing projects led by the Commercial Aircraft Corporation of China (Comac), the leading state-owned aerospace manufacturer in China, have acknowledged the importance of these noise abatement measures. Last but not

[93] Article 59 of the Regulation of Civil Airport Management, (2009).

[94] *Supra* note 91.

[95] Standards for Aircraft Noise Around Airports, (《机场周围区域飞机噪声环境标准》, 21 August 2013).

least, operating restrictions at airports should focus on specific types of aircraft, the use of runways with significant noise impact, night curfews, and flight frequency limitations. However, operating restrictions should not be the first resort for noise management at airports.

Thirdly, regulatory authorities can implement supplementary measures to reinforce the application of concrete rules, thereby creating an effective, self-standing, and comprehensive regulatory framework for airport noise management. For example, regulatory authorities could introduce noise-related charges as part of a broader noise management programme. In line with the ICAO Balanced Approach, individual airports should address noise most cost-effectively by exploring the four key elements: noise reduction at the source, land-use planning and management, noise reduction operational procedure, and, as a last resort, operating restrictions.[96] Consequently, decisions on noise-related measures should follow a thorough assessment of the airport's noise issues, an evaluation of the costs and economic impact of available measures, and consultation with relevant stakeholders.[97] If, after the appropriate analyses and consultations, regulatory authorities consider noise-related charges necessary, the charging methods should be straightforward, auditable, and consistent across airports. Additionally, charges should align with the ICAO Policies on Charges for Airports,[98]ensuring they are cost-related, non-discriminatory, and equitably distributed among all users.

The liability regime is another example. In cases of bodily injury or property damage, victims can seek compensation under Article 65 of the Tort Liability Law of the People's Republic of China (Chinese Tort Liability Law (2009)).[99] This provision establishes that environmental pollution can result in tort liability. However, determining who qualifies as a polluter under this provision, particularly in the context of airport noise pollution, has proven challenging. Airport noise originates from aircraft operated by various airlines, making it seemingly logical to hold airlines liable as polluters. However, given the large number of airlines operating at airports, both domestic and foreign, it would be difficult for residents living near airports to file lawsuits and claim compensation. Aligning the liability regime with noise-related charges could offer a practical solution whereby airlines would be required to pay landing and take-off fees to airports.

---

[96] IATA, 'Noise-Related Charges', available at < https://www.iata.org/contentassets/fa95ede4dee24322939d396382f2f82d/noise-related_charges.pdf > Last visited, 23 August 2024.

[97] *Id.*

[98] ICAO, *ICAO's Policies on Charges for Airports and Air Navigation Services*, (Doc 9082, 1974), Section II, Article 4.

[99] The Tort Liability Law of the People's Republic of China, (《中华人民共和国侵权责任法》, Chinese Tort Liability Law, (2009).

5 Conclusion

Civil aviation operations generate significant noise, particularly affecting those living near airports. Aviation noise is a critical issue that impacts the commercial viability of both international and domestic air transportation, necessitating regulatory solutions. Airport noise pollution presents a complex challenge that evolves with advancements in aviation technology and the growth of global air traffic.

The ICAO Balanced Approach to Aircraft Noise Management provides a structured framework for addressing airport noise, focusing on four key elements: noise reduction at the source, land-use planning and management, noise reduction operational procedures, and operating restrictions.

In China, the regulatory landscape for airport noise has developed significantly, progressing from basic airworthiness standards to more comprehensive regulations. Despite these advancements, significant gaps and inconsistencies remain in the current framework. The fragmented nature of regulations, along with delayed updates and a lack of alignment with international standards, has impeded effective noise management. The regulatory approach has been marked by minimal updates and slow adoption of international best practices, leading to ongoing noise pollution problems around airports. To improve the effectiveness of airport noise management in China, a three-pillar domestic framework comprising fundamental principles, concrete rules, and supplementary measures can be adopted to implement SARPs related to the ICAO Balanced Approach. This approach, which the Chinese regulatory authorities should pursue, would address various aspects of environmental protection from airport noise pollution, including advanced airport planning, noise measurement, and the use of charges to mitigate airport noise. By closing regulatory gaps and integrating international best practices, China can more effectively manage the environmental impacts of aviation and enhance the quality of life for communities affected by airport noise.

Chapter 5
Airport Governance in Sri Lanka: An Overview of the Regulatory Landscape

Anusha Wickramasinghe and Lasantha Hettiarachchi

Abstract Sri Lanka has ratified and given effect to the Chicago Convention on Civil Aviation by enacting domestic legislation. The Chicago Convention, its Annexes together with the Standards and Recommended Practices (SARPS) formulated under the Chicago Convention have been given the effect and force of law in Sri Lanka. This has been done through multiple statutory instruments; inter alia, the Civil Aviation Authority Act No 34 of 2002, the Civil Aviation Act 14 of 2010 and the Air Navigation (Special Provisions) Act 2 of 1982. A state-owned corporate body is also established to manage and operate international and customs aerodromes in Sri Lanka. Aerodromes in Sri Lanka are also subject to and are indirectly impacted by quasi-rules and regulations formulated by international non-governmental organizations such as International Air Transport Association (IATA) and Airports Council International (ACI), particularly when serving as customs aerodromes into which international airlines operate. This chapter provides an overview of all statutory and regulatory provisions applicable to the operations of international customs aerodromes in Sri Lanka. It also examines the regulatory oversight and compliance levels of the main international airport as reported in ICAO audits. Discussions on some operational problems and suggestions on remedies are also part of this chapter.

Keywords Air navigation act · Airports and aviation of Sri Lanka limited (AASL) · Airports authority act · Bandaranaike international airport (BIA) · Civil aviation act · Colombo international airport (CIA) · Department of civil aviation · Director of civil aviation (DCA) · Mattala Rajapaksa international airport (MRIA)

A. Wickramasinghe (✉) · L. Hettiarachchi
McGill Institute of Air & Space Law, Colombo, Sri Lanka
e-mail: anushawickramasinghe@yahoo.com

© The Author(s), under exclusive license to Springer Nature Singapore Pte Ltd. 2025

S. Bhat B. (ed.), *Aerodrome Governance in Asia*,
https://doi.org/10.1007/978-981-96-7568-5_5

1 History of Airports in Sri Lanka

The Sanskrit epic Ramayana[1] attributed to sage Valmiki refers to Raavana, the king of Lanka (modern-day Sri Lanka), who strode the skies between Lanka and India in a flying machine some 4000 years ago. Despite the incidence of manned flight in Ramayana being woven into the historical and social fabric of many South and East Asian countries, its narrative is treated more as historical legend rather than fact, presumably due to the absence of empirical evidence. If, on the other hand, manned flight as told in the Ramayana was a historical fact it would lend credence to the numerous places in Sri Lanka which folklore and legend recognize as ancient "airports" from where the King Raavana's flying machine did take-off and land during flights.

Despite the colourful ancient history of aviation in the country attributed to legend, a manned flight is said to have taken place in the Sri Lanka (then known as Ceylon) only around 1912. A Bleriot monoplane with an Anzani 25 horsepower engine, the first airplane had been freighted on a ship into Ceylon in 1911, eight years after the first manned flight operated in 1903 and a mere two years after Louis Bleriot whose company made the Bleriot plane had flown across the English Channel from Calais to Dover in 1909.[2] The airplane brought into the country in September 1911 on board a ship was not flown but merely exhibited to the public at different locations. A German pilot, Franz Oster, who also brought a monoplane called the Etrich-Taube into the country, operated the first flight to lift off into the Sri Lankan skies from the Colombo Race Course on Christmas day of 1911, which, however, crashed as he was unable to control the flight.[3]Repeat attempts thereafter by Franz Oster using the same aircraft and the Bleriot, the first airplane brought into the country, also resulted in crash landings although there were no reported injuries from these attempts.[4] The first successful flight to have taken off and landed was operated on the 7 December 1912 by two French nationals, Georges Vermink and Marc Pourpre. As there was no formal airport in Ceylon at the time, the initial attempts and the successful manned flight had all been performed from the Racecourse Grounds in Colombo, where the city elite in the British colonial era gathered to watch horse races.

---

[1] The ancient Sanskrit epic of Hindu literature attributed to author and sage Valmiki recounted in numerous Indian dialects including Buddhist and Jain adaptations and its narrative retold in many versions across vast geographical expanses of South and East Asia such as Cambodia, Indonesia, Philippines, Thailand, Laos, Burma, Nepal, Maldives, Vietnam, Tibet and Malaya (Malaysia and Singapore).

[2] Capt. Elmo Jayawardena, 'A Centenary Sky 100 years of Aviation in Sri Lanka', Civil Aviation Authority of Sri Lanka, 2012 at p. 33. Also see Civil Aviation Authority of Sri Lanka, 'Sri Lankan Aviation History', *CAASL*, January 2024, available at < https://caa.lk/en/about-us/sri-lankan-aviation-history > Last visited, 29September 2024.

[3] *Id.*, at p. 35.

[4] *Id.*, at p. 37.

With the outbreak of World War I, no further developments had been recorded in civil aviation in Sri Lanka until 1931.[5] The Colombo Racecourse (CRC) continued to be used as an airfield to facilitate aircraft operations as there were no proper 'airfields' to accommodate aerial activities. The first international flight landed at the CRC in 1931[6] carrying mail from Mumbai, India.[7] In 1934, the proposal to build an 'airport' in Ceylon had been submitted to the State Council and the Kandawala Estate of Ratmalana, a 242 acre property, a part of which was owned by Sir John Kotalewela[8] already gifted to the Government, was selected for that purpose as it was close to Colombo, the capital of the country. Construction of the runway and other structures were built[9] by 1935 to welcome the first flight, a de Havilland Puss Moth from Mumbai.[10] After the construction of the airport was completed,[11] it was named the Colombo International Airport (CIA) and was declared opened in 1938.[12] The first international operations at this airport were airmail flights between Colombo and Mumbai.[13] In 1947, Ceylon's first airline, Ceylon Airways commenced flights to London from the Colombo International Airport (Ratmalana) which was already busy with inbound flights from Western carriers KLM, BOAC and TWA.[14]After Katunayake International Airport was selected for international flights Colombo International Airport at Ratmalana ceased to be used for international operations and was mostly used for operation by the air force and flying schools. Although designated an international airport and CIA Ratmalana today sees only a limited number of international operations and at present is mainly used by domestic charter and scheduled operators, flight schools and other private aircraft owners.

---

[5] *Id.*

[6] Roger Thiedeman, 'Ceylon's first flights', *The Sunday Times*, December 2012, available at < https://www.sundaytimes.lk/121202/plus/ceylons-first-flights-22757.html > Last visited, 12 August 2024.

[7] *Id.*

[8] General Sir John Kotelawala who later became Prime Minister of Ceylon, is said to have owned an aeroplane and had a runaway built in his vast estate. It is also reported that when Lord Vevel from England visited Sri Lanka,and his aircraft needed a place to land Sir John had extended the length of the runway in his back garden to 700 yards to accommodate that plane. It is this home-made aerodrome, and the surrounding land gifted by Sir John to the Government that was to become the Ratmalana airport or the first international airport of Ceylon. See, Capt. Elmo Jayawardena, Supra, note 2 at p. 55.

[9] The new aerodrome was a large area cleared and leveled but without any markings to indicate where to land in which direction to take off from. The runway was simply a wide-open grass patch, and the original administrative buildings were sheds with galvanized sheets for the roof. *Supra*note 2 at page 57. See, *Supra*note 2.

[10] *Id.*

[11] By this time a three storied airport terminal building and hangars had been constructed for sheltering aircraft and an engineering workshop had been added for aircraft maintenance and repairs. *Supra* note 2, at p. 59. Also see, 'History of Colombo International Airport', *airport.lk*, available at < https://www.airport.lk/rma/about_rma/history_of_rma > Last visited, 12 August 2024.

[12] *Id.*

[13] *Id.*

[14] *Id.*

The second large airport in the country at Katunayake was built for the exclusive use of the Royal Air Force (RAF) in mid 1940s,[15] and named the Royal Airport Katunayake for World War II related activities of the RAF.[16] After Ceylon gained her independence in 1948, the Katunayake airport was transferred to Royal Ceylon Air Force of Sri Lanka.[17] In 1970, the Katunayake airport was named the Bandaranaike International Airport (BIA) but changed its name again to Katunayake International Airport in 1977.[18] The airport was renamed as Bandaranaike International Airport (BIA) in 1995.[19] The infrastructure development of the BIA took place at different stages since 1960s.[20] The airport was equipped with a 3368 M long runway, terminal building, taxiways, and navigation services under the Department of Civil Aviation of the Government. In 1983, the operations of airports in Sri Lanka were entrusted to a government-owned company named the Airports and Aviation of Sri Lanka Limited (AASL).[21] This being the busiest airport handling the largest content of international operations, it was further developed with the addition of a domestic terminal, a second runway, expanded passenger lounges, a dedicated cargo village, a pier with eight aero bridges and facilities to accommodate larger aircraft operations.[22]

The next large international airport of Sri Lanka is an eco-friendly modern airport built with the capacity to accommodate larger aircraft was named the Mattala Rajapaksa International Airport (MRIA) and was inaugurated in 2013.[23] Located in the southernmost part of the island, the MRIA has seen more than its share of controversy. With the change of governments in 2015, the new government utilised the MRIA facilities to store paddy[24] to mock the previous government for building an airport alleging that it was a failure for not generating expected levels of air traffic. However, due to public protests the stored paddy was removed from the MRIA airport

---

[15] K. Somasundaraswaran, 'Bandaranaike International Airport', *AERLINE Magazine*, Issue 39, available at < https://research.usq.edu.au/download/847e1e4b82b9caa36b5b35c085fbbefe1ae35c0a90c56454781403f1e0c84309/434556/Somasundaraswaran_A_i39_PV.pdf > Last visited, 12 August 2024.

[16] *Id.*

[17] *Id.*

[18] *Id.*

[19] *Id.*

[20] 'Colombo Airport and Ratmalana Air Force Museum', *oldjets.net*, available at < https://www.oldjets.net/colombo-airport.html > Last visited, 13 August 2024.

[21] *Supra* note 11.

[22] *Id.*

[23] 'Sri Lanka Air Navigation Plan 2022–2036', *CAASL*, September 2022, p. 33, available at < https://caa.lk/images/stories/pdf/guidance_materials/subject_specific/air_traffic_services/SLANP_Final_Book_30092022.pdf > Last visited, 13 August 2024.

[24] 'PM justifies paddy storage at Mattala', *Daily Mirror*, October 2019, available at < https://www.dailymirror.lk/print/breaking-news/PM-justifies-paddy-storage-at-Mattala/108-176629 > Last visited, 13 August 2024.

in 2016.[25] Currently, the MRIA serves as the main airport for charter operators and budget carriers as well an alternative airport for emergency diversions.

The Palaly airport situated at Jaffna the northern most city in Sri Lanka was originally built by the Royal Air Force in 1940 and was used as a military airfield until 2019. In 1947, the Palaly airport served an intermediate stop in Air Ceylon's inaugural flight when it operated to Madras via Palaly.[26] The Palaly airport was utilized by the military as well as domestic civil aviation operations during the 30-year civil war in Sri Lanka.[27] This airport was formally designated as an international aerodrome in 2019, named the "Jaffna International Airport" (JAF)[28] thus increasing the number of international airports in the country to four. International flights have been operated from Jaffna to Chennai and Chennai to Jaffna since commencement in 2022.[29]

Currently, the BIA, MRIA, JAF and the Colombo International Airport Ratmalana (CIA) are the four international airports serving Sri Lanka.

2 The Legal Landscape and the Evolution of the Regulatory Structure Relating to Airports

Regulations applicable to air navigation in Ceylon (then a British Colony) were first promulgated with effect from the 1 September 1937.[30] These regulations contained very basic rules only for the licensing of aerodromes, but they did not contain detailed provisions governing aerodromes.[31] When the Ratmalana Airport was inaugurated on 28 February 1938, for civil aviation, the Director of Public Works was appointed Director of Civil Aviation, and the airports' management was entrusted to the Director of Civil Aviation. In 1946, after World War II, the development of Civil Aviation in

[25] P.D. De Silva, 'Warehouses at MRIA Mattala being cleared of controversially stored paddy stocks', *DailyFT*, January 2016, available at < https://www.ft.lk/shippingaviation/warehouses-at-mria-mattala-being-cleared-of-controversially-stored-paddy-stocks/21-519437 > Last visited, 13 August 2024.

[26] *Id.*

[27] *Id.*

[28] 'Palaly Airfield', *airport.lk*, available at < https://www.airport.lk/jaf/about_us/history_of_jaffna_international_airport > Last visited 13 August 2024.

[29] 'Connecting Jaffna and Chennai', *airport.lk*, December 2022, available at < https://www.airport.lk/jaf/flight_info/flight_schedule > Last visited 13 August 2024.

[30] Order No. 8310, dated Friday August 20th, 1937, containing the direction issued by the Officer Administering the Government (Governor General of Ceylon) by virtue of the powers vested by the Air Navigation (Colonies, Protectorates and Mandated Territories) Order 1927, as amended by Amendment No. 2, Order of 1936.

[31] *Id.*, Regulations 80–83.

the country was assigned to the Ministry of Transport and the Ratmalana aerodrome was taken over from the Royal Air Force for civil flying.[32]

The Department of Civil Aviation (DCA) in the Country was established in 1946.[33] In the year 1948, Sri Lanka (then Ceylon) became a member of the International Civil Aviation Organization (ICAO) by acceding to the Chicago Convention on Civil Aviation and, within a period of two years completed the domestic legislative steps required to ratify and give effect the Chicago Convention[34] and the Warsaw Convention of 1929[35] relating to the air carrier liability the provisions of which were formally adopted as law with the promulgation of the Air Navigation Act No. 15 of 1950.[36]

Under the Air Navigation Act No. 15 of 1951 (later repealed and replaced by the Civil Aviation Act 14 of 2010), the Minister in charge of the subject of civil aviation was empowered *inter alia* to make regulations for the licensing, inspection, regulation and control of aerodromes and to prohibit the use of unlicensed aerodromes.[37] The Minister in charge of the subject of civil aviation was also empowered to establish aerodromes and acquire land for aerodromes,[38] and to make orders for apparatus and equipment to be installed and operated to warn of any buildings and obstructions near aerodromes and where necessary to alter, remove or demolish obstructions near aerodromes.[39]

Detailed regulations giving effect to the Annexes of the Chicago Convention and the Standards and Recommended Practices (SARPS) promulgated there under were brought into effect by the Air Navigation Regulations of 1955[40] wherein the several SARPS contained in the Annexes of the Chicago Convention relating to aerodromes were formally introduced into the regulatory landscape of the country. The 1955 Air Navigation Regulations repealed the Air Navigations Regulations of 1937 previously made for the Colony of Ceylon by the British Governor General.[41] The 1955 Regulations also contained detailed provisions relating to the licensing

[32] Airports & Aviation Services Ltd., 'History of Aviation', available at < https://www.airport.lk/aasl/company_overview/aviation_history>Last visited, 10 September 2024.

[33] 'Evolution of CAASL', *CAASL*, available at < https://www.caa.lk/en/about-us/history-of-caasl/evolution-of-caasl#:~:text=Accordingly%2C%20Air%20Lanka%20Ltd.%2C,air%20navigation%20services%20in%201983 > Last visited, 15 August 2024.

[34] Convention on International Civil Aviation signed at Chicago on the 7th of December 1944. Available at < https://treaties.un.org/doc/publication/unts/volume%2015/volume-15-ii-102-english.pdf > Last visited 15 September 2024.

[35] Convention for the Unifications of Certain Rules Relating to International Carriage by Air signed at Warsaw on 12th October 1929. Available at < https://www.mcgill.ca/iasl/files/iasl/warsaw1929.pdf > Last visited Last visited 15 September 2024.

[36] Air Navigation Act No. 15 of 1951, see the Preamble and Section 3 thereof which empowered the Minister in charge of the subject of Civil Aviation to make regulation and in particular, to give effect to the Annexes of the Chicago Convention.

[37] *Id.*, Sec. 3(2) (c).

[38] *Id.*, Sec. 8.

[39] *Id.*, Sec. 13.

[40] Air Navigations Regulation of 1955, Chapter 365, Subsidiary Legislation of 1956.

[41] *Id.*, Regulation 295.

of aerodromes,[42] regulating of noise near aerodromes,[43] and prescribing of customs aerodromes for international flights.[44] Most importantly, a specific provision therein gave effect to ICAO, Annex 14 formulated under the Chicago Convention whereby it was stated that:

> The physical characteristics of aerodromes, aeronautical ground lights and surface marking colours, obstruction clearing and markings, visual ground aids and aerodrome equipment shall conform to the standards prescribed in Annex 14 to the Convention, and the recommended practices therein shall be implemented as far as possible.[45]

It was also postulated that any additions or amendment adopted by the Council of the ICAO (to the relevant SARPS) shall have the same force as if prescribed under this regulation.[46]

This makes it clear that the international aerodromes in Sri Lanka were governed by, regulated and bound to comply with the standards formulated in Annex 14 of the Chicago Convention relating to aerodromes which standards had been given legislative and regulatory force in Sri Lanka as far back as the year 1955.

In 1979, a statutory body was established by an Act of Parliament named as the Airport Authority of Sri Lanka.[47] The duties of the Airport Authority under that statute was to assume full responsibility and management of airports and to provide all facilities and services required for the safe operation of airports.[48] With the creation of the said Airports Authority all movable and immovable properties (at all existing civil airports) hitherto managed and controlled by the Director of Civil Aviation (DCA) were vested in the said Airports Authority.[49] Despite the property and lands of the airports being vested in the control of the Airports Authority, the powers of the DCA to supervise and regulate matters relating to the aerodromes to ensure due compliance of standards in Annex 14, as mandated in the Air Navigation Act No. 15 of 1951 and the Regulation of 1955 were not affected and remained with the DCA.

Before the Airports Authority Act[50] and its provisions were fully implemented the Parliament introduced a new piece of legislation titled the Air Navigations (Special Provision) Act.[51] By this statute the authority for the development, maintenance and administration of aerodromes and airports, the provision of airports and aerodrome facilities at airports, the maintenance of air navigation services and facilities and the provision of fire-fighting services at airports was to be conferred upon an "Agent" of

---

[42] *Id.*, Regulation 106.

[43] *Id.*, Regulation 108.

[44] *Id.*, Regulation 126.

[45] *Id.*, Regulation 282(1).

[46] *Id.*, Regulation 282(2).

[47] Airport Authority Act No. 46 of 1979.

[48] *Id.*, Sec. 14.

[49] *Id.*, Sec. 37.

[50] *Id.*

[51] Air Navigation (Special Provisions) Act No. 2 of 1982, amending Section 20 of the principal enactment, by adding a new provision as Section 21A.

the Government, to be incorporated as a company under the existing company law, of which the majority control of 95% equity was to be held by the Government and the balance 5% equity to be held by a company or body operating the national airline.[52] This statute repealed the Airports Authority Act, which had been legislated a mere two years prior to that, and made provision to divest all property (lands, buildings, facilities and equipment at all airports) held by the Airports Authority back to the Civil Aviation Department.[53]

The "Agent" of the Government contemplated in the Air Navigations (Special Provision) Act No. 2 of 1982 referred to above, was incorporated thereafter in 1983 under the name of "Airports and Aviation Services (Sri Lanka) Limited" (AASL) as 100% Government owned company, and has since its incorporation functioned under the statutory mandate conferred upon it by law as the "Agent" of the Government to develop, manage, maintain and to provide air navigations related services and facilities at civil airports in Sri Lanka. AASL today is one of the leading public business undertakings making a significant contribution to the national economy.

Further amendments were introduced in 1992 by the Air Navigation (Special Provisions) Act,[54] which created the statutory office of the Director General of Civil Aviation (DGCA)[55] in place of the DCA. This amendment made a specific provision that all movable and immovable property (relating to airports) previously vested in the DCA and made available to the Agent (AASL) by the Minister was deemed to be held by the Agent on behalf of the State with effect from the 20 January 1982.[56] Whilst this amendment conferred authority upon the AASL to deal with movable and immovable property of the airports being managed and controlled by it, the AASL was precluded from leasing any property for more than 10 years without the approval of the Minister.[57]

In December 2002, a significant change was brought about to the regulatory scheme of civil aviation in the country by the conversion of the Department of Civil Aviation, which was hitherto under the direct control of the Government and the Minister in charge of the subject of aviation, to an autonomous authority named as the Civil Aviation Authority of Sri Lanka (CAASL).[58] This Act also re-established the office of the Director General of Civil Aviation (DGCA) as chief executive officer of the CAASL and an independent statutory office with prescribed duties, functions, authority and power under the Act and other applicable laws.[59] The CAASL Act also made provisions for the transfer and vesting of all movable and immovable properties (including airports) in the DGCA which had hitherto been held and possessed by

[52] *Id.*, Sec. 3.

[53] *Id.*, Sects. 7 & 8.

[54] Air Navigation (Special Provisions) Act No. 55 of 1992.

[55] *Id.*, Sec. 2 repealing and replacing Section 20 of the principal enactment.

[56] *Id.*, Sec. 3 amending Section 21A of the principal enactment and substituting subsections 21A (8) & (9) with new provisions.

[57] *Id.*, new Sec. 21A (9).

[58] Civil Aviation Authority of Sri Lanka Act No. 34 of 2002.

[59] *Id.*, Sec. 11.

the DCA under Sect. 20 of the Air Navigation Act No. 15 of 1951.[60] This was a progressive step towards regularising the governance of civil air transport in Sri Lanka. Section 9 of the Civil Aviation Authority Act granted powers to the Minister to vest, by way of a gazette, the aerodromes listed in the second schedule and the aeronautical facilities and land appertaining thereto as per the third schedule to the Act to the CAASL.[61] The second schedule included all the airports and airfields that existed in 2002.[62] Schedule 3 listed a number of facilities, including training centers, radio navigational aid facilities, communication centers, radar stations etc.[63]

These provisions taken in toto affirmed the legal position that the proprietary interests and ownership of all movable and immovable properties and assets relating to airports in the country are vested and held within de jure ownership of the office of DGCA which holds them on behalf of the State whilst the de facto and regular management and control of the airports in Sri Lanka are exercised by the AASL.

In November 2002, an interim regulation having much significance was issued by the Minister under the authority of the Air Navigation Act No. 15 of 1951.[64] This regulation specifically postulated that:

> Subject to any differences filed with the ICAO council by the DGCA, the international standards contained in the current annexes of the Chicago Convention, shall be enforced and implemented in Sri Lanka and it is the responsibility of the DGCA to take all necessary measures for effectively enforcing and implementing the same.[65]

Under the above regulation, all 18 Annexes of the Chicago Convention including Annex 14 (Volumes I & II) containing the international standards applicable to aerodromes were specifically listed.

As the Sri Lankan state has so far not filed any difference or departures with the ICAO council in relation to any of the international standards contained in the 18 Annexes of Chicago Convention as required in terms of Article 38 of the Chicago Convention, the effect of this domestic regulation is that the Sri Lankan DGCA would be required by law to take all necessary measures to effectively enforce and implement all of the standards as set out in the 18 Annexes of the Chicago Convention including all the standards in Volumes I & II of Annex 14, of the Chicago Convention relating to aerodromes.

Therefore, the implementation of all published standards of Annex 14 relating to aerodromes is not only an obligation assumed by the State of Sri Lanka vis-a-vis the international aviation community under its multilateral obligation of the Chicago Convention, but also a statutory duty cast upon the DGCA by domestic legislation.

---

[60] *Id.*, Sec. 8.

[61] *Id.*, Sec. 9.

[62] *Id.*, Schedule 2.

[63] *Id.*, Schedule 3.

[64] Civil Aviation (Interim) Regulation No. 01 of 2002, issued under the Section 24 read with Sect. 3 of the Air Navigation Act No. 15 of 1951 and amending the Ceylon Air Navigations Regulation of 1955. Government Gazette No. 1264/33 dated 28 November 2002.

[65] *Id.*, Regulation 2.

This regulatory landscape once again was subject to significant change with the enactment of the Civil Aviation Act[66] in 2010 which was intended to unify into a coherent body of the laws made under several previous legislative instruments. The Civil Aviation Act No. 10 of 2014 repealed the Air Navigation Act No. 15 of 1951 and the Air Navigation (Special Provisions) Act No. 55 of 1992, except Part III of the former and Part II of the latter, which respectively gave effect and legal force to the air carrier liability regimes of the Warsaw Convention of 1929 and amendments made thereto by the Hague Protocol of 1955,[67] whilst once again giving effect to the Chicago Convention which had been in force in the country since the year 1951 and specific provisions thereof as set out in the Schedule of the Act.[68] With the enactment of this statute, a wide and extensive scope of matters relating to public law and regulatory oversight of civil aviation in the country were captured within its ambit.[69] These matters pertained, inter alia, to the provision and use of aeronautical services within the country,[70] and the regulation, administration and safety oversight of all civil aviation within the country.[71] This statute also legislated for other matters relating to the safe and orderly operation and development including the economic development of civil air navigation.[72] However, provisions in the statute expressly excluded its operation to military aircraft and aerodromes.[73]

The Civil Aviation Act made further provision that all regulations made under the repealed statutes (Air Navigation Act No. 15 of 1951 and the Air Navigation (Special Provisions) Act No. 55 of 1992), which were in force at the time of its enactment shall be deemed to be regulations made under the Civil Aviation Act 14 of 2010 in so far as such regulations not being inconsistent with the provisions thereof. It is noteworthy that the Ceylon Civil Aviation Regulation of 1955[74] as well as the Civil Aviation (Interim) Regulation No. 01 of 2002[75] which were in force at the time the Civil Aviation Act was made law in 2010, neither of which had been repealed or amended, therefore, continue to be in force and applicable within the rubric of regulations governing civil aviation in the country today.

Therefore, it is clear that the international standards postulated in Annex 14 (Volumes I & II) applicable to aerodromes under the Chicago Convention apply in full and without change to the aerodromes in Sri Lanka. Hence, the DGCA Sri Lanka is duty bound under the laws of the State to take all measures to give effect and implement all Annex 14 standards that are applicable in relation to aerodromes in full and without reservation.

---

[66] Civil Aviation Act No. 14 of 2010.

[67] *Id.*, Secs. 126(1) (a) & 126(1) (b).

[68] *Id.*, Sec. 2.

[69] *Id.*, Sec. 3.

[70] *Id.*, Sec. 3 (1) (b) & (d).

[71] *Id.*, Sec. 3 (1) (c).

[72] *Id.*, Sec. 3 (1) (e).

[73] *Id.*, Sec. 3 (2).

[74] *Supra* note 39.

[75] *Supra* note 60.

From a legal perspective, the operation of the above regulation and the compliance burden cast upon the State of Sri Lanka as a signatory of the Chicago Convention to fully implement all standards set out in the 18 Annexes thereof, including the Annex 14 standards that are applicable to aerodromes can be deemed onerous. Sri Lanka as a state party to the Chicago Convention had expressly professed and undertaken to implement within its territory all standards (SARPS) set out in the Annexes of the Chicago Convention. Therefore, if any shortcoming is found in the implementation the SARPs, it will tantamount firstly a failure of the multilateral legal obligations assumed by Sri Lanka. Secondly, the compliance levels of the Sri Lanka at ICAO periodic audits would inevitably result in negative findings when the comparison benchmark for evaluation would be the measurement against full compliance with all standards in the ICAO Annexes, which have been expressly undertaken and committed to by the State of Sri Lanka.

The Civil Aviation Act 14 of 2010 introduced progressive changes in the laws that govern civil aviation in the country and enacted new provisions particularly applicable to the appointment, governance and regulations of "Service Providers" for aeronautical services, which include the operation of aerodromes and providing of associated aeronautical services at aerodromes.[76]

Accordingly, the Minister in charge of the subject of aviation in consultation with the Civil Aviation Authority of Sri Lanka (CAASL) is empowered by an Order published in the Gazette to appoint Service Providers in respect of aeronautical services defined in Sect. 31 of the Act on such terms and conditions to be stipulated in such Order.[77]

However, the Minister can appoint only the "Statutory Service Provider" in respect of the aeronautical services of the development, operation and maintenance of international aerodromes; the provision and maintenance of search, rescue and fire-fighting services; and the provision and maintenance of aviation security services, at any international aerodrome.[78] Further, only the Statutory Service Provider can be appointed for the provision of Air Traffic Services, provision of Aeronautical Information Services, provisions of Aeronautical Communication Services, and the provision of aeronautical aids for communication, navigation and surveillance at any aerodrome.[79]

The Civil Aviation Act, made specific provisions to ensure that the "Statutory Service Provider" who is identified as the "Agent" appointed under Sect. 21A of the Air Navigations Act to be given the exclusive monopolistic economic opportunities of operating aerodromes in the country. Establishing and operating international aerodromes, providing fire-fighting and security services at international aerodromes, providing Air Traffic, Aeronautical Information and Communication and related services at all aerodrome in Sri Lanka, can thus be carried out only by the "Statutory

[76] *Supra* note 62, Chapter II.
[77] *Id.*, Sec. 6(1).
[78] *Id.*, Sec. 6(3) (a) (i) read with Secs. 31(a), 31(c) & 31(d).
[79] *Id.*, Sec. 6(3) (a) (ii) read with Secs. 31(e), 31(f), 31(g) & 31(h).

Service Provider".[80] Therefore, the exclusive economic rights granted to Airports and Aviation Services (Sri Lanka) Limited (AASL)[81] as the "Agent" of the Government in connection with international as well as domestic airports by past legislation, have been preserved and protected by the current statute. The AASL, which is the Statutory Service Provider referred to in the Act, by operation of law, thus became entitled to be issued with necessary licenses to enable it to continue to provide all such aeronautical services it had provided and operated at the time the Civil Aviation Act No. 14 of 2010 was enacted into law.[82]

These exclusive rights preserved for the AASL by being named the "Statutory Service Provider" under the Civil Aviation Act was confirmed by an Order made by the Minister and published in the Government Gazette, whereby AASL, the "Agent" of the Government was formally appointed as the Statutory Service Provider.[83]

If the Statutory Service Provider (the AASL) consents to develop, operate and maintain any airport or aerodrome other than international aerodromes, the Minister can then appoint only the Statutory Service Provider (AASL) to provide fire-fighting and security service at such aerodromes.[84] The Minister can appoint a Service Provider other than AASL only in respect of aerodromes which are not designated as international aerodromes and only to provide aeronautical services which the AASL has not been appointed to provide at such aerodromes.[85] Further, only one service provider can be appointed to provide the aeronautical services relating to fire-fighting and security at any aerodrome.[86]

It is important to note that, the Minister can only appoint a company or corporation whose majority shares are owned by the Government to provide the aeronautical services of supplying aviation fuel and lubricants to aircraft, providing assistance or equipment for dispatch of aircraft on the apron and aircraft cleaning, ground handling and related facilities, catering services to aircraft and the supply of any other services other than the services specified above, unless such Government owned company does not consent to provide such services in which case any other Service Provider (a private entity not owned or controlled by the Government) may be appointed to provide such services.[87] All Service Providers (both government controlled and private) appointed to provide the aeronautical services of supplying fuel and lubricants, providing equipment and assistance for the dispatch of aircraft on the apron, aircraft cleaning, ground handling and catering services are required to enter into agreements with the aerodrome operator appointed for the aerodrome at which the

[80] *Id.*, Sec. 127.

[81] *Supra* notes 50 and 56.

[82] Civil Aviation Act No. 14 of 2010, *Supra*, Sec. 127.

[83] Gazette 1727/12 dated 13 October 2013, Order made on the 12 October 2013 in terms of Sect. 127(2) of the Civil Aviation Act No. 14 of 2010.

[84] Civil Aviation Act No. 14 of 2010, *Supra*, Sec. 6(3) (b).

[85] *Id.*, Sec. 6(3) (c).

[86] *Id.*, Sec. 6(3) (d).

[87] *Id.*, Sec. 6(3) (e) & the Proviso thereof.

relevant aeronautical service is to be performed.[88] Where a Service Provider, other than AASL (the Statutory Service Provider), is appointed to operate any aerodrome (other than international aerodromes) then persons providing Air Traffic Services, Aeronautical Information Services, Aeronautical Communication Services and aeronautical aids for communication, navigation and surveillance at such airports must enter into agreements with the AASL, where such services can have a direct impact to the safety and security of services provided by the AASL.[89]No person can be appointed to provide aeronautical services described above, if the person is likely to pose a threat to the public security of Sri Lanka or international civil aviation.[90] Once an appointment is made as aforesaid of an aeronautical Service Provider a license will be issued to such person by DGCA or the CAASL whilst a separate license is required to be issued in respect of each type of aeronautical service.[91] The licenses so issued by the DGCA or the CAASL are subject to an annual license fee and can be suspended or revoked on the grounds of non-compliance of the license conditions, non-payment of the license fees or any other reason which can affect the smooth operation of the service or the safety of the operations for which the license was granted.[92]

Whilst the Civil Aviation Act makes provision in general for the licensing of aerodromes and for providing different types of aeronautical services as described in detail above what is to be borne in mind is that the DGCA is duty-bound to ensure that all aerodromes and aeronautical services provided at international airports in Sri Lanka are compliant to the maximum extent with the standards stipulated in Annex 14 of the Chicago Convention. Therefore, the standards that have to be complied with in relation to matters such as the classification of aerodromes (land or water aerodromes) and the essential attributes that have to be established and maintained at such aerodromes, aerodrome data and physical characteristics such as runways, strips, taxiways, aprons, lights, aeronautical ground lighting, obstruction clearing, signs, marking, visual ground aids, signaling, emergency lighting, aids to locations, electrical systems, aerodrome operational services, equipment, installations and aerodrome maintenance,[93] safety, security at aerodromes, and operations etc., as well should be in line with the standards stipulated in Annex 14 of the Chicago Convention.

Given this regulatory backdrop and the international obligations assumed by Sri Lanka under the Chicago Convention, it has formulated an aviation policy and therein

---

[88] *Id.*, Sec. 7(1).

[89] *Id.*, Sec. 7(2).

[90] *Id.*, Sec. 9.

[91] *Id.*, Sec. 10.

[92] *Id.*, Sec. 11(4) read with Sec. 26.

[93] Annex 14 to the Chicago Convention, Aerodromes, Vol. I, Aerodrome Design and Operations, (8th Edn.) July 2018, ICAO International Standards & Recommended Practices, available at < https://www.iacm.gov.mz/app/uploads/2018/12/an_14_v1_Aerodromes_8ed._2018_rev.14_01.07.18.pdf > Last visited, 15 September 2024.

attempted to capture wide -ranging initiatives in relation to aerodromes and their development.

The National Civil Aviation Policy for Sri Lanka (Aviation Policy), approved by the Cabinet of Ministers and published in 2016, presents a progressive policy framework for aviation in general and includes specific tasks and proposals in relation to aerodromes, including their establishment and development.[94] Whilst noting that the development of airports is essential for the growth of aviation and tourism sectors, the Aviation Policy commits to the development of existing and proposed domestic and international airports in the country according to required standards and foreseeable demand based on traffic forecasts.[95] All domestic aerodromes except those used by the military are to be developed and maintained according to the prescribed standards, whilst clear segregation of land and space facilities at military airports which are used for civil aviation is to be done to ensure safe, regular and economic civil aviation under the regulatory oversight of the CAASL.[96] Construction of new aerodromes, including heliports and helipads, are to be carried out and located subject to technical feasibility based on tourism, trade, commerce, industrial and social needs.[97] The policy also encourages the use of inland water bodies as water aerodromes for the use of floatplanes in consultation with the authorities in charge of water bodies without prejudice to the primary use of such water bodies.[98] Construction of Helipads in major cities and near Highways is to be promoted to facilitate efficient transfers of needy passengers, including medical evacuation.[99]

The policy provides for the development of new airports and the renovation and expansion of existing airports and related infrastructure to be carried out through systematic planning and design with the assistance of AASL and all other stakeholders and in dialogue with the local communities.[100] It is interesting to note that the Aviation Policy proposes the building four regional airports covering North, East, South and West of Sri Lanka to improve external as well as internal connectivity[101] and to initiate domestic terminal facilities at the international airports to facilitate passenger transfers at domestic airports and thereby promote domestic air travel.[102] The Policy also proposes the construction of low-cost terminals at airports recognizing the significant economic contributions made by low-cost or budget carriers towards the growth in air traffic.[103]

---

[94] 'A National Civil Aviation Policy for Sri Lanka—November 2016', *CAASL*, November 2016, available at <https://caa.lk/images/Civil_Aviation/NCAP_SL_CabinetApproved.pdf> Last visited, 15September 2024.

[95] *Id.*, Policy 12.1, at p. 11.

[96] *Id.*, Policy 6.2, at p. 9.

[97] *Id.*, Policy, 6.3, at p. 9.

[98] *Id.*, Policy 6.4, at p. 10.

[99] *Id.*, Policy 6.7, at p. 10.

[100] *Id.*, Policy 12.3, at p. 11.

[101] *Id.*, Policy 12.4, at p. 12.

[102] *Id.*, Policy 12.6, at p. 12.

[103] *Id.*, Policy 12.7, at p. 12.

The Policy also makes provisions for the airport facilitation and efficient management of the flow of passengers, baggage, cargo and mail through the airport facilities, ensuring that services are delivered in a healthy, safe and secure environment.[104] It also incorporates the State Aviation Safety Programs (SAAP) and aviation security initiatives in line with applicable standards and recommended practices.[105]

The regional and international airports embodied in the Aviation Policy have become a partial reality, with the Jaffna International Airport (JAF) being developed and categorised as an international airport. Further, the Batticaloa airport has also been commissioned as a regional airport for civil aviation.[106] There are two international airports for Western province, i.e., the Bandaranayake International Airport (BIA) and the Colombo International Airport (CIA) at Ratmalana. Another airport at Koggalain the South of the country, already a hub for domestic civil aircraft and military operations,[107]which is currently managed by the Sri Lanka Airforce, could also developed as a regional airport for the Southern province along with the Mahinda Rajapakse International Airport (MRIA). Therefore, the country has a sufficient number of airports locations to accommodate the current needs of civil aviation as well as projected growth in the long term, provided that these airports are developed with proper facilities and in compliance with applicable international standards.

As at date all international and regional airports in the country are operated and developed by the AASL. There are no privately operated airports in the country, whilst there are several airfields operated by the Air Force around the country.[108]

Apart from the above statutory and regulatory provisions, other statutes enacted relating to aviation also have implications for aerodromes. The Offences against Aircraft Act No. 24 of 1982 which gave effect to the Montreal Convention 1971.[109] The Suppression of Unlawful Acts of Violence at Airports Serving International Airports Act No. 31 of 1996 was enacted to give effect to the Protocol Supplementary to the Montreal Convention 1971.[110] This Act specifies the penalties applicable for endangering the safety of airports with a statutory maximum fine and

---

[104] *Id.*, Policy 20, at p. 16.

[105] *Id.*, Policy 17 & 18, at pp. 14 & 15.

[106] Gazette Notification under Civil Aviation Act No. 14 of 2010 on DGCA Instructions relating to Batticaloa Airport, *CAASL*, March 2023, available at < https://caa.lk/images/stories/pdf/regulations/2323-44_E-_DGCA_Instructions.pdf > Last visited, 29 September 2024.

[107] 'Sri Lanka Air Force Koggala', *airforce.lk*, available at < https://www.airforce.lk/pages.php?pages=koggala > Last visited, 13 August 2024, 'Strategic development plan for domestic airports', *news.lk*, September 2018, available at < https://news.lk/news/business/item/22440-strategic-development-plan-for-domestic-airports > Last visited, 13 August 2024.

[108] For example—Air Field in Wirawila, 'Sri Lanka Air Force Wirawila', *airforce.lk*, available at < https://www.airforce.lk/pages.php?pages=wirawila > Last visited, 13 August 2024; Air Field in Katukurunda, 'Sri Lanka Air Force Katukurunda' *airforce.lk*, available at < https://www.airforce.lk/pages.php?pages=katukurunda > Last visited, 13 August 2024.

[109] Convention for the Suppression of Unlawful Acts Against the Safety of Civil Aviation, signed at Montreal, on 23 September 1974, 974 UNTS 177.

[110] Suppression of Unlawful Acts of Violence at Airports Serving International Civil Aviation Act No. 31 of 1996.

imprisonment.[111] Furthermore, the Extradition Law of 1977 of Sri Lanka was also amended by the Suppression of Unlawful Acts of Violence at Airports Serving International Airports Act No. 31 of 1996 Act, to include the offences under the latter Act concerning unlawful acts of violence at airports and any act that endangers the safety of airports and the destruction or damage of the facilities at airports serving international civil aviation.[112] The Civil Aviation Act No. 14 of 2010 was amended by the Civil Aviation (Amendment) Act No. 12 of 2018[113] to introduce measures to prevent passengers at airports from being subject to intimidation or nuisances by touting of any form. This amendment to the Civil Aviation Act introduced provisions to make touting of inbound or outbound passengers to be an offence punishable by law and empower the employees of security service providers at the airport to apprehend or arrest offender and hand them over to the police for appropriate procedures to report facts to a Magistrate who upon inquiry is empowered to impose a fine or imprisonment on the offender.[114] Civil Aviation (Amendment) Act No. 24 of 2023 was the latest amendment of the principal enactment that is directly relevant to aerodrome governance.[115] Prior to this amendment, the minister could appoint only one service provider, which was a public corporation or company owned and controlled by the government, to provide aeronautical services of supplying equipment for dispatch of aircraft at the apron, aircraft cleaning, ground handling, catering, and any other services to aircraft at international and domestic airports. Any service provider to provide such aeronautical services could be appointed only if the government corporation or government- controlled entity did not consent to provide such services. However, with the aforementioned amendment of the law,[116] the requirement of appointing a Government corporation or Government controlled body to provide such services in the first instance, has been removed whilst also making room for more than one service provider for such aeronautical services to be appointed to provide such services at international as well as domestic airports.[117]

Apart from the general stipulation whereby Sri Lanka has formulated regulations undertaking to comply with all standards prescribed in the Annexes of the Chicago Convention to the fullest extent possible,[118] as adverted to above, the DGCA of Sri Lanka, in the exercise of his statutory authority vested under law[119] from time to time has also issued orders for implementing standards to give effect to Articles of the Chicago Convention and the regulations and rules including those set out in Annexes thereof. Several Implementing Standards issued by the DGCA of Sri Lanka

---

[111] *Id.*, Sec. 3.

[112] *Id.*

[113] Civil Aviation (Amendment) Act No. 12 of 2018.

[114] *Id.*, new Sec. 18A.

[115] Civil Aviation (Amendment) Act No. 24 of 2023, repealing and replacing Sect. 6(3) (e) of the principal enactment with a new provision.

[116] *Id.*

[117] *Id.*

[118] Civil Aviation (Interim) Regulation No. 01 of 2002, *Supra* notes 64 & 65.

[119] See Sec. 120, Civil Aviation Act No. 14 of 2010.

pertain to the subject of aerodrome governance and cover *inter alia* matters such as Aerodrome Standards in Sri Lanka,[120] Criteria to Regulate the Use of a Pavement by an Aircraft with ACN higher than the Reported PCN (Overload Operations),[121] Requirements to be Satisfied by the Aerodrome Operators for the Certification of Aerodromes in Sri Lanka,[122] Heliport Standards in Sri Lanka,[123] and Requirement for Facilities and Services to be provided by Aerodrome Operator.[124]In addition to these, several other implementing standards issued by the DGCA also have relevance to the subject of aerodrome governance, such as the implementing standard on competency certification of the aeronautical service provider maintaining an aviation security service[125]; air traffic services in compliance with Annex 11,[126] licensing of ground handling arrangements and facilities and services to aircraft,[127] certification of air navigation service providers[128] etc.

The initial regulation on the zoning of aerodromes in Sri Lanka provided for zoning limits in relation to the three aerodromes of Ratmalana (presently CIA), Katunayaka (presently BIA), and Kankesanturai (presently the JAF) airports as they then existed.[129] The zoning regulations relating to MRIA airport were published in 2012.[130] The regulation in relation to the classification of aerodromes was issued in 2018, which included a more precise classification of aerodromes in Sri Lanka.[131] The classifications were based on the designs of aerodromes, types of use, scope of use, operating conditions and approach and landing aids provided in available aerodromes.[132] Specific regulations are available for commissioning international

---

120 Aerodrome Standards of Sri Lanka, CAASL Doc No: SLCAIS-030, IS Reference Code CA-IS-2022-AE-02 dated 22 November 2022, available at < https://caa.lk/en/regulations-policies/subsidiary-legislation/implementing-standards#implementing-standards-on-aerodromes > Last visited, 15 September 2024.

121 *Id.*, CAASL, CA-IS-2014-ANS-005. SN: 32, 11 August 2014.

122 *Id.*, IS Reference Code: CA-IS-2022-AE-001, CAASL Doc. No: SLCAIS-037, 15September 2022.

123 *Id.*, IS Reference Code: CA-IS-2024-AE-001, CAASL Doc No: SLCAIS-041, 20 March 2024.

124 *Id.*, Reference No: IS-09-(1, 2, 3, 6, 7, 8) SLCAIS: 060, 25 July 2017.

125 *Id.*, IS Reference Code: CA-IS-AVSEC-01, CAASL Doc. No: SLCAIS 078, 1 December 2020.

126 *Id.*, IS Reference Code: IS-11—all, CAASL Doc. No: SLCAIS 025, 5 April 2021.

127 *Id.*, CA-IS-2016-OPS-001; CAASL Doc. No: SLCAIS 046, 1 December 2021.

128 *Id.*, CA-IS-2018-ANS-087, CAASL Doc No: SLCAIS 087, 10 April 2023.

129 Sri Lanka Aerodromes (Zoning) Regulations of 1975, Order No. 1 of 1975, General Gazette, Part I, Sec I, 18 April 1975, CAASL, April 1975, available at < https://caa.lk/images/Civil_Aviation/6sri_lanka_aerodromes_zoning__regulations_order_no_01_of_1975_1975_04_14.pdf > Last visited, 29 September 2024.

130 Zoning Instructions Hambantota International Airport, No. 01 of 2012, available at < https://caa.lk/en/regulations-policies/subsidiary-legislation/regulation#regulations-on-aerodromes-zoning-and-commissioning > Last visited, 15 September 2024.

131 Civil Aviation (Classification of Aerodromes) Regulations of 2018, *CAASL*, September 2018, available at < https://caa.lk/images/Civil_Aviation/2087-27_E_AE_Classification.pdf > Last visited, 29 September 2024.

132 *Id.*

airports[133] as well as regional airports. The 2022 regulation on water aerodromes opened up the opportunity for service providers[134] to apply for a license to maintain and operate water aerodromes.[135] The availability of water aerodromes has significantly enhanced the development opportunities for domestic civil aviation in the country and for inland air transportation using biplanes, particularly to the regions of the hill country such as Kandy and Nuwara-Eliya which are mountainous terrain and do not have the possibility of accommodating landing strips or runways for the operation of larger aircraft.

3 Sri Lanka Air Navigation Plan 2022–2036

The latest development on enhancing air services in Sri Lanka is the Air Navigation Plan 2022–2036. Responding to the ICAO's Air System Block Upgrade (ASBU) and Asia Pacific Seamless ANS Plan, the Sri Lanka Air Navigation Plan (SLANP) has been drafted under five areas, namely, airport operations, communication navigation and surveillance, air traffic management, aeronautical information management and meteorology.[136] This plan gives effect to a series of ICAO docs[137] addressing the aforementioned aspects and proposes to achieve the results through a phased framework.[138] The SLANP further responds to the ICAO Asia Pacific Office (APAC) regional implementation of ABSU elements and APAC regional implementation elements.[139]

4 Legal and Practical Issues

The above discourse relating to the regulatory structure and the landscape governing aerodromes in Sri Lanka will clearly demonstrate to the reader that, at present, ownership and the operation of aerodromes in Sri Lanka are primarily vested within

[133] Commissioning of Mattala Rajapaksa International Airport (Gazette No. 1795/52 dated 01–02-2013), *CAASL*, February 2013, available at < https://caa.lk/images/Civil_Aviation/16_gazette_no_1795_52_01_feb_2013.pdf > Last visited, 13 August 2024.

[134] Sri Lanka Water Aerodromes Regulation No. 1 of 2022 (Extra Ordinary Gazette No. 2292/34 dated 09/08/2022)-S/T, Article 2, *CAASL*, August 2022, available at < https://caa.lk/images/stories/pdf/regulations/2292_34_E_Water_Aerodrome.pdf>Last visited, 13 August 2024.

[135] *Id.*

[136] *Supra* note 23, at p.4.

[137] *Supra* note 23, ICAO Docs 9750 on Global Air Navigation Plan, ICAO Doc 9854 on Global ATM Operational Concept, ICAO Doc 10,004 on Global Aviation Safety Plan (GASP), ICAO 9882 on Manual on ATM System Requirements, ICAO 9883 on Global Performance of the Air Navigation System, ICAO Doc 9673 on Asia/Pacific Regional Air Navigation Plan.

[138] See generally, *supra* note 23.

[139] *Supra* note 23, Appendix B.

the ownership and control of the government and or reserved for companies/entities controlled and owned by the government.

At present, all primary aeronautical services such as operating the aerodromes, firefighting and aviation security at all international airports in Sri Lanka are provided by AASL, whilst the said government-owned company also provides a large majority of associated aeronautical services, such as aeronautical communication and information services, aids for communication navigation and surveillance, air traffic control etc., at all international as well as domestic airports in Sri Lanka.

Sri Lankan Airlines, the national carrier, has been appointed by AASL under the direction of the Government of Sri Lanka to act as the sole ground handling "agent" for all International Airlines operating to Bandaranayaka International Airport at Katunayaka (BIA) and Mattala Rajapaksa International Airport (MRIA). At present, Sri Lankan Airlines, the national carrier, is also the only catering services provider to all international airlines that operate to BIA and MRIA. Ground handling at the other international airports is presently carried out by AASL whilst no formal arrangements operate for airline catering services at the international airports of CIA at Ratmalana and JAF in Jaffna. Fits Air, registered in Sri Lanka operating both domestic and international scheduled passenger services, which is privately owned and controlled, has been granted the dispensation and license to perform ground handling services and catering for its own flights at BIA and CIA in Ratmalana.

The monopoly of ground handling services, as well as airline catering, presently enjoyed by Sri Lankan Airlines as at BIA and MRIA has given rise to many complaints of the national carrier having abused its dominant position in providing these aeronautical services by charging exorbitant or unreasonable rates for such ground handling services. At times, the provision of ground handling and associated services such as aircraft cleaning and supply of equipment for the dispatch of aircraft by Sri Lankans carried out as a monopoly at BIA have given rise to serious complaints of inequitable treatment. Complaints of such nature could lead to a foreign government whose airline operates international flights to Sri Lanka under a bilateral air services agreement alleging that Sri Lanka is in violation of Article 15 of the Chicago Convention for allowing non-uniform user charges to be recovered at BIA Airport by its national airline.

Therefore, for the equitable and efficient development of aerodromes in the country to take place it is imperative that appropriate regulations are introduced to ensure that primary aeronautical services, as well as secondary aeronautical services, are made available at regionally competitive and comparable service levels and rates whereby multiple service providers are allowed entry into providing such services at aerodromes to facilitate both international and domestic aviation.

Another area where practical difficulties have been encountered is the absence of proper coordination between the aerodrome operator and the numerous divisions of its aeronautical service provider, including the aviation security service or the air traffic control. Two instances where such lack of coordination resulted in foreign passenger aircrafts being arrested and detained at BIA need mention. In both these instances the arrested aircraft had to be released only through the intervention of courts.

On the first occasion, in the year 2002, arose from a dispute between a foreign aircraft owner and a Sri Lankan domestic operator who wet-leased an aircraft. The wet lease had been terminated, but the lessee, the Sri Lankan company, had not returned the aircraft to its owner on termination. The aircraft owner, whose crew was operating the aircraft, then directed the crew to fly the aircraft out of Bandaranayake International Airport (BIA). However, in the meantime, the lessee had influenced the local police of Katunayake, the area in which BIA is situated, and the Officer in Charge of the local police station had telephoned the air traffic control tower at BIA and ordered the air traffic controller not to clear the aircraft for takeoff. Heeding the said order of the local police air traffic controller had not granted clearance for the relevant aircraft to take off although the DGCA at that time had confirmed in writing to the aircraft that there was no legal impediment for the aircraft to be flown out of Sri Lanka. This ultimately led to litigation where the relevant aircraft was permitted to leave several only after the intervention of the Commercial High Court.

A second incident occurred in June of 2022, which also involved a dispute between an international aircraft leasing company in Europe and the Aeroflot, the international airline of Russia. In this dispute also, the aircraft leasing company is alleged to have terminated the aircraft lease following the embargo placed by the European Union applicable to companies within the European Union being compelled to cease or terminate commercial transactions with Russian companies. As a subsequent directive by the aircraft leasing company requiring Aeroflot to return the aircraft had not been heeded, the leasing company had chosen to institute action in Sri Lanka, a third-party country, which had no privity or connection to the leasing contract, merely on the grounds that the relevant aircraft was anticipated perform a flight and to land in Sri Lanka. Having thus filed action and supported its claim *ex parte,* the foreign leasing company court had obtained an enjoining order restraining Aeroflot Airlines from departing or flying the aircraft out of Sri Lanka. As the order of the court had been obtained by the aircraft lessor in anticipation of the aircraft landing at BIA at the time the order was issued by the court, the relevant aircraft operated by Aeroflot had not yet entered Sri Lankan airspace. When the aircraft landed at BIA, it disembarked the passengers travelling to Colombo and thereafter emplaned the large number of passengers returning from Colombo to Moscow who were ready to depart. The court order issued as aforesaid restraining Aeroflot from flying its aircraft out of Sri Lanka had not been served on Aeroflot (the defendant) in the manner prescribed by law, and as such, there was no binding obligation on Aeroflot to comply with the said order. In these circumstances, the representatives of the aircraft leasing company head entered the restricted area at the BIA and exerted pressure on the air traffic control authorities to prevent the aircraft from being cleared for takeoff. As a result, the Aeroflot aircraft about to take off with a load of passengers on the tarmac was illegally arrested and the passengers on board had to be deplaned and sent to hotels until alternate arrangements were made for them to return to Moscow. This incident created a serious international controversy, particularly for the aviation authorities of Sri Lanka, as the DGCA of Sri Lanka had shortly prior to that incident confirmed in writing to Aeroflot that its aircraft were not subject to seizure or arrest in Sri Lanka because of the embargo placed on Russia by the European Union. Subsequently, the order of the court was vacated on the factual circumstances being presented regarding the irregular manner in which the order of the Court had been by abused or misused by the aircraft leasing company representatives to illegally detain the aircraft.

In both the incidents described above, the lead author of this article was personally involved in the litigation to obtain the release of the two aircraft illegally and unlawfully arrested in Sri Lanka. Therefore, from a firsthand perspective, the main issue that became starkly evident from both incidents was the absence of coordination and the demarcation of the lines of authority between the different divisions of service providers providing aeronautical services at the airports. Both these unpleasant incidents, which created adverse and negative publicity for the country, could easily have been avoided if the respective structures of authority governing the different aeronautical service providers at aerodromes had been clearly demarcated and the relevant personnel performing services had proper instructions and protocols regarding a clear line of authority from whom they were obliged to take and follow orders. In the first case discussed above, the air traffic control personnel had acted on the instructions of a local police officer who had no regulatory authority to give any directions or instructions to air traffic controls, and in the subsequent instance, air traffic controllers had unduly yielded to a representative of the aircraft leasing company who improperly used and misrepresented a court order issued on a foreign airline Aeroflot, but not on the relevant officer or the aerodrome authorities who were coerced to implement the said court order on the threat of being found in contempt of court.

5 Conclusion

From an exposition of history and a narrative of the progressive development, the above discourse has attempted to present a general description of the laws and regulations presently applicable to the establishment, operation, administration and regulation of aerodromes in Sri Lanka. Due to the dynamic nature of the airline industry and the rapid growth in air traffic, the need for parallel development of essential infrastructure facilities including airports and related services is of paramount importance. As a signatory to the Chicago Convention and having expressly undertaken to give effect to all applicable SARPs, it would behove upon Sri Lanka to develop its airport infrastructure and to update its laws and regulations in alignment with international standards to meet the needs of the airline industry.

The IATA implements many policies, initiatives and programmes relating to airports including, airport infrastructure and development, airport charges, air traffic management, ground operations, baggage operations, fuel, and airport slot management, etc. IATA resolutions have on many occasions been the catalyst to regulatory initiatives adopted by States through the ICAO. The soft laws of IATA, considered as best practices in the industry, are followed by member airlines all over the world even where domestic laws and regulations have not been made. As many international carriers who are members of IATA operate into Sri Lanka, IATA resolutions are also followed and applied across the airline industry in Sri Lanka including at its airports.

Therefore, service providers to the airline industry including the airline consumers who are not members of IATA indirectly become subject to IATA's scheme of quasi-rules when interacting with airlines. IATA's industry initiatives have thus compelled the airline industry in the country to also follow best industry practices at its airports even where the national legislative efforts are lagging behind.

Chapter 6
Aerodrome Safety and Security Governance in Malaysia: Issues and Solutions

Haris Zuan and Zamri Sulaiman

Abstract This chapter examines Malaysia's approach to aerodrome safety and security governance, highlighting the country's efforts to comply with international standards set by the International Civil Aviation Organization (ICAO). It explores the various challenges Malaysia faces in modernising its aviation safety and security framework, focusing on the role of key initiatives such as the Civil Aviation Regulation (Security) 2019, the Security Management System (SeMS), and the Advance Passenger Screening System (APSS). The article discusses how Malaysia has adopted a risk-based approach to improve the efficiency of aviation governance and enhance passenger experiences while addressing significant challenges such as inter-agency coordination, infrastructure costs, and skilled personnel shortages. The discussion underscores the importance of integrating safety measures across all levels of aviation operations, from airside to landside areas. The article highlights how the SeMS and APSS systems, particularly, are designed to ensure that Malaysia's aviation security framework is robust and compliant with international standards. However, implementation delays due to administrative restructuring, legal reforms, and the need for global cooperation are also examined. The findings suggest that while Malaysia has made substantial progress, it still needs to achieve ICAO compliance, particularly in data privacy, cybersecurity, and inter-agency collaboration. This article concludes that ongoing reforms and enhanced cooperation between government bodies, industry stakeholders, and international organisations are crucial for positioning Malaysia as a leading global aviation hub with solid safety and security standards at the core of its operations.

Keywords Advance passenger screening system (APSS) · Annex 17 · Civil aviation act (CAA) · Kuala Lumpur international airport (KLIA) · Malaysia

H. Zuan (✉)
Institute of Malaysian and International Studies (IKMAS), National University of Malaysia, Bangi, Malaysia
e-mail: hariszuan@ukm.edu.my

Z. Sulaiman
Civil Aviation Authority of Malaysia (CAAM), Putrajaya, Malaysia

© The Author(s), under exclusive license to Springer Nature Singapore Pte Ltd. 2025

S. Bhat B. (ed.), *Aerodrome Governance in Asia*,
https://doi.org/10.1007/978-981-96-7568-5_6

airports holding berhad (MAHB) · Ministry of transport (MOT) · Safety and security · Security management system (SeMS)

1 Introduction

In Malaysia, there are 40 operational airports across the country, comprising 6international airports, 16 domestic airports, and 18 airstrips, also known as Short Take-Off and Landing Ports (STOL ports), to accommodate the growing demand for passengers and the operation of various types of aircraft. Kuala Lumpur International Airport (KLIA), encompassing Terminals 1 and 2, has become Malaysia's primary airport and a regional hub for national airlines such as Malaysia Airlines and Asia's leading low-cost airline, AirAsia groups.

In 2023, the total number of passengers travelling in and out of Malaysia reached 50.2 million. In July 2024, air passenger traffic was recorded at 8.8 million, marking a robust year-on-year increase of 14.3 percent compared to 7.7 million passengers in July 2023 and a month-on-month increase of 7.7 percent compared to 8.1 million passengers in June 2024. This growth was primarily driven by a rise in international travel, supported by the continued recovery of international routes, the implementation of a 30-day visa exemption for tourists from China and India, and the launch of new international destinations in July 2024. Overall, this brought July 2024 traffic to 91.7 percent of pre-pandemic levels in July 2019, when traffic reached 9.6 million, with international traffic leading the recovery.[1]

Domestic air passenger traffic in July 2024, which accounted for 48.4 percent of the total, recorded 4.3 million passengers. This represents 88.0 percent of the traffic in July 2019, which stood at 4.8 million. International air passenger traffic comprised 51.6 percent of the total, with 4.5 million passengers in July 2024. This reflects a strong month-on-month (MoM) increase of 11.1 percent and a year-on-year (YoY) rise of 26.6 percent, reaching 95.4 percent of July 2019 levels, indicating an almost complete recovery.[2]

Regarding traffic distribution, ASEAN and non-ASEAN routes have contributed almost equally to international traffic growth. ASEAN traffic reached 2.3 million passengers, reflecting a 4.5 percent month-on-month (MoM) increase and a 16.3 percent year-on-year (YoY) rise. Non-ASEAN traffic grew stronger, with 2.3 million passengers, marking an 18.5 percent MoM increase and a 39.0 percent YoY increase. This high passenger volume highlights the recovery of the aviation and tourism sectors following the COVID-19 pandemic, with growth in both international and

[1] MAVCOM, 'MAVCOM Reports Strong Air Traffic Growth for July', 2024, available at < https://www.mavcom.my/en/2024/08/26/mavcom-reports-strong-air-traffic-growth-for-july/ > Last visited, 8 August 2024.

[2] *Id.*

domestic movements.[3] These statistics indicate that Malaysia's airports, particularly KLIA, are key regional airports experiencing a significant increase in aircraft and passenger traffic. This highlights the need for Malaysia to enhance governance efficiency at the country's primary entry points.

However, Malaysia still needs to modernise its air transport management, including airport operations. Malaysia's recent plans to secure international funding have faced heavy criticism from the public and opposition, often linked to political sentiments shrouded in national security rhetoric—yet this is only a tiny part of Malaysia's issues. The next section of this article will provide a broader overview of the governance framework for air transport management in Malaysia, helping to understand the challenges the country is currently dealing with more comprehensively.

2 Governance Background of Malaysia's Air Transport

Air transport has played a significant role in global economic and social development. Generally, there is an ongoing debate over whether air transport should be viewed as a strategic state asset or a public utility, especially at the public and policy levels. As a state instrument, air transport is often regarded as a tool to achieve political and strategic goals. Countries use national carriers and major airports to project soft power, strengthen diplomatic relations, and enhance national security. A clear example can be seen in national airlines such as Singapore Airlines and Emirates, which not only serve to transport passengers but also promote the country's image on the international stage.[4] On the other hand, as a utility, air transport is viewed as a service that provides public access to mobility and supports the economy by connecting cities and countries. In this context, the focus is on how air transport can be accessible, affordable, and efficient for general use. This model requires regulations that ensure fair competition, safety, and cost-effectiveness, as often seen in more liberalised air markets such as the European Union.[5]

Both concepts are not mutually exclusive and often operate along a spectrum. For instance, in ASEAN, the liberalisation of air transport under the ASEAN Single Aviation Market (ASAM) framework demonstrates a combination of these two elements. ASEAN member states strive to balance their roles as regulators and market facilitators while maintaining aspects of national sovereignty concerning security and economic interests.[6] However, the role of air transport as either a state instrument

[3] *Id.*

[4] Alejandro Portes, 'A Tale of Three Cities: The Rise of Dubai, Singapore, and Miami Compared', *Sustainability*, Vol. 12, 2020, 8566. https://doi.org/10.3390/su12208566.

[5] Megersa Abera Abate & Panayotis Christidis, 'The impact of air transport market liberalization: Evidence from EU's external aviation policy', *Economics of Transportation*, Vol. 22, 2020. https://doi.org/10.1016/j.ecotra.2020.10016.

[6] Haris Zuan, Darren Ellis & Romano Pagliari, 'Geopolitics and the ASEAN single aviation market: Aspirations versus realities', *Transportation Research Procedia*, Vol. 59, 2021, pp. 95–104.

or a utility depends on the national and regional context. Countries with greater economic and political capacity tend to leverage air transport as a state tool, while nations with more limited capacity may view it primarily as a utility.[7] Therefore, these concepts must be understood within a broader geopolitical and economic framework, as they significantly impact the governance of air transport security. This context is crucial for understanding air transport governance, including in Malaysia. Air transport authorities constantly face the dynamic tension between market demands and the sensitivities of security, safety, and national interests.

Malaysia, formerly known as Malaya, gained independence in 1957, and in the same year, Malaya joined the International Civil Aviation Organization (ICAO). On 16 September 1963, Malaya and two Borneo territories (Sabah and Sarawak) united to form the Federation of Malaysia. The formation of Malaysia had governance implications for aviation, particularly with special provisions for Sabah and Sarawak, especially in terms of immigration control, including at airports. Malaysia enforced the Civil Aviation Act (CAA) in 1969. In 1976, the Department of Civil Aviation (DCA) became a 'self-accounting department' under the Ministry of Transport, overseeing 22 airports, including four international airports in Malaysia at that time.

In 1992, the government implemented its national privatisation policy, which led to the partial privatisation of the Department of Civil Aviation with the establishment of Malaysia Airports Holding Berhad (MAHB). This led to the operation of two main organisations: MAHB, which manages and administers terminal operations and aircraft parking, and the Department of Civil Aviation, which manages airspace and oversees the enforcement of civil aviation laws and regulations. MAHB was granted the sole authority to manage and operate commercial airports in Malaysia. MAHB became the sixth airport operator in the world and the first in Asia to be listed on a stock exchange when it was established as a public limited company and listed on the Malaysian Stock Exchange (Bursa Malaysia) in 1999.[8] Malaysia subsequently announced the strategic plan for constructing Kuala Lumpur International Airport (KLIA) in Sepang in 1991, officially opening on 27 June 1998. By 2011, Malaysia

[7] Heymann, Hans 'Air Transport and Economic Development: Some Comments on Foreign Aid Programs, *The American Economic Review*, Vol. 52, No. 2, 1962, pp. 386–95.

[8] 'Our Profile', *Malaysia Airports*, available at < https://www.malaysiaairports.com.my/en/about-us/corporate-profile/our-profile > Last visited, 14 December 2024.

Airports Holdings operated and managed 39 international, domestic, and Short Take-Off and Landing (STOL) airports.[9] Currently, only two airports in Malaysia are not managed by MAHB.[10]

The primary goal of the Department of Civil Aviation Malaysia has been to remain competitive and aligned with other ICAO member countries by providing services equipped with modern and advanced technology, including offering specific training for all department staff. As a result, in 2015, Malaysia's civil aviation sector was divided into two entities: the Civil Aviation Authority of Malaysia (CAAM) and the Malaysian Aviation Commission (MAVCOM), both of which fall under the responsibility of the Ministry of Transport (MOT). As a contracting state, the establishment of CAAM is in line with ICAO's recommendations for contracting states to the 1947 Chicago Convention, which called for creating autonomous civil aviation authorities to ensure more efficient oversight and safety management of civil aviation. Regarding the division of powers, MOT serves as the primary policy maker for the aviation industry in Malaysia. At the same time, MOT is also responsible for negotiating bilateral air service agreements between governments.

The responsibility for regulating technical aspects of civil aviation lies with the CAAM. CAAM's primary role is to contribute to the development of Malaysia's civil aviation technical sector, and it is mandated to comply with ICAO standards to ensure safe, secure, and efficient aviation operations. Among its essential functions are regulating, facilitating, and promoting the nation's aviation and aerospace industry while ensuring that Malaysia meets both national and international obligations related to civil aviation. This includes adhering to and maintaining global standards for aviation safety and oversight, as recommended by ICAO. The establishment of CAAM also aims to ensure that all matters related to the civil aviation industry in the country comply with the safety standards and procedures recommended by ICAO.

On the other hand, the MAVCOM functions as the economic regulator overseeing commercial and economic matters in Malaysia's civil aviation industry. Its key responsibilities include economic regulation, consumer protection, dispute resolution, management of air traffic rights, and serving as an advisor to the government on civil aviation matters.

In June 2024, the Malaysian government tabled a bill to dissolve the MAVCOM, agreeing in principle to merge the regulatory bodies of the Malaysian aviation

---

[9] In line with this success, Malaysia remains committed to upholding and advancing civil aviation safety, innovation, and sustainability on the global stage through the development of strategic infrastructure and the enhancement of institutional capacity to meet the needs of the next generation of aviation professionals. Following the recent vote, Malaysia improved its position in ICAO's Category III, moving from 13 to 11th place, with an increase of 14 votes compared to the previous assembly in 2016. Overall, Malaysia received 143 votes (81%) from the participating countries, marking the highest number of votes Malaysia has ever achieved and its best performance since joining the ICAO Council. For the record, Malaysia's previous results were 92 votes (2007), 137 votes (2010), 128 votes (2013), and 129 votes (2016).

[10] The first is Senai International Airport in Johor Baharu, operated by Senai Airport Terminal Services SdnBhd (SATS). The second is Kerteh Airport in Terengganu, owned and operated by Petronas, a government-owned oil and gas company. The primary purpose of Kerteh Airport is to manage air transport for workers from offshore oil and gas platforms in the South China Sea.

industry under a single entity. This would see MAVCOM dissolved, with all its functions transferred to the CAAM. According to the Minister of Transport, who presented the bill, this merger aims to reduce bureaucratic red tape and improve the efficiency of service delivery in civil aviation, particularly in licensing services. With the merger of MAVCOM and CAAM, the need for two separate regulatory bodies will no longer exist. A single regulatory mechanism is also adopted in most major global aviation sectors, including in countries like the United States, the United Kingdom, Germany, Singapore, and China. This consolidation is expected to optimise using existing human and financial resources while enhancing governance efficiency and improving service delivery systems.[11]

3 The Concept of Safety and Security in Air Transport Governance

Aviation security refers to protecting airports and aircraft from criminal activities. However, the definition in Annex 17 of the 1944 Chicago Convention describes it as a combination of human measures and other material resources aimed at safeguarding civil aviation from unlawful acts. The term "aviation security threats" generally refers to acts or attempts to compromise the safety of civil aviation, as well as the safety of passengers and aircraft. However, this is not limited to these threats alone, as it also includes (1) aircraft hijacking, (2) sabotaging or damaging aircraft, (3) taking hostages on board an aircraft or within airport premises, (4) unauthorised access to an aircraft while in restricted areas of an airport or any aeronautical facility, (5) carrying weapons or dangerous items within airport premises with the intent to commit a crime, (6) using an aircraft as a weapon to cause fatalities, injuries, or serious damage to property and the environment, (7) providing false information or committing cybercrimes that could jeopardise the safety of aircraft on the ground or in the air. These elements highlight the broad scope of aviation security measures required to protect the industry from a wide range of unlawful activities.

To this day, the civil aviation sector continues to face security threats from criminals and terrorists. However, before exploring the specifics of security threats at airports, it is essential to understand the terms 'safety' and 'security', as there are significant differences between the two. 'Safety' refers to the condition in which risks related to air traffic directly associated with aircraft and their operational support are reduced to an acceptable minimum level.[12] The term 'security' encompasses the protection of international civil aviation from unlawful acts. This objective is achieved through a combination of measures, human resources and material resources

[11] Parliament of Malaysia, Parliament Hansard for Lower House of 26 June 2024, available at <https://www.parlimen.gov.my/hansard-dewan-rakyat.html?uweb=dr&lang=bm> Last visited, 9 August 2024.

[12] Annex 19—Safety Management, Second Edition, July 2016.

aimed at preventing and mitigating security threats.[13] Thus, within the context of Malaysia's air transport governance, the operational definitions used are as follows:

- Aviation safety: The safety of air transport, encompassing the safe execution of processes related to aircraft operations, aircraft control, design, maintenance, manufacturing, and human factors, procedures, tools, and organisational structures.
- Flight safety: The human factors, tools, and procedures required for the safe execution of flight as a process.
- Aviation security: The protection of aircraft operations, instruments, procedures, and human factors from intentional, unlawful, or accidental threats to aircraft operations, design, maintenance, and manufacturing. This definition considers aviation as a whole, with a focus on external threats.
- Airport safety: The tools, procedures, buildings, and human factors needed for the safe execution of all flights within airport aerodromes, primarily addressing internal threats within the organisation, focusing on one aviation element—airports.
- Airport security: The tools, procedures, organisations, and human factors required to safeguard the infrastructure for transporting goods, passengers, and luggage, with security solutions aimed at airports, but applicable to external threats.

Effective safety and security management in air transport is critical to maintaining passenger confidence. This confidence not only influences their willingness to fly but also has a significant economic impact on airlines and the broader economy, particularly in industries like tourism and international business, especially when there is a decline in safety ratings. Airport security threats can also lead to diplomatic implications and political tensions. For example, in 2017, Kim Jong-nam, the half-brother of North Korean leader Kim Jong Un, was assassinated in a planned attack at Kuala Lumpur International Airport 2 (KLIA 2). Jong-nam's murder led to diplomatic tensions between Malaysia and North Korea, with North Korea strongly opposing the autopsy results as autopsy was conducted without its permission. Malaysia maintained that the death occurred within its jurisdiction and had the right to investigate and take action. Both sides engaged in a diplomatic standoff, resulting in the expulsion of the North Korean ambassador following his provocative statements.[14]

[13] Annex 17—Aviation Security, Twelfth Edition, July 2022.

[14] Mustafa Izzuddin, 'Reviewing Malaysia's Relations with North Korea', *Journal of Perspective*, No. 30, 2017, pp. 1–10.

4 The Decline of Malaysia's Aviation Industry and Issues of Safety and Security Threats

Based on the discussion above, it is clear that there are negative implications for a country if airport security is not adequately regulated, as this may result in the International Civil Aviation Organization (ICAO) assessment of "Significant Security Concern" (SSeC).[15] The ICAO certification for Standards and Recommended Practices (SARPs) represents the pinnacle of safety and security benchmarks in the global aviation sector. While individual ICAO member states have their respective aviation authorities overseeing domestic operations, international certification is crucial to verify an airline's compliance with global standards. Malaysia faced this issue when the United States Federal Aviation Administration (FAA) determined that the CAAM fell short of ICAO's safety requirements. Consequently, on 11 November 2019, the FAA, as part of its routine International Aviation Safety Assessment (IASA) audit, downgraded Malaysia's aviation safety rating to Category 2.

A Category 2 rating indicates that the country's aviation sector does not meet at least one of three key standards regarding organisational management or operational procedures, namely safety measures, human resource management, or data management issues. The FAA specifically stated that the downgrade of Malaysia's aviation industry was due to non-compliance by the regulator rather than the absence of necessary safeguards airlines.[16] While international authorities such as ICAO often collaborate to enhance civil aviation security guidelines, their implementation is still perceived as lacking in rigour.

The primary reasons that make it challenging for airports to comply with international standards fully can be observed from the findings of the 2019 audit conducted by ICAO.[17] This report highlighted that the sustainability indicator for contracting states in the Asia–Pacific region was only at 65.9%, based on the Critical Elements (CE) framework. This demonstrates that the sustainability level in compliance and implementation of ICAO's guidelines remains less than satisfactory and sustainable among Asia–Pacific countries, including Malaysia.

Based on the Corrective Action Plan (CAP-Malaysia), developed following the 2019 Universal Security Audit Programme (USAP) audit conducted in Malaysia, five critical elements were identified that require attention from the Malaysian government. These elements include aviation security programmes and regulations (CE-2), provision of technical guidance, tools, and critical safety information (CE-5), certification and approval obligations (CE-6), quality control obligations (CE-7), and the

[15] Wakimoto Takuya, 'Ensuring the Safety of Commercial Space Transportation through Standardization: Implications of the Chicago Convention and ICAO Standards', *Space Policy*, Vol. 49, 2019. https://doi.org/10.1016/j.spacepol.2019.05.004.

[16] Tamat Sarmidi, Nurul Aishah Khairuddin & Muhamad Rias K.V. Zainuddin, 'The Economic Impacts of Air Safety Rating Downgrade for Malaysia', *Malaysian Journal of Economic Studies*, Vol. 58, 2021, pp. 21–43.

[17] ICAO Universal Security Audit Programme Continuous Monitoring Approach (USAP-CMA), Ninth Edition, 31 December 2019.

resolution of security concerns (CE-8) (CAAM, 2022). Among these, CE-5 and CE-8 were highlighted as critical elements requiring more in-depth focus, as prioritised in the USAP 2019 audit report. Through the audit, ICAO identified several deficiencies, particularly concerning weaknesses in compliance with Annex 17 guidelines.

First, there were areas for improvement in compliance with the National Training Program, where non-compliance issues included a lack of skilled personnel to conduct inspections beyond passengers, such as inspecting carried items, and searching suspected vehicles in airport areas and the items contained within them. Additionally, there were areas for improvement in inspecting baggage, cargo, and mail at the airport level, as well as insufficient oversight of training provided to all entities delivering aviation security training. This included identifying training needs and gaps in the training process conducted by airline and airport operators, among other issues highlighted in the USAP 2019 (Malaysia) report.

Second, weaknesses in the country's compliance with thenational security directive known as the National Civil Aviation Security Program (NCASP) require immediate attention. These issues include the inadequate implementation of a risk assessment methodology to determine aircraft security during inspections or searches, considering established factors. Additionally, there are concerns related to foreign aircraft operators making transit stops at airports in Malaysia, where no standards are in place to ensure that any items left behind by passengers disembarking from transit flights are either removed from the aircraft or adequately handled before the aircraft departs. Other issues, such as those outlined in the USAP 2019 (Malaysia) report related to NCASP, also need addressing.

Furthermore, non-compliance with the National Quality Control Program (NQCP) shows significant gaps in the regulator's function related to quality control activities. These include the lack of airport-level procedures for re-screening passengers and their cabin luggage before boarding, as well as the failure of airport operators to develop appropriate methods for screening cargo and mail. Consideration must be given to activating threat techniques such as decompression chambers, full-flight simulation systems, and cooling-off periods (for example, storing cargo for 24 to 48 h). These methods are not valid screening procedures for cargo and mail and cannot be used as substitutes for screening. Additional issues related to NQCP were also noted in the USAP 2019 (Malaysia) report.

This clearly demonstrates that the level of compliance with and implementation of ICAO guidelines in aviation security legislation and regulations in Malaysia still needs improvement. The weaknesses in complying with these guidelines pose potential risks to national security, particularly in the civil aviation sector.

These shortcomings expose the difficulties encountered by local authorities, Malaysian security agencies, airport operators, and airline operators in enforcing and adhering to ICAO guidelines and civil aviation security laws in Malaysia. Typically, government and private entities' administration and management approaches, such as airline operators and airport handlers, differ significantly. Private companies prioritise organisational profit over compliance, while government bodies focus on regulation. The obligation to comply with any guidelines challenges airline operators, airport handlers, and aviation authorities in Malaysia. These challenges arise due to differences in priorities, legal issues, financial constraints, a shortage of skilled personnel, extended administrative and management implementation delays due to political debates, and confusion regarding government objectives and evaluation criteria. These are some of the recurring issues that entangle stakeholders in Malaysia.

The next section of this article will discuss (1) the response of Malaysia's air transport authorities and improvements in governance to meet international standards and (2) proposed new approaches currently under review by CAAM and the challenges in the implementation.

5 Shift to a New Risk-Based Approach

In response to the abovementioned challenges, Malaysia's air management authorities have adopted a modernised regulatory governance approach by implementing risk-based oversight. This approach allows for the optimal allocation of resources, ensuring that supervisory functions have the greatest impact on improving civil aviation safety. This approach is expected to enhance the efficiency of safety and security governance, improve the passenger experience at airports, and ultimately boost the confidence of passengers, the aviation industry, and international regulatory bodies.

The ongoing threats have driven the Civil Aviation Authority of Malaysia (CAAM) to intensify its efforts, aspiring to introduce new aviation safety and security regulations aligned with international standards. These regulations must be carefully reviewed and refined to protect passengers, company assets, air cargo, mail, and airports. Moreover, the rules will be extended to include the landside areas of airports.[18] The government's strategic defence and security assessment must be strengthened to ensure that Malaysia's civil aviation security remains in a state of readiness. Users' perception requires careful attention, and it is essential to build strong confidence in the safety operations of airports and airlines. This is the challenge faced by CAAM as the regulatory authority, in collaboration with the aviation industry, to enhance safety while minimising inconveniences to passengers when using air transport services.

The best practices established in the 2019 regulations saw CAAM's new administration begin modernising governance with a focus on a risk-based approach.[19] This approach gives the industry greater flexibility in delivering better solutions, concentrating on achieving safety and security outcomes rather than adhering to prescriptive

[18] The landside areas of airports have been officially included in Annex 17 of ICAO, recognising that these areas also require attention in security controls, not just the airside zones. Examples of landside areas include airport car parks, airport hotels, and access roads. These areas are crucial for overall airport security and safeguarding them is essential for preventing potential threats before they reach airside operations.

[19] The new regulations on aviation security will be known as the Civil Aviation Regulation (Security) 2019, issued under the Civil Aviation Regulation 2016. These regulations are designed to enhance the security framework within the aviation sector, aligning with international standards and addressing evolving security challenges.

measures. While maintaining high safety and security standards, this approach aims to be more efficient and passenger-centric. This aligns with Malaysia's decentralisation policy, emphasising strategic and intelligent security control for those interacting with passengers daily.

The government will continue to assume its primary responsibility for aviation security by clearly understanding threats and risks and setting safety standards to facilitate industry implementation. This includes prioritising a risk list, where operators must have mitigation plans developed as effectively as possible. Effective government monitoring is required to ensure that the responsibilities entrusted to the aviation industry are carried out effectively. This approach fosters a smart partnership between the government and the industry, maintaining the highest aviation safety standards without compromising passenger comfort. A close relationship between CAAM and the industry, which understands the threats of terrorism and unlawful activities in the air transport sector, is crucial in positioning Malaysia as a global hub for civil aviation security.

Updating the regulatory framework for aviation security is a key element of a collaborative, cross-departmental strategy to strengthen aviation safety, as detailed in the government's strategic review of defence and security. Effective aviation security, guided by more comprehensive new regulations, will complement broader border security roles, including land and sea, for example, through passenger screening, contributing to aviation security, raising safety standards, and indirectly improving the passenger experience.

Under this revised framework, the current 'direct and inspect' regulatory system will transition to an outcome-focused, risk-based (OFRB) approach. This shift aligns with contemporary regulatory practices and mirrors Malaysia's methodology to oversee aviation safety.

Through the OFRB approach, the focus on safety and security outcomes is more effective than rigidly following specific processes. Agencies can establish overall requirements based on the level and nature of threats at any given time. The industry will have the flexibility to design safety and security processes driven by safety and security outcomes rather than strict adherence to detailed regulations. Basic regulatory requirements, such as CAAM's standard norms, will still be necessary, and the agencies responsible for their implementation must collaborate closely with the authorities. The direction set for aviation safety and security must align with and comply with the Civil Aviation Act 1969 (CAA—1969) and its related regulations.

However, one of the main objectives of the OFRB approach is to give the industry broader ownership of security operations and greater freedom to integrate safety and security into day-to-day business activities while remaining under strict regulatory oversight. This method is more likely to offer passengers a better travel experience. The proposed new approach focuses on transitioning towards a system that prioritises risk-based inspections and incentivises the industry to improve overall safety and security performance collectively.

6 Security Management System (SeMS)

Under the OFRB approach, the responsibility for implementing regulations falls on all parties outlined in the NCASP. SeMS and NCASP complement each other in ensuring aviation security. The Security Management System (SeMS) is a tool for aviation organisations to comply with and implement security measures established in the NCASP. Through SeMS, aviation organisations can integrate security practices into their daily operations, ensuring alignment with the standards and requirements set out in the NCASP. Additionally, SeMS aids in evaluating and continuously improving security measures, ensuring that organisations consistently meet and exceed national security expectations. SeMS allows operators to plan and deliver their security processes effectively. It is a systematic approach that ensures security standards remain high, and it incorporates critical components such as:

- Risk assessment and mitigation: Identifying potential threats and taking measures to reduce them.
- Security policy: Including management accountability and responsibility.
- Documenting security measures: Recording the appropriate measures implemented across the organisation.
- Security assurance: Ensuring regular reporting, data analysis, reviews, internal and external audits, covert testing, and arrangements for continuous improvement.
- Security awareness: Providing training and seminars to staff as a strong communication tool to foster a robust security culture.

SeMS is a dynamic management process that will be continuously monitored and reviewed to account for changes in the threat environment, organisational shifts, and the results of ongoing analyses. A key feature of SeMS is that the industry must provide detailed reports on its security performance, increasing the amount of performance data available to regulators. Serious lapses in reporting will still result in penalties in line with existing laws. As mentioned earlier, all entities are required to comply with the basic standards set by CAAM and will continue to do so.

Under the current approach, the authorities determine detailed requirements, directly verify compliance, and conduct inspections. The authorities will outline the desired safety and security outcomes and then assess the effectiveness of the proposed system to meet the control requirements more efficiently through a quality assurance process. While the industry remains subject to basic monitoring and compliance by the authorities, CAAM will also examine how a risk-based approach can become more effective. The aim is to reward good performance and compliance with greater autonomy. Conversely, increased oversight by the authorities will be necessary if there is a decline in performance by any agency or operator.

The shift towards the OFRB approach is part of regulatory reform, transitioning the day-to-day security oversight functions from CAAM to the operators. Under this proposal, compliance with aviation security regulations will be directly managed by the industry, with CAAM accepting reports from the industry itself. This approach must be consistently financed to ensure the sustainability of aviation security regulations and other aviation safety aspects, with the cost ultimately borne by the 'end users.' This transfer of responsibilities will go through a legal process, subject to scrutiny and debate at the highest levels. However, once the relevant ministry focuses on this issue, industry feedback will also be considered as part of the discussions.

7 Implementation of the Advance Passenger Screening System (APSS)

Following an audit conducted by ICAO in April 2019,[20] one of the key findings was that Malaysia lacked an Advance Passenger Screening System (APSS), also known as the Advance Passenger System (APS). ICAO emphasised the need for Malaysia to focus on developing an APS that aligns with international standards. This is a critical component of the corrective action plan that Malaysia must implement in preparation for the USAP-CMA audit scheduled for December 2024. Ensuring the successful development and implementation of this system is vital to prevent Malaysia from being at risk of receiving a Significant Security Concern (SSeC) designation from ICAO in the upcoming audit.

APSS is an early screening system for passengers travelling to Malaysia. It assists the Malaysian Immigration Department in conducting comprehensive security analyses of Advance Passenger Information (API) and Passenger Name Records (PNR) by examining passenger travel patterns, including those transiting through Malaysia. The system can provide early warnings to Malaysian authorities, specifically Immigration, to identify high-risk passengers. Additionally, it ensures that the information and number of travellers arriving and departing are accurately coordinated with those reporting during entry and exit checks at immigration counters.

Many countries have implemented this system worldwide to address the issue of high-risk passengers, such as those with criminal records or involvement in terrorist activities. Implementing APSS is also aligned with international recommendations and standards, such as UN Security Council Resolution 2396, UN Security Council Resolution 2178, and Annex 9 (Facilitation) and Annex 17 (Security) of the Chicago Convention. As a contracting state to ICAO, Malaysia is bound by the standards and audits established by ICAO, including those concerning civil aviation security.

[20] Audit Universal Security Audit Programme—Continuous Monitoring Approach (USAP-CMA), April 2019.

8 Challenges in Implementing APSS and SeMS

Implementing the APSS and SeMS in Malaysia has faced numerous challenges, leading to delays. The responsibility for rolling out the APSS primarily lies with the Malaysian Immigration Department (IM) and the Ministry of Home Affairs (MOHA). Due to its multi-agency involvement, this process necessitates significant updates to existing policies and procedures, including drafting new legislation. Agencies such as MOHA, IM, the Royal Malaysian Police (RMP), the Chief Government Security Office (CGSO), the Ministry of Transport (MOT), the CAAM, and the Malaysian Customs and Border Protection Agency (MCBA) are key stakeholders in this initiative.

Similarly, implementing the Security Management System (SeMS) requires close collaboration among government bodies, including the Immigration Department, Royal Malaysian Customs, RMP, CAAM, CGSO, and airline operators. However, challenges in inter-agency coordination, particularly in information sharing and aligning security operations, have hampered progress. Each agency operates within its own framework and culture, which can create barriers to seamless cooperation. This has been evident in incidents of passengers being denied entry into Malaysia (Not-to-Land or NTL cases) at major international airports such as KLIA, Kota Kinabalu, and Kuching, Sarawak. Introducing the APSS is expected to mitigate such issues by enabling pre-screening of high-risk passengers before they board their flights, thus enhancing overall security and operational efficiency.

Malaysia is undertaking significant institutional reforms in the aviation sector, including the reintegration of MAVCOM into CAAM, as part of broader efforts to improve agency coordination. These changes align with the current administration's large-scale restructuring initiatives, emphasising border security and enforcement bodies. Such transformations require extensive public dialogue and legal adjustments, including parliamentary approval.

Implementing the Advanced Passenger Screening System (APSS) further underscores the need for strong international cooperation. Sharing information with other nations necessitates the establishment of agreements and mechanisms, which require substantial time and diplomatic engagement. Additionally, the infrastructure and financial demands of implementing APSS and SeMSare challenges. Developing advanced technology systems, training personnel, and maintaining these systems involve significant costs. For example, although the government has committed to major upgrades at KLIA after its 25th anniversary, the improvements will not commence until 2026. Other international airports are undergoing gradual upgrades, extending the timeline for system implementation.

Risk assessments also play a crucial role in determining the urgency of APSS deployment. If Malaysia perceives the current security threat as low, prioritisation may shift to other areas—moreover, data privacy and security present significant hurdles. APSS requires collecting personal passenger data, and safeguarding this information is paramount. Recent legislative progress, such as the Cyber Security Act 2024, aims to bolster data protection and replace older laws like the Personal

Data Protection Act 2010 and the Police Act 1967. While these measures strengthen cybersecurity and public trust, they also highlight the complexities of balancing security needs with privacy concerns.

Implementing the Security Management System (SeMS) also faces notable obstacles, including compliance with ICAO's stringent aviation safety standards under Annex 17. Meeting these standards requires highly trained personnel proficient in aviation security and surveillance technologies. However, Malaysia lacks a sufficient number of such experts. For instance, as of late 2023, CAAM had only 19 aviation security officers, many of whom had not completed ICAO-certified training for auditors and inspectors. This resource gap makes managing the growing number of airport operators, airlines, and foreign carriers a formidable challenge.

Fostering a safety culture within the aviation industry is another critical area. Instilling a deep commitment to safety protocols across all levels of staff and management requires significant shifts in attitudes and practices. This cultural transformation demands a consistent and integrated approach to ensure safety remains a top priority.

Finally, continuous monitoring and auditing are essential for SeMS to function effectively. Malaysia has struggled with ensuring consistent audits and maintaining compliance across all stakeholders. Weak oversight risks exposing vulnerabilities in the aviation security framework, underscoring the need for robust and sustained monitoring to safeguard civil aviation.

9 Conclusion

In summary, Malaysia's efforts to enhance aerodrome safety and security governance underscore its dedication to meeting international standards, particularly those outlined by ICAO. Initiatives such as implementing the Civil Aviation Regulation (Security) 2019 and adopting risk-based strategies through systems like the Security Management System (SeMS) mark significant progress. These reforms aim to modernise the regulatory framework, optimise resource utilisation, and improve oversight to ensure that safety and security protocols are reactive and proactive in addressing potential threats.

However, these advancements come with considerable challenges. Delays in deploying critical systems such as the Advance Passenger Screening System (APSS) illustrate the complexities of inter-agency coordination, legislative adjustments, and infrastructure readiness. These issues are further exacerbated by a shortage of skilled professionals, financial limitations, and the need for more effective collaboration among agencies to ensure integrated security operations. Data privacy and cybersecurity also remain pressing concerns, necessitating robust legal protections and public trust to safeguard sensitive information.

Overcoming these challenges is vital for Malaysia, as its aviation sector is a cornerstone of the country's economic growth, particularly in tourism and global trade. Successfully implementing systems like APSS and SeMS, coupled with enhanced security protocols across airport operations, will improve the passenger experience and solidify Malaysia's position as a safer and more competitive player in the global aviation industry.

Looking ahead, cultivating a strong culture of safety and security throughout the aviation sector remains a priority. This requires ongoing training, rigorous monitoring, and consistent auditing to ensure alignment with ICAO standards and to adapt to emerging threats. As Malaysia continues to refine its regulatory framework and upgrade aviation infrastructure, fostering collaboration among government agencies, private stakeholders, and international partners will be critical to sustaining high levels of safety and security in the future.

Chapter 7
Governance of Airports and Aerodromes in the Republic of Korea

Jinyoung Choi

Abstract The Republic of Korea, with a landmass of 100,188 km^2, boasts a robust aviation infrastructure comprising 15 airports—eight international and seven domestic—and numerous aerodromes, including five privately established facilities. These numbers reflect the significant development of the country's aviation industry despite its relatively small geographical size. Governed initially by the Air Law of 1961, airports and aerodromes have since come under the purview of the Airport Facility Act of 2017, which provides a comprehensive framework for their regulation and management. This contribution sketches the legal framework for the airport facilities. It also examines key governance issues, including the privatisation debate surrounding Incheon International Airport, which recorded 780,635 landings and take-offs in 2023. By focusing on compliance with international standards such as the Chicago Convention 1944 and ICAO Annex 14, this study sheds light on the strengths and challenges of the Republic of Korea's aviation governance system. Furthermore, it explores the integration of safety, sustainability, and operational efficiency within the legal framework, offering insights into areas of potential improvement and how Republic of Korea aligns with global best practices while addressing local needs.

Keywords Airport expansion · Airport facility act · Airport operators · Annex 14 · Dual-use · Facility management · Korea Airports Corporation (KAC) · Safety standards

---

The views and opinions expressed in this contribution are those of the author(s) and do not necessarily reflect the official policy or position of any other agency, organisation, employer, or company.

J. Choi (✉)
International Institute of Air and Space Law, Leiden University, Leiden, Netherlands
e-mail: j.choi@law.leidenuniv.nl; jin.choi@nlr.nl

Department of Aerospace Operations Safety & Human Performance, Royal Netherlands Aerospace Centre - NLR, Amsterdam, Netherlands

© The Author(s), under exclusive license to Springer Nature Singapore Pte Ltd. 2025

S. Bhat B. (ed.), *Aerodrome Governance in Asia*,
https://doi.org/10.1007/978-981-96-7568-5_7

1 Introduction

1.1 Context

Some of the 15 'aerodromes' in the Republic of Korea (Korea, or South Korea) attract a significant volume of traffic internationally and domestically.[1] Its international and domestic traffic volume is ranked as the world's 9th per revenue tonne-kilometres for passengers, freight and mails among 101 States recorded,[2] which appears to be impressive for a country with a land mass of 10,043ha.[3] Aerodromes are critical infrastructure to facilitate such traffic in Korea.

These aerodromes, either civil or military, or both, are governed and operated by a public, private, or both bodies. Regardless of the governance and operation body, Korea is a party to the Convention on International Civil Aviation 1944 (Chicago Convention).[4] Korea, therefore, as a State, is bound by certain obligations laid in the Chicago Convention. Especially under Article 44 of the Chicago Convention, as part of the ICAO, States are encouraged to cooperate for "international air navigation" and "international air transport", which includes the development of airports. Under Article 6 of the Constitution of Korea, the Chicago Convention that is concluded and promulgated have the same effect as domestic laws of Korea.[5] Therefore, Article 44 of the Chicago Convention becomes the legal basis for states to facilitate the governance and operation of aerodromes in Korea.

Among other provisions laying obligations in the Chicago Convention, this contribution focuses on specific obligations under Articles 37 and 38 of the mentioned Convention. Obligations laid under these two provisions are related to Standards and Recommended Practices (SARPs). Article 37 requires States to adopt "international standards and procedures" while Article 38 lays how States depart there from. When it comes to aerodromes, the most relevant SARPs are contained in Annex 14 to the Chicago Convention.[6]

This contribution aims to explore the status of the aerodrome governance of South Korea in the specific context of compliance with the SARPs contained in ICAO Annex 14 and demonstrate how specific domestic legislation governs aerodromes and

[1] The term 'aerodrome' referred to in Sect. 1.1 needs some discussion in the context of this scholarly contribution, which is going to take place in Sect. 1.2.

[2] ICAO, 'Presentation of 2022 Air Transport Statistical Results', 2023, available at < https://www.icao.int/sustainability/WorldofAirTransport/Pages/presentation-of-2022-air-transport-statistical-results.aspx > Last visited, 15 September 2024. This presentation is referred to as the most recent statistical record.

[3] Korean Statistical Information Service, 'Land Area',2023, available at < https://kosis.kr/statHtml/statHtml.do?orgId=101&conn_path=I2&tblId=DT_2KAA101 > Last visited, 15 September 2023.

[4] Convention on International Civil Aviation, (Chicago Convention), Signed 7 December 1944, 15 UNTS 295, (Entered into force 4 April 1947).

[5] Constitution of the Republic of Korea [Wholly Amended by Constitution No. 10, Oct. 29, 1987].

[6] ICAO, Aerodrome Design and Operation, Annex 14, Air Traffic Services, Vol. I, (2022, 9thedn.), [ICAO Annex 14].

airports facilities. This aspect has never been discussed, and hence, it is worthwhile to visit.

1.2 Terms and Definitions—Airports and Aerodromes in Republic of Korea

This subsection attempts to define the very important term 'aerodrome'. To a large public, the term 'airport' may be more widely used, primarily referring to the specific facilities airlines utilise to transport passengers, cargo and mail by air. While the connotation attached to both terms may be similar internationally, they are used differently domestically in Korea and its legal system. Hence, this section is dedicated to defining these principal terms before exploring compliance.

First and foremost, the international definitions of these terms are a good reference to lay the groundwork for the local definitions. By international definition, I refer to the definition provided in ICAO Annex 14. This Annex defines 'aerodrome' as "[a] defined area on land or water (including any buildings, installations and equipment) intended to be used either wholly or in part for the arrival, departure and surface movement of aircraft."[7] However, the same Annex does not define 'airport', even though the term appears frequently.

Nevertheless, Article 2 of the Airport Facility Act of Korea contains a domestic reference to the terms 'aerodrome' and 'airport'.[8] 'According to this provision, the definitions of the terms are as follows:

> 2. The term "aerodrome" means a certain area of land or water surface prescribed by Presidential Decree, used for taking off (including taking off from water surface; hereinafter the same shall apply) and landing (including landing on water surface; hereinafter the same shall apply) of aircraft, light sport aircraft, and ultra-light vehicle;
>
> 3. The term "airport" means a public aerodrome with airport facilities, whose name, location, and area are designated and publicly notified by the Minister of Land, Infrastructure and Transport;

The relevant presidential decree lists the 'airport facilities' to include aircraft take-off and landing facilities such as runways, taxiways, aprons, and landing strips, passenger facilities and cargo handling facilities such as terminals, air navigation safety facilities, communication facilities such as control tower, meteorological observation facilities, parking facilities and security and guard facilities for airport users, and promotional and information facilities for airport users.[9] From this, it

---

[7] ICAO, Annex 14, Air Traffic Services, Volume I - Aerodrome Design and Operation, (2022, 9thedn.), 1.1 Definition.

[8] Airport Facility Act of Korea, Law No. 20291, 13 February 2024, (Enforcement date: 14 August 2024), (Partially revised). The translation used in this contribution is provided by the Korea Legislation Research Institute.

[9] Enforcement Decree of the Airport Facilities Act, Presidential Decree No. 34836, 13 August 2024, (Enforcement Date: 14 August 2024), (Partially revised), Art. 3.

is possible to conclude that an airport is a subset of aerodromes and not all aerodromes can be airports according to the Korean law. These two terms are not always interchangeably used when exploring the facilities in the Korean context. The same applies to the discussion on 'aerodromes', rather than 'airports'.

There are further similarities and differences between airports and aerodromes in Korea. The main similarity is that airports and aerodromes must be equipped with aircraft take-off and landing facilities per relevant standards. Also, they must comply with all safety regulations, such as altitude restrictions. The airport operation requires prior permission from the Minister of Land, Infrastructure and Transport of Korea. As to the main difference, while airports are public goods that are expected to be utilised by the general public, aerodromes can be established and operated by private entities or individuals. These private entities or individuals may independently implement everything from planning to construction.

1.3 Aerodromes of the Republic of Korea

1.3.1 Overview of the Airports

In South Korea, there are eight international airports:

Governing entity	Name	Civil/Dual use	IATA/ ICAO code
Incheon International Airport Corporation	Incheon International Airport	Civil	ICN/ RKSI
Korea Airports Corporation	Gimpo International Airport	Civil	GMP/ RKSS
	Gimhae International Airport	Dual use	PUS/ RKPK
	Jeju International Airport	Civil	CJU/ RKPC
	Daegu International Airport	Dual	TAE/ RKTN
	Cheongju International Airport	Dual	CJJ/ RKTU
	Muan International Airport	Civil	MWX/ RKJB
	Yangyang International Airport	Civil	YNY/ RKNY
	Gwangju Airport	Dual	KWJ/ RKJJ
	Ulsan Airport	Civil	USN/ RKPU

(continued)

(continued)

Governing entity	Name	Civil/Dual use	IATA/ICAO code
	Yeosu Airport	Civil	RSU/RKJY
	Sacheon Airport	Dual	HIN/RKPS
	Pohang Gyeongju Airport (Korean Navy, US Navy, Korean Airport Coperation)	Dual	KPO/RKTH
	Gunsan Airport	Dual	KUV/RKJK
	Wonju Airport (Korean Airforce)	Dual	WJU/RKNW
	Guangju Airport	Dual	KWJ/RKJJ

1.3.2 Overview of Aerodromes

There are also several aerodromes which are established and operated by private entities or individuals. The table below shows the list of some of the aerodromes established and operated by private entities.

Governing entity	Name	Code
Korea Aerospace University	Susaek Airfield (Dual)	KSK/RKRS
Hanseo University	Taean Airfield (Civil)	QDY/RKTA
KoreanAir	Jeongseok Airfield (Civil)	JDG/RKPD
Korea Airports Corporation	Uljin Flight Training Center (Civil)	UJN/RKTL

1.3.3 Remarks

There are 20 aerodromes in total, 16 of which are considered airports. Some airports are governed by multiple bodies, while private bodies exclusively run aerodromes and are not always used by large passenger traffic volumes. Those aerodromes featured in Sect. 1.3.2 are mostly used for education purposes by approved training organisations under ICAO.

1.4 *Institutional Framework for Airport Governance*

1.4.1 Overview of Institutions

There are several vital governmental and non-governmental agencies involved in the governance of airports and aerodromes in Korea. Some of these are mentioned in Sect. 1.3 since they are governing entities of the facilities. The governing entity is part of the unofficial criteria for the airports and aerodromes to be called private or public. In addition, the governing body to be civil and military is also relevant for the airports and aerodromes to be civil or military. This section contains the description of those entities, while some do not directly operate the airports and aerodromes.

1.4.2 Civil Public Entity

Ministry of Land, Infrastructure, and Transport

Ministry of Land, Infrastructure, and Transport (MOLIT) is the central public body involved in the governance of airports and aerodromes in Korea. It is the competent authority and primary regulatory authority for aviation and transport infrastructure within Korea. Therefore, MOLIT is solely responsible for implementing Standards and Recommended Practices, which Sects. 1.5 and 2 describe this contribution to the domestic framework through the legal and policy framework.

MOLIT is also involved in the governance of Korea Airports Corporation (KAC) and Incheon International Airport Corporation (IIAC).

Regional Government

Certain regional governments are also mandated to be involved in the governance of airports and aerodromes. Those are mostly related to the construction of the airports and aerodromes and also their maintenance. The role of regional government is featured further in Chapter 2 of this contribution.

1.4.3 Airport Corporation

Korea Airports Corporation (KAC)

KAC manages and operates most public airports in Korea, which include Gimpo, Gimhae and Jeju Airports,[10] except for Incheon International Airports.[11] Established

---

[10] These can be considered the main public major airports in Korea. See Sect. 1.3.1.

[11] Korea Airports Corporation Act, Law No. 20299, 13 February 2024, (Enforcement date: 13 February 2024), (Partially revised), Art.9.

based on the Korean Airport Corporation Act,[12] the legislation itself refers to KAC's responsibility as "efficient construction, management, and operation of airports."[13] Until the enactment of the Incheon International Airport Corporation Act in 1999, which led to the establishment of Incheon International Airport Corporation, will be discussed below.

Incheon International Airport Corporation (IIAC)

IIAC is a market-oriented public enterprise established under the Incheon International Airport Corporation Act.[14] As the Act provides, the establishment's central role and purpose is to manage and operate Incheon International Airport exclusively. While independently managed like a private corporation, it remains under government ownership and management,[15] reflecting its dual mission of public service and financial performance.

1.4.4 Military Authorities

Military authorities operate and manage certain aerodromes and airports in Korea. Those are listed in Sect. 1.3 of this contribution. These bases are primarily operated by the Air Force and Military of Korea. Key installations include Osan Air Base, jointly operated with U.S. forces, which serves as a hub for allied operations, and Cheongju Air Base, housing advanced F-35A stealth fighters. Some bases, such as Gwangju, Daegu, and Gimhae, are dual-use facilities, accommodating both military and civil aviation. These dual-use facilities are important for the purposc of both defence and public transportation.

1.5 Applicable Legal Frameworks

This contribution visits how the aerodrome governance of Korea relates to international obligations, including compliance with SARPs. For that, among others, the following international legal frameworks apply to the aerodrome governance of Korea:

- Chicago Convention
- ICAO Annex 14
- Technical contributions of ICAO regarding Annex 14

[12] *Id.*

[13] *Id.*, Art. 1.

[14] Incheon International Airport Corporation Act, Law No. 20297, 13 February 2024, (Enforcement Date: 14 August 2024), (Partial Amendment).

[15] *Id.*, Art. 16.

Next to these, the following domestic legal frameworks are referred to in this contribution:

- Airport Facility Act[16]: The Airport Facility Act of Korea, which came into force on 30 March 2017 but recently revised in 2024, provides a comprehensive framework for the development, management, and operation of airport facilities in Korea. Its primary objectives are to ensure airport safety, efficiency, environmental sustainability, and service competitiveness. The act regulates the classification of airports, sets standards for facility maintenance, and promotes government oversight while encouraging private sector involvement. It also includes provisions for land use, noise control, and environmental protection around airports. The latest revisions focus on digitalisation, green airport initiatives, and enhanced disaster response systems.
- Enforcement Decree of the Airport Facility Act[17]: Based on the legal foundation of the Airport Facility Act, the Enforcement Decree of the Airport Facility Act provides detailed rules and guidelines necessary to implement and enforce the provisions of the Act. It covers regulations on the construction and maintenance of airport infrastructure, designation of airport zones, operational standards, public–private cooperation and government support. The decree also emphasises environmental protection and ensures that airport facilities comply with international aviation standards. The recent amendment likely reflects updates to technological, environmental or administrative aspects to meet evolving industry needs.

1.6 Structure of This Contribution

The present contribution is divided into three parts.

Section 1, which is the current part, is dedicated to introducing this research, including the terms and definitions, aerodromes of Korea, the applicable framework and the current subsection on the research structure.

Section 2 of this study is dedicated to the compliance of aerodromes in Korea with the international and domestic legal framework. The appendix of the study provides the list of aerodromes in Korea that are discussed in this study.

Section 3 provides remarks regarding the analysis done in Sect. 2. It summarises the previous analysis and provides a synthesis of the analysis.

---

[16] Airport Facilities Act [Enforcement Date: 14 August 2024] [Law No. 20291, 13 February 2024, Partial Amendment].

[17] Enforcement Decree of the Airport Facilities Act [Enforcement Date: 14 August 2024] [Ministry of Land, Infrastructure and Transport Decree No. 1381, 14 August 2024, Partially Revised].

2 Regulatory Compliance and International Alignment

2.1 Overview Provisions of the Airport Facility Act

The Airport Facilities Act consists of a total of 69 provisions contained in Chapter 1 on the general provisions, Chapter 2 on airport and airfield development, Chapter 3 on the airport and airfield management and operation, Chapter 4 on the navigational safety facilities, Chapter 5 on supplementary provisions, and Chapter 6 on penalties. The organisation of chapters is appropriate for the purpose of enacting the Airport Facilities Act (draft), and navigational safety facilities correspond to airport facilities that constitute airports or airfields, but this part seems to have been organised as a separate chapter because it is recognised as an especially important part for aviation safety.

2.2 Compliance with the Chicago Convention and Annexes

As indicated in Sect. 1.1, several provisions, namely Articles 28, 37, 38, and 44 in the Chicago Convention relate to essential features of aerodrome compliance in Korea. These provisions are directly applicable to aerodromes therein based on Article 6 of the Constitution. While the relevance of Article 44 is already mentioned, a short discussion on the relevance of Article 28 of the Chicago Convention prepares this contribution to expand further into the obligations under Articles 37 and 38.

If Article 44 of the Chicago Convention obliges States to cooperate for international civil air navigation and transport, Article 28 focuses on a more specific aspect: the air navigation facilities and standard systems. The provision provides that Contracting States, including Korea, must provide air navigation facilities and adopt and operate the "appropriate standard systems" concerning air navigation. While Article 28 may be more related to air navigation facilities, including Procedures,[18] it is a good basis to make the connection between the obligation to adopt and operate under specific standardised systems and SARPs, which contain the systems based on Articles 37 and 38 of the Chicago Convention.

Again, Articles 37 and 38 of the Chicago Convention mostly relate to compliance and non-compliance with SARPs. According to Article 37, Korea should adopt SARPs contained in ICAO Annex 14. This Annex, at least when it comes to Volume I on Aerodrome Design and Operations, contains SARPs concerning "physical characteristics and obstacle limitations surfaces to be provided for at aerodromes, and

[18] See Ruwantissa Abeyratne, *Convention on International Civil Aviation - A Commentary*, (Cham: Springer International Publishing AG, 2013); See also Frans G. Von der Dunk, 'Navigating Safely through the 21st Century: ICAO and the Use of GNSS in Civil Aviation', *Indian Journal of International Law*, Vol. 47, 2007, 1–8.

certain facilities and technical services normally provided at an aerodrome."[19] Under Article 38, there is room for States to depart from SARPs if the State notifies differences between the domestic legal framework and SARPs, which in this case are contained in ICAO Annex 14, of ICAO.[20]

The Supreme Court of Korea interpreted that the Chicago Convention does not force its Contracting States to implement and enforce SARPs in the relevant domestic jurisdiction. Still, it only has a recommendatory effect, as ICAO 'announces' the adoption and revision of SARPs, only, despite the legal force under Article 6 of the Constitution of Korea demonstrated under Sect. 1.1. Regardless of this interpretation, however, since this contribution does not intend to analyse the legal force of SARPs but rather analyse the governance of aerodromes in Korea, I do not go into further details of the case concerning the legal force.

Despite the potential issues regarding the SARPs, Korea has implemented more than 98.48% of the existing SARPs. The operation of aerodromes in Korea can be perceived as standardised with "international standards." Under the Korean legal system, these standards are contained in the Enforcement Decree of the Airport Facility Act, which supports the Airport Facility Act.

2.3 Details of the Domestic Legal Framework

2.3.1 Chapter 1[21]

The first chapter of the Airport Facility Act on airports outlines the purpose of regulating the installation and operation of airports, airfields, and navigation safety facilities to promote the aviation industry and public welfare. It provides detailed definitions for terms such as airports, aerodromes, associated facilities, development areas and operators and describes various infrastructure components, including runways, landing areas, and navigation aids. The chapter also specifies development projects related to constructing or upgrading airport and airfield facilities and highlights measures for ensuring safety and operational efficiency through designated zones and regulatory oversight.

2.3.2 Chapter 2[22]

Chapter 2 of the Airport Facility Act on airport and airfield development focuses on establishing comprehensive and basic development plans for airports. The Minister

[19] ICAO, 'Aerodromes Design and Operations', Annex 14 Aerodromes, Vol. I, (2022, 9th edn.), 1–1 Introductory note.

[20] *See* Supreme Court of Korea, Judgment 2002Do 850, 27 June 2003.

[21] Airport Facility Act, Chap. 1, General Provisions.

[22] *Id.*, Chap. 2, Development of Airports and Aerodrome.

of Land, Infrastructure, and Transport is required to create a comprehensive airport development plan every five years, which includes forecasts of air traffic demand, plans for developing significant airfields with a government support threshold, and resource allocation strategies. The plans must align with other national transportation and aviation policy frameworks. Additionally, any significant changes to these plans require revisions, consulting local governments and relevant agencies, and must undergo review by the Aviation Policy Committee. The basic development plans for specific airport or airfield projects also need to include aspects like current status analysis, safety assessments, scale and layout, environmental management and financial plans.

The law further details the implementation process, including the role of the Airport Development Technical Review Committee in advising on construction and related impacts. It outlines the authority and responsibilities of project implementers, ensuring the need for detailed execution plans, necessary approvals, and notifications for public awareness. Provisions for land entry, usage, and potential expropriation for development purposes are specified, along with measures for public consultation and coordination with local and national bodies. The chapter also includes financial support provisions from the state for development projects and standards for constructing airport-related facilities.

2.3.3 Chapter 3[23]

Chapter 3 of the Airport Facility Act on the management and operation of airports and aerodromes outlines the regulatory framework for maintaining and overseeing these facilities. MOLIT is empowered to establish and manage rights related to airport and aerodrome facilities, including collecting usage fees and implementing registration and security measures.[24] These rights are subject to special provisions for mortgage settings and transfers. The Act is also set for maintaining records, compliance with operational standards, and conducting inspections to ensure the facilities meet required safety and functionality standards.[25] Additionally, guidelines for preventing ground safety incidents, training requirements, and the responsibilities of aviation-related organisations and personnel are specified to uphold operational safety.

The chapter emphasises procedures for reporting and handling usage suspensions, facility closures, or reactivations,[26] along with stipulations for removing obstacles near airports to prevent interference with air navigation.[27] It also details the installation of aviation warning lights and restrictions on lights that might mimic

[23] *Id.*, Chap. 3, Management and operation of airports and aerodromes.

[24] *Id.*, Art. 26.

[25] *Id.*, Arts. 30 & 31.

[26] *Id.*, Arts. 32 & 33.

[27] *Id.*, Art. 34.

aviation signals.[28] Requirements for airport operators to acquire certification for safe operations are described, including compliance checks and potential penalties for violations.[29] The law also provides for the succession of roles when airport or airfield management changes hands,[30] ensuring continued oversight by the Ministry to uphold public safety and infrastructure integrity.

2.3.4 Chapter 4[31]

Chapter 4 of the Airport Facility Act focuses on the installation, management, and operation of navigation facilities. MOLIT holds the primary authority for setting up navigation facilities, with provisions for non-governmental entities to establish such facilities, contingent on receiving the Minister's approval and adhering to specific conditions.[32] Detailed processes are outlined for the creation and approval of implementation plans before the installation of these facilities, as well as requirements for performance checks, known as completion inspections, before their operational use.[33] This chapter emphasises that facilities must meet established safety and operational standards and pass performance tests to ensure safe and efficient functionality.

Chapter 4 also governs modifications to navigation facilities,[34] mandating approval from the Minister for any significant changes and completion inspections once alterations are made. The maintenance of these facilities must follow set criteria, with regular inspections conducted to verify compliance. Usage fees for these facilities can be imposed by the facility operators, subject to Ministry oversight.[35] Provisions for the suspension, resumption, or cessation of facility usage require approval to ensure the safety of air navigation.[36] The chapter further outlines the procedure for transferring management rights of navigation safety facilities and sets conditions for obtaining performance conformity certificates for specific safety equipment.[37]

2.3.5 Chapter 5[38]

Chapter 5 of the Airport Facility Act encompasses regulations regarding entry, inspections, and prohibited activities to ensure the safety and management of airports and

[28] *Id.*, Arts. 36 & 37.

[29] *Id.*, Arts. 37–41.

[30] *Id.*, Art. 42.

[31] *Id.*, Chap. 4, Navigation Facilities.

[32] *Id.*, Art. 43.

[33] *Id.*, Arts. 44 & 45.

[34] *Id.*, Art. 46.

[35] *Id.*, Art.50.

[36] *Id.*, Art. 49.

[37] *Id.*, Arts. 51–54.

[38] *Id.*, Chap. 5, Miscellaneous Provisions.

navigation facilities. MOLIT has the authority to require reports, access premises for inspections, and demand documentation from entities involved in aviation activities to uphold compliance. Strict entry restrictions are set for runways, taxiways, and facilities housing navigation safety equipment without appropriate authorisation.[39] Prohibited actions include damaging airport or airfield facilities, throwing objects at aircraft, and activities posing threats to navigation safety.[40] The Airport Facility Act provides for the authority to prevent or remove unauthorised activities, outlining permissible actions for safety, including intervention by government officials.

This chapter also establishes penalties and responsibilities for non-compliance, such as fines up to 1 billion KRW in lieu of operational suspensions or other orders when public convenience or safety may be compromised.[41] Provisions ensure compensation for damage caused by preventive actions, such as the neutralisation of unauthorised lightweight aircraft. The Ministry has the power to revoke permits or mandate corrective actions for violations, with stipulated procedures including holding hearings for significant decisions.[42] There is an emphasis on the delegation of authority, allowing tasks to be assigned to sub-agencies or relevant organisations, which include regional government,[43] which emphasises the role of regional government that are not strictly considered as airport operators mentioned in Sect. 1.4 of this contribution. Lastly, the chapter mandates a periodic review of regulatory measures for relevance and effectiveness every three years.[44]

2.3.6 Chapter 6[45]

Chapter 6 outlines the penalties for violations related to the operation and management of airports, aerodromes, and navigation facilities. Operating an airport without obtaining the required operation certification results in up to three years of imprisonment or fine of up to 30 million KRW.[46] Unauthorised installation or use of facilities related to airport development incurs fines of up to 20 million KRW.[47] Violations involving orders, such as unapproved construction or refusal to cooperate with inspections, can result in up to one year of imprisonment or fines of up to 10 million KRW.[48] Lesser offences, like obstructing inspections or not complying with requests

---

[39] *Id.*, Art. 55.
[40] *Id.*, Art. 56.
[41] *Id.*, Art.59.
[42] *Id.*, Art. 58.
[43] *Id.*, Art. 61.
[44] *Id.*, Art. 63.
[45] *Id.*, Chapter 6, Penalties.
[46] *Id.*, Art. 64.
[47] *Id.*, Art.65.
[48] *Id.*, Art. 66.

for reports, are penalised with fines of up to 5 million KRW.[49] Noncompliance with removal orders leads to a smaller penalty of up to 200,000 KRW or detainment.[50]

The law also establishes the dual liability of individuals and organisations,[51] holding corporate representatives or employees accountable for infractions unless proven that proper oversight was maintained. Administrative penalties, such as fines, range from less than 500,000 to 5 million KRW for violations involving unauthorised use or failures in operational compliance.[52] The imposition of compulsory fines is specified for non-compliance with correction orders, with amounts up to 1 million KRW,[53] repeatable annually until compliance is achieved.

2.3.7 Chapter 7[54]

Chapter 7 outlines special provisions for handling minor airport and aerodrome facility regulations violations. It defines "violations" as specified infractions and provides detailed rules on who qualifies as an "offender" for these provisions. Repeat offenders, or those whose actions warrant formal legal proceedings due to their nature or consequences are excluded.[55] If an individual receives a notice for a violation, they are expected to pay a specified fine within a designated timeframe, with provisions for appeals and additional charges if delayed.

If the notified offender fails to pay within the period or disputes the notice, authorities must initiate summary trials unless the individual pays an increased fine before the trial. Once the fine is paid or a summary judgment is rendered, the individual cannot be prosecuted further for the same act. These measures aim to streamline the process of handling minor infractions while ensuring adherence to aviation safety and operational standards.

2.4 *Remarks*

2.4.1 Overview

The Airport Facility Act of Korea reflects a comprehensive approach to the governance of aerodromes, focusing on improving safety, fostering infrastructure development through public–private partnerships, and promoting environmental sustainability. It is aligned with international standards and embraces modern technology

---

[49] *Id.*, Art. 67.

[50] *Id.*, Arts. 67(2).

[51] *Id.*, Art. 68.

[52] *Id.*, Art. 69.

[53] *Id.*, Art. 70.

[54] *Id.*, Chapter 7, Special Cases Concerning the Handling of Offenses.

[55] *Id.*, Art. 71.

to enhance operational efficiency. Furthermore, the Act balances central government oversight with localised governance structures, especially for regional airports, ensuring effective administration of aerodromes across the country.

The subsections below describe the strengths, challenges and considerations on the Airport Facilities Act of Korea and also relationship between the Airport Facility Act and ICAO Annex 14, based on the author's observation.

2.4.2 Strength of the Legal Framework

Clear Structure and Regulatory Compliance

The Act is well-structured, providing clear guidelines on the establishment, operation, safety, and security of airports and aerodromes. It ensures compliance with both domestic and international safety standards, particularly ICAO Annex 14. This alignment helps maintain the global credibility of Korean airport infrastructure and operational practices.

Comprehensive Safety and Security Provisions

The Act emphasises safety in terms of infrastructure, including lighting and signage, operational procedures, regular inspections, and emergency response planning. While it may not be obvious, the Act requires operators to include sections mentioned in these provisions that align with ICAO Annex14, which stresses the importance of safety measures like runway strip design, obstacle limitation surfaces, and aerodrome rescue and firefighting services.

Stringent Penalties and Enforcement Mechanisms

The penalty provisions in Chapters 6 and 7 of the Airport Facility Act demonstrate an enforcement framework for ensuring compliance. By including severe penalties, including fines, criminal charges, and potential suspension of operations for non-compliance, the law ensures that both public and private operators maintain high operational standards. The introduction of fines for violations and compulsory compliance fees shall ensure swift enforcement, incentivising compliance with operational safety standards.

Structured Approach to Facility Management

The provisions for the facility management set out specific rules for maintaining aerodrome infrastructure, ensuring regular inspections and safety checks. This helps ensure that the physical infrastructure meets high standards and is properly maintained throughout its operational life. Such provisions align with ICAO's emphasis on the regular safety inspections and facility maintenance to ensure compliance with international standards.

Integration with Local Government and ICAO Regulations

The Act also integrates local government officials, such as Jeju Special Self-Governing Province, in the enforcement of airport and aerodrome safety regulations, promoting a local level of accountability. This decentralisation is helpful in ensuring that specific regional needs and circumstances are considered, particularly in geographically unique areas like Jeju Island.

2.4.3 Potential Challenges

Complexity and Ambiguity in Penalty Enforcement

While the penalties are intended to enforce compliance, some of the provisions might create ambiguity in terms of how violations are treated. For example, the conditions under which compulsory compliance fees are applied and how they interact with criminal penalties may need further clarification. This could lead to inconsistencies in how penalties are levied, especially in complex cases or when multiple infractions occur.

Balancing Strict Regulations with Industry Flexibility

The Airport Facility Act includes several stringent safety and operational provisions, such as mandatory compliance with safety standards for lighting and obstacle marking (Articles 36–37), which are necessary for safety but may create operational constraints or additional costs for airport operators, especially at smaller or regional airports. There could be a need for flexibility or tiered implementation of such provisions, particularly for airports that may not handle large traffic volumes but still need to meet safety requirements.

Alignment with ICAO's Evolving Standards

The ICAO SARPs themselves are regularly updated to adapt to new technologies and safety concerns. The Korean Air Facility Act aligns well with ICAO SARPs, but it will need continuous updates to keep pace with emerging developments in aviation technology, like drone operations, sustainable airport infrastructure, and innovative airport technologies. ICAO's evolving guidance on cybersecurity and environmental sustainability might require more attention in future revisions of the Act.

Monitoring and Enforcement Mechanism

The Act sets out robust provisions for penalties, but the effectiveness of enforcement is dependent on the implementation mechanisms. Ensuring that inspectors and local authorities have adequate training and resources to monitor and enforce compliance will be critical in maintaining high safety standards. The inspection process (Article 31 and Article 47) is central to enforcement, but there may be concerns regarding adequate staffing and technical resources at smaller airports, which need attention.

2.4.4 Consideration

The Airport Facility Act provides a solid legal foundation for regulating airports and aerodromes in South Korea, particularly regarding operational safety, compliance with international standards, and penalties for non-compliance. Its alignment with ICAO Annex 14 may not be apparent, but it is present. The presence ensures that South Korea remains competitive on the international aviation stage while maintaining rigorous safety standards. However, to ensure the long-term success and relevance of the Act, periodic updates will be needed to address new challenges in aviation, such as technological advancements, environmental sustainability, and emerging threats to airport safety.

2.4.5 Relationship with ICAO Annex 14

The law concerning airport and aerodrome management in Korea shares significant connections with ICAO Annex 14 in its approach to safety, infrastructure, and operational standards. For instance, Chapter 3 emphasises the management, operation, and safety inspections of airports and aerodromes, paralleling Annex 14's SARPs for aerodrome certification and compliance. The Korean law's stipulations, such as the requirement for public airport operators to obtain an Airport Operation Certificate as outlined in Article 38, align with ICAO Annex 14's mandates for ensuring that aerodrome facilities meet both local and international operational and safety benchmarks. Moreover, provisions related to facility management standards in Articles 31 and 47 outline the importance of adherence to strict safety procedures, in relation to comprehensive safety management requirements ICAO Annex 14.[56]

Additionally, the Airport Facility Act's focus on obstacle limitation and safety measures, as seen in Articles 34 and 36, reflects ICAO Annex 14's emphasis on

[56] In fact, the safety management aspects require further adherence to Annex 19 to the Chicago Convention on Safety Management. This is outside the scope of this contribution.

safeguarding navigable airspace through regulated height restrictions and proper markings. Article 36 further discusses the installation and management of aeronautical obstacle lights and markers, which is a direct implementation of ICAO Annex 14's guidelines for ensuring visibility and reducing risks to aircraft during critical phases of flight.

3 New Challenges

3.1 Overview

The governance and operation of airports and aerodromes of Korea face several critical challenges that require focused attention to maintain safety, efficiency, and sustainability. Key challenges include the integration of transportation systems, managing airport expansion in urbanised areas, and balancing the operations of dual-use facilities.

3.2 Integrating Transportation Systems

Korea's efforts to enhance the accessibility and efficiency of airports are exemplified by existing multimodal transport initiatives, such as high-speed rail, metro systems, and dedicated bus routes to major airports like Incheon and Gimpo. However, as passenger volumes increase, particularly at international hubs, ensuring seamless connectivity becomes paramount.

3.3 Airport Expansion

As air traffic demand rises, expanding airport capacity is vital to maintaining Korea's position as a global aviation hub. However, expansion efforts face several hurdles. The first hurdle may be the land use and zoning. Urbanised regions, especially around Gimpo, face land scarcity, making it difficult to develop new infrastructure without disrupting surrounding communities. This is one of the reasons that Incheon Airport was established.

The second hurdle is relevant to the environmental concerns. Noise pollution and habitat disruption near airport expansion sites pose significant challenges, necessitating rigorous environmental assessments and community engagement. The Korean Airport Corporation has a specific team dealing with these societal concerns.

3.4 Dual-Use Facilities

Korea's reliance on dual-use airports—facilities shared by civilian and military operations—introduces complexities in governance and operations, regarding the operational coordination between civil-military authorities, safety concerns, and infrastructure limitations where necessary infrastructure for the military airport may be understood as an obstacle according to the civil rule.

4 Conclusion

Korea has successfully managed to balance its rapid industrial growth with compliance to international obligations under the Chicago Convention and ICAO Annex 14. The transition from the Air Law of 1961 to the Airport Facility Act of 2017 marks a significant evolution in Korea's legal and regulatory approach, prioritising safety, efficiency, and environmental sustainability. Key achievements include a comprehensive regulatory framework that facilitates public and private sector involvement, stringent safety protocols, and the integration of modern technologies. Despite these strengths, challenges persist, such as ensuring ongoing compliance with ICAO's evolving standards, addressing environmental concerns, and integrating multimodal transport solutions. Additionally, managing dual-use facilities and navigating tensions between urban development and airport expansion requires careful balancing of competing priorities.

In conclusion, Korea's aviation governance model demonstrates a strong foundation for continued growth and innovation. At the same time, areas such as adaptability to emerging technologies, environmental impact mitigation, and regional inclusivity remain opportunities for future enhancement. As Korea continues to refine its aviation framework, it sets an example of how a country with a limited geographic size can achieve global competitiveness in the aviation sector.

Chapter 8
Airport Development in Indonesia: Legal and Policy Considerations

Ridha Aditya Nugraha and Rio Christiawan

Abstract As an archipelagic state, Indonesia relies on air transportation for seamless connectivity. The two main actors in this mode of transportation are airlines and airports. The latter is usually less highlighted compared to the former. After the COVID-19 pandemic, Indonesia opened new opportunities in the air transportation industry through the enactment of Law No. 11/2020. Also known as the Indonesian Omnibus Law, it aims to simplify the investment process in various sectors, including air transportation. Currently, investors can establish an airline with only three aircraft—whereas the minimum requirement used to be ten. The Indonesian Omnibus Law aims to welcome new entrants to the airline business, which will hopefully encourage airport development. Still, the foreign direct investment nationality clause remains, which upholds single majority concept. In addition, airport development in Indonesia has faced a new chapter during the last decade, which is the introduction of the public–private partnership scheme. There were two state-owned enterprises airport operators, namely Angkasa Pura I and Angkasa Pura II, which were merged into InJourney Airports in September 2024, and they have been pushed to enter joint ventures with private investors with the aim of finding best practices on fair competition and innovation. This step is important as Indonesia is facing a more complex ASEAN Open Skies as the region is increasingly integrating in accordance with the ASEAN Economic Blueprint 2025. Finally, Indonesian airports are facing a domestic situation where the ceiling and floor prices are still implemented at domestic routes, leading to questions regarding flexibility.

Keywords Angkasa Pura · ASEAN · Foreign Direct Investment (FDI) · Hub and spoke · Indonesian omnibus law · InJourney airports · Open skies · Public Private Partnership (PPP)

R. A. Nugraha (✉)
Air and Space Law Studies, Universitas Prasetiya Mulya, Jakarta, Indonesia
e-mail: ridha.nugraha@prasetiyamulya.ac.id

R. Christiawan
Faculty of Law, Universitas 17 Agustus 1945 Jakarta, Jakarta, Indonesia

© The Author(s), under exclusive license to Springer Nature Singapore Pte Ltd. 2025
S. Bhat B. (ed.), *Aerodrome Governance in Asia*,
https://doi.org/10.1007/978-981-96-7568-5_8

1 Introduction

Indonesia heavily relies on air transportation for inter-island transportation, noticing its archipelagic nature. Both land and water transportation have proven to be unable to replace air transportation on many routes. The country lifeline such as government affairs until healthcare depends on seamless air connectivity. Airport existence spread equally among Indonesia's five biggest islands namely Sumatera, Java, Kalimantan, Sulawesi, and Papua as well as lesser islands from time to time becomes more essential for domestic air transportation.

Indonesia is the biggest Member State of the Association of Southeast Asian Nations (ASEAN)—a region of 650 million people. As the region is facing the ASEAN Economic Blueprint 2025[1] which promotes economic growth through air transportation, the current situation strengthens the importance of airport presence in Indonesia. The International Air Transport Association (IATA) forecasted Indonesia to be one of the fastest-growing global markets in terms of additional passengers. It is expected to be the fourth largest market in 2039 supported by its rapidly increasing middle-class.[2]

Until August 2024, there were only two leading airport operators in Indonesia. Both were Angkasa Pura I and Angkasa Pura II which hold status as state-owned enterprises (*Badan Usaha Milik Negara or BUMN*). State funding allocations were legal and had been granted to them from time to time. Angkasa Pura I managed 17 airports, most of which are located in the central and eastern parts of Indonesia. Angkasa Pura II managed 20 airports, with most of them located in western and central parts of Indonesia, including Soekarno-Hatta International Airport (CGK) as the country's primary gateway. In total, about 119 million domestic passengers and 31 million international passengers were transported in 2023.[3] In terms of cargo, 928 million tons of domestic cargo and 337 million tons of international cargo were transported in 2023, which was facilitated by both state-owned airport operators.[4] On 9 September 2024, both state-owned airport operators merged into InJourney Airports which operates 37 airports across the archipelagic.

InJourney holding company (PT Aviasi Pariwisata Indonesia) is established for management and financial consolidation purposes. It is a giant state-owned aviation and tourism holding company. As of May 2024, InJourney also has state-owned hotels as its members and plans to welcome the flag carrier Garuda Indonesia to join

[1] The ASEAN Economic Community Blueprint 2025 was adopted by ASEAN Leaders at the 27th ASEAN Summit on 22 November 2015 in Kuala Lumpur, Malaysia.

[2] Mardika Parama 'Indonesia to have world's fourth-largest air passenger market by 2039: IATA', available at <https://www.thejakartapost.com/news/2020/11/11/indonesia-to-have-worlds-fourth-largest-air-passenger-market-by-2039-iata.html> Last visited, 6 August 2024.

[3] Arvin Lienardi, 'Daiwa Capital Markets-Bahana Sekuritas Indonesia Corporate Access PT Angkasa Pura', 26 November 2024.

[4] *Id.*

the holding.[5] In parallel, Citilink (as a part of Garuda Indonesia Group) and Pelita Air, as two Indonesian airlines owned by state-owned enterprises, are in the same talk.[6] The three airlines represent around half of the domestic market shares. Thus, it could potentially have a significant impact if the airlines decide to join. However, the plan with Garuda Indonesia has been shelved pending the flag carrier improving finances.[7]

In the last decade, the Indonesian Government has encouraged more private investment in airports across the archipelagic. This initiative aims to attract foreign investors with its global network to expand Indonesian airport connectivity in ASEAN, Asia–Pacific, and beyond. At this stage, InJourney presence means a coordination forum to set new strategy for both state-owned airport operators competing with well-established airports in the region, among others are Suvarnabhumi Airport (Thailand), Changi Airport (Singapore), and Kuala Lumpur International Airport (Malaysia).

For Indonesia, the Covid-19 pandemic has led to a momentum in liberalising air transportation sector. Consolidation through liberalisation is one of the survival keys in aviation. The Indonesian Job Creation Law of 2020[8] (also known as the Indonesian Omnibus Law of 2020) is enacted to boost economic recovery by amending many laws to encourage ease of doing business. In the airline sector, this initiative is translated into reducing the entry barrier by reducing aircraft minimum requirements by amending the Indonesian Aviation Law of 2009.[9] Previously, a scheduled airline must operate a minimum of ten aircraft with five of them owned and another five aircraft in possession (leasing). The Indonesian Omnibus Law reduces the aircraft minimum requirements from ten in three for scheduled airlines. Such liberalisation ensures that the Indonesian aviation business can be sustained and attractive for Foreign Direct Investment (FDI), as the previous ten aircraft minimum requirements portrayed the country's heaviest investment barrier in ASEAN.[10] This initiative is considered as a game-changer in the airline sector.

---

[5] Dimas Waraditya Nugraha, 'Untung-Rugi Bergabungnya Garuda ke InJourney', available at <https://www.kompas.id/baca/ekonomi/2024/07/30/untung-rugi-bergabungnya-garuda-ke-injourne?open_from=Search_Result_Page> Last visited, 7 September 2024.

[6] Dimas Waraditya Nugraha &Yosepha Debrina Ratih Pusparisa, 'Integrasi Bisnis Citilink Indonesia dengan Pelita Air Bikin Untung atau Buntung?', available at <https://www.kompas.id/baca/ekonomi/2023/11/05/menanti-integrasi-bisnis-citilink-indonesia-dengan-pelita-air?open_from=Section_Artikel_Terkait> Last visited, 7 September 2024.

[7] Tenggara Statistics, 'Analysis: Airport firms merged to create one the world's biggest operators', available at <https://www.thejakartapost.com/opinion/2024/09/20/analysis-airport-firms-merged-to-create-one-the-worlds-biggest-operators.html> Last visited, 28 September 2024.

[8] Indonesia, Law No. 11/2020 on Job Creation (2 November 2020) (also known as the Indonesian Omnibus Law).

[9] Indonesia, Law No. 1/2009 on Aviation (12 January 2009).

[10] Ridha Aditya Nugraha, 'ASEAN Integration Through the Skies: The Current Progress in Preparation for 2025', ASEAN Prosperity Initiative (API), Briefing Paper No. 02, 2020, pp. 1–19 at p. 7 & 8.

There are a few legal frameworks related to airports. The Indonesian Aviation Law of 2009 lays down the foundation,[11] and its revision through the Indonesian Omnibus Law of 2020 on airport provisions has a significant impact on the airline sector. Among others, in terms of liberalisation, a room is now open to avoid the single majority concept for Indonesian nationals in FDI pertaining to airport operators. More foreign capital is welcomed, including from other ASEAN Member States. This initiative becomes essential, noticing that the construction of Indonesian airports has relied heavily on the state budget—either national or provincial—for many decades. FDI liberalisation in the Indonesian airport sector means reducing reliance on the state budget as they are also needed for many sectors' recovery post-pandemic. Now in terms of infrastructure, Indonesian state budget focuses on the new capital Nusantara construction.

Finally, the Indonesian aviation sector is now facing new opportunities with the increasing demand for seamless connectivity. ASEAN integration with reference to ASEAN Economic Blueprint 2025 and the full enactment of the ASEAN Single Aviation Market since 2016 are among the encouraging factors. Furthermore, the world's biggest bloc-to-bloc open skies arrangement between ASEAN and European Union (EU) is also in the pipeline regarding its implementation, which is something that ASEAN will face soon. Indonesian airports' development needs to strive towards eliminating regulatory hurdles to compete in the region and maximize in grasping opportunities.

2 Liberalisation of the Indonesian Airline Sector

The Indonesian aviation boom started at the beginning of the 1990s. The tightly regulated industry gradually came to loosen after the allowance of private enterprises to establish an airline serving domestic as well as international flights.[12] Within a half-decade, a more liberal policy of allowing foreign carriers to perform cabotage (8th and 9th Freedom of the Air) or serving the Indonesian domestic market was being raised. Such plan on cabotage was never be realised. The 1997 national economic crisis led to the privatisation of Garuda Indonesia as the Indonesian flag carrier stalled.

The Indonesian aviation industry liberalisation led to the growing number of airlines, namely from 7 airlines (1999) that rose to 27 airlines (2004).[13] Almost 400% increase irrespective of the total fleet each airline had. Another factor to support the Indonesian growth was the 9/11 attack (2001), which resulted in an abundant supply of leased aircraft for international market, and thus, decreased lease prices. The

[11] *Supra* note 9, at Chapter 9.

[12] Danang Parikesit, et al., 'Developing a Policy Decision Tool for a Domestic Airline Company: A Case of Indonesia', *Journal of the Eastern Asia Society for Transportation Studies*, Vol. 5, 2003, pp. 572–586 at p. 573.

[13] Organization for Economic Co-operation and Development, OECD Report No. DAF/COMP/WD(2014)70 (121st meeting of OECD Competition Committee, June 2014).

Indonesian Aviation Law of 1992[14] allowed to set up an airline with Indonesian nationality without any obligation to own a single aircraft. The only condition was to have a minimum of two aircraft in lease.[15] Unsurprisingly, the Indonesian airline business was booming at that time. However, the facts showed a lack of supervision, which ended in a few consecutive incidents and tragic accidents, among others were Adam Air Flight KI-574 (2007) and Garuda Indonesia Flight GA-200 (2007).[16]

A new chapter in the Indonesian aviation began in 2009. As an aftermath of the consecutive accidents in Indonesia, all Indonesian airlines were banned from flying to the European Union (EU) due to unaddressed safety concerns in 2007.[17] Efforts to improve aviation safety were raised, including through legislation as one of the eight aspects of International Civil Aviation Organization (ICAO) Universal Safety Oversight Audit Program Continuous Monitoring Approach (USOAP-CMA).[18] This was the reason behind the speedy enactment of the Indonesian Aviation Law of 2009,[19] which covered both public and private air law provisions.

The Indonesian Aviation Law of 2009 has raised the condition to establish an airline performing scheduled flight, which is to own a minimum of five aircraft and to lease (or in a possession of) a minimum of another five aircraft.[20] Such ten aircraft minimum rule should fit the routes served—or plan to be served as stated within the airline's expansion plan. This tight benchmark is an indirect saying that only those with adequate funding and management capability could operate. Within the last fifteen years, the Indonesian Aviation Law of 2009 has resulted in the decrease of privately owned national airlines.

The Indonesian aviation industry (especially Indonesian airlines) was hit hard during the COVID-19 pandemic. The introduction of the Indonesian Omnibus Law in 2020 led to less barrier for either domestic or foreign investor to set up an airline from minimum number of aircraft requirements perspective. Currently, a fleet of three aircraft for performing commercial scheduled flight is the minimum. The aim is to maintain FDI competitiveness in airline business with other ASEAN Member States.[21] At the same time, the single majority concept in ownership portrayed within

---

[14] Indonesia, Law No. 15 Year 1992 on Aviation (May 25, 1992). Came into force on 25 May 1992, remained until 11 January 2009.

[15] Indonesia, Minister of Transportation Decree No. KM 11/2001 on Performing Air Transportation, Art. 15(1b).

[16] Ridha Aditya Nugraha, 'Improving Aviation Safety in Indonesia: How Many More Accidents?', *Hasanuddin Law Review*, Vol. 2, Issue 3, 2016, pp. 328–348.

[17] 'EU Lifts Flight Ban on All Indonesian Airlines', *Cabinet Secretariat of the Republic of Indonesia*, June 2018, available at <https://setkab.go.id/en/eu-lifts-flight-ban-on-all-indonesian-airlines/> Last visited, 24 October 2024.

[18] International Civil Aviation Organization <https://www.icao.int/safety/CMAForum/Pages/default.aspx> Last visited, 24 October 2024. See also International Civil Aviation Organization <https://www.icao.int/safety/CMAForum/Pages/background.aspx> Last visited, 24 October 2024.

[19] *Supra* note 9.

[20] *Id.*, Art. 118.

[21] *Supra* note 10.

the Indonesian Aviation Law of 2009 remains untouched by the Indonesian Omnibus Law. Thus, a status quo pertaining to ownership and control issues is maintained.

This policy resulted in the establishment of BlueBird Nordic Airlines, also known as BBN Airlines Indonesia, in 2022. The airline is a part of the group holding based in Ireland. Since September 2024, the airline served three domestic trunk routes with Soekarno-Hatta International Airport (CGK) in the Greater Jakarta Area as its base. BBN Airlines Indonesia became the second Indonesian airline established under the FDI scheme after Indonesia AirAsia. The latter is a part of AirAsia Group with roots in Kuala Lumpur, Malaysia—and is listed on the Indonesia Stock Exchange (Bursa Efek Indonesia –stock code: CMPP).

The liberalisation efforts with relaxed FDI conditions and restrictions live in parallel with protectionism pertaining to domestic routes' tariff. Indonesia is among the only few in Asia–Pacific that still implements floor price (*tarif batas bawah*) and ceiling price (*tarif batas atas*) policies only when it comes to domestic flights.[22] The lowest floor price could not be less than 35% of the determined ceiling price.[23] Prior to 28 March 2019, it was lower at 30% of the ceiling price.[24] The background of such tariff concept is to prevent airlines from gaining too much profit from passengers, while at the same time to prevent airlines compromising safety aspects in terms of promotions especially during low season. A conservative business model mindset leads to disbelief in income diversification, which made low ticket price possible. Both ceiling and floor price concepts only apply to economy class and are not applicable to business class.

The floor and ceiling price concept for domestic flights has faced multiple tests since 2018. The situation has become more challenging for the aviation sector following skyrocketing oil prices due to a few international conflicts in the last few years. The depreciation of the Indonesian Rupiah (IDR) against the United States Dollar (USD) in the last five years also added a burden to airlines especially due the use of USD in aircraft maintenance and purchase of spare parts.[25] As airline revenue from passengers is valued in IDR with the ceiling price as maximum, it leaves not much room for airlines seeking revenue during high seasons (such as Christmas and Eid al-Fitr) to make up losses suffered during low seasons. The thin margins or potential of flying for a loss has led to the closure of several non-trunk routes to many

---

[22] Ridha Aditya Nugraha, 'Akankah Harga Tiket PesawatTerjangkau Kembali?' available at <https://www.kompas.id/baca/opini/2024/01/12/akankah-harga-tiket-pesawat-terjangkau-kembali> Last visited, 24 September 2024.

[23] Indonesia, Minister of Transportation Regulation No. PM 20/2019 on Procedure and Formula to Calculate Ceiling Price on Economy Class as Applicable for Domestic Flights.

[24] Indonesia, Minister of Transportation Regulation No. PM 14/2016 on Mechanism of Calculation and Determination of the Upper and Lower Tariff Limits for Economy Class Passengers in Domestic Scheduled Commercial Air Transport Services. Existed between 28 January 2016 and 27 March 2019.

[25] When the Minister of Transportation Regulation No. PM 20/2019 was enacted in 2019, USD 1 is around IDR 14,000. In November 2024, USD 1 is around IDR 15,900. IDR has been depreciated around 12–14% to USD. Despite such situation, there has not been any change towards floor and ceiling price formula since 2019.

(smaller) Indonesian airports. This factor contributes to slowing down recovery in the aviation sector.

Finally, the Indonesian airline liberalisation policy, which has been conducted in a few stages within the last two decades, has shown a positive impact amid current challenges. Such a policy and its implementation have provided direct and indirect impacts toward the Indonesian airport operator or InJourney Airports.

3 State of Play of the Indonesian Airport Operator

On 9 September 2024, the Indonesian Government, through the Ministry of State Owned Enterprises (*Kementerian Badan Usaha Milik Negara (BUMN)*) merged the two state-owned airport operators into PT Angkasa Pura Indonesia.[26] Such an entity is known to the public in the name of InJourney Airports as a part of the state-owned InJourney holding (PT Aviasi Pariwisata Indonesia).The merger led to InJourney Airports being the world's fifth-biggest airport operator from a passenger traffic perspective with a total of 37 airports.[27] As of November 2024, 16 of 37 airports serve international flights, and most of them are located in the western and central parts of Indonesia.[28] A few airports with international exposure, among others, are (i.) Soekarno-Hatta International Airport (CGK) in Greater Jakarta Area; (ii.) I Gusti Ngurah Rai International Airport (DPS) in Bali; (iii.) Yogyakarta International Airport (YIA) in Greater Yogyakarta Area; and (iv.) Sultan Aji Muhammad Sulaiman Sepinggan International Airport (BPN) in Balikpapan, which serves the new Indonesian capital. The first two airports mentioned above are among the largest serving international travellers, which stand as the gateway to Indonesia.

The Jokowi administration, which ended in October 2024, decided to run an integrated but also centralised model of airport management under the tourism umbrella. Such integration is aimed at improving efficiency and reducing logistics costs; as official data show, air transportation contributes 5.7% of total domestic logistics costs.[29] Liberalisation seems to become a key to ensure innovation and competitiveness are in place in seeking profitability. There have been talks on InJourney Airports' corporate action plan to conduct an initial public offering (IPO). A few domestic investors have shown interest in the airport business.[30] However, it seems the IPO is pending a better performance of InJourney Airports in terms of passenger volume and financial performance.

---

[26] In terms of corporate action, InJourney first renamed PT Angkasa Pura II as PT Angkasa Pura Indonesia. Then PT Angkasa Pura I was merged into PT Angkasa Pura Indonesia. The rebranding effort goes with the latter known in public as InJourney Airports. In addition, PT stands for *Perseroan Terbatas* or Limited Liability Company established under the Indonesian Law No. 40/2007 (also known as the Indonesian Company Law).

[27] *Supra* note 3.

[28] *Id.*

[29] *Supra* note 7.

[30] *Id.*

Numerous International Air Transport Association (IATA) reports in the past years concluded global aviation has not yet reached the pre-pandemic 2019 level. This premise applies to Indonesia. In 2023, Angkasa Pura I reported passenger volume reaching only 85% of 2019; and also, a comparison of 450 aircraft serving domestic routes in September 2023 to around 50% higher capacity of 650 aircraft in 2019.[31] In total, Angkasa Pura I and Angkasa Pura II transported 173 million passengers in 2019 compared to 150 million passengers in 2023.[32] However, in terms of cargo there is an increase of domestic traffic from 712 million tonnes in 2019 to 928 million tonnes in 2023.[33] After the September 2024 merger, InJourney Airports accounted 90% of total passengers in the country.[34] These data show a promising future for Indonesian airports post-pandemic.

There are countries that have only one gateway, such as, Brunei Darussalam (Brunei International Airport), the Netherlands (Schiphol Airport), and Singapore (Changi Airport). Such a situation leads to more advantage in terms of recovery for airports rather than the competing airlines. Indonesia is a different case since the archipelagic contour leads to its domestic flights dominating over international flights. With 37 airports and many other smaller airports, a different situation exists for Indonesian airports compared to one-gateway cases. Although they are now under the InJourney Airports umbrella, these airports are competing with each other as supply and demand are still far from equilibrium.

As of 2024, two main factors that hamper the recovery of the Indonesian domestic aviation market are still high ticket prices and insufficient aircraft availability post-pandemic.[35] Specific to the high ticket prices in domestic routes, in August 2024, the Coordinating Minister of Maritime and Investment Affairs mentioned that Indonesian airfares are the second most expensive in the world after Brazil as well as much higher than other ASEAN Member States.[36] Indonesian middle and lower classes find it hard to travel as a return flight ticket (in economy class) accounts for more than half of the minimum monthly wage in many provinces. The ongoing situation has delivered a direct impact, which put Indonesian airports at a disadvantage pertaining to losing potential revenue in short, medium, and long-term plans.

The Indonesian airport state of play, as seen in 2024, comes with a long history behind it. The time-to-time national airport regulations and policy developments have played a definitive role. The Ministry of Transportation Decree No. 31/2024[37]

---

[31] *Id.*

[32] *Supra* note 3.

[33] *Id.*

[34] *Id.*

[35] Ridha Aditya Nugraha, 'The never-ending high airfares on Indonesian domestic routes', available at <https://www.thejakartapost.com/opinion/2024/08/08/the-never-ending-high-airfares-on-indonesian-domestic-routes.html> Last visited, 23 October 2024.

[36] '4 Alasan Tiket Pesawat RI Termahal Kedua di Dunia Setelah Brasil', *CNN Indonesia*, August 2024, available at <https://www.cnnindonesia.com/ekonomi/20240808111024-92-1130647/4-alasan-tiket-pesawat-ri-termahal-kedua-di-dunia-setelah-brasil> Last visited, 23 October 2024.

[37] Indonesia, Minister of Transportation Decree No. KM 31/2024 on Determination of International Airports (April 2, 2024).

(MoT Decree No. 31/2024) is the latest one pertaining to national airport policy. In furtherance of Article 256 of the Indonesian Aviation Law of 2009, which regulates airports, MoT Decree No. 31/2024 determines 17 airports to bear international airport status. In addition, Halim Perdanakusuma Airport (HLP) in Jakarta is among them, which is designated as international airport but only for charter or non-scheduled commercial flights. As a consequence, airports that are not granted international status can only serve domestic flights. A grace period starting from 2 April 2024 is guaranteed to airports that still serve international flights until the period (season) ends. However, this policy draws a setback in liberalisation efforts pertaining to airports and goes back to protectionism.

Recent polemic pertaining to the reorganisation of Angkasa Pura Indonesia within InJourney holdings and the granting of international status for selected Indonesian airports by the Ministry of Transportation are just the tip of the iceberg. Further fundamental issues and complex challenges of Indonesian airport developments are described in the next part.

4 Challenges to Indonesian Airport Development

The year 2017 marked one of the peaks in the Indonesian aviation business in terms of traffic, passengers' volume and number of airlines. About 14 national airlines were serving 374 routes from 128 domestic airports in 2017.[38] Low-cost carriers maintained its domination in the archipelagic skies, transporting about 55% of the domestic market share (approximately 52.3 million passengers). A total of 19 airports served international flights to 59 cities around the world—transporting around 31.5 million passengers.[39] As the Indonesian middle class population continues to grow and more new airports are opened in many Indonesian islands—not only Java, the Indonesian aviation market was expected to be among the biggest in Asia–Pacific. During Covid-19 pandemic, still there was a need to travel by air noticing the archipelagic nature and mountainous terrain. Such a fact speeds up aviation business recovery post-pandemic, albeit skyrocketing ticket price at domestic routes.

The foregoing highlights the crucial link of Indonesian aviation policies on airline at national stage towards airport development. No wonder domestic routes became the backbone for Indonesian airlines prior to Covid-19 pandemic with approximately 96.8 million passengers in 2017, while international flights only achieved around 30% of such number.[40] The growth of the airline business has a direct and significant impact towards Indonesian airport development. However, policies on airports are

---

[38] Indonesia National Air Carriers Association (INACA), *Annual Report 2017*, (Jakarta: INACA, 2017) p. 10.

[39] *Id.*

[40] Ridha Aditya Nugraha, 'Reviewing Ownership and Control of the Indonesian Airlines', ASEAN Aviation Integration Platform (AAIP) Institut Kajian Malaysia dan Antarabangsa (IKMAS) Universiti Kebangsaan Malaysia, Policy Paper No. 2, 2019.

not that much developed, noticing the airline-centric approach.[41] There are a few legal frameworks and policies which have impacted Indonesian airport development in the last decade. The subsequent parts of this chapter delve into them.

4.1 ASEAN Open Skies Implementation and Impact on Indonesian Airport

ASEAN has introduced liberalisation in aviation market (namely market access) through three multilateral agreements, namely (i.) Multilateral Agreement on Air Services of 2009[42] (MAAS); (ii.) Multilateral Agreement for the Full Liberalisation of Air Freight Services of 2009[43] (MAFLAFS); and (iii.) Multilateral Agreement for the Full Liberalisation of Passenger Air Services of 2010[44] (MAFLPAS). Only up to the 5th Freedom of the Air is allowed, and the situation will never change until April 2025.[45] Due to concerns of losing market share for its national airlines—especially flag carriers, Indonesia and some of ASEAN Member States were delaying the ratification of the three multilateral agreements for around a half-decade. This delayed the initial plan.[46] Finally, Indonesia became the last ASEAN Member State to sign the ASEAN MAFLPAS as the latest unratified instrument on 7 April 2016. This action led to the full enactment of an open skies or single aviation market in the region since then. It is based on the need for a collective act to realise the ASEAN Economic Community Blueprint 2025 goals, whereas seamless air connectivity becomes one of the pillars of a highly integrated regional economy.

There is no universally accepted definition for open skies.[47] However, the world seems to agree that the open skies concept aims to relax restrictions on market access, and among others is the access to designated airports. In a more practical approach, the open skies concept could be defined as freedom of air traffic rights and flexibility of business practices, which include; (i.) flight capacity (or flight frequency); (ii.) tariff (or airfare); (iii.) choice of aircraft type; (iv.) designated route(s); and (v.) designated

---

[41] Peter Forsyth, 'Chapter 21 Economic Evaluation of Air Services Liberalization: The New Calculus', in Peter Forsyth, et al. (eds.), *Liberalization in Aviation: Competition, Cooperation and Public Policy*, (Farnham: Ashgate, 2013) p. 403.

[42] Ratified on 24 November 2011.

[43] Ratified on 31 August 2015.

[44] Ratified on 7 April 2016.

[45] With limitations on capacity, ASEAN Member States airlines designated by an ASEAN Member State is allowed to operate both passenger and cargo scheduled services between its home country and a point with international airport in another ASEAN Member State, and then to a point with international airport of a third ASEAN Member State.

[46] Ridha Aditya Nugraha, 'The Indonesian Aviation Sector in the Realm of Liberalisation: The Long and Winding Road', in Jae Woon Lee (ed.), *Aviation Law and Policy in Asia: Smart Regulation in Liberalized Markets*, (Leiden: Brill Nijhoff, 2020) pp. 253–268 at pp. 255–257.

[47] Jae Woon Lee, *Regional Liberalization in International Air Transport: Towards Northeast Asian Open Skies*, (The Hague: Eleven International Publishing, 2016) p. 3.

airline(s).[48] These conditions are available within bilateral and multilateral air service agreements, whereas the number usually varies from each other—depending on the different characteristics and connectivity needs of each state.

The question is how far ASEAN Open Skies could bring an advantage to Indonesian airports and not merely to its national airlines. First, the number of international passengers shows a steady increase from 31 million passengers in 2017 (the first year of ASEAN Open Skies full implementation in Indonesia) to 38 million passengers in 2019.[49] The Covid-19 pandemic decreased the passenger volume between 2020 and 2022. The number returned to 31 million passengers in 2023, and potentially, it will further increase by the end of 2024.[50] In terms of international cargo, the peak was reached in 2019, with 475 million tons (40% of the total) served at Angkasa Pura I and II airports.[51] Post-pandemic international cargo volume has not yet returned to the 2019 level. In short, the prospect for airport operators seems promising from a quantitative perspective.

The disadvantage for Indonesian airports in ASEAN Open Skies also comes from the multilateral agreements that paved the way for the single aviation market itself. During the ASEAN Open Skies drafting stage, Indonesia was reluctant to adopt it, noticing its negative impact on its national airline competitiveness in the region as well as the potential loss of domestic market share. The Indonesian Government has exercised its reservation rights by opening only five of its major cities to participate in the ASEAN single aviation market—as strengthened under MAFLPAS.[52] These cities are Jakarta, Denpasar (Bali), Makassar, Medan, and Surabaya. Such limitations are not an infringement of the ASEAN MAAS, MAFLAFS, and MAFLPAS per se, but it is not in line with open skies vision. One of the main aims is to relieve designated airport provisions and let airlines determine based on their business model. This situation opens the possibility for private airlines to overcome flag carriers on international routes.

As a consequence of the waiver policy, Indonesian airport development in areas other than those five cities is not optimal. They mainly rely on revenues from domestic traffic. International flights could still come to these Indonesian airports but face barriers to market access. Such international routes, including intra-ASEAN routes, rely on existing bilateral air service agreements. Thus, bilateralism is still in force, although multilateralism through ASEAN Open Skies has been fully enacted for a decade.[53]

There are at least two main reasons to challenge the reservation policy of the five Indonesian airports—either conducted under the MAFLPAS legal framework or

---

[48] Brian F. Havel, *Beyond Open Skies: A New Regime for International Aviation*, (Alphen aan den Rijn: Kluwer Law International, 2009).

[49] *Supra* note 38.

[50] The number of international passengers has reached 31 million passengers as of 10M2024. *Supra* note 3.

[51] *Id.*

[52] Supra note 46, at p. 255.

[53] *Id.*

at the implementation stage. First, the construction of the new capital, Nusantara, where Sultan Aji Muhammad Sulaiman Sepinggan International Airport (BPN) in Balikpapan serves its connectivity. As Balikpapan is not enlisted for ASEAN Open Skies full implementation, increasing international flights from any ASEAN Member States point(s) to the new capital in Kalimantan Island will soon face the capacity limit issue.

Second, the Indonesian Government, through Angkasa Pura Indonesia, is encouraging tourism growth across the archipelagic by building new airports and increasing existing airports' capacity. This is happening with a huge national state budget allocation in the last decade. The two big airports constructed, currently in operation, are; i.) Yogyakarta International Airport (YIA) in Kulon Progo, Yogyakarta; and ii.) Kertajati Airport (KJT) in Majalengka, West Java. Both airports are aimed to become the entrance gate to each province. However, there is a lack of international (intra-ASEAN) flights as of 2024—especially at the Kertajati Airport.[54]

Realising foreign tourist visit targets means increasing international flights to the designated area, the Silangit Airport (DTB) in North Tapanuli, North Sumatera, was revitalised and allowed to serve international routes between January 2017 and April 2024. Providing direct connectivity to Lake Toba was the aim[55]; which otherwise required additional three to five hours with transit at Soekarno-Hatta International Airport (CGK), Jakarta Greater Area. Unfortunately, like the Yogyakarta International Airport (YIA) and the Kertajati Airport (KJT), the initiative to welcome foreign tourists faced protectionism from the airport perspective at the Silangit Airport. These three airports did not enjoy liberalised market access—in terms of unlimited capacity—unlike the five above-mentioned Indonesian airports.

The latest breakthrough with ASEAN Open Skies, which might help Indonesian airports gain more traffic, is Protocol 4 on Co-Terminal Rights[56] under MAFLPAS as introduced in 2018. Indonesia became the last ASEAN member state to ratify it on 15 July 2024. Except for Cambodia, which ratified in 2021, the other ASEAN Member States ratified it during 2019-2020.

Article 2(1) of the ASEAN Open Skies Protocol 4 on Co-Terminal Rights stipulates that "[t]he designated airline(s) of each Contracting Party shall be allowed to exercise co- terminal rights, provided that there shall be no exercise of cabotage rights."

The co-terminal rights concept allows ASEAN Member States' airlines to carry out international traffic from their home base in one ASEAN Member State (A) to more than one airport in another ASEAN Member State (B1, B2). However,

[54] 'Flight Schedule and Routes in Kertajati International Airport', Kertajati International Airport, available at <https://bijb.co.id/schedule> Last visited, 30 November 2024.

[55] 'Menteri Pariwisata: Pembangunan 10 Destinasi Baru Untuk Ciptakan 10 Bali Baru', Cabinet Secretariat of the Republic of Indonesia, February 2016, available at <https://setkab.go.id/menteri-pariwisata-pembangunan-10-destinasi-baru-untuk-ciptakan-10-bali-baru/> Last visited, 30 November 2024.

[56] ASEAN Open Skies Protocol 4 on Co-Terminal Rights Between Points Within the Territory of Any Other ASEAN Member States. Done at Bangkok on 9 November 2018. In force since 16 August 2019.

there is no right to sell tickets or transport passengers solely from B1 to B2. For example, a Thai Airways (Thailand national airline) departing from Bangkok (BKK), Thailand, could fly to Jakarta (CGK), Indonesia, then end the journey in Balikpapan (BPN), Indonesia. Thai Airways is only allowed to disembark passengers during the transit in Jakarta, but not to embark any new passenger. Thus, Protocol 4 does not represent 5th Freedom of the Air per se—and not meant to open new competition with the Indonesian airlines serving the Jakarta-Balikpapan domestic route in this example. There is no cabotage[57] right while at the same time increasing traffic to more airports. This breakthrough could become a solution to increase connectivity to many Indonesian airports as the country currently lacks aircraft in operations, and the fleet has not returned to 2019's capacity.

Unfortunately, as a condition for Protocol 4 acceptance, Indonesia clearly mentions only opening its five major cities to exercise co-terminal rights, namely Denpasar (Bali), Jakarta, Makassar, Medan, and Surabaya.[58] Indonesia had become the only ASEAN Member State to reserve within a legal framework, but this is still accepted by the region as a gesture of the so-called ASEAN Way. Such a situation is a disadvantage for other Indonesian airports from a seamless connectivity perspective. Furthermore, the implementation of the concept of co-terminal rights is also questioned either in Indonesia or in other ASEAN Member States with some reluctant gestures. Aviation stakeholders in the region need to understand better that ASEAN Open Skies Protocol 4 emphasises cabotage as an economic rather than physical (foreign aircraft) presence issue.[59] If calculated correctly from an air transport economics perspective, the Protocol could become a solution to increase traffic to many Indonesian airports, noticing the limited aircraft available during the first years after the pandemic and the slow progress of FDI pertaining to airline investment.[60]

In the end, current Indonesian protectionism measures in implementing ASEAN Open Skies have hampered many Indonesian airports' potential growth. The scarcity of intra-ASEAN direct flights (unlimited 3rd and 4th freedoms of the air) to and from Indonesian airports outside the five cities—Denpasar (Bali), Jakarta, Makassar, Medan, and Surabaya—is one significant factor. Current Indonesian case shows that ASEAN internal market has not been fully forged. When the disadvantage lies with airport operators, unfortunately, there is no regional mechanism to help ASEAN Member States to move forward.[61]

---

[57] The term "cabotage rights" includes the holding out of air services for sale on purely domestic routes by the designated airlines(s) of that ASEAN Member States. For further reading on cabotage, see Pablo Mendes de Leon, *Cabotage in Air Transport Regulation*, (Dordrecht: Martinus Nijhoff, 1992).

[58] *Supra* note 56, at Art. 2(3).

[59] *Supra* note 46, at p. 257.

[60] Rio Christiawan, Haris Zuan, Sufian Jusoh & Ridha Aditya Nugraha, 'Foreign Direct Investment in Airline Industry', *Hasanuddin Law Review*, Vol. 10, Issue 1, 2024, pp. 43–63 at p. 59.

[61] Alan Khee-Jin Tan, 'The New ASEAN-E.U. Comprehensive Air Transport Agreement (CATA)', in Jae Woon Lee (ed.), *Aviation Law and Policy in Asia: Smart Regulation in Liberalized Markets*, (Leiden: Brill Nijhoff, 2020) pp. 285–301 at pp. 297–300.

4.2 National Law and Policy on Indonesian Airport

4.2.1 Public Private Partnership and Foreign Direct Investment

Airport presence is a basis for establishing seamless national air connectivity. As of April 2024, the Indonesian Directorate General of Civil Aviation (DGCA) performed monitoring of 256 airports—wherein 17 airports are allowed to serve international flights and 239 airports to serve domestic routes only.[62] With airstrips included, in total, 582 airports under DGCA supervision served across the archipelagic.[63] Previously, in 2023, 32 airports were classified as international airports.[64]

Most airports in Indonesia are built and renovated with full funding from the national or provincial state budget. Unfortunately, not all airports can operate effectively, and more importantly, they failed to open new routes. The J.B. Soedirman Airport (PWL) in Purbalingga, Ngloram Airport (CPF) in Blora, Wiriadinata Airport (TSY) in Tasikmalaya, and Kertajati Airport (KJT) in Majalengka—all of them located in Java Island and inaugurated between 2019 and 2021—are examples of state-funded airports lacking passengers. Some airports even have closed their scheduled flights. The Kertajati Airport is even known for its huge investment, which totals IDR 2.6 trillion.[65] Until the end of 2024, these airports remain far from their ideal capacity, thus making the state investment meaningless.

A Public Private Partnership (PPP) scheme could reduce the burden of state and provincial budget financing. The Presidential Regulation No. 38/2015[66] as PPP legal ground allows government and private enterprise collaboration in infrastructure sector, which also includes airport construction. The main challenge is to build a new airport from empty grounds, which has more difficulties then just finding a PPP strategic partner for renovating an existing airport. Shifting new airport development to islands other than Java should be a priority in ensuring equal access for all Indonesians.[67]

---

[62] Erwina Rachmi Puspapertiwi & Rizal Setyo Nugroho, 'Kemenhub Pangkas Bandara Internasional dari 34 Jadi 17, Ini Daftarnya', available at <https://www.kompas.com/tren/read/2024/04/28/180000465/kemenhub-pangkas-bandara-internasional-dari-34-jadi-17-ini-daftarnya?page=all> Last visited, 30 November 2024.

[63] Indonesia, Directorate General of Civil Aviation Ministry of Transportation, <https://hubud.dephub.go.id/hubud/website/bandara> Last visited, 1 December 2024.

[64] Yaries Mahardika Putro & Ridha Aditya Nugraha, 'Challenges for Airport Development: Is PPP an Answer?', available at <https://www.thejakartapost.com/opinion/2023/06/09/challenges-for-indonesian-airport-development-is-ppp-an-answer.html> Last visited, 30 November 2024.

[65] Nadya Zahira, 'Empat Bandara Ini Mati Suri Setelah Habiskan APBN Triliunan Rupiah' available at <https://katadata.co.id/berita/industri/6323dbd87cd5c/empat-bandara-ini-mati-suri-setelah-habiskan-apbn-triliunan-rupiah> Last visited, 30 November 2024.

[66] Indonesia, Presidential Regulation No. 38/2015 on Partnership between Government and Business Entity on Infrastructure Construction.

[67] *Supra* note 64.

Another relevant legal framework which encourages PPP is the Indonesian Positive Investment List of 2021,[68] which allows a maximum of 49% foreign share in the air transport sector. It does not specifically mention airport operators per se but when interpreted together with the Indonesian Aviation Law of 2009, the single majority concept still applies towards the whole national aviation business.

These legal frameworks establish legal certainty for investment in the airport business. As of November 2024, there is foreign investment in airports based on the PPP scheme, which includes (i.) GMR Airport Consortium from India, which set up a joint venture with Angkasa Pura II (now Angkasa Pura Indonesia) in operating the Kualanamu International Airport (Sumatera Island)[69]; (ii.) Incheon International Airport Corp. from South Korea in a joint venture with Angkasa Pura I (now Angkasa Pura Indonesia) in operating and developing both passenger and cargo capacity at Hang Nadim Airport (Riau Island)[70]; and (iii.) on a smaller scale—Changi International Airports from Singapore under Cardig Aero Service Consortium which operates the Komodo Airport (Flores Island).[71] A PPP scheme could reduce the burden on both state and provincial budgets in financing airport construction as well as increasing its passenger and cargo capacity.

The three PPP realisations, as mentioned above, mark a new chapter on FDI pertaining to the Indonesian airport business. Not only foreign investors who participated, but also locals showed interest in airport investments. Local private investor participation in the construction of the newly operated Singkawang Airport (SKJ) is an example of this. As a second-tier city located in Kalimantan Island, the total construction amount of the Singkawang Airport is IDR 427 billion, with 74% allocation from the state budget and 36% from private investors—which also includes

---

[68] Indonesia, Presidential Regulation No. 49/2021 on Investment Sector. See the Third Attachment, point 31 (KBLI 51,109).

[69] The PPP period is 25 years since 2021. The investment from GMR Airport Consortium accounted for at least IDR 15 trillion. See See Muhammad Said, 'GMR Airport Jadi Mitra Pengelolaan Bandara Kualanamu', available at <https://www.antaranews.com/berita/2542689/gmr-airport-jadi-mitra-pengelolaan-bandara-kualanamu> Last visited, 30 November 2024; Stefanus Osa Triyatna, 'GMR Airports Consortium Jadi Mitra Strategis Pengelolaan Bandara Kualanamu', available at <https://www.kompas.id/baca/ekonomi/2021/11/23/gmr-airports-consortium-jadi-mitra-strategis-pengelolaan-bandara-kualanamu> Last visited, 30 November 2024; 'Kualanamu International Airport', GMR Aero, available at <https://gmrinfra.com/airport-kualanamu.aspx> Last visited 30, November 2024.

[70] The PPP period is 25 years since 2021. The PPP is worth of IDR 6.8 trillion. See Lee Hae-rin, 'Incheon airport seeks to develop Batam airport into ASEAN's next gateway', available at <https://www.koreatimes.co.kr/www/culture/2024/11/135_363723.html> Last visited, 30 November 2024; Fadli, 'Consortium involving Incheon operator starts running Batam airport', available at <https://www.thejakartapost.com/business/2022/06/28/consortium-involving-incheon-operator-starts-running-batam-airport.html> Last visited, 30 November 2024.

[71] The PPP period is 25 years since May 2020. The investment is worth of IDR 1.23 trillion. See Hari Widowati, 'Lima Fakta Bandara Komodo yang Dikelola Changi Airports', available at <https://katadata.co.id/berita/industri/5e9a495ce528c/lima-fakta-bandara-komodo-yang-dikelola-changi-airports> Last visited, 30 November 2024.

corporate social responsibility (CSR) funds.[72] As of December 2024, the Singkawang Airport operates at its initial stage and serves a direct flight to Soekarno-Hatta International Airport (CGK)—as the runway is capable of flying Airbus A320 and Boeing 737 series. People living in Singkawang and its surroundings could save costs and reduce travel time by at least three hours, while previously, they needed to fly via Supadio Airport (PNK) located in Pontianak as the provincial capital.[73]

As the latest development, the financing scheme for the Dhoho Airport (DHX) in Kediri construction has gained national attention. With its soft launching on April 2024, the Dhoho Airport became the first airport in Indonesia to be constructed by the full private sector funding from Surya Dhoho Investama.[74] The partnership of Surya Dhoho Investama with Angkasa Pura I is scheduled for 50 years, with a total investment of at least IDR 12 trillion.[75] The airport is capable of welcoming wide-body aircraft such as the Boeing 777-300ER series and aims to reach 1.5 million passengers annually in the first few years.[76]

Initiatives through the national legal framework on PPP and FDI, which has liberalised the airport business, are facing challenges from DGCA Ministry of Transportation's recent policies. Like other ASEAN Member States, Indonesia is protecting its own national airlines in the domestic market. This policy has been translated by enacting the hub and spoke policy for a long time in Indonesia. The number of airports serving international flights decreased by half from 32 to 17 in April 2024. Such a half-reduced number of international airports is not due to commercial issues, but by a legal framework, namely the Ministry of Transportation Decree No. 31/2024[77] (MoT Decree No. 31/2024). The reasoning is to ensure domestic market recovery is on track by maximising national airlines' passenger load factor. This method means stopping international connectivity to many airports. In some routes, it is more affordable to depart from a non-Java Island point to a place of destination

[72] Laksmi Pradipta Amaranggana & Ahmad Naufal Dzulfaroh, 'Baru Saja Diresmikan Jokowi, Berikut Profil Bandara Singkawang', available at <https://www.kompas.com/tren/read/2024/03/20/191500965/baru-saja-diresmikan-jokowi-berikut-profil-bandara-singkawang > Last visited, 30 November 2024.

[73] Filemon Agung, 'Permintaan Tinggi, Bandara Singkawang Ditargetkan Beroperasi September 2024', available at <https://jelajahekonomi.kontan.co.id/ekonomi-infrastruktur/news/permintaan-tinggi-bandara-singkawang-ditargetkan-beroperasi-september-2024> Last visited, 30 November 2024.

[74] Surya Dhoho Investama is a subsidiary of Gudang Garam Tbk. as one of the leading companies within the cigarette industry in Indonesia. Dhoho airport focuses on air cargo and could be designated for pilgrimage (hajj or umrah) point in East Java.

[75] Ministry of Transportation of the Republic of Indonesia, 'Bandara Dhoho Kediri Diresmikan: Bandara Pertama yang Dibangun Tanpa APBN', available at <https://dephub.go.id/post/read/bandara-dhoho-kediri-diresmikan--bandara-pertama-yang-dibangun-tanpa-apbn> Last visited, 30 November 2024.

[76] *Id.*

[77] *Supra* note 37.

in Java or Bali Island via Singapore (SIN) or Kuala Lumpur (KUL) rather than transit in Jakarta (CGK or HLP).[78]

MoT Decree No. 31/2024 is issued when the number of aircraft in operation is far from optimal. Not a single airline wants to fly routes which are commercially not viable. Airlines aim to serve domestic trunk routes during the current high-ticket prices. In this situation, the MoT Decree No. 31/2024 might help national airlines to recover, but for many Indonesian airports, it is at a cost. The decree outcome is in contrast with the right to travel—both domestic and international routes—of each Indonesian national. As the country has committed to realising ASEAN Economic Blueprint 2025 through seamless connectivity under ASEAN Open Skies, and the sunset clause is also not familiar in the Indonesian legal framework, there is a strong ground for the judicial review of MoT Decree No. 31/2024.Hence, legal certainty and transport economics need immediate attention. Otherwise, investors shall be discouraged from venturing into PPP or FDI in the Indonesian airport sector.

4.2.2 The Hub and Spoke Concept

In parallel, the Minister of Transportation Regulation No. 40/2023[79] (MoT Regulation No. 40/2023), which amends a few provisions of the Minister of Transportation Regulation No. 39/2019[80] (MoT Regulation No. 39/2019) is also in force. MoT Regulation No. 39/2019 becomes the ground for hub (*bandar udara pengumpul*) and spoke (*bandar udara pengumpan*) concept implementation.[81] There are three different status of hub airports, namely; (i.) primary (*primer*) status for an airport that serves a minimum of five million passengers annually; (ii.) secondary (*sekunder*) status for airports serving between one million to five million passengers annually; and (iii.) tertiary (*tersier*) status for airports serving between 500 thousand to one million passengers annually.[82] A spoke criterion is granted indirectly to airports with less than 500,000 passengers annually, which are connected to hub airport(s).The enactment of MoT Regulation No. 40/2023 does not amend the hub and spoke criteria pertaining to passenger volume as introduced four years earlier.

MoT Regulation No. 40/2023 has simplified national airport policy by strengthening DGCA's role to speed up and be more agile in planning. Previously, consideration from aviation stakeholders through a public test forum was obliged to be held, which is now done away with. The other important provision in the new Regulation is regarding the criteria to change airport status from domestic to international.

---

[78] The authors own assessment through official airline websites from Indonesia, Malaysia, and Singapore. Conducted in between July to November 2024.

[79] Indonesia, Minister of Transportation Regulation No. PM 40/2023 on National Airport Management (1 August 2023).

[80] Indonesia, Minister of Transportation Regulation No. PM 39/2019 on National Airport Management (23 May 2019).

[81] *Id.*, Art. 17(1).

[82] *Id.*, Art. 17(2).

While previously an approval from the Minister of Defense was mandatory, now the "approval" is changed into merely a "consideration".[83] These two steps are encouraging FDI and PPP, especially in search of new airport construction from zero across the archipelagic.

As of today, a few major Indonesian airports are originally military airbases (*pangkalan udara*) of the Indonesian Air Force (*Tentara Nasional Indonesia or TNI Angkatan Udara*).Now, all operated by Angkasa Pura Indonesia, such airports, among others, are Husein Sastranegara Airport (BDO) in Bandung, I Gusti Ngurah Rai (DPS) in Denpasar or Bali, Halim Perdanakusuma (HLP) in Jakarta, Adisutjipto (JOG) in Yogyakarta, El Tari (KOE) in Kupang, and Juanda (SUB) in Surabaya. The last mentioned airport is owned by the Indonesian Navy (*Tentara Nasional Indonesia or TNI Angkatan Laut*). Although there are 42 military airbases, around 21 of them are functioning dually as civil enclaves. Their presence is significant as in most of the cases they are the biggest airports in each province.[84]

The dual use of Indonesian Air Force' military airbases has proven to play a significant role in increasing the local economy. Still, the Indonesian Air Forces are reluctant to further liberalise their air bases via FDI and PPP. It is normal as the security perspective should also be looked into and an equilibrium between business and security needs to be established. Such an initiative is becoming far more important as more airbases are being forced to open for scheduled flights due to airport infrastructure constraints in many regions.[85] There is also a need for considering problems could arise in civil-military relationships in case such an airport is levelled up as a hub or even levelled as an international airport.

It is also important to note that there is no precise definition of a "secondary airport". Neither ICAO/IATA nor Airport Council International (ACI) has defined what a secondary airport means.[86] Hence, there is no precise indication or clear answer as to whether Halim Perdanakusuma (HLP) Airport or Soekarno-Hatta International Airport (CGK) is the secondary airport of the Greater Jakarta Area. This situation leads to uncertainty for investors as the next due diligence is to determine which airport could become a hub and perform international flights. No investor would like to be on the losing side with the least opportunity, and this becomes the reason why FDI and PPP in airports often stalled.

[83] *Supra* note 79, at Art. 1(2).

[84] *Supra* note 46, at p. 265.

[85] *Id.*

[86] Ridha Aditya Nugraha, 'Quo Vadis Pembangunan dan Investasi Bandara', available at <https://www.kompas.id/baca/opini/2022/08/11/quo-vadis-pembangunan-dan-investasi-sbandara?open_from=Search_Result_Page> Last visited, 30 November 2024.

5 Conclusion

Liberalisation of the Indonesian aviation industry has paved the way for airport sector growth. To ensure such progress, ASEAN Open Skies based on multilateralism should prevail over bilateralism in Indonesia. This action shall secure connectivity to all Indonesian airports via more international flights.

Funding for airport infrastructure from the state and provincial budgets shall remain limited in the future as the new Ibu Kota Nusantara becomes a focus. Private participation is essential, and this requires legal certainty. Hence, the legal framework harmonisation between the Ministry of Transportation, the Ministry of Investment, and the Indonesian Air Force is essential. While the current equilibrium seems shifting to a higher level of protectionism with the hub and spoke policy as well as the limitation on airports serving international flights, the interests of airport are compromised. This needs to be addressed carefully. Indonesian success in overcoming these challenges shall determine FDI and PPP in Indonesian airports.

Chapter 9
Airport Economic Oversight in Thailand: A State Enterprise Challenge

Lalin Kovudhikulrungsri and Navatasn Kongsamutr

Abstract Effective airport economic oversight plays a crucial role in promoting efficiency, fairness, and competition within the aviation industry, ultimately benefiting airlines, passengers, end users, and the economy as a whole. The International Civil Aviation Organisation (ICAO) provides guidance to States and airport operators on regulatory mechanisms and governance on airport economics. Its core values on non-discrimination, cost-relatedness, transparency, and consultation with users are essential because airports often operate as monopolies or oligopolies within their regions, which can lead to market power abuses if left unchecked. Thailand presents an interesting case study in relation to economic oversight of a state enterprise operator. The Airports of Thailand Public Company Limited (AOT), corporatised from the state-owned entity in 2002, with the government retaining a 70% shareholding, operates six out of seven international airports in Thailand. This chapter explores how Thailand implements ICAO economic oversight framework into its national regulations and practices. Particular attention is paid to the law and policy applying to the state enterprise airport operator. Hence, it analyses how the AOT's state enterprisc status affects governance in both aeronautical and non-aeronautical activities, and how the abovementioned core values and airport performance management mechanisms, enshrined in ICAO documents, are translated into domestic practice, especially in case of airport charges.

Keywords Airports Authority of Thailand (AAT) · Airport charges · Airport ownership · Civil Aviation Board (CAB) · Doc 9562 · Performance management · Suvarnabhumi Airport

L. Kovudhikulrungsri (✉)
Faculty of Law, Thammasat University, Bangkok, Thailand
e-mail: lalin@tu.ac.th

N. Kongsamutr
Faculty of Engineering, Kasetsart University, Bangkok, Thailand
e-mail: navatasn.k@ku.ac.th

© The Author(s), under exclusive license to Springer Nature Singapore Pte Ltd. 2025

S. Bhat B. (ed.), *Aerodrome Governance in Asia*,
https://doi.org/10.1007/978-981-96-7568-5_9

1 Introduction

Economic oversight is defined as "the function by which a State supervises commercial and operational practices of an airport".[1] The national regulatory framework for commercial airport economics presents a multifaceted challenge. On one hand, ensuring user protection from exorbitant charges and potentially anti-competitive practices exercised by airports leveraging their monopolistic positions is paramount. Conversely, the established principles of a free market remain acknowledged as crucial drivers of economic growth and attracting private investment in large-scale infrastructure projects, such as airport expansions.[2]

In addition, airport operates among diverse stakeholder interests, leading to negotiation dynamics and conflicting priorities. Determining fair airport charges requires a careful analysis of operational costs, market conditions, and competitive factors and might face further challenges in allocating costs transparently and avoiding cross-subsidisation. Especially, when airport requires significant investment in infrastructure, which must be recovered over long periods, creating risks for investors and oversight challenges for regulators.

Lastly, there may be the rise of secondary airports or new entrants can disrupt traditional economic oversight models and lead to new market dynamics and competitive landscape. Adoption of technologies like automation and digitisation changes cost structures and operational models, challenging the oversight frameworks. Demand fluctuations from events like pandemics, geopolitical crises, or economic downturns can disrupt demand patterns, making pre-set regulatory assumptions obsolete. The demand for sustainable practices and compliance with environmental regulations often increases both capital and operational costs, while there are limited mechanisms to ensure that such sustainability-driven costs are shared fairly among stakeholders.

2 ICAO Policies

The Convention on International Civil Aviation 1944 (Chicago Convention) consists of four main parts: air navigation, the International Civil Aviation Organisation (ICAO), international air transport, and final provisions. Among several articles in Part I, Article 15 together with Articles 68 and 28 forms the bedrock of economic regulations on airport. These articles oblige Contracting States to provide services for air navigation and airports in their territory and they can charge for airport services. Article 15 establishes fundamental principles on airport charges mandating that aircraft operators regardless of nationality shall be charged on a non-discriminatory

[1] ICAO Doc 9562, Airport Economics Manual, 3rd edn., 2013, p. xiv, available at < https://www.icao.int/sustainability/documents/doc9562_en.pdf> Last visited, 18 November 2024.

[2] Isabelle Lelieur & Charles E. Schlumberger, *'Airport Business and Regulation'*, in Paul Stephen Dempsey & Ram S. Jakhu (eds.), *Routledge Handbook of Public Aviation Law,* (New York: Routledge, 2017), pp. 114–136 at p.128.

basis. In addition, such charges must be informed to the ICAO and are subject to a review by the ICAO Council.[3]

While the legal provisions in the Convention itself may not be exhaustive, the Chicago Convention empowers ICAO to provide further details. The Chicago Convention establishes ICAO as an organisation composed of an Assembly, a Council and other bodies.[4] The significance of the Chicago Convention lies in its creation of ICAO, which serves to develop rules for international civil aviation. Even though its objectives cover mainly on safety and orderliness in international civil aviation, the economic aspects of air transport are not neglected. This is evident in Articles 44(d), 44(e), and 44(g), which clearly state the objectives of preventing 'economic waste caused by unreasonable competition', and avoiding 'discrimination between contracting States'.[5] These three objectives naturally lead to a discussion of economic aspect in the ICAO Assembly. The Assembly has continuously resolved and consolidated the ICAO policies in the air transport field including policy on the economic aspects of airport services.[6] It must be noted that safety techniques are adopted and compiled in the Annex to the Chicago Convention. For airport, specifications relating to safety and technical issues are compiled and updated in Annex 14; however, nothing therein covers economic oversights. Economic policy on airports is not included in the Annex, but rather contained in ICAO documents, which have a softer legal force. As Abeyratne rightly pointed out, the legal status of ICAO policies contained in documents is only authoritative in practice.[7]

This section examines the role of the ICAO and its policies on economic oversight of airports. Strictly speaking, it mainly focuses on two ICAO documents, they are, the ICAO's Policies on Charges for Airports and Air Navigation Services (Doc9082) and the Airport Economic Manual (Doc 9562).

2.1 *Overview of Documents*

The Council, a permanent body responsible to the Assembly, plays a crucial role in airport economic oversight. Beyond reviewing charges that states submit, the Council appoints the Air Transport Committee to specifically address this area. The focus on airport economic oversight can be historically traced back to 1986 when the ICAO

[3] Convention on International Civil Aviation, 7 December 1944, 15 UNTS 295 [Chicago Convention], Art. 15.

[4] *Id.*, Art. 43.

[5] *Id.*, Art. 44 (d), (e), (g).

[6] For example, see ICAO resolutions on consolidated statement of continuing ICAO policies in the air transport field, such as resolutions A32-17, A33-19, A35-18, A36-15, A37-20, A40-9, A41-27, etc.

[7] Ruwantissa Abeyratne, 'A Critical Look at ICAO Policies on Charges Levies for Airports and Air Navigation Services', *Air and Space Law*, Vol. 34, No. 3, 2009, pp. 177–188 at p. 180.

Air Transport Committee developed a manual on airport economics, which is now known as the Airport Economic Manual (Doc 9562).[8]

The significant event shaping economic policy on airports was the Conference on the Economics of Airports and Air Navigation Services (CEANS) held in 2008.[9] Thailand, along with over hundred Contracting States of ICAO, attended the CEANS.[10] The conference's recommendations played a pivotal role in revisions to both Doc 9082 and Doc 9562, essentially forming the foundation for these documents.

Originally published in 1974, Doc 9082 has undergone periodic updates to reflect evolving practices. Its latest tenth edition in 2024 contains three sections: general, ICAO's policies on airport charges, and ICAO's policies on charges for air navigation services. The document also provides guidelines to assess the costs of facilities and services in airports and air navigation services.

The Airport Economic Manual or Doc 9562 has been revised twice in 2006 and 2013 after its initial publication in 1991. Its latest edition contains six chapters. It begins with ICAO policies on charges and States' responsibilities and discusses the foundation in Article 15 of the Chicago Convention. Chapter 2 focuses on the ownership, control and governance of airports as airport operators can be either government-owned or private-owned. Chapter 3 discusses the financial management of airport. Chapter 4 delves into the details of airport charges, while Chapter 5 addresses non-aeronautical activities. Last, Chapter 6 explores the financing of airport infrastructure projects.

2.2 *Economic Oversight on Airport*

It is the responsibility of a State to provide service, in an equal manner, for aircraft landing at airports in their territory. This obligation applies regardless of whether airports are operated by public or private entities. To ensure airport operators comply with the principles of the Convention, particularly in situations where they hold a dominant market position, international regulations mandate the concept of "economic oversight" by governments. This oversight encompasses preventing airport operators from exploiting their power; promoting non-discrimination and transparency in pricing practices; evaluating future investment based on a cost-effective manner; and safeguarding the interests of passengers and shippers.[11]

[8] *Supra* note 1, at Foreword.

[9] *Supra* note 7, at 182.

[10] ICAO Doc 9908, Report of the Conference on the Economics of Airports and Air Navigation Services, (CEANS), 20 September 2008, p.4 available at <https://www.icao.int/Meetings/ceans/Documents/Doc9908_en.pdf> Last visited, 18 November 2024.

[11] *Supra* note 1, at 1–6.

Economic oversight can be implemented through legislation including competition law, market regulation and cost of service regulation.[12] The latter also known as the rate of return regulation is designed to curb excessive profits from airports, which usually have a monopoly on services; as a result, airport may need approval for the fees they charge and their investments.[13] Owing to a diverse range of available approaches, ICAO suggests that States take into account several factors when selecting an oversight measure. These factors include the potential costs and benefits, the legal and institutional environment, and the existing governance framework.[14]

Two facets of economic oversight—airport ownership, control, and governance—and airport charges will be the main topics of discussion in this section.

2.2.1 Ownership, Control and Governance of Airports

Historically, airports have functioned as public services, leading to their initial ownership and management by States. However, a distinct trend towards airport privatisation has emerged since the 1990s.[15] This has resulted in a spectrum of ownership models ranging from full state control to private ownership.

Regardless of the ownership structure, effective airport governance remains crucial. Economic oversight plays its role to ensure that public or private airport operators are subject to governance. For example, a key governance concern for government-owned autonomous airport entities lies in ensuring their financial independence from undue government influence.[16] Corporate governance principles provide a vital framework for the management of airports, irrespective of ownership models. These principles can be applied to privatised airports, as well as those owned or controlled by governments.[17]

2.2.2 Airport Charges

Airport charges, regardless of whether the airport is government-owned or privately operated, constitute a key source of revenue. Both Doc9082 and Doc9562 are interrelated because Doc9082 is one of the main sources for developing the current edition of Doc9562 and they share common core principles derived from the CEANS, which are non-discrimination, cost-relatedness, transparency, and consultation with users.

---

[12] *Id.*, at 1–7.

[13] *Id.*, at 1–7.

[14] ICAO Doc 9082, ICAO's Policies on Charges for Airports and Air Navigation Services, 10th edn., 2024, p.1–2 – 1–3, available at <https://www.icao.int/publications/Documents/9082_10ed_en.pdf> Last visited, 18November 2024.

[15] *Supra* note 2, at 119.

[16] *Supra* note 1, at 2–5.

[17] *Id.*, at 2–10.

The non-discrimination principle, enshrined in Article 15 of the Chicago Convention and further elaborated in CEANS and both ICAO Documents, dictates that airport charges must be uniformly applicable to every air carrier. State aircraft should bear the cost proportionately as well.[18] Nevertheless, certain exceptions exist. For example, charges for international flights may differ from those for domestic flights, even if both utilise the same terminal facilities. This distinction often reflects the increased security requirements associated with international air travel.[19] Differential charges can also be introduced in specific circumstances. In specific instance, to incentivise service expansion or novel technology adoption, airport operators may implement discount or incentive schemes.[20] Since differential charges depart from the core principle of non-discrimination and, as such, are subject to additional requirements. First, transparency must be complied with through the publication of the purpose, criteria, and State aid (if any).[21] Second, cross-subsidisation for other services is prohibited. Third, users that meet the same criteria must enjoy the differential charges equitably.[22] In other words, subject to non-discrimination, users in the same category cannot be arbitrarily excluded from enjoying the benefits of the differential charges. Last, as an exception, the differential charges must be applied temporarily.[23]

The cost-relatedness intends to guarantee that airport operators will not make profit from tariffs, rather the calculation should be based only on the full cost of the provided services and functions.[24] Lelieur and Schlumberger point out that the public service nature of airports serves as a justification for regulating airport charges and preventing them from becoming overly burdensome.[25] As domestic and international civil traffic can be subject to dissimilar charges, they must be calculated on the basis of the service they use.[26] While cost-relatedness is a core principle, gradual implementation of charge increases can help minimise disruption to the industry.[27]

Third, transparency requires airport operators to maintain clear and accessible data to facilitate users understanding of charges. Particularly, this includes ensuring transparency in the purpose and criteria applied to any differential charging schemes.[28]

While the first three principles deal with the substance of tariffs, consultation involves the procedure in setting charges. Consultation between regulators, airport operators, and users can foster mutual understanding and create a thriving air transport

[18] *Supra* note 14, at 2–1.
[19] *Supra* note 1, at 4–20.
[20] *Id.*, at 4–29- 4–30.
[21] *Id.*, at 4–30.
[22] *Id.*, at 4–29–4–30.
[23] *Id.*, at 4–29—4–30; *Supra* note 14, at 2–2.
[24] *Supra* note 2, at 131.
[25] *Id.*, at131.
[26] *Supra* note 1, at 4–20.
[27] *Supra* note 14, at 2–2.
[28] *Id.*, at 2–2.

industry.[29] Consultation should be done throughout the charge-setting process even in times of no changes in charges.[30] In the case of revising charges or imposing new charges, ICAO recommends notifying stakeholders at least four months in advance to ensure sufficient opportunity to gather public opinion.[31] When the final decision is reached, a one-month notice period is also recommended.[32] Moreover, even after the amount of charges has been announced, the appeal process should be provided.[33] In case of directly collecting passenger service charges from passengers at the airport, consultation should encompass both the amount of the charge and the collection method.[34]

3 Airport System Overview in Thailand

Thailand is the third largest land area among ASEAN countries in Southeast Asia, bordered by Myanmar (Burma) to the northwest, Laos to the northeast, Cambodia to the southeast, and Malaysia to the south. Its capital is Bangkok, and major cities are Chiang Mai in the north, Udon Thani and Khon Kaen in the northeast, Chonburi in the east, and Phuket and Nakhon Si Thammarat in the south. The topography of the country is a diverse landscape including mountains in the north, the central plains, the Korat Plateau in the northeast, and coastal regions along the Gulf of Thailand and the Andaman Sea. The population is approximately 70 million people.

The first commercial airport in Thailand is Don Mueang International Airport, located in Bangkok, and it is one of the world's oldest international airports. It officially opened on 27 March 1914 as a Royal Thai Air Force base. The airport started serving commercial flights in 1924, which marked the beginning of its role in civil aviation.[35] Don Mueang remains in operation today, primarily handling low-cost domestic and international flights. Currently, Thailand's commercial airport network consists of 29 domestic and 7 international airports, including three airports without air services.[36] The top five busiest airports are all international airports, which are Bangkok-Suvarnabhumi, Bangkok-Don Mueang, Phuket, Chiang Mai, and Samui. In 2023, 13 of the 39 airports (one-third) served more than 1 million passengers per annum (mppa).

---

[29] *Supra* note 1, at 1–11.

[30] *Id.*, at 1–12.

[31] *Supra* note 14, at 1–4.

[32] *Id.*, at 1-I-4.

[33] *Supra* note 2, at131.

[34] *Supra* note 14, at 2–3.

[35] The Standard, 2023, *The First Opening of Don Mueang Airport*, available at <https://thestandard.co/onthisday27032457-2/> Last visited, 8 September 2024.

[36] Civil Aviation Authority of Thailand (CAAT), 2023, *Air Transport Statistics,* available at <https://www.caat.or.th/th/archives/65098> Last visited, 8 September 2024.

3.1 Airport Network: Market, OwnershipandRole

During the period from 2012 to 2019, before the COVID-19 pandemic began, the country's airport increased its available seats remarkably and continuously, rising from 82.9 mppa to 159.7 mppa (93%). The international market size is more than double (2.5 times) of domestic one. From 2020 to2023, the pandemic caused the worst years for the air transport industry. Since 2000, it was the first time that the number of seats produced in domestic market exceeded that of the international one. Regarding the domestic market, seven of the top ten busiest airports are all popular tourist destinations. For the international market, top region pairs are between Asia and Europe.

Thailand has several types of airport operators managing different airports across the country. There are four commercial airport operators in Thailand, which are Airport of Thailand PCL (AOT), operating six airports; Bangkok Airways PCL (BKP), operating three airports; Department of Airport (DOA), operating 29 airports; and Royal Thai Navy (RTN), operating one airport. Three of them are government-owned airport operators, AOT is a state-owned enterprise as well as a listed company with 30% of its shares floated for the public, DOA and RTN are purely government entities under the Ministry of Transport (MOT) and the Ministry of Defence consecutively. BKP is the only private operator as well as a listed company. One of its most famous and lucrative airports is Samui International Airport, located in Samui Island.

Regarding Thailand's airport classification, four categories of airport are defined by the Civil Aviation Authority of Thailand (CAAT). They are primary hub, secondary hub, regional and local airport. The primary and secondary hub airports are those serving the air service network for both domestic and international, linking the global as well as regional hub airports. Most of the connecting traffic is served by these hub airports. The regional airports serve multi provincial areas as their air services are better served with more choices of destinations, frequencies and airlines and are mostly located in the major province in each region. Lastly, local airports are located in medium-small provinces, where air services are limited.

3.2 Airport Market Structure and Concentration

Among the four airport operators, AOT, with its six airports, is the market leader, having the biggest share of passenger numbers in both domestic and international markets. In contrast, the DOA operates the largest number of airports (29 airports) around the country but holds 20.96% of domestic and only 0.81% of international traffic. BKP owns three airports and holds 3.68% and 0.29% of domestic and international market shares respectively. Noticeably, the airport market structure is considerably concentrated, especially in the international market where Herfindahl–Hirschman Index (HHI) is nearly 10,000, indicating a pure monopoly market.

4 Airport Ownership and Control: Evolution and Implications

Airport ownership and control have significant implications that affect the operation, management, and development of airports, as well as their broader impact on the economy, society, and the environment. This impact depends on whether an airport is publicly or privately owned and controlled. Airports owned by the government often focus on public service objectives, such as accessibility, safety, and national infrastructure. However, they may face bureaucratic challenges, which can lead to inefficiencies in management and operations.

4.1 Evolution of Airport Ownership and Control

The evolution of airport ownership and control has been shaped by a complex interplay of economic, political, and social factors over the past century and reflects shifts in governance, economic models, and regulatory approaches over time. This evolution can be traced through several key phases, shaped by the growing complexity of the aviation industry, government policies, and broader economic trends.

4.1.1 Governmentalisation and Centralisation (Early to Mid-20th Century)

In the early days of civil aviation, for example, in the United States, airports were typically owned by local authorities or the private sector. Immense increases in passenger volume, as well as aircraft size, weight, and technology, required huge investments beyond the capabilities of private finance at that time.[37] Therefore, airports were primarily developed and controlled by national governments or local municipalities, closely tied to national defence and postal services. This was due to the strategic and economic importance of air travel infrastructure, which governments viewed as public goods essential for national security, defence, and economic development. After World War II, airports expanded rapidly, with governments continuing to own and control these assets, often treating them as extensions of public transportation networks.[38] Like most of the other places in the world, in Thailand, the government

---

[37] Norman J. Ashford, Saleh Mumayiz, & Paul H. Wright, *Airport Engineering: Planning, Design, and Development of 21st Century Airports*, Fourth edition, (New Jersey: John Wiley& Sons, 2011) p. 7.

[38] Anne Graham, *Managing Airports: An International Perspective*, Fourth edition, (Abingdon: Routledge, 2014) p. 9.

had to take responsibility for developing civil aviation in addition to maintaining a military air service.[39]

4.1.2 Corporatisation and Decentralisation (1970s - 1990s)

Starting in the 1970s, many governments began to corporatise airports, transitioning them from government agencies into independent public entities with commercial mandates. This shift was driven by the increasing complexity and costs of running airports, along with the desire for more commercially oriented management. This is illustrated by the British Airport Authority (BAA), established in 1966, Australia's establishment of the Federal Airports Corporation (FAC) in 1987 and India's Airports Authority of India (AAI) in 1986.[40] The successful corporatisation of BAA provided an example for other governments to follow the BAA development path. Some national airport authorities were established and modelled on the BAA as it was prior to privatisation. The Airports Authority of Thailand (AAT), set up in 1979, the Israeli Airports Authority, the Mexican Airports Authority and Aer Rianta (the Irish Airports Authority) are examples of such institutional establishment.[41] Some governments also transferred airport ownership to local or regional authorities, especially in the United States, where municipal ownership became common. This allowed for more localised decision-making and management flexibility.[42]

4.1.3 Privatisation and Commercialisation (1980s - Present)

The 1970s oil crises and the subsequent economic challenges led governments to reconsider the financial sustainability of state-owned enterprises, including airports. The global trend towards privatisation in the 1980s and 1990s, inspired by neoliberal economic policies, also impacted the airport sector. Government decisions on privatisation involve assessing their influence over strategic planning decisions against the obligations and risks of ownership, and the benefits by transferring operational and financial responsibilities to the private sector.[43]

The UK pioneered airport privatisation, with the 1987 privatisation of the British Airports Authority (BAA), which controlled major airports like Heathrow. This marked a shift towards private ownership and operation, with the belief that

[39] Edward M. Young, *Aerial Nationalism: A History of Aviation in Thailand*, (Washington: Smithsonian Institution Press, 1994) p.14.

[40] PaulHooper, 'Privatization of Airports in Asia', *Journal of Air Transport Management,* Vol. 8, No. 5, 2002, pp. 289–300 at p. 294.

[41] Rigas Doganis, *The Airport Business,* (Florence: Taylor and Francis 2005) p. 12.

[42] Tae H. Oum, Nicole Adler, & Chunyan Yu, 'Privatization, Corporatization, Ownership Forms and Their Effects on the Performance of the World's Major Airports', *Journal of Air Transport Management,* Vol. 12, No. 3, 2006, pp. 109–121 at p. 111.

[43] Anne Graham, 'Airport Privatisation: A Successful Journey?',*Journal of Air Transport Management,* Vol. 89, 2020, pp. 1–9 at p. 2.

private companies could operate more efficiently. This move set a precedent for airport privatisation worldwide. In Australia, three major airports were privatised in 1995–1997: Brisbane, Melbourne, and Perth (Sydney Airport was privatised in 2002).[44] Many airports adopted public–private partnership models, where governments retained ownership of land and regulatory authority, while private companies managed operations. These models became popular in countries like India, Brazil, and some European nations, for example, the privatisation of Delhi and Mumbai airports in India through concession agreements attracted global private investment.[45]

4.1.4 Global Airport Groups and Competition (1990s—Present)

In the 1990s and 2000s, large global airport management companies such as Fraport, VINCI Airports, and Groupe ADP emerged. These companies manage and operate multiple airports worldwide, introducing more competition among airports in international markets.[46] As airports became privatised and corporatised, competition between them intensified, particularly in regions with multiple airports serving the same or nearby markets. This led airports to focus more on customer service, efficiency, and increasing non-aeronautical revenues, such as retail and parking.[47]

4.1.5 Privatisation in Emerging Markets and Greenfield Airports (21st Century)

As air travel expanded in fast-growing economies, many governments in countries like China, India, and the Middle East embarked on large-scale airport construction projects. This often involved private sector participation through concession agreements or full privatisation.[48] Governments in developing regions, constrained by fiscal limitations, turned to privatisation to finance the construction and operation of airports. Latin America and Southeast Asia saw significant foreign investment in their airports.[49]

The evolution of airport ownership and control has shifted from government-run infrastructure to increasingly privatised and corporatised models. These changes have led to a more commercially driven industry with greater competition and efficiency. Emerging markets and new technologies are likely to continue influencing how airports are owned and operated in the future. In addition, as passenger numbers

---

[44] David Gillen, 'The Evolution of Airport Ownership and Governance', *Journal of Air Transport Management,* Vol. 17, No. 1, 2011, pp. 3–13 at p. 5.

[45] *Supra* note 41, at p.14.

[46] Robert W. Poole JR, 'Annual Privatization Report: Aviation', *Reason Foundation,* 2021, pp. 6 & 7.

[47] *Id.*

[48] *Supra* note 48.

[49] *Supra* note 43.

increase and customer expectations evolve, airports are integrating advanced technologies to streamline operations, improve security, and enhance the customer experience. Airports have partnered with tech companies to introduce biometric screening, automated check-in processes, and smart infrastructure.[50] The focus on sustainability and reducing carbon footprints is reshaping airport management and ownership strategies. Future developments include green airport design, renewable energy usage, and partnerships for environmental innovation.[51]

4.2 *From Airport Authority of Thailand (AAT) to Airport of Thailand PCL (AOT)*

AAT, established by law in 1979 as a state-owned enterprise, was tasked with operating international airports.[52] Initially, the AAT managed Don Mueang Airport in Bangkok, expanding its portfolio to include other key airports like Chiang Mai International Airport, Hat Yai International Airport, Phuket International Airport, and Mae Fah Luang-Chiang Rai International Airport. Plans to develop a new international airport in Bangkok led to the creation of New Bangkok International Airport in 1996, with AAT holding a majority stake.[53]

One year later, the 1997 Asian financial crisis forced the privatisation of many state enterprises including the AAT. Despite this trend, the government opted for corporatisation rather than full privatisation of AAT.[54] This process involved several years of study and proposed various structuring options, including the establishment of a holding company, separate companies for Bangkok and regional airports, or a subsidiary structure with Don Mueang Airport as the parent company.[55]

Finally, in 2002, the winds of change finally transformed the AAT into a public company limited. This new entity, the Airports of Thailand Public Company Limited (AOT), assumed responsibility for managing all six existing airports—including the New Bangkok International Airport—without creating any regional subsidiaries.

---

[50] Airport Technology, (2021), 'Contactless Airport Boarding: Biometric Technology with SITA', available at <https://www.airport-technology.com/features/contactless-airport-boarding-biometric-technology-with-sita/> Last visited, 8 September 2024.

[51] 'Innovation and Technology in Airport Sustainability: ECO Airport Toolkit 2023', ICAO, 2023, p.7.

[52] Airports Authority of Thailand Act, B.E. 2522 (1979), Arts. 5 & 9.

[53] ICAO, 'Case Study: Thailand', available at <https://www.icao.int/sustainability/Documents/Thailand.pdf> Last visited, 5 September 2024.

[54] *Id.*

[55] Serirat Prasutanond, 'State Enterprise Privatisation: Privatising the Airports Authority of Thailand to Airports of Thailand Public Company Limited', available at <http://kpi-offscan.kpi.ac.th/elib/cgi-bin/opacexe.exe?op=mmvw&db=Main&skin=u&mmid=4885&bid=6034> Last visited, 8 September 2024 at pp. 12–13.

Furthermore, the corporatisation mandated an initial public offering (IPO) to raise funds for the new airport's construction.[56]

The AOT was formally established on 30 September 2002, and was listed on the Stock Exchange of Thailand in 2004. The Thai government retained a 70% ownership stake, while the remaining 30% was held by private investors.[57] Prior to its stock exchange listing, AOT published a prospectus detailing its revenue, categorised as aeronautical and non-aeronautical. The prospectus revealed that aeronautical revenue constituted approximately 60% of its revenue, with passenger service charges contributing 40% of that revenue.[58] The calculation formula for landing charges and passenger service charges was based on the consumer price index minus a factor determined by the Civil Aviation Board (CAB) to gauge the performance and efficiency of airport operations. Additionally, it incorporated a constant that accounted for the necessary and appropriate capital expenditures of the airport over a specific period, as determined by the CAB.[59] Notably, the prospectus also declared AOT's intention to adjust airport usage fees to maintain operational profit due to the significant capital expenditure incurred for the construction of Suvarnabhumi Airport. However, the prospectus specified that AOT would not apply the CPI formula to adjust the airport usage fee.[60]

5 Airport Economic Oversight in Thailand: Practices and Problems

Airport Economic Oversight in Thailand refers to the regulatory framework and policies that ensure the efficient, fair, and transparent operation of airports while maintaining economic balance, and public–private cooperation, all while aiming to maintain high operational standards and economic viability. Key elements of oversight in Thailand include; (1) the MOT providing general policy direction and being involved in approving airport fees and charges, (2) the CAB approving rates and conditions for collection of service charges, and (3) the CAAT, primarily responsible for aviation safety and security but also plays a role in overseeing as well as promoting economic aspects related to air traffic and airport operations.

---

[56] *Id.*, at 15–16, 24. See Royal Decree Defining the Authority, Rights and Benefits of Airports of Thailand Public Company Limited, B.E.2545, (2002).

[57] *Supra* note 56.

[58] 'Prospectus of Airports of Thailand Public Company Limited', available at < https://capital.sec.or.th/webapp/corp_fin2/cgi-bin/final69.php?txt_compid=0684&txt_offerid=000432&txt_secuid=01&txt_offertypeid=07&txt_language=T&start_date=2004-02-04 ≥ Last visited, 8 September 2024, at p. 111.

[59] *Id.*, at112.

[60] *Id.*, at 114.

5.1 Airport Economic Regulations

The core legislation for airport economic regulations in Thailand is the Air Navigation Act, B.E. 2497 (1954). The Act has undergone 14 amendments to adapt to evolving circumstances. Airport economic regulations are mainly outlined in Chapter 6 and 6bis thereof, which were recently revised in the 11th amendment in 2008. Chapter 6, on Aerodrome and Air Navigation Facility, underlines that airport operators can only charge specified fees or charges: (1) departure passenger service charge, (2) aircraft takeoff and landing service charge, (3) aircraft storage service charge, (4) ramp services charge, and (5) other charges determined by the Royal Decree, as a sweeping clause.[61]

The Act is designed to regulate the amount charged for each type of charge. The first charge is the departure passenger service charge, which is detailed in a chapter devoted to it. It can be collected for the purposes related to aerodromes and its facilities for passengers as well as environmental pollution objectives.[62] In order to oversee the charge amount, approval by the Minister of Transport with recommendations of the CAB is required. The airport operator must submit a comprehensive application to the Director of the CAAT who will forward the application to the Minister. The CAA Trequires the following documents: work plan or project outlining the implementation including the estimated costs, funding sources, and a plan for using the collected fees to support airport operations; financial statements for the current fiscal year and forecast for the next five years; fee rates for all types of passengers; passenger statistics for the past five years and a projection of passenger numbers for the next five years; a five-year airport development plan; result from consultation with representatives from users or relevant stakeholders; fee collection details describing collection methods; and any other additional documents required by the Director.[63] The air operator may collect this charge on behalf of the airport operator to facilitate passengers.[64]

The Act imposes restrictions on how the collected revenue can be spent, primarily for airport maintenance.[65] In addition, a portion of the revenue from the departure passenger service charge, at a rate not exceeding ten percent, can be remitted to a working fund for the DOA; however, in practice, the Minister has not yet ordered such transmission.[66] Thus, this means that one source of the DOA's income comes from other airports' passenger charges. To guarantee financial accountability, airport operators must prepare and submit an annual budget and a financial report to the Director of the CAAT within a specified period. Nevertheless, there are currently no

---

[61] Air Navigation Act, B.E. 2497 (1954), Art. 56 para. 1.

[62] Air Navigation Act, B.E. 2497 (1954),Arts. 60/37, 60/39.

[63] Civil Aviation Authority of Thailand Regulation No. 51 Passenger Service Charge Approval.

[64] Air Navigation Act, B.E. 2497 (1954),Art.60/41;Civil Aviation Authority of Thailand Regulation No. 50, an aircraft owner or registrant, or an air operator collecting a departure passenger service charge on the behalf of the owner or operator of a licensed aerodrome.

[65] Air Navigation Act, B.E. 2497 (1954), Art. 60/39.

[66] Air Navigation Act, B.E. 2497 (1954), Arts. 60/43, 60/44.

penalties for non-compliance with this requirement. Certain categories of individuals are exempt from passenger service charges, including members of the royal family, religious leaders, heads of state, government guests, children under two years of age, and transit passengers under specific conditions.[67]

The second and third types of remuneration are the aircraft takeoff and landing service charge and the aircraft storage service charge. The regulatory framework for these charges employs a two-tiered approach to limit airport operator discretion. Firstly, operators are prohibited from setting rates that exceed those established in the Ministerial Regulations.[68] Secondly, the CAB issues regulations prescribing maximum rates, which in turn cannot exceed the limit set by the Ministerial Regulation.[69] Significantly, the maximum rates for these two charges have remained unchanged since 2011, despite amendments to other rates within the Ministerial Regulations in 2016 and 2024.[70] Notably, neither the Act nor the Ministerial Regulations provide a clear rationale or methodology for determining these rates. In 2017, with CAB approval, the CAAT published rates for these charges. The published rates are based on the maximum takeoff weight of the aircraft and vary among different airport operators.[71] However, the regulations lack transparency regarding the underlying justification and objectives for this differentiation. The Ministerial Regulation provides exemptions for specific categories of aircraft including State aircraft of the Thai government, foreign military aircraft, aircraft used in International Red Cross services, and a broader clause permitting case-by-case exemptions granted by the Minister of Transport.[72] Two instances of ministerial exemption are noteworthy. The first exempts all commercial aircraft at specified regional airports operated by the DOA to attract operators.[73] The second case grants an exemption for medical service flights carrying donated organs for the Thai Red Cross Society.[74]

---

[67] Ministerial RegulationRe: Fees and Maximum Rates for Services in Airport, B.E. 2554 (2011), Art. 5.

[68] Air Navigation Act, B.E. 2497 (1954), Art. 56.

[69] Air Navigation Act, B.E. 2497 (1954), Art. 56 para. 2.

[70] Ministerial RegulationRe: Fees and Maximum Rates for Services in Airport, B.E. 2554 (2011); Ministerial RegulationRe: Fees and Maximum Rates for Services in Airport (No. 2), B.E. 2559 (2016); Ministerial RegulationRe: Fees and Maximum Rates for Services in Airport (No. 3), B.E. 2567 (2024).

[71] Office of the Civil Aviation Authority of Thailand Regulation No. 5 Re: Aircraft Takeoff and Landing Service Charge and Service Charges collected to Aircraft at Licensed Aerodrome or Temporary Takeoff and Landing Area for Aircraft.

[72] Ministerial RegulationRe: Fees and Maximum Rates for Services in Airport, B.E. 2554 (2011), Art. 6(7).

[73] Ministry of Transport Notification Re: Exemption of Aircraft Takeoff and Landing Service Charge, and Aircraft Storage Service Charge at Aerodromes of Department of Airports, B.E. 2560 (2017).

[74] Ministry of Transport Notification Re: Exemption of Airport Fees for Passengers and Aircraft of the Volunteer Pilot Club, Civil Aviation Training Unit, Royal Thai Air Force Conducting Missions for the Thai Red Cross Society in Travelling for Donation and Organ Transplantation, B.E. 2563 (2020).

Table 1 Regulations on airport charges in Thailand

	Departure passenger service charge	Aircraft takeoff and landing service charge and aircraft storage service charge	Ramp services charge, and (5) other charges
Legal basis	Section 56 and Chapter 6 bis	Section 56 paragraph 2 and ministerial regulation	Section 56 paragraph 3
Criteria	Required documents to prove the propriety of the proposed rate	Not specified	Fairness to consumers and the competitiveness of that airport
Approval process	Approval by the Minister of Transport with recommendations of the CAB	–	–
Rate	Proposed by airport operator	Not exceeding the rate set in the Ministerial Regulation and regulations of the CAB	Pursuant to the rules approved by the CAB
Consultation process	Required documents to show consultation result	–	–
Publication	Royal gazette	Royal gazette	Royal gazette

Ramp service charges and any other service charges must adhere to conditions and rates outlined in rules approved by the Director. The law imposes limitations on the Director's discretion, requiring them to consider consumer fairness and the competitive landscape of the aerodrome.[75] The CAB, with ministerial approval in 1979, established maximum rates for ramp service charges. These hourly rates are capped based on the available passenger seats in passenger aircraft and the MTOW for cargo aircraft.[76] However, before implementing ramp service charges, the Minister of Transport must designate specific ramps at an airport and publish this information in the Royal Gazette.[77] Despite the legal provisions, there has been no formal ramp service charge implemented until 2024 due to the lack of such a publication. This legal vacuum has created potential vulnerabilities, as airport operators may offer ramp services without any regulatory oversight under different names.

This analysis examines the legal provisions governing airport charges in Thailand through the lens of ICAO principles: non-discrimination, cost-relatedness, transparency, and consultation with users. It reveals varying degrees of adherence for each type of charge, as shown in Table 1.

[75] Air Navigation Act, B.E. 2497 (1954), Art. 56.

[76] Civil Aviation Board Regulation No. 23, Ramp Service Charges.

[77] Air Navigation Act, B.E. 2497 (1954), Art. 60 quarter.

The non-discrimination principle is reflected in the phrase 'fairness to consumers', which explicitly addresses only two categories of charges: the aircraft takeoff and landing service charge, and the aircraft storage service charge. These charges are capped by rates set in Ministerial Regulations, suggesting an attempt to prevent arbitrary variations. Nonetheless, for the departure passenger service charge, it is ambiguous whether consultation with users for this charge is conducted in a manner that upholds non-discriminatory practices.

For the cost-relatedness, the requirement for airport operators to submit detailed documentation, including cost projections and funding sources, when applying for approval of the departure passenger service charge suggests a regulatory concern. However, for the aircraft take-off and landing service charge and aircraft storage service charge, there are no specified criteria for determining rates. Additionally, there is no public record of cost justifications or deliberations during the rule-making process. These factors make it difficult to assess whether these charges are indeed based on actual costs incurred by airport operators. In addition, the working fund from other airport operators to support the work of the DOA, a governmental operator for regional airports, can be considered cross-subsidisation which raises debate over whether it contradicts the principle of cost-relatedness.[78]

Transparency is partially achieved through the publication of all charge rates in the Royal Gazette. The Act on Legislative Drafting and Evaluation of Law B.E. 2562 (2019) mandates public hearings for proposed legislation, followed by the publication of a summary report.[79] These measures represent positive steps towards increased transparency. However, the extent of transparency during the public consultation process for the departure passenger service charge is unclear due to the lack of publicly accessible minutes or resolutions of the CAB.

Consultation with users is a mandatory precondition and one of the required documents before seeking approval for a departure passenger service charge. Moreover, a public hearing is required under the Act on Legislative Drafting and Evaluation of Law B.E. 2562 (2019). However, this requirement may not be fully effective in ensuring meaningful user consultation for airport charges. Since the legislation and public hearing processes are conducted solely in Thai, foreign air carriers potentially subject to these charges may be disadvantaged due to language barriers. This limitation hinders meaningful participation and could potentially lead to a discriminatory approach.

[78] *Supra* note 1, at 2.36–2.37.

[79] See The Civil Aviation Authority of Thailand, 'Report of the Public Consultation on Draft Ministerial Regulation Regarding Maximum Fees', available at <https://www.caat.or.th/wp-content/uploads/2022/05/%E0%B8%AA%E0%B8%A3%E0%B8%B8%E0%B8%9B%E0%B8%9C%E0%B8%A5%E0%B8%81%E0%B8%B2%E0%B8%A3%E0%B8%A3%E0%B8%B1%E0%B8%9A%E0%B8%9F%E0%B8%B1%E0%B8%87%E0%B8%84%E0%B8%A7%E0%B8%B2%E0%B8%A1%E0%B8%84%E0%B8%B4%E0%B8%94%E0%B9%80%E0%B8%AB%E0%B9%87%E0%B8%99%E0%B8%A3%E0%B9%88%E0%B8%B2%E0%B8%87%E0%B8%81%E0%B8%8E%E0%B8%81%E0%B8%A3%E0%B8%B0%E0%B8%97%E0%B8%A3%E0%B8%A7%E0%B8%87.pdf> Last visited, 5 September 2024.

5.2 *ICAO Policies Versus Thai Practices*

In April 2024, the passenger charges at all AOT airports increased by 30 THB per person, sparking controversies over airport governance and the role of economic oversight in Thailand. This section compares and analyses domestic implementation by reviewing the case of AOT.

5.2.1 Airport Charge Oversight Scheme

ICAO's Policies on airport charges are described in Doc 9082, as discussed in Sect. 2.2.2 above, airport charge oversight refers to the regulatory mechanisms used to monitor and control the fees that airports charge airlines, passengers, and other service providers for using airport infrastructure and services. Airport charges typically include landing fees, passenger service charges, aircraft parking fees, and other service-related charges. These fees are critical to an airport's revenue, but they must be balanced with the interests of airlines, passengers, and other stakeholders. The Airport Economics 2023 Report illustrates three main sources of airport revenue which are aeronautical revenue, non-aeronautical revenue, and non-operating revenue.

In ICAO Doc 9562, there are three options for airports to recover their operating costs and essential non-aeronautical services. These approaches are commonly referred to as: (a) single-till or the residual method; (b) dual-till or the compensatory method; and (c) hybrid-till; noting however that the characterisation of aeronautical versus non-aeronautical activities may vary from State to State.[80]

(a) The Single-till: Under the single-till approach, both aeronautical and non-aeronautical revenues are considered when setting airport charges. In this model, all revenues generated by the airport, including those from activities like retail, parking, and real estate, are pooled together to help cover airport operating costs. The overall revenue reduces the fees charged to airlines for using aeronautical services like runways and terminals. ICAO also states in its DOC 9562, paragraph 4.127 that, by the application of this single-till or the hybrid-till approach, which will be discussed later, the airport charge (derived from the summation of cost of capital and depreciation of assets, as well as the cost of maintenance and operation and management and administration expenses) may be offset by non-aeronautical revenue. Therefore, it typically results in lower charges for airlines and passengers because non-aeronautical revenue subsidises aeronautical costs.

(b) Dual-Till: The dual-till approach separates the revenues and costs associated with aeronautical and non-aeronautical activities. In this model, only aeronautical revenues are used to determine charges for airlines. Non-aeronautical revenues, such as those from shopping or parking, are not factored into the calculation of airport charges, meaning airlines pay fees based solely on the costs associated with aeronautical operations. This often leads to higher fees

[80] *Supra* note 1, at 4–26.

for airlines, as they must cover the full cost of aeronautical services without any subsidies from non-aeronautical revenues. Many privatised or commercially focused airports prefer dual-till as it allows for more profit from non-aeronautical activities without reducing aeronautical charges.[81]

(c) Hybrid-Till: The hybrid-till approach is a middle-ground model that allocates part of the non-aeronautical revenues to offset aeronautical costs, but not as extensively as in the single-till system. A portion of the non-aeronautical revenue is used to reduce airline charges, but the airport retains some of the non-aeronautical profits. This model balances the interests of both the airport and airlines, ensuring some cost recovery for airlines while allowing the airport to benefit from non-aeronautical activities.[82]

There is an ongoing debate regarding the most effective method for economic regulation. Airports and airlines often tend to have opposing views. The single-till approach offers the advantage of lower charges for airlines; however, it leaves little incentive for airports to be flexible on building up its competitive advantage and value through non-aeronautical activities. On the other hand, the dual-till method may result in higher charges for airlines but it keeps non-aeronautical revenue separate and provides airports with incentives to develop the commercial side of their business which effectively is unregulated. This is unlike the single- till approach, since developments in commercial areas need not be accompanied by reductions in aeronautical charges.[83] The hybrid approach may become a viable alternative for inclusion of benefit from both single and dual till approaches with an appropriate setting ratio of non-aeronautical revenue to reduce the charges. Ultimately, the choice of model often depends on the regulatory environment of the country and the specific goals and business context of the airport and its stakeholders.

In Thailand, there is no government's official evidence indicating which till method the Minister of Transport chose under the advisory of CAB as primary law. The only evidence available is the ICAO's Case study: Thailand, which states that "Thailand airports operate under the dual-till regime."[84] This can be confirmed by comparing AOT's charge levels with those of the leading airport operators in the region, namely Incheon Airport, Hong Kong Airport, and Changi Airport. The results evidently show that AOT's charges are higher than those of Incheon and Hon Kong airport, which standat around 41.4% and 29.68% respectively. Although Changi Airport's charges are higher than AOT's (see Table 2), the cost of living in Singapore as well as level of service quality must be considered, which is much higher than in Thailand and at AOT. This leads to the conclusion that AOT's charges may be too high and could result from the dual-till approach that the government adopted.

[81] David Starkie, 'Reforming UK Airport Regulation', *Journal of Transport Economics and Policy*, Vol. 35, No. 1, 2001, pp. 119–135.

[82] *Supra* note 41.

[83] Anne Graham, *Managing Airports: An International Perspective*, Fifth edition, (Abingdon, Oxon: Routledge, 2018) p. 137.

[84] *Supra* note 56.

Table 2 Comparison of airport charges between AOT's airports, Incheon airport, Hong Kong airport, and Changi airport

Airport	International departing passenger charge		
	Local currency	Converted to USD[*]	± comparing with AOT's charge (USD)
All AOT's airports[**]	*730 THB*	*22.34*	
Changi airport[***]	*43 SGD*	*33.87*	*+11.53*
Incheon airport[****]	*17,000 KRW*	*13.09*	*−9.25*
Hong Kong airport[*****]	*120 HKD*	*15.71*	*−6.63*

[*] Calculated by using currency converter of VISA (https://www.visa.co.uk/support/consumer/travel-support/exchange-rate-calculator.html)accessed on 07/09/2024 at 08:20 GMT
[**] https://corporate.airportthai.co.th/storage/2024/06/Airport-Charges.pdf
[***] https://www.changiairport.com/content/dam/cacorp/documents/changiairportgroup/List%20of%20Fees%20and%20Charges.pdf
[****] https://www.airport.kr/ap_cnt/en/dep/depche/depche.do
[*****] https://www.hongkongairport.com/en/passenger-guide/departures/air-passenger-departure-tax.page

Moreover, the level of charges, which is currently used and is already higher than selected world leading airports in the region, has been approved by CAB since 2003and officially adopted since 2007.[85] For the past 18 years of adopting this charge level, the government has never determined a regulatory period to review and evaluate the appropriation of charge level, whether it is too high or too low. Under the dual-till scheme, airport operators are incentivised to invest and manage non-aeronautical activities independently, keeping all return in their own pocket, without having to share it with aeronautical operations. Interestingly, the approach of AOT for managing its highly lucrative non-aeronautical revenue, mainly generated by running duty-free and commercial areas, is the "master concessionaire" approach,[86] rather than other alternatives such as category concession or direct leasing[87] which allows airport to be in charge. Moreover, it is more effective in managing these vital areas and activities, which are very important for passenger experiences as well as for its own financial returns, similar to the practices of many world leading airports. This could imply that, either intentionally or unintentionally, AOT leaves significant business opportunities to the private sector rather than exploiting them by itself. This is because the till approach government selected makes AOT already satisfied with its return and have no interest in reducing the aeronautical charges. More or less, the

[85] *Supra* note 61.

[86] Bangkok Post, 'AOT told to Delay Airport Duty Free Bid', available at <https://www.bangkokpost.com/thailand/general/1645244/aot-told-to-delay-duty-free-bid≥ Last visited, 8 September 2024.

[87] Transportation Research Board of the National Academies, 'ACRP Resource Manual for Airport In-Terminal Concessions', available at <https://crp.trb.org/acrpwebresource2/wp-content/themes/acrp-child/documents/045/original/ACRP_54_Resource_Manual_for_Airport_In-Terminal_Concessions.pdf> Last visited, 8 September 2024.

political interest group could be part of the design of such policies, regulations, and the charge regulatory system, on the expense of public interest.

5.2.2 Cross Subsidies

According to ICAO Doc 9562, Chapter 2, Section D-Airport Systems, Networks and Groups, when a single airport owner/operator operates multiple airports in its system or network, the owner/operator needs to ensure that airport charges accurately reflect the cost of providing the service. "The airport owner/operator should ensure that an equilibrium is achieved between the interests of airports and users, and especially those of current and future end-users. In cases where cross-subsidisation within a national network is applied, full transparency is necessary."[88] This means that cross subsidisation among airport system/networks is allowed, under specific conditions, from ICAO's perspective.

AOT's aeronautical charges for all its six airports, which are Bangkok Suvarnabhumi Airport, Bangkok Don Mueang International Airport, Chiang Mai International Airport, Mae Fah Luang—Chiang Rai International Airport, Hat Yai International Airport, and Phuket International Airport, are the same. This includes landing charges, parking charges, boarding bridge charges, and passenger service charges, despite the size and traffic volume of those six airports which are very diverse. Furthermore, all cost occurred at each individual airport could not be the same for both capital and operational expenses. For example, Mae Fah Luang—Chiang Rai International Airport and Hat Yai International Airport are the only loss-making airports,[89] despite both handling 3.1 mppa and 1.9 mppa in 2023.[90] If AOT is now allowed to adopt a uniform charge rate for all its airports, it may try to find the solution to make these two airports profitable, such as spinning off and running the airports individually but integrally with its network, with the localised cost structure. This can confirm the argument about the negative side of cross-subsidisation that hinder efforts of the airport operator to achieve cost reduction and cost efficiency.[91]

5.2.3 Airport Economic Performance Management

To promote the four objectives of airport economic oversight, as detailed in ICAO's Doc 9562 Airport Economic Manual, States should ensure that airport

88 *Supra* note 1.

89 Airport of Thailand PLC, 'Financial Statement as of 30 September 2023', available at <https://investor.airportthai.co.th/misc/financials/20231120-aot-fs-fy2023-th.pdf> Last visited, 8 September 2024.

90 Airport of Thailand PLC, '2023 Airport Traffic Report', available at <https://www.airportthai.co.th/wp-content/uploads/2024/07/ANNUAL-REPORT-2023.pdf> Last visited, 8 September 2024.

91 IATA, 'Cross Subsidization', available at <https://www.iata.org/contentassets/fa95ede4dee24322939d396382f2f82d/cross-subsidization.pdf> Last visited, 8 September 2024.

operators maintain consultation with users and appropriate performance management systems.[92] The framework for airport economic performance management is described in Part B of Chapter 3 in ICAO Doc 9562 as well as in Appendix 1: Measuring Airport Economic Performance. The key processes of performance management are (1) identification of key management areas (KPAs), (2) definition of performance objectives, (3) selection of performance indicators, (4) establishment of performance targets, (5) creation and implementation of a plan, (6) assessment of performance results, and (7) publication of performance report. The processes 2–4 involve consultation with users and stakeholders. For transparency purposes, performance reports should be readily obtainable and be made available to all interested parties on a timely basis, subject to national regulations.

Under the above-mentioned primary legislation in topic 5.1, there is no clause that mandates a performance management system as an obligation for airport operators after the charges have been approved. This means that airport operators in Thailand are free from commitments to deliver a certain level of service quality, making an appropriate investment in capacity, or protecting the interests of passengers and other end-users. There was a remarkable growth in pre-tax earnings, which increased from 1.37 billion THB in 2010 to the highest amount in 2019 of 31.48 billion THB.[93] This is directly related to revenue generated from both regulated aeronautical and nonregulated non-aeronautical revenues. On other hand, Skytrax rankings of Suvarnabhumi Airport, the largest airport under AOT's management and the kingdom's primary hub airport, show almost continuous decline, from the 10th place in 2010 to a fall to 68th in 2022.[94] This may be the result from the absence of airport performance management system that should be in place and being overseen by the regulator (CAAT).

5.2.4 Departure Service Charge Adjustment

In 2020, the AOT, planning to use information technology to support airport management, signed a ten-year contract with Sky ICT for the provision of service and system maintenance of the Common Use Passenger Processing System (CUPPS). This system encompasses six subsystems concerning common use terminal equipment, common use self-service, common use self-bag drop, passenger validation system, self-boarding gate, and automated biometric identification system, deployed across its airports.[95]

---

[92] *Supra* note 1.

[93] Airport of Thailand PCL, 'Annual Report 2010–2023', available at <https://investor.airportthai.co.th/ar.html> Last visited, 8 September 2024.

[94] Skytrax, 'Top 100 Airports', available at <https://www.worldairportawards.com/> Last visited, 8 September 2024.

[95] 'SKY Acquires a Common Use Passenger Processing System Project from AOT Worth ฿8.62bn', available at <https://www.kaohoon.com/breakingnews/369099> Last visited, 8 September 2024.

Concerns have been raised regarding the transparency and adherence to government procurement regulations during the contract awarding process. As a consequence, AOT stated that the contract incorporates a risk management strategy to prevent private companies from charging excessively high fees for managing passenger volume fluctuations, by establishing a risk tolerance threshold of 90%.[96] Recently, the Deputy Minister of Transport confirmed that the bidding process was conducted appropriately and additionally, the service fees are reportedly based on actual costs, and any profits generated will be reinvested in AOT's airports and the broader community through social activities.[97] However, a potential contradiction emerges when considering the ICAO principle of cost-relatedness outlined in Sect. 2.2.2 above. This principle suggests that the airport charges should not excessively be collected for profit. As such, this statement casts doubt on the collected amount, even if it is ultimately used for corporate social responsibility projects.

As pointed out in Sect. 5.1, the CAB's documents and resolutions are not publicly available. AOT notifies air carriers responsible for collecting passenger service charges on its behalf approximately four months in advance of its increased amount.[98] This notification applies to all passengers, regardless of whether they successfully purchased and paid for tickets prior to the notification date but are travelling after the adjustment becomes effective. This practice differs from other airport operators, such as those in Hong Kong and Malaysia, both of which exempt passengers holding tickets issued before the effective date, even for travel on or after such date.[99] The AOT's practice can negatively affect airline operators, since they have to absorb the cost difference unless they explain the situation and request extra payment from passengers after the transaction is completed. For passengers, this extra retroactive charge can be perceived as unfair. Nevertheless, excluding the collection of the new rate from tickets issued before the adjustment cannot be treated as discriminatory, since at the time of the contract, the applicable charge was the lower amount, and neither a mistake nor a fraudulent activity was involved.

While the Air Navigation Act does not explicitly mandate the public disclosure of CAB resolutions approving airport charge adjustments, the MOT typically publishes a notification outlining the new rates in the Royal Gazette. However, these notifications are primarily intended for informational purposes and do not specify an effective

[96] 'Tracing back AOT's Explanation on the Passenger Boarding System Concession', available at <https://www.thansettakij.com/business/economy/575807#google_vignette> Last visited, 8 September 2024.

[97] 'MP Wirach of Pheu Thai Party Raises a Question about the Value of Using the PVS System at Airports. The Deputy Minister of Transport Confirms that AOT Calculates the Cost of the Service System and Opens a Transparent Bidding Process, Aiming to Improve Safety Efficiency', available at <https://www.tpchannel.org/news/26416> Last visited, 8 September 2024.

[98] 'Passenger Service Charge at Six Thai Airports to be Hiked by THB30', available at <https://www.nationthailand.com/thailand/general/40033200> Last visited, 8 September 2024.

[99] 'Passenger Security Charge to be Adjusted in Phases at Hong Kong International Airport', available at <https://www.hongkongairport.com/en/media-centre/press-release/2024/pr-1716≥ Last visited, 8 September 2024.; 'Mavcom Announces Revised PSC Rates Effective June 1, 2024', available at <https://www.thestar.com.my/business/business-news/2024/03/12/mavcom-announces-revised-psc-rates-effective-june-1-2024≥ Last visited, 8 September 2024.

date for the rate adjustments. For instance, AOT applied a new rate in April 2024, but the corresponding MOT Notification was published in the Royal Gazette in June 2024, without mentioning an effective date for the new rate.[100] While the notifications serve an informative purpose, their delayed publication can hinder transparency.

6 Conclusions and Recommendations

The legal framework for airport charges in Thailand exhibits a mixed adherence to ICAO principles. While the black-letter law indicates certain compliance, the actual implementation falls short of full conformity. The publication of rates in the Royal Gazette offers some transparency in the outcome. Nevertheless, the lack of publicly available CAB resolutions raises concerns about the transparency of the process, which is, if not more important, equally significant in ensuring transparency throughout. The cost-relatedness is difficult to validate owing to the absence of publicly available documentation. Only AOT and politicians have confirmed the link between charges and actual costs. Nonetheless, passengers and even airlines should not bear costs they do not use, and justifying the collection of charges for charitable activities does not align with the core purpose of charges, which should be used for airport service improvement.

The dual-till approach makes AOT focus and rely mainly on aeronautical revenue, which results in high and non-competitive airport charges and allows the private entity to leverage its interests in lucrative non-aeronautical activities instead, by adopting concession contracts, especially for duty-free and retail activities. As a state-owned enterprise, AOT should balance its commercial goals with public responsibilities. Abandoning the stake in non-aeronautical activities does not benefit either commercial goals or the public interest.

Cross subsidisation among AOT's six airports refers to the financial practice where revenues generated from more profitable airports (typically larger, busier hubs like Bangkok Suvarnabhumi or Bangkok Don Mueang airport) are used to support non-profitable regional airports (such as Chiang Rai airport and Hat Yai airport). While this approach can help maintain service levels across all airports, it also presents distortions of economic efficiency and discourages AOT from putting more effort into creating appropriate long-term solution for those loss-making airports, such as spinning off the non-profitable airport to let them have operational autonomy, focus on their own business objectives and design their localised business model and cost structure.

Furthermore, when the airport charge level is approved in the absence of a performance management system, AOT may struggle to demonstrate that its airport charges are cost-related and transparent. AOT may not have the data to show that it is maximising efficiency, which is critical for justifying charges to airlines and other

[100] Office of the Civil Aviation Authority of Thailand Notification Re: Departure Passenger Service Charges at Public Licensed Aerodrome, B.E. 2567 (2024).

stakeholders, and to monitor key operational metrics which make it difficult to identify and address inefficiencies, leading to increased operational costs that are passed on to airlines and passengers through higher charges.

In order to effectively promote economic oversight objectives, a performance management system needs to be in place. CAAT should require airport operators to demonstrate that its charges are aligned with its performance in areas such as safety, security, service quality, and operational efficiency. A lack of performance management system hinders the justification of these charges, increasing the risk that they will be rejected or modified. In addition, the system will help CAAT to monitor the operators and ensure that they operate efficiently. It does not impose undue costs on airlines, passengers and other users, and also prevent charging fees that are not linked to performance metrics.

Regarding the legislative framework, the Air Navigation Act and its subordinate regulations should be amended to align with ICAO policies. Ramp areas should be designated to enable the implementation of ramp service charges, and the working fund should be utilised as intended. In the short term, CAAT should develop a clear, transparent, and structured set of guidelines that governs airport consultations. These guidelines must align with ICAO Doc 9082 and ICAO Doc 9562 and focus on cost-relatedness, stakeholder engagement, transparency, and performance-based management. By establishing a robust framework for consultations, CAAT can ensure that airport charges are fair, justifiable, and aligned with both national regulations and international best practices. Moreover, all processes should be transparent, with the publication of results and underlying reasoning. All of these measures will enhance the credibility of Thailand's airports and maintain their competitiveness in the global aviation market.

Chapter 10
Airport Governance in the United Arab Emirates: Latest Facilities and Future Developments

Hassan Barman and Attila Sipos

Abstract The strategic management of the aviation sector of the United Arab Emirates (UAE) focuses on key areas such as infrastructure expansion, integration with urban mobility networks, technological innovation, and sustainability initiatives in alignment with the international standards set forth by the International Civil Aviation Organisation (ICAO) and the UAE's General Civil Aviation Authority (GCAA). The UAE positions itself as a global aviation hub, home to six international airlines and eight international airports, including the world's busiest international airport in Dubai (DXB). The UAE's main airports, such as Dubai International (DXB), Abu Dhabi International (AUH), and Sharjah International (SHJ) play a critical role in achieving the nation's broader economic and developmental objectives. The long-term vision of the UAE for aviation is outlined in Vision 2021 and Vision 2030. These frameworks focus on enhancing airport capacity, streamlining air traffic management, and adopting advanced technologies such as artificial intelligence and biometrics to improve passenger experience and operational efficiency. The authors also discuss the integration of airports with urban mobility networks to facilitate seamless, environmentally friendly, "smart" transportation systems to and from the airports, highlighting key airports infrastructure projects and their expansion. Sustainability is a core focus, as the UAE's aviation performers invest in "green airport" practices, sustainable aviation fuels (SAF), and carbon emission reduction initiatives in compliance with ICAO's and ACI's (Airports Council International) environmental guidelines and procedures. The opportunities and strategic priorities, such as technological advancement, are also analysed while emphasising the UAE's proactive cybersecurity and safety standards investments. It is concluded that the

H. Barman
College of Law, Master in Air and Space Law (MASL), University of Sharjah (UOS), Sharjah, United Arab Emirates

A. Sipos (✉)
Institute of Aerospace and Telecommunications Law, Ludovika University of Public Service, Eötvös József Research Centre, Budapest, Hungary
e-mail: sipos.attila@uni-nke.hu

Adv. LL.M. International Air and Space Law, Leiden University, Leiden, The Netherlands

© The Author(s), under exclusive license to Springer Nature Singapore Pte Ltd. 2025
S. Bhat B. (ed.), *Aerodrome Governance in Asia*,
https://doi.org/10.1007/978-981-96-7568-5_10

UAE's strategic management, grounded on ICAO and GCAA standards, is shaping its aviation sector and positioning the nation as a leader in global aviation.

Keywords Air navigation services (ANS) · Carbon Offsetting and Reduction Scheme for International Aviation (ICAO - CORSIA) · Dubai International Airport (DXB) · General Civil Aviation Authority (GCAA) of the UAE · Net Zero targets · Smart airports · Sustainable aviation fuels (SAF)

1 Introduction

The United Arab Emirates (UAE) has established itself as a key player in the global aviation industry, serving as a crucial hub connecting the East and West. Its strategic location at the crossroads of major international trade and travel routes has attracted significant passenger and cargo traffic in the UAE. The country's aviation sector is characterised by rapid growth, world-class infrastructure and commitment to innovation, making it a preferred transit point for millions of travellers worldwide.

The authors carry out a comprehensive analysis of the UAE's airport management practices, highlighting the strategic initiatives, technological innovations, infrastructure, latest developments and regulatory framework that have propelled the country's airports to the forefront of the global aviation industry. It explores the distinctive management approaches adopted by each of the UAE's key airports, examining how they have leveraged advanced technologies and sustainable practices to enhance operational efficiency, passenger experience, and overall competitiveness.

This part of the book delves into various aspects of airport management, including safety and security measures, customer service excellence, digital transformation, air navigation services and environmental sustainability. By providing a detailed overview of these elements, the chapter seeks to illustrate the UAE's commitment to maintaining its status as a global aviation leader and its ongoing efforts to adapt to the evolving dynamics of the aviation sector.

2 Major International Airports in the United Arab Emirates

In the aerodrome field, eight international airports require licensing in the United Arab Emirates. The Zayed International Airport (AUH) in Abu Dhabi,[1] Dubai International Airport (DXB), and Sharjah International Airport (SHJ) are the primary

[1] Abu Dhabi Airports (ADA) own and operate 5 airports: (1) Zayed (Abu Dhabi) International Airport (AUH); (2) Al Ain International Airport (AAN); (3) Al Bateen Executive Airport (AZI); (4) Delma Island Airport (ZDY) and (5) Sir Bani Yas Island Airport (SBY). Available at <www.adairports.ae/en>. Last visited 20 November 2024.

gateways that facilitate the UAE's status as a global aviation hub. Further important ones are the Al Ain International Airport (AAN), Ras Al Khaimah International Airport (RKT) and Al Bateen Executive Airport (AZI).[2]

2.1 Dubai International Airport (DXB)

DXB is one of the busiest airports globally, managing international passenger traffic, consistently ranking among the top airports for passenger throughput and cargo volumes. Dubai Airport operates both Dubai's International Airport, DXB and Al Maktoum International (DWC). The DXB functions as the home base for Emirates Airlines (EK), the UAE's national carrier, which operates a wide-ranging network of flights that connect to various destinations across six continents. DXB has been ranked the world's busiest hub for international passengers for ten consecutive years.[3] In 2024, DXB handled over 92 million international passengers, highlighting its significant role in global air travel.[4]

The airport's growth trajectory has been marked by continuous investments in infrastructure and technology, enabling it to handle increasing passenger volumes and deliver seamless travel experiences. Key initiatives include the deployment of biometric technology for immigration purposes (passport control process),[5] expedited check-ins and boarding, extensive use of automated baggage handling systems [such as Self Baggage Drop (SBD) systems including automated baggage scanning and weighing],[6] and sustainable practices aimed at reducing the airport's carbon footprint. The latter respect is vitally important as DXB had the highest carbon footprint

---

[2] For more information about these airports, visit <www.holidify.com/pages/airports-in-uae-2073.htmly> Last visited 20 November 2024.

[3] 'DXB Remains World's Busiest International Airport', *ARN News Staff*, 15 April 2024, available at <www.dubaieye1038.com/news/business/dxb-remains-worlds-busiest-international-airport2> Last visited, 20 November 2024.

[4] 'Top 10 busiest airports in the world shift with the rise of international air travel demand: (1) Dubai DXB; (2) London LHR; (3) Incheon (ICN); (4) Singapore SIN; (5) Amsterdam AMS', etc. *ACI Press Releases* about Airports Ranking regarding International Passenger Traffic. 14 April 2025, available at <https://aci.aero/2025/04/14/the-busiest-airports-in-the-world-defy-global-uncertainty-and-hold-top-rankings/> Last visited, 20 April 2025.

[5] At Dubai International Airport (DXB), passport control procedures take between 5 and 9 s without human intervention, depending on the movement and steps of the passenger. Mansoor Zainab, 'Passport control at Dubai Airports can now be completed in 9 s'. The new service that uses AI technology was launched to expedite immigration processes. *Gulf Business*, 25 May 2021, available at <www.gulfbusiness.com/fast-track-service-at-dubai-airports-reduces-passport-control-processing-time-up-to-9-seconds> Last visited, 20 November 2024.

[6] At Dubai International Airport (DXB), '32 self-service bag drop machines and 16 check-in kiosks can be controlled completely by personal mobile devices without touching the screens, thereby providing a safe and convenient airport experience'. 3 February 2021, *Emirates Media Centre*, available at <www.emirates.com/media-centre/emirates-enhances-smart-contactless-journey-with-touchless-self-check-in-kiosks> Last visited, 20 November 2024.

(carbon dioxide, CO_2) among international airports in 2019.[7] Therefore, numerous initiatives and achievements in airport management have been implemented to significantly reduce the carbon footprint and promote a more sustainable, eco-friendly environment at this leading global hub airport.[8]

2.2 *Zayed International Airport (AUH)*

Zayed International Airport (AUH) is the hub for Etihad Airways (EY), UAE's other national carrier. It complements Dubai's capabilities by focusing on connecting passengers to key markets in Europe, Asia, and the Americas. The airport has undergone substantial expansion to accommodate growing passenger numbers and enhance customer experience, including the development of the state-of-the-art Midfield Terminal (Terminal A). Zayed International Airport (AUH) has positioned itself as a key player in connecting global markets through its strategic expansions and partnerships. The launch of the newly opened Midfield Terminal, designed to accommodate up to 45 million passengers annually, underscores the airport's ambition to enhance its capacity and provide world-class amenities.[9]

2.3 *Sharjah International Airport (SHJ)*

Sharjah International Airport (SHJ) has a crucial role in the UAE's aviation ecosystem, particularly in the cargo and low-cost passenger segments. The SHJ Airport handled record numbers of passengers—more than 13 million in 2023. The airport serves as the primary hub for Air Arabia (G9), the Middle East's first and largest low-cost carrier, which connects to numerous destinations across the Middle East, North Africa, and South Asia. Additionally, SHJ airport's strategic focus on cargo operations has made it an important centre for freight traffic, contributing significantly to the UAE's economy and supporting global supply chains.

---

[7] Ian Tiseo, 'Airports with the highest carbon dioxide emissions worldwide in 2019', *Statista*, 26 February 2024, available at <www.statista.com/statistics/1453299/airports-with-the-highest-co2-emissions worldwide/#statisticContainer> Last visited, 20 November 2024.

[8] 'Partnership with Dubai Airports and ENOC introduces biodiesel as the exclusive fuel for all non-electric vehicles. This initiative cuts CO_2 emissions by 3,500 tonnes annually'. 'Dnata further reduces carbon footprint with fleet-wide transition to biodiesel in UAE', *Dnata Media Centre*, available at <www.dnata.com/media-centre/dnata-further-reduces-carbon-footprint-with-fleet-wide-transition-to-biodiesel-in-uae> Last visited, 20 November 2024.

[9] Ben Schlappig, 'Abu Dhabi Airport Terminal A: Etihad's Gorgerious New Home', *One Mile at a Time*, 6 December 2023, available at <www.onemileatatime.com/reviews/abu-dhabi-airport-terminal-a> Last visited, 20 November 2024.

2.4 Air Navigation Services (ANS) Serving the Airports

In the UAE, multiple entities provide air navigation services (ANS) to ensure comprehensive coverage and efficient management of the country's airspace. The General Civil Aviation Authority (GCAA), as a federal authority, is responsible for ANS in the upper airspace covering areas over the high seas in addition to offshore areas for the provision of en-route services through the Area Control Centre [located at Sheikh Zayed Air Navigation Centre (SZC)] in Abu Dhabi.[10] Additionally, ANS at airports are managed by the designated authorities for each Emirate through their respective Air Navigation Service Provider (ANSP), as detailed below:

- Global Air Navigation Services (GANS): Provides aerodrome control and approach control services for Abu Dhabi, Al-Ain and off-shores specifically for rotary-wing aircraft operations.[11]
- Dubai Civil Aviation Authority (DCAA): Oversees ANS in Dubai to ensure alignment with the GCAA requirements, while Dubai Air Navigation Services (DANS) manages ANS in Dubai.[12]
- Fujairah Department of Civil Aviation: Oversees ANS in Fujairah to ensure alignment with the GCAA requirements, while Fujairah Air Navigation Services (FANS) manages ANS in Fujairah.[13]
- RAK Department of Civil Aviation: Oversees ANS in Ras Al Khaimah to ensure alignment with the GCAA requirements, while SERCO manages ANS in Ras Al Khaimah.[14]
- Sharjah Department of Civil Aviation (DCA): Oversees ANS in Sharjah to ensure alignment with the GCAA requirements, while SERCO manages ANS in Sharjah.[15]

This collaborative structure ensures efficient airspace management and safe navigation services across the UAE.

---

[10] General Civil Aviation Authority (GCAA), available at <www.gcaa.gov.ae/en/home> Last visited, 20 November 2024.

[11] <www.gans.aero> Last visited, 20 November 2024.

[12] <www.dans.gov.ae/What-We-Do/ATM-Services> Last visited, 20 November 2024.

[13] <www.fans.ae> Last visited, 20 November 2024.

[14] <www.serco.com/me/sector-expertise/our-clients/cs-rak-airport> Last visited, 20 November 2024.

[15] <www.serco.com/me/media-and-news/2022/serco-and-sharjah-department-of-civil-aviation-celebrate-75-years-of-partnership> Last visited, 20 November 2024.

3 Significant Developments in UAE Airport Infrastructure

The UAE's aviation sector continues to demonstrate robust growth, driven by substantial investments in airport infrastructure aimed at accommodating rising passenger and cargo demands. This growth trajectory is underpinned by several major expansion projects currently underway or planned for the foreseeable future. These projects underscore the UAE's strategic intent to fortify its position as a preeminent global aviation hub, enhancing its capacity and operational capabilities. The UAE's airport expansion is designed to accommodate increasing passenger and cargo volumes, aligning with the International Civil Aviation Organisation's (ICAO) and Airports International Council's (ACI) global standards for passenger experience and capacity optimisation.

3.1 Dubai International Airport (DXB) and Al Maktoum International Airport (DWC)

Dubai International Airport (DXB) is recognised as one of the world's busiest airports. The airport's recent expansions encompass the development of new concourses and the extension of existing terminals aimed at managing increased passenger traffic more efficiently. Al Maktoum International Airport (DWC), also known as Dubai World Central, represents a monumental development in the UAE's aviation landscape. DWC opened its doors on 27 October 2013, while cargo operations had been launched on 27 June 2010.[16] As DXB will not be able to accommodate the projected and futuristic growth, the Dubai Government, in May 2024, announced an expansion of DWC airport, involving a record investment of USD 35 billion. The DWC aims to reshape the aviation landscape and revolutionise global air travel,[17] as it is envisaged to become the world's largest airport hub upon its completion. Its planned capacity will manage up to 260 million passengers and 12 million tonnes of cargo annually. These goals will be reached via facilities such as 400 aircraft gates, 5 parallel runways and 5 passenger terminal buildings at the airport, which will be five times bigger than the current DXB.[18] The expansion project is scheduled for delivery by 2028. The airport's strategic location and advanced infrastructure are expected to make it a pivotal hub for international travel and logistics.

---

[16] <www.dubaiairports.ae/corporate/our-story/dwc-dubai-world-central> Last visited, 20 November 2024.

[17] Bell Jennifer, 'Dubai's new Al Maktoum International Airport will be world's biggest and best: CEO'. *Al Arabiya English*, 13 June 2024, available at <www.english.alarabiya.net/News/gulf/2024/06/13/dubai-s-new-al-maktoum-international-airport-will-be-world-s-biggest-and-best-ceo> Last visited, 20 November 2024.

[18] 'Dubai World Central Airport Expansion', *Airport Technology*, Dubai, available at <www.airport-technology.com/projects/al-maktoum-international-airport-expansion-dubai/?cf-view> Last visited, 20 November 2024.

3.2 *Zayed International Airport (AUH)*

Zayed International Airport (AUH) opened in Abu Dhabi in November 2023, and it is one of the world's fastest-growing airport hubs. It is home to Etihad Airways (EY), Air Arabia Abu Dhabi (3L) and Wizzair Abu Dhabi (5W). AUH combines great design and technology to ensure all passengers experience at world-class levels of service and comfort whilst visiting the capital's airport.[19] AUH is the only airport in the world to incorporate a comprehensive 'Smart Travel' system that involves 5 steps: (1) Self-check-in; (2) Self-bag drop-off; (3) E-registration; (4) E-border gate; (5) Self-boarding.[20] The AUH airport's annual capacity is 45 million passengers (11,000 passengers/hour), with 65 gates (+14 remote), 140 check-in counters, 14 self-service counters, etc.[21]

3.3 *Sharjah International Airport (SHJ)*

Sharjah International Airport (SHJ) is also subject to an ambitious expansion project to bolster its capacity and service offerings. The project will be completed in 2027 and aims to elevate the airport's passenger handling capacity from 12 to 20 million passengers annually, with the possibility of increasing it further to 25 million in the future. Its higher capacity is needed urgently. According to the statistics for 2023, the SHJ handled record numbers of passengers: 15.3 million.[22] The main goals are strengthening its role within the UAE's aviation network and supporting the growth of Air Arabia (G9), the region's foremost low-cost carrier. The key components of the expansion include the construction of a new passenger terminal, the expansion of the current terminal and significant upgrades to the airport's runway and taxiway systems. These enhancements are designed to improve operational efficiency and boost the overall passenger experience.

---

[19] Available at <www.adairports.ae/en/OurExpertise/ZayedInternationalAirporty> Last visited 20 November 2024.

[20] *Id.*

[21] Joe Bates, 'Abu Dhabi's Game Changer', *Airport World*, 23 September 2024, available at <https://airport-world.com/game-changer-2> Last visited 20 April 2025.

[22] Alan Dron, 'Sharjah on the charge', Sharjah Airport has embarked on the next step of its major expansion programme', *Times Aerospace*, 7 August 2024, available at <www.timesaerospace.aero/features/airports/sharjah-on-the-charge-0> Last visited, 20 November 2024.

4 Technological Advancements

4.1 Integration of Cutting-Edge Technology

The UAE's airports are in the vanguard of integrating advanced technologies to enhance operational efficiency and optimise passenger experiences. Dubai International Airport (DXB) and Zayed Abu Dhabi International Airport (AUH) have been pioneers in deploying biometric screening technologies, which utilise facial (face and iris) recognition to expedite the boarding process. This technology not only bolsters security but also substantially reduces waiting times. AI-driven services, including predictive maintenance and automated customer service, are being implemented to optimise airport operations and deliver personalised services to travellers. For example, AI-powered chatbots provide passengers with personalised travel assistance, real-time flight information, baggage tracking, and airport navigation, thereby contributing to enhanced customer satisfaction and operational efficiency.[23]

4.2 Smart Airport Initiatives and Their Impact

Smart airport initiatives are integral to the UAE's strategy of establishing itself as a global leader in the aviation sector.

These initiatives encompass a wide range of cutting-edge technologies, including the support of passengers from check-in to boarding: e.g., (1) Automated gates and security checkpoints; (2) Self-check-in; (3) Self-baggage drop-off systems; (4) Automation of immigration processes; (5) Facial recognition; Digital guidance, Way finding support; (6) Health monitoring and alert systems,[24] etc.

There are also several smart solutions to support the airports' operational staff and management: e.g., (1) Intelligent cleaning systems and Waste Management, (2) Autonomous Vehicles (AV) systems, (3) Autonomous Mobile Robots (AMRs) for inspection, maintenance and repair (use for remote maintenance activity and

---

[23] Serhii Uspenskyi, 'Taking Flight into the Future or How Chatbots Make a Difference in Aviation: Discover the impact of chatbots in aviation and explore their examples, benefits and features', *Springs*, 4 June 2024, available at <www.springsapps.com/knowledge/taking-flight-into-the-future-or-how-chatbots-make-a-difference-in-aviation> Last visited, 20 November 2024.

[24] For example, to prevent the spread of infectious diseases and the outbreaks of pandemics, such as measuring body temperature with heat cameras. 'The communicable diseases which have many times affected civil aviation worldwide: e.g., Serious Acute Respiratory Syndrome (SARS-CoV coronavirus) 2003; Highly Pathogenic Avian Influenza (bird flu) (H5N1) 2005; Swine Influenza Virus (SIV) (H1N1) 2009; Middle Eastern Respiratory Syndrome (MERS-CoV coronavirus) 2012; Novel Virus of the Avian Influenza (H7N9) 2013; Western-African Ebola-Virus (EVD) 2014; ZikaVirus 2016; Severe Acute Respiratory Syndrome Coronavirus 2 (SARS-CoV-2) 2019'. Sipos Attila, 'The Liability of the Air Carrier for Damages and the State of Health of the Passenger: Accidents and Diseases (COVID-19)', *Hungarian Journal of Legal Studies—Acta Juridica Hungarica*, Vol. 61, No.1, 2021, pp. 87 & 88.

equipment monitoring tasks); (4) Rostering and Optimization of the movements of air carriers, ground handling and maintenance services, the work of operational staff, and even mass transportation within terminals.[25,26]

All these modern initiatives are aimed at creating a seamless travel experience. Smart solutions such as automated systems, data and biometric verification, Artificial Intelligence (AI), and the Internet of Things (IoT) devices in airport operations represent a significant frontier in the technological evolution of UAE airports.[27] These modern technologies contribute to faster processing times, minimise human errors, ensure more reliable and efficient airport operation and reduce costs.

4.3 Airport Sustainability Initiatives and Environmental Measures

The United Arab Emirates (UAE) is committed to advancing sustainability within the aviation industry, including airports. Airports are extremely energy-intensive. Therefore, airports must introduce various sustainable and energy-saving initiatives and measures. The main focus of airport operators is to ensure the passengers' comfortable and fast movement within the airport via efficient passenger service and efficient aircraft ground handling. To control the total carbon emission of the airport and to ensure environmentally friendly operations, the UAE's airports focus on adopting environmentally friendly technologies in their operations.

Sustainability is a fundamental priority for UAE airports. All UAE airports have implemented several green practices (e.g., energy-efficient lighting, waste management programs, and water conservation measures). Sharjah Airport (SHJ) ground handling team launched "Go Green" initiatives to generate cleaner air, lower emissions, and increase energy efficiency by replacing its existing diesel and petroleum-driven vehicles with environmentally friendly electric/solar vehicles. Sharjah Airport (SHJ) has a waste management policy which guarantees zero landfill waste at the Airport. The technical initiatives adopted by Sharjah Airport (SHJ) to reduce power consumption include energy-efficient airfield, passenger and cargo terminal lighting systems, energy-efficient chiller replacement, new software and sensors for A/C Units, solar reflectors and panel installation, etc. Sharjah Airport (SHJ) was the first airport within the UAE and second in the Middle East to have been accredited with Airport Carbon Accreditation Level 3+ *Neutrality* granted by the Airport Council International (ACI).[28]

---

[25] Global Infrastructure Hub, Smart Airports, available at <www.cdn.gihub.org/umbraco/media/3599/45-smart-airports.pdf> Last visited, 20 November 2024.

[26] Alketbi Khalifa & Sipos Attila, 'The Role of Smart Technology in Airport Facilitation and Security Control: ICAO Annex 9 and 17 Requirements', *Journal of Infrastructure, Policy and Development*, Vol. 8, 2024, pp. 1–17.

[27] *Id.*

[28] 'The second in the Middle East Achievement of Level 3+ Neutrality of the ACI's Airport Carbon Accreditation Programme: Sharjah Airport becomes the first carbon neutral airport in GCC', *Sharjah*

The Airport Carbon Accreditation (ACA)[29] is the only internationally recognised accreditation granted to airports by ACI for mapping and reporting, reducing, optimizing and offsetting their carbon footprint. The Airport Carbon Accreditation is designed to encourage and enable airports to implement best practices in carbon management with the ultimate objective of becoming carbon neutral.[30] Zayed International Airport (AUH) received the Airport Carbon Accreditation Level 3 *Optimization* certification. This certification recognised AUH Airport's efforts towards achieving carbon neutrality through the implementation of energy-saving measures, for example, 7,540 solar panel parking shades have been installed in the long- and short-term car parks in the whole new Terminal A, which saves 5,300 tonnes of carbon dioxide emissions per year, etc.[31]

4.3.1 The UAE's Role in Global Aviation Sustainability Initiatives

The UAE's aviation sector aligns with global sustainability efforts by incorporating the United Nations Sustainable Development Goals (SDGs) into its operational strategies. Particularly, SDG 13 (Climate Action)[32] guides the UAE's policies in order to reduce greenhouse gas emissions, enhance energy efficiency, and adopt sustainable aviation fuels (SAF). In line with SDG 7 (Affordable and Clean Energy),[33] UAE airports, including DXB, have implemented renewable energy projects, such as solar panel installation, to reduce their carbon footprint.

Airport Media Center, 16 August 2020, available at <www.sharjahairport.ae/en> Last visited, 20 November 2024.

[29] Airport Carbon Accreditation is owned and governed by ACI EUROPE in close cooperation with four ACI regions and with the support of ACI World. The seven levels of accreditation are as follows:

Level 1: MAPPING; Carbon footprint measurement.

Level 2: REDUCTION; Carbon management towards a reduced carbon footprint.

Level 3: OPTIMIZATION; Third-party engagement in carbon footprint reduction.

Level 3+: NEUTRALITY; Carbon neutrality for direct emissions by offsetting.

Level 4: TRANSFORMATION; Transforming airport operations and those of its business partners to achieve absolute emissions reductions.

Level 4+: TRANSITION; Compensation for residual emissions with reliable offsets.

Level 5: The Topmost level in the Airport Carbon Accreditation Programme, available at <www.airportcarbonaccreditation.org/about/7-levels-of-accreditation> Last visited, 20 November 2024.

[30] *Id.*

[31] 'Abu Dhabi International Airport completes new solar-powered car park', *Airport Technology*, 1 June 2021, available at <www.airport-technology.com/news/abu-dhabi-solar-car-park>. Last visited 20 November 2024.

[32] United Nations—Department of Economic and Social Affairs. Sustainable Developments. The 17 Goals, available at <www.sdgs.un.org/goals> Last visited, 20 November 2024.

[33] *Id.*

The UAE Government also announced the Net Zero targets by 2050 in November 2021. Following the Government initiative, the aviation sector established the Aviation Net Zero Task Force in May 2022 to explore and elaborate an internal solution toward Net Zero within the industry.[34] In January 2024, the UAE submitted its first long-term strategy (LTS) to the United Nations Framework Convention on Climate Change (UNFCCC),[35] including its 2050 Net Zero targets.[36]

The UAE is a strong advocate of ICAO's Carbon Offsetting and Reduction Scheme for International Aviation (CORSIA).[37] CORSIA seeks to reduce aviation's carbon emissions by 50% by 2050 through carbon–neutral growth. The UAE actively participates in CORSIA by investing in Sustainable Aviation Fuel (SAF) and carbon offset programs, ensuring that its airports not only comply with international environmental regulations but also serve as leaders in sustainable aviation.

The UAE's involvement in international forums and its proactive stance on environmental issues reflect its dedication to mitigating the aviation sector's environmental impact. One of the key platforms where the UAE has demonstrated its commitment to sustainability is the ICAO's Committee on Aviation Environmental Protection (CAEP). Within this framework, the UAE has actively participated in shaping global policies and practices aimed at reducing aviation's carbon footprint. This engagement was particularly evident during the Third Conference on Aviation and Alternative Fuels (CAAF/3), which the UAE hosted in Dubai in November 2023.[38] This event showcased the UAE's leadership and commitment to Sustainable Aviation Fuel (SAF) and other green initiatives. During CAAF/3, the UAE actively supported the adoption of ambitious targets for SAF production and deployment, emphasising the need for international cooperation and investment in new technologies to meet the aviation sector's carbon reduction goals. CAAF/3 underscored its strategic vision for sustainable aviation and its dedication to fostering innovation in green technologies.

Sustainable Aviation Fuel (SAF) is a cornerstone of the UAE's strategy to contribute to global aviation sustainability. SAF can significantly reduce the lifecycle carbon emissions of aviation fuels, providing an effective means for airlines to reduce their environmental impact. The UAE has been at the forefront of SAF research and development, investing in the production of alternative fuels that can be used in existing aircraft engines without significant modifications. One of the notable initiatives in SAF production in the UAE is the collaboration between Etihad Airways and

---

[34] ICAO A41-Working Paper (WP)/520 P/14 Assembly—41st Session Plenary, Agenda Item 5: Election of Member States to be represented on the Council, Candidature of United Arab Emirates (Presented by United Arab Emirates), 13 September 2022, 1. UAE Aviation Sector, 1.7. p. 2, available at <www.icao.int/Meetings/a41/Documents/WP/wp_520_en.pdf> Last visited 20 November 2024.

[35] <www.unfccc.int> Last visited, 20 November 2024.

[36] 'Net Zero targets—UAE Summary', April 2024, available at <www.climateactiontracker.org/countries/uae/net-zero-targets> Last visited, 20 November 2024.

[37] ICAO Annex 16 on Environmental Protection—Volume IV, CORSIA (2nd edn.), July 2023.

[38] ICAO, Committee on Aviation Environmental Protection (CAEP) and the Third Conference on Aviation and Alternative Fuels (CAAF/3), 2023, Montreal, Canada.

various international partners to develop and test sustainable fuels. Etihad Airways (EY), based in Abu Dhabi Airport (AUH), has been actively involved in several SAF initiatives, including the pioneering flight using fuel derived from plants grown in the UAE's desert.[39] The other great example is that Emirates Airlines (EK) has become the world's first airline to operate an A380 demonstration flight using 100% Sustainable Aviation Fuel (SAF).[40]

Beyond SAF production, the UAE advocates policies that support the adoption of green technologies and sustainable practices across the aviation sector. This includes efforts to improve aircraft fuel efficiency, enhance air traffic management systems, and promote the use of alternative energy sources at airports. As the aviation sector faces increasing pressure to reduce its carbon footprint and meet international climate goals, the UAE's efforts provide a valuable model for other countries and regions.

5 Integration of Airports with Urban Mobility Networks

5.1 Transportation Connectivity

Effective connectivity between airports and urban centres is crucial for the smooth movement of passengers and cargo. In the UAE, airports like Dubai International Airport (DXB), Abu Dhabi International Airport (AUH), and Sharjah International Airport (SHJ) are well-integrated with their respective cities through a range of transportation options. These include metro systems, buses, taxis and dedicated airport shuttle services. The rapid advancement of technology has led to the introduction of innovative solutions aimed at improving the integration of airports with urban transport networks.

[39] This project, integral to the Sustainable Bioenergy Research Consortium (SBRC) led by the Khalifa University of Science and Technology, aims to produce SAF using halophyte plants irrigated with seawater, demonstrating the potential for innovative, sustainable solutions in aviation fuel production. The world's first commercial flight using locally produced sustainable fuel was carried out by an Etihad Airways Boeing 787 powered by GE's GEnx-1B engines. 'Etihad Airways Flies the World's First Flight Using Fuel Made in the UAE from Plants Grown in Saltwater by Khalifa University', available at <www.advancedbiofuelsusa.info/etihad-airways-flies-the-worlds-first-flight-using-fuel-made-in-the-uae-from-plants-grown-in-saltwater-by-khalifa-university> Last visited, 20 November 2024.

[40] On 22 November 2023, this Emirates Airline (EK) flight, proudly commanded by Capt. Khalid Binsultan and Capt. Philippe Lombet, 'took off from Dubai International Airport (DXB) with one of four engines powered by 100% SAF, helping demonstrate its potential as a drop-in replacement that matches jet fuel's technical and chemical requirements, while being a more sustainable alternative. SAF can reduce carbon emissions by up to 85% over the fuel's life cycle when compared to conventional jet fuel'. 'Emirates world's first airline to operate an A380 demonstration flight with 100% Sustainable Aviation Fuel', *Emirates Media Centre*, available at <www.emirates.com/media-centre/emirates-worlds-first-airline-to-operate-a380-demonstration-flight-with-100-sustainable-aviation-fuel> Last visited, 20 November 2024.

There are other promising innovations for transport, such as autonomous self-driving vehicles (driverless taxis), flying taxis, and hyperloop.

- Autonomous self-driving vehicles are emerging as a potential solution for reducing traffic congestion and improving the efficiency of transportation to and from airports. In Dubai, 5 fully autonomous electric robot taxis are already in testing.[41]
- Another development confirmed by the Road and Transport Authority (RTA) is the flying (aerial) taxi prototype. The stations will connect four crucial points of Dubai: Downtown Dubai, Dubai Marina, Palm Jumeirah and Dubai International Airport (DXB). Projected to be 'launched by 2026, the taxis travel up to 300 kms per hour, with the capacity to hold four passengers with one pilot'.[42]
- Hyperloop is a new futuristic technology being explored in the UAE, which promises to significantly reduce travel times between cities and airports. Hyperloop systems are currently under development in the UAE and could drastically reduce the time taken to connect the cities with their respective airports.[43]

There are planned developments to integrate airports with urban transport networks further. Dubai's metro system is undergoing continual expansion, with new lines being planned to better serve the city's growing population and tourist traffic. There are also proposals to extend the metro to Dubai World Central (DWC), which is designed to become the city's primary airport in the future. Abu Dhabi's new Terminal A is a crucial part of the airport's strategy to expand its capacity and accommodate increasing passenger numbers. This expansion aligns with the country's broader development objectives, including major infrastructure projects like the Etihad Rail network, currently under construction to enhance connectivity across the UAE.[44]

The UAE Government has implemented several policy frameworks to support the development of integrated urban mobility systems. The Dubai Urban Plan 2040 and Abu Dhabi Economic Vision 2030 are two key strategic documents that outline the nation's commitment to improving urban transport and integrating it with airport infrastructure. Both plans emphasise sustainability, aiming to reduce reliance on private cars and promote the use of public transport.[45] The UAE is also investing heavily in smart city technologies, which aim to integrate transportation with digital

---

[41] *See*, Aimee, 'Dubai to start robotaxi trials next month in major autonomous push', *CNN*, 27 September 2023, available at <www.edition.cnn.com/2023/09/27/tech/dubai-rolls-out-robotaxis-mime-intl/index.html> Last visited, 20 November 2024.

[42] 'Dubai's Hyperloop Project: Revolutionizing Transportation in the City', *HiDubai Newswire*. Focus, 7 July 2023, available at <www.focus.hidubai.com/dubais-hyperloop-project-revolutionizing-transportation-in-the-city> Last visited, 20 November 2024.

[43] *Id*.

[44] Bovenizer Noah, 'Abu Dhabi Airports working on rail connection to new terminal—CEO'. 21 May 2024, available at <www.railway-technology.com/news/abu-dhabi-airports-rail-connection-terminal> Last visited, 20 November 2024.

[45] 'The UAE's Future Roadmap', available at <www.u.ae/en/about-the-uae/uae-in-the-future/uae-future> Last visited, 20 November 2024.

infrastructure. This will allow for real-time data collection and monitoring, improving the efficiency of transportation networks and ensuring smoother connections between airports and urban centres.[46]

5.2 UAE Vertiport Initiative

The electrical Vertical Take-Off and Landing (eVTOL) aircraft needs new infrastructure, networks and regulatory approaches. Regarding this new challenge, the AAM Business Park was built by ground infrastructure group VPorts at the Mohammed Bin Rashid Aerospace Hub (MBRAH) in Dubai.[47] Under this partnership, Archer and Falcon Aviation starts by developing state-of-the-art Vertiport infrastructure at *Falcon Heliport* at Atlantis, the Palm in Dubai and the *Marina Mall Heliport* in Abu Dhabi's Corniche.[48]

The UAE supports the Advanced Air Mobility (AAM) sector. Therefore, it has pioneered and long-maintained the oversight of helipads, a new generation of clean, sustainable and dynamic eVTOL aircraft, owing to which initiatives to reach non-traditional aviation stakeholders have accelerated, novel regulations have been developed, and forecasting models to cater for an Urban Air Mobility (UAM) sector within the UAE has been expanded. This new mode of transportation has many advantages, such as:

- providing fast movements and reducing congestion on the road;
- shifting time-consuming and inefficient cultural practices to smarter, faster and error-free methods;
- supporting efficient logistics background in emergencies;
- ensuring easy access to markets;
- search and rescue missions;
- multiple benefits for the military and police departments;
- flexibility to operate from anywhere.

[46] Nandkeolyar Karishma, 'Dubai's smart city plans accelerated due to huge cash injection', *TimeOut*, 18 December 2023, available at <www.timeoutdubai.com/news/dubai-digital-strategy-2023-2030> Last visited, 20 November 2024.

[47] 'VPorts links landmark agreement to create world's first advanced air mobility integrator centre in Dubai. VPorts announces agreement with GCAA and MBRAH', *Government of Dubai Media Office*, 8 December 2022, available at <www.mediaoffice.ae/en/news/2022/December/08-12/VPorts-inks-landmark-agreement-to-create-world> Last visited, 20 November 2024.

[48] 'Archer Aviation and Falcon Aviation are to jointly Develop a Vertiport network in Dubai and Abu Dhabi', *Falcon Aviation*, available at <www.falconaviation.ae/2024/03/12/archer-aviation-and-falcon-aviation-are-to-jointly-develop-a-vertiport-network-in-dubai-and-abu-dhabiy> Last visited, 20 November 2024.

5.2.1 Vertiports Regulations

Despite very limited ICAO guidance in this area, the UAE has developed the world's first national regulation on Vertiports. The new Civil Aviation Regulation for Heliports and Vertiports (CAR-HVD)[49] is in compliance with ICAO Annex 14 on Aerodromes—Volume II—Heliports,[50] FAA Engineering Brief No. 105 Vertiport Design,[51] and EASA Vertiports regulation.[52]

The new regulation focuses more on the design, operations, certification and oversight of Vertiports. The rules cover the certification requirements for publicly and privately used Vertiports.[53] Applications will be processed by the General Civil Aviation Authority (GCAA) by assessing physical aspects, operational procedures, the safety management system, the airspace, training, etc. The regulatory oversight and certification frameworks provide a roadmap for the safe and controlled integration of Vertiports into the civil aviation system while expanding critical national infrastructure to unleash the potential offered by VTOL aircraft.[54]

The GCAA relaunched its Heliport dashboard to include all certified Vertiports in the country. This database provides general information and technical details of each Heliport and Vertiport within the UAE.[55]

---

[49] UAE Civil Aviation Regulations (CARs) for Heliports (Onshore/Offshore), Vertiports (Onshore) (CAR-HVD), GCAA, Issue 1, March 2023, pp. 1–695. Effective from 1 September 2023.

[50] ICAO Annex 14—Aerodromes—Volume II—Heliports, (5th edn.), July 2020, ICAO Doc 9261 Heliport Manual, 2021.

[51] Federal Aviation Administration (FAA), Engineering Brief (EB) # 105, Memorandum, 21 September 2022, available at <www.faa.gov/sites/faa.gov/files/eb-105-vertiports.pdf> Last visited, 20 November 2024.

[52] European Union Aviation Safety Agency (EASA): Vertiports. Prototype Technical Specifications for the Design of VFR Vertiports for Operation with Manned VTOL-Capable Aircraft Certified in the Enhanced Category (PTS-VPT-DSN), March 2022, available at <www.easa.europa.eu/sites/default/files/dfu/PTS-VPT-DSN.pdf> Last visited, 20 November 2024.

[53] Use of Vertiport: (1) Public Vertiport; (2) Hospitality and tourism; (3) Private Vertiport; (4) Flight training; (5) Hospitals/Clinics/Helicopter Emergency Medical Services (HEMS); (6) Corporate facility; (7) Shipboard Vertiport; (8) Emergency Evacuation Helipad (Vertipad); (9) Temporary use. UAE CAR-HVD, Appendix III-A: Certificate or Landing Area Acceptance, 2023, pp. 652–653.

[54] ICAO Fifth Meeting of the Aerodrome Safety, Planning & Implementation Group (ASPIG/5), *UAE Vertiport Regulation*, Agenda Item 2: Regional Performance Framework for Aerodrome Safety, ASPIG/5-WP/9, Doha, Qatar, 13–15 June 2023.

[55] *Id.*

6 ICAO Standards and UAE Airport Governance

6.1 Regulatory Framework

The international civil aviation regulatory framework is guaranteed by ICAO and it is based on the Standards and Recommended Practices (SARPs).[56] The ICAO Council has the mandatory function to adopt the SARPs rules and, for convenience, "designate these as Annexes to the Convention".[57] SARPs constitute a complex regulatory mechanism which ensures uniform rules and procedures and enhances the safety of international air navigation for the civil aviation industry worldwide. The Paris Convention Relating to the Regulation of Aerial Navigation[58] with its 8 Annexes,[59] was the first international air law treaty adopted by the contracting States in 1919. The Chicago Convention on International Civil Aviation superseded the Paris Convention in 1944. The framework rules of SARPs are adopted in 19 separate Annexes to the Chicago Convention.[60] The Annexes of at least 4,000 pages contain more than 12,000 Standards.[61] It is the elementary interest and obligation of the contracting States to incorporate the SARPs rules set forth under the Annexes encompassing all major areas of civil aviation into their national law.[62]

Annexes 1 (Personal Licensing), 2 (Rules of the Air), 6 (Operation of Aircraft), 8 (Airworthiness of Aircraft), 11 (Air Traffic Services) and 14 (Aerodromes) are

---

[56] 'A Standard implies any specification, the uniform observance of which has been recognized as generally practicable and necessary to facilitate and improve the safety and regularity of international air navigation, and to which the contracting States will conform in accordance with the Convention'.

'A Recommended Practice is any specification, the observance of which has been recognized as generally practicable and as highly desirable to facilitate and improve the safety, regularity and efficiency of international air navigation, to which the contracting States endeavour to conform in accordance with the Convention'. ICAO Doc 10075 Assembly Resolutions in Force, Appendix A, 6 October 2016.

[57] Chicago Convention, Art. 54 (l).

[58] Convention Relating to the Regulation of Aerial Navigation, signed at Paris, 13 October 1919 (Paris Convention), Journal of Air Law & Commerce 94 (1930), available at <www.scholar.smu.edu/jalc/vol1/iss1/6> Last visited, 20. November 2024.

[59] *Id.*, Annex (A): The Marking of Aircraft; Annex (B): Certificates of Airworthiness; Annex (C): Log Books; Annex (D): Rules as to Lights and Signals. Rules of the Air; Annex (E): Minimum Qualifications Necessary for Obtaining Certificates as Pilots and Navigators; Annex (F): International Aeronautical Maps and Ground Markings; Annex (G): Collection and Dissemination of Meteorological Information; Annex (H): Customs Regulations.

[60] The most recent Annex to the Convention, that is, Annex 19 on Safety Management, has been applied worldwide since 14 November 2013. From the viewpoint of the regulation, Annex 19 does not contain new elements, but summarises the safety prescriptions which had been applicable formerly in the relevant areas of air transport under all the Annexes concerned by aviation safety (with the exception of Annex 17 on aviation security), ICAO Annex 19, Safety Management, (2nd edn.), July 2016.

[61] Sipos Attila (Rev.), '*Milde's International Air Law and ICAO*', Eleven International Publishing, The Hague, (4th edn.), May 2023, p. 20.

[62] *Id.*

of extremely great significance because of the operative implementation of flights, therefore, they mainly consist of Standards. The treaty-maker highlighted that "each contracting State shall undertake to collaborate in securing the highest practicable degree of uniformity in regulations, standards, procedures and organisation in relation to aircraft, personnel, airways and auxiliary services in all matters in which such uniformity facilitates and improves air navigation".[63] ICAO SARPs and procedures deal with various aspects of civil aviation, including the "characteristics of airports and landing areas; rules of the air and air navigation control practices; licensing of operating and mechanical personnel; collection and exchange of meteorological information; aeronautical maps and charts; customs and immigration procedures, etc., and such other matters concerned with the safety, regularity, and efficiency of air navigation as may from time to time appear appropriate".[64]

Standards are legally effective *erga omnes* (towards all), that is, they have binding effect for all Member States (they are valid in case of provisional differences communicated by the Member States to, and publicised by, ICAO). The binding effect of this legal institution springs primarily from the entirety and spirituality of the Chicago Convention and the commitment of the Member States, not from continued practice followed as law or from customary law.[65] Therefore, the effective implementation of SARPs rules is a basic requirement for the Member States worldwide. For the purpose of the most efficient support of implementation and familiarisation with problems deriving from the deficient implementation of SARPs rules, ICAO has set up the Universal Safety Oversight Audit Programme (USOAP),[66] and later, the Universal Security Audit Programme.[67] All Member States are obligated to participate in the safety and security oversight audit system.

[63] Chicago Convention, Art. 37.

[64] *Id.*

[65] Sipos Attila, '*International Aviation Law. Regulations in Three Dimensions*', Springer Nature, Switzerland, Cham, (1st edn.), September 2024, p. 210.

[66] ICAO Assembly Resolution A32-11, Establishment of an USOAP, September 1998.; ICAO Assembly Resolution A33-8, Expanded the USOAP to include audits of Annexes 11, 13, 14, September 2001.; ICAO Assembly Resolution A35-6 USOAP/CSA; ICAO Assembly Resolution A37-5 USOAP/CMA.

[67] ICAO Doc 9807 Universal Security Audit Programme Continuous Monitoring Manual, (3rd edn.), 2021.; ICAO Assembly Resolution A37-17, Appendix E refers; ICAO Doc 10,010-C/1172 Council Decision, 197th Session, C.MIN 197/1, Subject No. 52.1, 2013, pp. 11–12.

6.2 Compliance with ICAO Annexes

The UAE has been an ICAO Member State (since 1972)[68] and an ICAO Council Member (since 2007),[69] following ICAO's stringent safety oversight system to ensure that its airports comply with international regulations for aerodrome certification, flight safety and air navigation services. The UAE further integrates ICAO's cybersecurity guidelines to safeguard critical airport infrastructure amid increasing reliance on technologies.

The UAE's commitment to safety and security in aviation is rooted in its adherence to ICAO's Annexes, particularly Annexes 14 and 17. ICAO Annex 14 governs the design and operation of aerodromes, focusing on runway safety, infrastructure and operational efficiency. UAE airports strictly follow the guidelines provided in Annex 14, ensuring that all runways, taxiways, and lighting systems are maintained at the highest standards. This includes a runway debris monitoring system (RDMS),[70] foreign object debris (FOD) management,[71] and regular safety audits. ICAO Annex 17 emphasises "aviation security measures to safeguard civil aviation against acts of unlawful interference".[72] UAE airports comply with Annex 17 by integrating state-of-the-art security technologies, including biometric identification, advanced surveillance and real-time monitoring systems. These measures help ensure that both passengers and staff are protected while maintaining smooth operations at high-traffic airports like DXB.

---

[68] Date of notification of adherence 25 April 1972, available at <www.icao.int/publications/Documents/chicago.pdf> Last visited, 20 November 2024.

[69] The 36th Session of the Assembly of the ICAO completed the election of its new Council members. In PART III, the United Arab Emirates was elected on 25 September 2007. *ICAO Press Release*, PIO 09/07, available at <www.uae-icao.gcaa.gov.ae/en/Pages/Home.aspx> Last visited, 20 November 2024.

[70] Dubai International Airport (DXB) has implemented an advanced Runway Debris Monitoring System (RDMS) to enhance runway safety by detecting Foreign Object Debris (FOD), which can include materials like aircraft parts or luggage pieces that pose serious risks during take-off, landing, or taxiing. The RDMS detects FOD on the runways, continuously scanning for debris and providing real-time alerts to airport authorities, enabling immediate action to mitigate potential risks. This system's primary purpose is to prevent aircraft damage and improve safety by ensuring that runways remain clear of hazardous debris. Brannigan Laura, 'FOD Detection Systems Supporting Runway Safety', Airside Project Manager Dubai Airports, 2 June 2014, available at <www.icao.int/MID/Documents/2014/MID-RRSS> Last visited, 20 November 2024.

[71] *Id.*, The DXB Airport uses Tarsier FOD detection technology, which deploys radar and cameras to identify debris and notify ground staff in real-time.

[72] *Supra* note 67.

6.3 UAE's Regulatory Environment for Aerodromes

The UAE continues to maintain the number1 global ranking for compliance in the ICAO USOAP and USAP audits.[73]

The UAE Federal Act No. 20 on Civil Aviation Law (1991) addresses the applicability of the provisions of this Law to civil airports in the State and refers to some technical activities.[74] The Civil Aviation Law and the Federal Law No. 4 regarding the General Civil Aviation Authority (GCAA)[75] had been promulgated before the requirement of certification for aerodromes in ICAO Annex 14, Volume I became applicable. The GCAA had accordingly developed regulations and promulgated their implementation to give effect to the provisions of the Civil Aviation Law.[76] Thus, the regulatory framework contains the Civil Aviation Regulations (CARs) and other publications. The CARs are divided into nine parts. In the aerodrome field, the GCAA has developed and promulgated regulations in Part IX of the CARs. These regulations are comprehensive and establish the requirements for the State with respect to the provisions of ICAO Annex 14, including the regulatory framework for the certification of aerodromes.

Aerodromes' safety oversight functions fall within the ANS Regulations Section. In accordance with Part IX of the CARs, all international aerodromes require a licence. There are no domestic aerodromes that operate scheduled passenger services in the UAE. The GCAA has so far issued interim licences to all international airports. These were granted based on a set of minimum requirements. A timetable for the verification/approval of the different elements of the aerodrome manuals developed by the service providers is being followed in order to assist the airports in developing a manual in accordance with the requirements established by the GCAA.

6.4 IATA Standards and Operational Efficiency

IATA's Standards significantly influence the UAE's operational frameworks, especially regarding passenger experience and cargo handling. The IATA Operational Safety Audit (IOSA) certification[77] is applied across the UAE's major air carriers, which affect the airports' operations, ensuring best practices in safety and efficiency.

---

[73] The UAE has recorded the best results in an ICAO safety audit, rating it the highest in the world for compliance. *Times Aerospace*, February 2015. <www.timesaerospace.aero/news/atm-and-regulatory/uae-is-on-top-of-the-world-for-aviation-safety-compliance>.; <www.icao.int/safety/scripts/USOAP-Results.html>. Last visited, 20. November 2024.

[74] UAE Federal Act No. 20 (1991), Art. 3.

[75] UAE Federal Law No. 4 (1996) regarding the General Civil Aviation Authority.

[76] *Id.*, Arts. 6 & 7.

[77] The IATA Operational Safety Audit (IOSA) Program is an internationally recognized and accepted evaluation system designed to assess the operational management and control systems of an airline. <www.iata.org/en/programs/safety/audit/iosa> Last visited, 20 November 2024.

The UAE also benefits from IATA's Fast Travel initiatives,[78] promoting automation and self-service technologies like biometric screening and self-check-in systems, which have been deployed at Dubai International (DXB) and Abu Dhabi International (AUH) Airports. These advancements streamline passenger movement, reduce congestion, and enhance overall customer satisfaction. Moreover, IATA's global sustainability campaigns, particularly regarding CO_2 emissions reduction, align with the UAE's green initiatives. By adopting IATA's guidance on Sustainable Aviation Fuel (SAF)[79] production and carbon offsetting programs, the UAE remains competitive within the global aviation landscape.

7 Aerodrome Operations

The UAE plays a pivotal role in regional and international airspace management, collaborating with neighbouring countries and global stakeholders to enhance air traffic efficiency. UAE's General Civil Aviation Authority (GCAA) has been instrumental in optimising air routes and reducing congestion in busy airspaces. By working with regional airspace partners, the UAE has contributed to the redesign of air routes, improving safety, reducing fuel consumption, and ensuring smoother flight transitions. This collaborative approach aligns with global airspace management efforts spearheaded by ICAO. With 187 Air Services Agreements (ASAs), of which 159 are Fully Liberal and Liberal, the UAE is connecting many parts of the world.[80] Out of a total of 430 foreign operators registered with the UAE, over 190 airlines operate regularly at UAE airports and enjoy the benefits of the Open Skies policy.[81]

7.1 *Best Practices in Aerodrome Operations at UAE Airports*

UAE airports adhere to ICAO and GCAA regulations and incorporate the following best practices:

[78] 'IATA's Fast Travel Programme: Smoother travelling with facial recognition', available at <www.futureairport.com/companies/iatas-fast-travel-programme-smoother-travelling-with-facial-recognition> Last visited, 20 November 2024.

[79] 'Developing Sustainable Aviation Fuel (SAF)', available at <www.iata.org/en/programs/sustainability/sustainable-aviation-fuels> Last visited, 20 November 2024.

[80] *Supra* note 34 at ICAO A41-WP/520 P/14 Assembly—41th Session Plenary, Agenda Item 5, 13 September 2022, 1. UAE Aviation Sector, 1.5, p. 2.

[81] *Id.*

- Runway and Taxiway Safety Management: Advanced foreign object debris (FOD) detection systems like the Tarsier FOD radar ensure continuous runway scanning.[82] Regular inspections and the use of ICAO-compliant markings and lighting systems enhance operational safety.
- Ground Operations and Aircraft Movement: Airport—Collaborative Decision Making (A-CDM)[83] is employed at DXB and AUH, ensuring real-time communication between air traffic control (ATC), airlines and ground services to optimise aircraft movement.
- Air Traffic Management (ATM): UAE airports use next-generation ATC systems, supported by Performance-Based Navigation (PBN),[84] to optimise airspace use and enhance runway throughput.
- Emergency Response: ICAO-compliant Emergency Response Plans (ERP)[85] are regularly updated, with full-scale exercises conducted every two years to ensure readiness in case of emergencies.
- Sustainability Initiatives: UAE airports invest in eco-friendly infrastructure, including energy-efficient lighting and electric ground service equipment, aligning with ICAO's environmental guidelines.
- Passenger Flow and Terminal Efficiency: Biometric systems and Radio Frequency Identification (RFID) baggage tracking technologies at DXB and AUH enhance terminal efficiency, improving passenger flow and reducing congestion.

7.2 Drone Detection Systems in the UAE

The UAE has developed and implemented sophisticated drone detection systems to address the increasing risk posed by unauthorised drone activities near its airports. This is especially crucial given the potential disruption to air traffic and threats to aviation safety. With a growing number of drone-related incidents worldwide, the UAE has become a global leader in adopting stringent drone regulations and deploying advanced detection and mitigation technologies to safeguard its airspace, particularly in highly trafficked areas such as Dubai International Airport (DXB) and Abu Dhabi International Airport (AUH).

The UAE has employed a combination of radar, optical, and radio frequency (RF) detection technologies to monitor its airspace and detect unauthorised drone activity.

---

[82] *Supra* note 70.

[83] ICAO Doc 9971 Manual on Collaborative Decision-Making (CDM), (3rd edn.), 2018.; EUROCONTROL A-CDM Implementation Manual, Version 5 March 2017.; Airport—Collaborative Decision Making (A-CDM), IATA Recommendations.

[84] ICAO Doc 9613 Performance-Based Navigation Manual, Vol. I, Concept and Implementation Guidance and Vol. II, Implementing RNAV and RNP Operations (5th edn.), 2023.

[85] ICAO Guidance Material on Emergency Response and Contingency Planning. Annex 11. Vol. 1. Chapter 9, available at <www.icao.int/sustainability/ERP/Pages/default.aspx> Last visited, 20 November 2024.

These systems are part of a larger air traffic and safety management framework aligned with both ICAO Standards and the GCAA regulations.

The key features of the UAE's drone detection systems are as follows:

- Radar and Optical Detection: The UAE uses radar-based systems that can detect low-flying objects, such as drones, within a defined perimeter of the airport. These radars are coupled with electro-optical sensors, which provide real-time visuals of drone activity. This combination enhances accuracy, allowing operators to confirm the presence of drones and their exact locations.
- Radio Frequency (RF) Detection: RF detection systems track the communication signals between a drone and its operator. By identifying these signals, authorities can determine the direction and proximity of the drone's operator, which is critical for swift intervention and apprehension.
- Geofencing Integration: The UAE has implemented geofencing technology to prevent drones from entering restricted areas around airports. This technology, supported by GPS and RF systems, ensures that drones programmed with geofencing restrictions cannot enter the vicinity of airports, thus preventing unauthorised drone flights.
- Counter-Drone Systems: In addition to detection, the UAE has adopted drone mitigation systems, which can disable unauthorised drones. These systems use jamming technology to disrupt communication between a drone and its operator, effectively neutralising the threat by forcing the drone to land safely.
- Integration with Air Traffic Control (ATC): Drone detection systems in the UAE are integrated with existing air traffic management systems, ensuring that any detected drone activity is immediately communicated to Air Traffic Control. This integration allows for quick rerouting or the temporary halting of air traffic to prevent potential accidents.

The UAE's drone detection systems are fully compliant with the ICAO's guidelines on Unmanned Aerial Systems (UAS).[86] These guidelines emphasise the importance of protecting controlled airspaces from unauthorised drones. The GCAA has further enforced regulations on drone use, requiring mandatory registration for drones and adherence to strict operational guidelines. Unauthorised drone use near airports is met with severe penalties, ensuring that UAE airspace remains among the safest in the world.

There have been instances of unauthorised drone activity near UAE airports, leading to flight disruptions. In response, the UAE has significantly enhanced its drone detection capabilities and raised public awareness of the risks of flying drones near airports. Public awareness campaigns, along with legal measures, have significantly reduced unauthorised drone activity.

[86] ICAO Doc 10019 Manual on Remotely Piloted Aircraft Systems (RPAS), AN/507, (1st edn.), 2015.

8 Future Directions and Strategic Plans

8.1 Visions 2021, 2030 and Beyond

The United Arab Emirates has articulated a bold and far-reaching vision for the aviation industry sector, including airport management, driven by comprehensive strategic frameworks like UAE Vision 2021, Abu Dhabi Economic Vision 2030, Dubai Industrial Strategy 2030 and the vision 'We the UAE 2031″. These initiatives emphasise a transition towards a knowledge-based economy, with a focus on innovation, sustainability and enhanced global connectivity. The aviation sector, a key pillar of the UAE's economic growth (over 13% of the GDP),[87] is expected to play a central role in achieving these broader national objectives.

The Vision 2021 initiative[88] set the foundation for modernising the UAE's aviation sector. The primary goals included improving airport infrastructure, providing a sustainable environment, optimising air traffic management, and elevating passenger satisfaction. As the deadline approached, Dubai International Airport (DXB), Zayed International Airport (AUH) and Sharjah International Airport (SHJ) made notable advancements in increasing their capacity, adopting user-friendly business and innovative technologies.[89]

Looking forward, the Abu Dhabi Economic Vision 2031 framework[90] outlines a trajectory toward sustainable growth and leadership that will be reflected in aviation. The strategic initiatives outlined in Abu Dhabi Vision 2030 provide a clear roadmap for growth, emphasising innovation, sustainability and capacity expansion. While challenges such as global competition and environmental regulations will require careful navigation, the UAE's proactive approach to addressing these issues places it in a strong position to maintain its role as a global aviation hub. Key projects such as the Abu Dhabi Midfield Terminal and Dubai's Al Maktoum International

---

[87] 'The civil aviation sector contributes over 13% to the country's Gross Domestic Product (GDP), a percentage expected to multiply in the coming years due to significant investments by the country to continue developing this vital sector'. Basel El Sayed Mansour Nasr, 'The UAE Civil Aviation Sector: An Admirable Journey of Excellence and Leadership', 31 January 2024, available at <www.u.ae/en/participate/blogs/blog?id=1113> Last visited, 20 November 2024.

[88] UAE National Charter 2021, In the Golden Jubilee Year 50, available at < www.energystream-wavestone.com/wp-content/uploads/2015/11/UAE_Vision_2021_English.pdf> Last visited, 20 November 2024.

[89] As per the Global Competitiveness Report 2019 issued by the World Economic Forum (WEF), the UAE was ranked 7th in the efficiency of air transport services indicator and 12th in the infrastructure pillar. Infrastructure and Vision 2021, available at <www.u.ae/en/information-and-services/infrastructure/infrastructure-and-vision-2021> Last visited, 20 November 2024.

[90] The UAE will have achieved Abu Dhabi Economic Vision 2030, Environment Vision 2030 (Abu Dhabi), Plan Abu Dhabi 2030, Abu Dhabi Transportation Mobility Management Strategy, Surface Transport Master Plan (Abu Dhabi), Dubai Autonomous Transportation Strategy, Dubai Industrial Strategy 2030, Dubai 3D Printing Strategy and UN's 2030 Agenda, etc., available at <www.actvet.gov.ae/en/media/lists/elibraryld/economic-vision-2030-full-versionen.pdf> .; <https://u.ae/en/about-the-uae/strategies-initiatives-and-awards/strategies-plans-and-visions/industry-science-and-technology/dubai-industrial-strategy-2030>. Last visited, 20 April 2025.

Airport will significantly enhance passenger and cargo handling capacities. These projects not only aim to support the UAE's position as a global hub but also align with sustainability targets. The UAE's vision is also deeply committed to integrating advanced technologies to streamline airport operations. The development of smart airports is a cornerstone of this strategy.

The next step forward is the vision: 'We the UAE 2031', which represents a national plan through which the UAE will continue its development path for the next 10 years, with a focus on social, economic, investment and development aspects.[91]

8.2 *Opportunities*

The UAE has identified several strategic priorities to ensure continued success and competitiveness in the global aviation sector: (1) Airport Infrastructure Expansion, (2) Sustainability Initiatives, and (3) Technological Innovation. These areas determine the opportunities that will support the sector's growth trajectory.. The ever-increasing global passenger traffic and cargo volumes align with the UAE's continuous approach to increasing its investments in technology, customer service and competitive pricing to maintain its strategic advantage.

The UAE plays a pivotal role in regional and international airspace management, collaborating with neighbouring countries and global stakeholders to enhance air traffic efficiency. UAE's General Civil Aviation Authority (GCAA) has been instrumental in optimising air routes and reducing congestion in busy airspaces. By working with regional airspace partners, the UAE has contributed to the redesign of air routes, improving safety, reducing fuel consumption, and ensuring smoother flight transitions. This collaborative approach aligns with global airspace management efforts spearheaded by ICAO.

The UAE fosters an open skies environment, granting unrestricted access to its aviation market, which is exceptionally compelling due to several quantifiable factors. These include its status as a global hub with extensive passenger traffic, its strategic geographic location connecting major international routes, and the remarkable economic contributions from the aviation sector, all of which collectively establish the UAE as an important gateway in the global aviation market.

The UAE is outstanding in terms of possessing a developed and pro-active robust strategy to manage and mitigate risks associated with technological disruption and cybersecurity within the aviation sector. As airports increasingly rely on advanced systems such as Artificial Intelligence (AI), automation, and Internet of Things (IoT) solutions, the UAE has been ahead of the curve in implementing robust cybersecurity measures. By proactively investing in cutting-edge technologies and comprehensive cybersecurity protocols, the UAE is safeguarding its critical infrastructure from potential threats like cyberattacks and system malfunctions.

[91] Available at <https://u.ae/en/about-the-uae/strategies-initiatives-and-awards/strategies-plans-and-visions/innovation-and-future-shaping/we-the-uae-2031-vision>. Last visited, 20 April 2025.

9 Conclusion

The UAE's aviation sector has demonstrated remarkable growth and innovation, supported by ambitious infrastructure projects, cutting-edge technological integration, and a strong focus on sustainability. The development of world-class airports like Dubai International Airport, Zayed International Airport, and Sharjah International Airport has positioned the UAE as a global leader in both passenger and cargo traffic.

Efforts to integrate urban mobility solutions, including metro systems and smart transport networks, have further enhanced airport accessibility and efficiency. The focus on environmental sustainability, through initiatives like SAF and green airport designs, aligns the UAE with international best practices in aviation. By leveraging its strategic location, investing in advanced technologies and prioritising sustainability, the UAE is well-positioned to set new benchmarks in airport management and aviation excellence.

In conclusion, the UAE's adherence to UN, ICAO, IATA, and ACI standards highlights its commitment to maintaining global best practices in airport governance. By integrating international safety, operational, and environmental standards into its aviation management framework, the UAE remains a leader in global aviation. These standards enable the country to continuously enhance its operational efficiency, sustainability initiatives, and overall airport governance while achieving the strategic objectives outlined in its Vision, particularly the vision "We the UAE 2031".

Chapter 11
Implementation of International Norms Relating to Airport Security in Bangladesh

Muhammad Ekramul Haque and Md. Jahid-Al-Mamun

Abstract The term "security" denotes safeguarding against negative events happening with malicious intent of causing harm or achieving evil goals. "Airport Security", more specifically, as defined by the International Civil Aviation Organization (ICAO), is the safeguarding of international civil aviation from unauthorised interferences. Airports serve as boundaries between the state where the airline passenger lands and the outside world. It is also the last location where someone can get checked before boarding an aircraft. Additionally, cargo is loaded onto an aircraft at the aerodrome before take-off. Therefore, it is imperative for Bangladesh to ensure airport security to defend national borders and sovereignty, defend against external threats, and ensure the safety of passengers, airline employees, and airport staff internally. International conventions like the Chicago Convention and its annex 17, the guidelines, regulations, and procedures set forth by international aviation organisations like the ICAO and the International Air Transport Association (IATA) comprise the international norms that govern airport security. These standards include things like emergency readiness, access control, perimeter security, cargo security, and screening of passengers and their belongings etc. This chapter aims to critically assess the implementation of these norms in the context of Bangladesh, which is paramount to ensuring safe and secure aviation operations. In doing so, this chapter will explore the discrepancies between established international standards and their eventual practical application in Bangladesh's airport security framework, the challenges to ensure effective implementation, and the way forward.

Keywords Air Navigation Order (ANO) · Airport security · Annex 17 · Civil Aviation Act · Civil Aviation Authority of Bangladesh (CAAB) · Hazrat Shahjalal International Airport (HSIA) · International Air Transport Association (IATA)

M. E. Haque
Faculty of Law, University of Dhaka, Dhaka, Bangladesh
e-mail: ekram.haque@du.ac.bd

Md. Jahid-Al-Mamun (✉)
Department of Law, University of Dhaka, Dhaka, Bangladesh
e-mail: jahid.mamun@du.ac.bd

© The Author(s), under exclusive license to Springer Nature Singapore Pte Ltd. 2025
S. Bhat B. (ed.), *Aerodrome Governance in Asia*,
https://doi.org/10.1007/978-981-96-7568-5_11

1 Introduction

The airport serves as the boundary between the state where the airline passenger lands and the outside world.[1] Therefore, it is imperative for a state to ensure airport security to defend national borders and sovereignty, to defend against external threats, and to ensure the safety of passengers, airline employees, and airport staff internally. The term "security" denotes safeguarding against negative events happening with malicious intent of causing harm or achieving evil goals.[2] "Airport Security" is, on the other hand, as defined by the International Civil Aviation Organization (ICAO), "safeguarding international civil aviation against acts of unlawful interference".[3] It refers to the measures, techniques and methods implemented at airports to protect airport and aircraft infrastructure, large number of passengers, airport staff, etc., from criminal activities and other threats, including terrorism, hijacking, sabotage, etc.[4] Putting it differently, Airport Security connotes "safety from man-made intentional harm".[5] Airports play a significant role in today's globalised world, they connect continents, states, and even small villages through 3,250 airports.[6] With the growing dependency of global economic growth and economic development on international air transportation,[7] ensuring airport security has become more significant than ever before. The international aviation sector, primarily governed by the International Civil Aviation Authority and supported by United Nations Security Council (UNSC) resolutions, has developed a comprehensive legal framework comprising norms, regulations, and standards to ensure effective airport security management worldwide.[8]

Since the inception of aviation, it has "imbued the public mind with feelings of awe accompanied by outsized fears regarding its associated dangers", which essentially

---

[1] Ruwantissa Abeyratne, *Law and Regulation of Aerodromes*, (Springer Science & Business Media, 2014) p. 169.

[2] Anders Pousette & *et.al.*, 'Aerodrome Security Climate: Development and Validation of the Aerodrome Security Climate Questionnaire (ADSECQ)' *Journal of Transportation Security*, Vol. 14, No. 1, 2021, pp. 19–39, at 19.

[3] ICAO, 'Security: Safeguarding International Civil Aviation against Acts of Unlawful Interference, Annex 17 to the Convention on International Civil Aviation', 2022, available at <https://store.icao.int/en/annex-17-security> Last visited, 23 April 2024.

[4] Carl Rizk, 'Contribution to the Evaluation and Optimization of Passengers' Screening at Airports', Institut National Polytechnique de Toulouse (INPT), 2019.

[5] Jung Sang Yool, *A Legal Analysis of Aviation Security under the International Legal Regime*, 2005, available at <https://trid.trb.org/View/854924> Last visited, 2 October 2024.

[6] Chehab Salih, *International Aviation Law for Aerodrome Planning*, (Cham: Springer Nature, 2020).

[7] Fangni Zhang & Daniel J. Graham, 'Air Transport and Economic Growth: A Review of the Impact Mechanism and Causal Relationships', *Transport Reviews*, Vol. 40, No. 4, 2020, pp. 506–528, at p. 506; Kenneth Button & Samantha Taylor, 'International Air Transportation and Economic Development', *Journal of Air Transport Management*, Vol. 6, No. 4, 2000, pp. 209–222, at p. 209.

[8] UNSC, 'S/RES/2309 (2016)—Threats to International Peace and Security Caused by Terrorist Acts: Aviation Security', available at <https://documents.un.org/doc/undoc/gen/n16/295/78/pdf/n1629578.pdf> Last visited, 10 January 2024.

includes airport security.[9] In response to these fears and concerns, States and aviation industries focus on safety and security measures within regulatory frameworks as set out by international laws and standards.

States have the ultimate responsibility for the operation of the airport and its security.[10] Although the Chicago Convention provides that "every State has complete and exclusive sovereignty over the air space above its territory", there is a general consensus amongst States that this principle is not absolute.[11] Every state must comply with international law and the normative framework regulating airport security. International conventions like the Chicago Convention and its annexes, the guidelines, regulations, and procedures set forth by international aviation organisations like the ICAO and the International Air Transport Association (IATA) comprise the international norms which govern airport security. These standards include things like emergency readiness, access control, perimeter security, cargo security, and screening of passengers and their belongings etc. These security measures are essential to ensure smooth international air travel. Furthermore, the United Nations Security Council (UNSC) has adopted resolutions requiring member states to adopt and implement stringent security measures, considering the imminent global threat of terrorism.[12]

Airport security is quite important for Bangladesh, given its geographic location nestled amongst South Asia and its proximity to major international air routes. Due to its strategically significant location, Bangladesh has the potential to become a regional air hub.[13] To become a successful regional air hub, Bangladesh must ensure airport safety and security. However, multiple states, including the United Kingdom, the United States of America and Australia, amongst others, have expressed their concerns regarding airport security in Bangladesh. It is essential for Bangladesh to ensure airport security to enhance Bangladesh's standing as a secure and reliable destination for global travel and commerce. Failure to ensure robust security could have serious consequences, including suspension of flights, harm to the country's reputation, and even sanctions from international regulatory bodies like ICAO. For example, in the past, Bangladesh was subjected to cargo restrictions from a variety of countries, including the United Kingdom, Australia, Germany, etc., as a result of inadequate airport security. Hence, Bangladesh must ensure airport security to be relevant in the global aviation industry.

Against this backdrop, this chapter aims to critically assess the implementation of international norms relating to airport security in the context of Bangladesh, which is paramount in ensuring safe and secure aviation operations. This chapter will explore

---

[9] Brian F Havel & Gabriel S. Sanchez (eds.), 'The International Law Regime for Aviation Safety and Security', *The Principles and Practice of International Aviation Law* (Cambridge: Cambridge University Press, 2014).

[10] *Supra* note 1, at p. 46.

[11] *Id.*

[12] *Supra* note 8.

[13] Rashidul Hasan, 'Shaping Bangladesh's Future as an Aviation Hub', *The Daily Star*, 7 October 2023, available at <https://www.thedailystar.net/supplements/charting-new-skies/news/shaping-bangladeshs-future-aviation-hub-3436701> Last visited, 2 October 2024.

the discrepancies between international standards and their practical application in Bangladesh's airport security framework, the challenges to ensure effective implementation, and the way forward. In doing so, this chapter will be divided into four parts: the first part focuses on international norms relating to airport security, the second part discusses on the issue of bilateral treaties between Bangladesh and other States to ensure airport security, the third part delves into the legislative framework of Bangladesh in ensuring airport security, and the fourth part is a case study on Hazrat Shahjalal International Airport (HSIA) to determine discrepancies in security protocols in practice. Finally, this chapter will conclude with the evaluation of differences between Bangladeshi laws and practices and international norms in ensuring airport security.

2 International Norms Governing Airport Security

Airport Security encompasses a wide range of measures, ranging from border control and body scanning to security for passengers, cargo, and aircraft. International conventions like the Chicago Convention and its annexes as well as the guidelines, regulations, and procedures set forth by international aviation organisations like ICAO and IATA comprise the international norms that govern airport security. These standards include things like emergency readiness, access control, perimeter security, cargo security, and screening of passengers and their belongings etc. This part will briefly reflect on the international norms of airport security under the Chicago Convention and its annexes, the guidelines, regulations, and procedures set forth by ICAO, IATA, and Airport Council International (ACI).

2.1 The Chicago Convention, Annex 17 and ICAO

The Chicago Convention is the landmark multilateral treaty establishing the framework for regulation of the global civil aviation industry, which essentially incorporates the regulation of airports. A specialised UN Agency, ICAO, has been established under this convention to oversee and regulate the international civil aviation industry. Bangladesh accessed the Chicago Convention on 22 December 1972, and became a member of ICAO.[14] Most important strategic objectives of ICAO are "safety, security, efficiency and environmental protection."[15] Therefore, ICAO has developed a series

[14] 'Status of Bangladesh With Regard To International Air Law Instruments', available at <https://www.icao.int/secretariat/legal/Status%20of%20individual%20States/bangladesh_en.pdf#:~:text=STATUS%20OF%20BANGLADESH.%20*%20Not%20in%20force> Last visited, 4 October 2024.

[15] Khalifa Alketbi & Attila Sipos, 'The Role of Smart Technology in Airport Facilitation and Security Control (ICAO Annex 9 and 17 Requirements)', *Journal of Infrastructure, Policy and Development*, Vol. 8, No. 8, 2024, pp. 5444–5460, at p. 5445.

of technical Annexes containing Standards and Recommended Practices (SARPs) to address safety and security concerns. The standard set out in the Annexes is a specification, and it contains only the minimum security requirements. ICAO has adopted 19 separate annexes to the Chicago Convention, among them; Annex 17 contains civil aviation security, which includes, in its ambit, airport security.

Annex 17 provides standard rules for preventing acts of unlawful interference, such as aircraft hijacking, terrorism, sabotage, etc. It outlines security measures for the airport, aircraft, cargo, mail and other goods security, as well as for the screening of passengers and baggage, crew and ground personnel.[16] These measures include access control to prevent unauthorised entry of weapons, explosives, or dangerous devices. Additionally, these security measures encompass the screening of passengers, baggage, and cargo, as well as the use of surveillance systems.

As a contracting party, Bangladesh is required to mandate that airports involved in civil aviation develop, implement, and maintain a comprehensive security protocol.[17] Furthermore, Bangladesh has an obligation to designate an authority at each airport to coordinate the implementation of security controls, supported by an airport security committee, which will ensure effective oversight of the security measures of the authority.[18] Additionally, Bangladesh is duty-bound to ensure that security considerations are incorporated into the architectural design and infrastructure development of new and existing airport facilities to facilitate the proper execution of security measures.[19] Annex 17 recommends the contracting State to use sudden, unpredictable and random security measures to create a deterrent effect in respect of security measures.[20]

To ensure better airport security, Bangladesh is obliged to ensure several security measures. Examples of such measures are: to establish security restricted areas at each airport; to establish an identity verification system at designated checkpoints; to ensure background checks on persons other than passengers who are granted unescorted access to security restricted areas; to ensure screening of both individuals and vehicles to prevent unauthorised entry and ensure the security of civil aviation operations, to ensure that passengers and their cabin baggage have been screened to an appropriate level, to ensure screening of hold baggage, etc.[21] Based on risk assessments by relevant national or local authorities, Bangladesh is obliged to ensure that "appropriate measures on the ground or operational procedures are established to mitigate possible attacks against aircraft using Man-Portable Air Defence Systems (MANPADS) and other weapons representing a similar threat to aircraft at or near an airport."[22] Furthermore, Bangladesh is duty-bound to establish security protocols to safeguard aircraft from unlawful interference, including providing timely notification

[16] *Id.*

[17] *Id.*, Chapter 3.

[18] *Id.*

[19] *Id.*

[20] *Id.*, Chapter 4.

[21] *Id.*

[22] *Id.*

to relevant authorities, conducting searches for dangerous items, making arrangements for handling potential hazards, developing and testing contingency plans, and ensuring trained personnel are available at airports to respond to suspected or actual incidents.[23]

2.2 IATA Guidelines on Airport Security

The International Air Transport Association (IATA) is a global trade association for airlines which represents over 330 airlines and more than 80% of global air traffic.[24] IATA plays a significant role in global airport security by developing international standards and providing guidance to ensure airlines operate safely, securely, and efficiently.[25]

IATA provides a comprehensive Security Management System (SeMS) to enhance airport security by integrating key processes into airport's daily operations.[26] SeMS have five essential components that promote a robust culture of airport security. They are: senior management and corporate commitment, Security training and awareness campaign, Threat assessment and risk management, Management of emergencies and incidents, and quality assurance and continuous improvement.[27] IATA also provides specialised training on SeMS to assist airports in complying with SeMS and IATA Operational Safety Audit (IOSA) requirements.

2.3 Airport Council International (ACI) Guidelines on Airport Security

ACI represents the collective interests of airports worldwide, and it advocates for promoting excellence in safety, security, and sustainability in the global aviation industry.[28] ACI collaborates with governments, international organisations like ICAO, and civil aviation industry stakeholders to develop policies and best practices that enhance airport operations and promote airport security.[29] By implementing risk-based security protocols and improved screening measures, ACI aims to enhance the Airport's ability to handle complex threats while maintaining a smooth passenger

[23] *Id.*, Chapter 5.

[24] 'About Us: IATA', available at <https://www.iata.org/en/about/> Last visited, 4 October 2024.

[25] *Id.*

[26] 'What You Need to Know about Aviation Security', available at <https://www.iata.org/en/publications/newsletters/iata-knowledge-hub/what-you-need-to-know-about-aviation-security/> Last visited, 4 October 2024.

[27] *Id.*

[28] 'About ACI | ACI World', available at <https://aci.aero/about-aci/> Last visited, 4 October 2024.

[29] *Id.*

experience.[30] ACI facilitates airports with tools, expertise, security assessments, training programs, and resources that develop best practices and ensure compliance with international standards relating to airport security.[31]

ACI guidelines on airport security have provided a comprehensive approach. It emphasises the critical role human elements may play in ensuring effective airport security. It highlights the significance of efficiently recruiting, training, and managing security staff to maximise their performance at designated screening checkpoints.[32] The guide also outlines organisational practices such as clear management structures, strategic resource planning, and fostering a supportive work environment to enhance airport security.[33] This guideline also suggests the integration of advanced technologies, proper facility design, and continuous performance assessments to ensure a smooth and secure passenger flow. This comprehensive approach is helpful for the airports to meet international security standards effectively.[34]

3 Bilateral Agreements Between Bangladesh and Other States Regarding Airport Security

Various bilateral agreements between Bangladesh and other States play important roles in ensuring airport security in Bangladesh. These agreements establish legal frameworks which regulate mutual assistance and cooperation between partner states in areas such as safety, including airport security. As airport security is an increasingly global concern, these Agreements play a significant role in combatting terrorism, hijacking and other unlawful activities. This part will discuss two major bilateral agreements between Bangladesh-US and Bangladesh-EU.

3.1 US-Bangladesh Air Transport Agreement

The US-Bangladesh Air Transport Agreement is a bilateral treaty that governs various aspects of international air transport, including aviation safety and security. Both Bangladesh and the United States (US) are parties to the Convention on International Civil Aviation 1944. Both Bangladesh and the United States (US) are parties

[30] 'Airport Security | ACI World', available at <https://aci.aero/airport-advocacy/security/> Last visited, 4 October 2024.

[31] *Id.*

[32] ACI, 'The ACI Guide to Airport Security: Assessment of Human Factors in Checkpoint Security' available at <https://store.aci.aero/wp-content/uploads/2018/05/Preview-ACI-Human-Factors-Checkpoint-Security.pdf#:~:text=Managing%20the%20checkpoint%20security> Last visited, 4 October 2024.

[33] *Id.*

[34] *Id.*

to the Convention on International Civil Aviation 1944. In this treaty, both States expressed serious concerns about actions or threats to aircraft security that endanger safety of persons or property, negatively impact air transportation operations, and erode public trust in civil aviation safety and pledged to ensure the highest level of safety and security in international air transport.[35] The primary focus on airport security is described in Article 7 of the treaty, wherein both parties agreed that it is their mutual responsibility to safeguard civil aviation security from unlawful interference as a fundamental component of this Agreement.[36] Article 7 reinforces the shared commitment of both States to safeguard the air transport system from acts of unlawful interference. This commitment is framed in conformity with the broader international legal framework, particularly the obligations under the Chicago Convention and other norms relating to airport security. Here, both parties committed to upholding their obligations in ensuring airport security under international treaties, where Article 7 specifically mentions the "Convention on Offenses and Certain Other Acts Committed on Board Aircraft, the Convention for the Suppression of Unlawful Seizure of Aircraft, the Convention for the Suppression of Unlawful Acts against the Safety of Civil Aviation, and the Protocol for the Suppression of Unlawful Acts of Violence at Airports Serving International Civil Aviation".[37] By mentioning these conventions, both parties reaffirmed their commitment to adhering to international norms regulating airport security, this coordinated approach is essential in combatting such security concerns.

Clause 2 of Article 7 speaks about cooperation between the States as it says that "[t]he Parties shall provide upon request all necessary assistance to each other to prevent [.....] unlawful acts against the safety [....] of airports and air navigation facilities".[38] Both Parties agreed to follow security standards laid down by ICAO and annexes to the Chicago Convention requiring that "operators of aircraft of their registry, operators of aircraft that have their principal place of business or permanent residence in their territory, and the operators of airports in their territory act in conformity with such aviation security provisions."[39] When a Party to this treaty requests that another Party observe the security provisions for entering, leaving, and while on the other Party's territory, the other Party must take appropriate precautions to safeguard aircraft and inspect passengers, crew, their baggage and carry-on items, cargo, and aircraft stores before and during boarding or loading.[40] When an incident or threat of an unlawful incident takes place, the Parties shall assist each other to terminate the incident or threat rapidly and safely.[41] This treaty basically focuses

---

[35] 'U.S.-Bangladesh Air Transport Agreement of September 30, 2020', Preamble, available at <https://www.state.gov/air-transport-agreements/u-s-bangladesh-air-transport-agreement-of-september-30-2020/> Last visited, 2 October 2024.

[36] *Id.*, Article 7.

[37] *Id.*

[38] *Id.*, Article 7 (2).

[39] *Id.*

[40] *Id.*, Article 7 (4).

[41] *Id.*,Article 7 (5).

on commitment to international security standards, compliance with international conventions dealing with airport security, and mutual assistance in security measures.

3.2 EU-Bangladesh Air Services Agreement

In 2024, Bangladesh and the EU have signed an agreement on certain aspects of air services.[42] This Agreement aims to establish a harmonised legal basis for air services between the EU Member States and Bangladesh.[43] Although this bilateral treaty does not contain any distinct, stand-alone provision on airport security, the provision of aviation safety is closely intertwined with security standards. Article 3 contains "safety standards", which essentially include airport security measures. Article 3 allows Bangladesh to exercise rights concerning "adoption, exercise or maintenance of safety standards".[44] It connotes that if an EU-designated air carrier fails to comply with the safety standards, Bangladesh has the right to suspend that carrier's operating authorisation. The EU and its member States retain similar rights under this Agreement. Thus, this bilateral agreement focuses on mutual rights and duties towards aviation safety, which includes airport security.

4 Legislative Framework Governing Airport Security in Bangladesh

In an interconnected and globalised world where threats from hijacking, terrorism, trafficking, and other unlawful activities pose a serious concern to the aviation industry, it is imperative for a State to undertake robust security measures to ensure security to passengers, crew, airport infrastructure, as well as to ensure national security. Moreover, as a party to several international conventions and as a member of several international organisations, as discussed above, Bangladesh has an obligation to adopt and implement globally recognised security measures. Bangladesh has adopted several laws, both primary and secondary, to ensure airport security. This part will discuss the position of airport security within the legislative framework of Bangladesh.

---

[42] 'Bangladesh Signs Air Transport Agreements with Switzerland, EU', *The Financial Express*, available at <https://thefinancialexpress.com.bd/trade/bangladesh-signs-air-transport-agreements-with-switzerland-eu> Last visited, 2 October 2024.

[43] 'Agreement between the European Union and the People's Republic of Bangladesh on Certain Aspects of Air Services', Preamble, available at <https://eur-lex.europa.eu/legal-content/EN/TXT/PDF/?uri=OJ:L_202401699#:~:text=RECOGNISING%20that%20consistency%20between%20the> Last visited, 2 October 2024.

[44] *Id.*, Article 3.

4.1 Civil Aviation Authority Act 2017 and Civil Aviation Act 2017

The Civil Aviation Authority Act 2017 has come into operation after repealing the Civil Aviation Authority Ordinance 1985.[45] This Act declared that the Civil Aviation Authority of Bangladesh (CAAB), established under the Civil Aviation Ordinance of 1985, shall continue to exist as if it were established under this Act.[46] CAAB is a statutory body with perpetual succession and a common seal, possessing the authority to acquire, hold, and transfer both movable and immovable property, and it has the legal capacity to sue and be sued in its own name.[47] CAAB's powers and functions include the management, planning, construction, operation, and maintenance of all airports in Bangladesh, along with their surrounding airspace.[48] Additionally, CAAB is responsible for ensuring security measures at these airports.[49]

The Civil Aviation Act 2017 came into effect in 2017 after repealing the Civil Aviation Ordinance 1960.[50] This new Act has been enacted to implement the International Civil Aviation Convention, focusing on enhancing the safety, security, and regulation of civil aviation and to modernise relevant provisions while repealing the Civil Aviation Ordinance of 1960.[51] This Act provides the Chairman of the Civil Aviation Authority of Bangladesh (CAAB) with wide discretionary power in relation to safety and security measures of civil aviation, including airports. To enforce the provisions of this Act and to ensure the safety and security of civil aviation/airport, the Chairman may exercise the powers and perform the duties entrusted to him in any manner he deems fit and appropriate.[52] If, either on his initiative or based on a complaint, it appears to the Chairman that immediate action is required to ensure the safety and security of civil aviation, he may issue an appropriate order or directive, citing the reasons for such action.[53] The Chairman, in accordance with the annexes of the Chicago Convention and applicable international practices, may issue and amend Air Navigation Order (ANO), orders, and directives to ensure the safety and security of civil aviation.[54]

An ANO may include one or more provisions, such as establishing standards to ensure the safety and security of civil aviation; defining methods for inspection and oversight to ensure civil aviation safety and security; ensuring the security of

[45] Civil Aviation Authority Act, 2017, Section 33.

[46] *Id.*, Section 3 (1).

[47] *Id.*, Section 3 (2).

[48] *Id.*, Section 4.

[49] *Id.*,

[50] Civil Aviation Act 2017, Section 48.

[51] *Id.*, Preamble.

[52] *Id.*, Section 13 (1).

[53] *Id.*, Section 13 (2).

[54] *Id.*, Section 14 (1).

airports, landing areas, surrounding areas, and other aviation-related facilities; regulating unlawful activities by allowing the search of passengers and related individuals at airports, including their belongings, weapons, explosives, or any other instruments, and providing screening provisions for all types of mail, including courier and express parcels; implementing necessary provisions to protect against aircraft hijacking, piracy, or terrorist activities; setting codes of conduct for air operators, their agents, and employees when conducting searches of individuals to ensure the safety of passengers and property during air transport; including any other provisions related to security and protection.[55] Section 15 empowers the Chairman to ensure compliance with the annexes related to dangerous goods mentioned in the Chicago Convention and the ICAO technical instructions for the safe transport of dangerous goods by civil aircraft.[56] Section 15 also empowers the Chairman to enter into agreements with the civil aviation authority of another state regarding the oversight of civil aviation safety, in accordance with Article 83 *bis* of the Chicago Convention. However, such agreements cannot be made with states that have failed to meet their international obligations related to safety oversight.[57] This Act also contains some penal measures to ensure better security. For example, under Section 31, wilfully transporting or attempting to transport dangerous goods by aircraft without meeting the specified conditions is a criminal offence, punishable by up to seven years of rigorous imprisonment, a fine of up to 5 million BDT, or both. Thus, the Civil Aviation Act 2017 has provided the Chairman of CAAB absolute power and responsibility to oversee the security protocols. This Act acknowledges Bangladesh's obligation under international conventions to ensure airport security.

4.2 *Civil Aviation Rules 1984*

These Rules were adopted under the Civil Aviation Ordinance of 1960, which has been repealed by the Civil Aviation Act 2017. However, these Rules are operative as Section 48 of the Act of 2017 says that the Rules made under the Civil Aviation Ordinance of 1960 shall be deemed to have been made under this Act.[58] The provisions of these Rules shall be applicable to the CAAB to address the prevailing threats of unlawful interference at each Bangladeshi airport. These Rules have been adopted to mitigate risks specific to the security vulnerabilities faced by individual airports. The objective of these Rules is to ensure "the safety of passengers, crew, ground personnel and the general public in all matters related to safeguarding against acts of unlawful interference."[59] Moreover, they empowered the Chairman of CAAB to adopt and implement regulations, practices and procedures to safeguard the airports

[55] *Id.*, Section 14 (2).

[56] *Id.*, Section 15.

[57] *Id.*

[58] *Id.*, Section 48.

[59] Civil Aviation Rules, 1984, Rule 280 (2).

from unlawful interference, and the Chairman will also ensure that "such regulations, practices and procedures protect the safety of passengers, crew, ground personnel and the general public."[60]

The Civil Aviation Rules 1984 requires the CAAB Chairman to ensure that the authority of each airport must create, implement and maintain a written airport security programs aligning with the national security program.[61] The Authority of the Airport shall be responsible for coordinating security measures, and an airport security committee must be established to oversee the implementation of these security measures.[62] Rule 283 empowers the Chairman to adopt security measures to "prevent weapons, explosives or any other dangerous devices, articles or substances, which may be used to commit an act of unlawful interference."[63] To prevent unauthorised entry, the Chairman shall take measures relating to access control in each airport which include establishing security restricted areas at each airport based on a security risk assessment, implementing identification systems for persons and vehicles to prevent unauthorised access to airside and security restricted areas; ensuring background checks are conducted on individuals granted unescorted access to security restricted areas; supervising the movement of persons and vehicles in security restricted areas to prevent unauthorised access to aircraft; screening a proportion of non-passenger individuals and items entering security restricted areas, based on a risk assessment; ensuring the validity and recognition of identity documents issued to aircraft crew for access to airside and security restricted areas; reapplying regular background checks for all individuals granted unescorted access to security in the restricted areas.[64] This Rules also contains detailed provisions on "measures relating to passengers and their cabin baggage", "Measures relating to aircraft", "Measures relating to hold baggage", security control measures "relating to cargo, mail and other goods", "Measures relating to special categories of passengers", etc.[65] These measures have resemblance with measures mentioned in Annex 17 of the Convention on International Civil Aviation.[66] However, these Rules do not cover emerging security threats like cyber security, which Annex 17 measures do. In light of the discussion above, it may be concluded that both primary and secondary legislations empowered the CAAB to oversee airport security measures. However, these Rules required CAAB to delegate its power to concerned airport authorities to take security measures. The next section will discuss the security measures at Hazrat Shahjalal International Airport (HSIA).

---

[60] *Id.*

[61] *Id.*, Rule 182 (2).

[62] *Id.*

[63] *Id.*, Rule 283.

[64] *Id.*

[65] Civil Aviation Rules, 1984.

[66] ICAO, 'Annex 17 to the Convention on International Civil Aviation' (ICAO 2017), 17, available at <https://ffac.ch/wp-content/uploads/2020/10/ICAO-Annex-17-Security.pdf> Last visited, 3 October 2024.

5 Security at Hazrat Shahjalal International Airport (HSIA)

Hazrat Shahjalal International Airport (HSIA) is the largest, and busiest, and one of the three international airports in Bangladesh, located in her capital city, Dhaka.[67] As a connecting hub of both domestic and international flights, it can handle 18.5 million passengers annually and 190 international flights daily.[68] The traffic is steadily increasing due to Bangladesh's expanding diaspora in foreign countries and its economic growth. HSIA also manages a good number of cargoes, mostly carrying garments, which are the lifeline of the Bangladesh's economy. As a result, it is imperative to ensure security for airport infrastructure, passengers, cargo, and airport personnel. This part will discuss the security measures at HSIA, breaches of security measures, challenges in the path to securing it and the way forward.

5.1 Security Protocols at HSIA

There is a separate and specialised body called the "Aviation Security (AVSEC) Division" at HSIA to oversee the security of passengers, cargo, crews, and aircraft at the Airport. The AVSEC Division's primary responsibilities are to screen passengers and their belongings for prohibited items such as weapons, explosives, and illegal drugs, to perform security checks on aircraft and cargo, to patrol the airport to deter and detect security threats, to respond to security incidents and emergencies, and to collaborate with other law enforcement agencies in order to ensure the safety of the aviation system.[69] The AVSEC personnel are skilled professionals and highly trained dedicated to secure travelling through the airport.[70] The AVSEC is also responsible for performing a wide range of duties, which include:

(a) Issuing and inspecting airport identification cards;
(b) Managing access to secure areas of the airport;
(c) Conducting training for other airport personnel on security matters;
(d) Maintaining security records and reports;
(e) Sharing the common goal of ensuring the safety of the aviation system;
(f) Supervising the movement of passengers, vehicles, and aircraft in secure areas;
(g) Responding to passenger inquiries and complaints;
(h) Maintaining a professional and courteous demeanour at all times;

---

67 'Hazrat Shahjalal International Airport (HSIA)', *Hazrat Shahjalal International Airport (HSIA)*, available at <https://www.hsia.gov.bd> Last visited, 2 October 2024.

68 *Id.*

69 Hazrat Shahjalal International Airport (HSIA): Aviation Security' *Hazrat Shahjalal International Airport (HSIA)*, available at <https://hsia.gov.bd> Last visited, 2 October 2024.

70 *Id.*

(i) Enforcing airport rules and regulations in accordance with International Civil Aviation Organization (ICAO)-17; and
(j) Ensuring passenger service to the respected passengers as per International Civil Aviation Organization (ICAO)-9.[71]

The HSIA website declares that firearms, ammunition, and realistic replicas of explosives are prohibited or restricted items.[72] It is prohibited to carry a list of goods, which are, fire guns, razor blades, meat cleavers, swords, axes, etc., in both cabin and Check-in luggage to ensure airport and aviation security.[73] HSIA has installed a new technology named AvSec ID System to enhance airport security and improve passenger experience.[74] The AvSec ID System monitors and controls access to sensitive areas. By digitising the pass application process, enabling location verification and real-time updates, and granting access only to authorised individuals. This system strengthens airport security, minimises security breaches, and improves overall aviation safety.[75] There is sufficient security personnel at HSIA, including, several hundred Aviation Security Force, Armed Police Battalion (APBN), a total of 850 air force personnel, 1500 aviation security forces personnel, 1000 Ansar members.[76]

5.2 Security Breaches at HSIA

Despite the implementation of above security measures, several incidents have occurred at HSIA which compromised its security protocols. Major security challenges at HSIA include the risks of unauthorised access, smuggling, and other forms of unlawful interference. Such security breaches have serious consequences, not only for the safety of passengers, crew, cargo and airport personnel but also for the country's reputation in the global aviation industry and compliance with its international obligations. This part will examine some of the security breaches at HSIA, and the next part will discuss the consequences of such breaches.

---

[71] *Id.*

[72] 'Hazrat Shahjalal International Airport (HSIA): Restricted Items', *Hazrat Shahjalal International Airport (HSIA),* available at <https://www.hsia.gov.bd> Last visited, 3 October 2024.

[73] 'Hazrat Shahjalal International Airport (HSIA): Prohibited in Cabin Luggage', *Hazrat Shahjalal International Airport (HSIA),* available at <https://www.hsia.gov.bd> Last visited, 3 October 2024.

[74] 'Dhaka Airport Gets 3 Digital Techs for Better Passenger Experience, Security', *The Business Standard*, 10 May 2023, available at <https://www.tbsnews.net/economy/aviation/dhaka-airport-gets-3-digital-techs-better-passenger-experience-security-629618> Last visited, 3 October 2024.

[75] *Id.*

[76] 'Security at Shahjalal Int'l Airport Beefed up', *The Financial Express*, available at <https://thefinancialexpress.com.bd/national/security-at-shahjalal-intl-airport-beefed-up> Last visited, 3 October 2024.

5.2.1 Unauthorised Access:

One of the most prevalent security concerns for HSIA is unauthorised access to the restricted zone. Access control to these areas is the cornerstone of airport security, which controls entry, restricts unauthorised access and maintains a secure environment. Access control prevents unauthorised access to terminals, runways, boarding gates, baggage handling areas, control towers, and other restricted zones.[77] Inadequate access control mechanisms and failures in monitoring security perimeters are liable for such unauthorised access. Unauthorised access may provide individuals with malicious intent to cause harm to passengers or other airport personnel, to airport infrastructure, or to engage in other illegal activities, including aircraft hijacking, terrorism, etc. Unauthorised access is common to HSIA. In September 2023, a notable incident of unauthorised access to HSIA occurred when a 12-year-old kid bypassed multiple security checkpoints, including immigration and boarding control procedures, and boarded a Kuwait-bound flight without a passport, ticket and boarding pass.[78] This kid managed to pass through at least five security layers, which showed that the access control system of HSIA is significantly vulnerable.[79] This incident highlighted a failure to enforce security protocols at HSIA, which posed a severe threat to both the operations of the airport and passengers' security.

5.2.2 Undetected Firearm Access

In March 2019, a significant security breach occurred at HSIA when Ilias Kanchan, a renowned actor in Bangladesh, passed undetected during the initial luggage scanning process, he was unintentionally carrying a licensed 9 mm pistol with nine bullets in his laptop bag.[80] The security scanner, as well as the responsible security personnel, failed to detect the loaded firearm.[81] This incident exposed serious flaws in the Airport's security protocols, particularly the negligence of the security personnel and the operational effectiveness of the scanners. It was a direct violation of the security measures, which mandated thoroughly inspecting all items passing through the airport checkpoints to prevent weapons, explosives, and other illegal, dangerous items from entering secure areas.

---

[77] 'Access Control at Airport—FDC',21 August 2024, available at <https://www.fdc.com/access-control-at-airport/> Last visited, 3 October 2024.

[78] Rashidul Hasan, 'Runaway Kid Lays Bare Airport Security Lapses', *The Daily Star*, 13 September 2023, available at <https://www.thedailystar.net/news/bangladesh/news/runaway-kid-lays-bare-airport-security-lapses-3417636> Last visited, 3 October 2024.

[79] 'How the Boy Who Evaded Security Has Now Had His Dream Fulfilled', *The Business Standard*, 22 September 2023, available at <https://www.tbsnews.net/bangladesh/how-boy-who-evaded-security-has-now-had-his-dream-fulfilled-704934> Last visited, 3 October 2024.

[80] 'Ilias Kanchan Crosses Airport Security with Revolver', available at <https://www.observerbd.com/news.php?id=187048> Last visited, 3 October 2024.

[81] 'Ilias Kanchan's Gun Undetected at Dhaka Airport', available at <https://www.daily-sun.com/printversion/details/375816> Last visited, 3 October 2024.

5.2.3 Attempt to Hijack Aircraft

The attempt to hijack "Biman Bangladesh Airlines Flight 147" in 2019, which had been travelling to Dubai from Dhaka, highlights severe violation of airport security protocols at HSIA.[82] Shortly after the Dubai-bound Boeing 737 took off from HSIA, the suspect pointed the "gun" at the passengers and crew members and threatened to shoot.[83]However, the forensic text by CID claimed that the firearm carried by the suspect was a non-functional plastic toy gun.[84]The accused managed to board the Dubai-bound plane with the said "gun" after four layers of security checks, including scanning at HSIA.[85] The CCTV footage did not capture anything out of the ordinary, and the scanner did not raise any alarm during the passage of the suspect.[86] Though the Special Forces finally managed to rescue the aircraft, passengers and crew after the suspect had been shot dead, the incident highlights significant flaws regarding how the security is managed, particularly with respect to the detection of firearms. This incident demands improved security protocols, advanced scanning technology, and sufficient training for the security personnel at HSIA.

5.3 Repercussions of Security Flaws at HSIA

Violations of security protocols at HSIA can have serious consequences as they may undermine the confidence the global community has in Bangladesh's airport security. Its serious repercussions came into play when Australia, the European Union (EU), the United Kingdom (UK) and Germany imposed a ban on direct cargo flights from HSIA in 2016–2017, citing that HSIA failed to implement global security standards.[87] Many other countries have threatened to implement such a ban, for instance, the United States has recently expressed concern over the security protocols at HSIA stating that "it will be difficult to resume Dhaka-New York direct flights if the security

[82] Julfikar Ali Manik, Mike Ives and Kai Schultz, 'Passenger Forces Bangladesh Plane to Land and Is Fatally Shot' *The New York Times*, 25 February 2019, available at <https://www.nytimes.com/2019/02/25/world/asia/bangladesh-plane-hijacking-biman-airlines.html> Last visited, 3 October 2024.

[83] bdnews24.com, 'Commando Blitz Ends Bangladesh Plane Hijack Drama; Suspect Dies, All Passengers, Crew Unharmed', (*Commando blitz ends Bangladesh plane hijack drama; suspect dies, all passengers, crew unharmed*), available at <https://bdnews24.com/bangladesh/police-surround-dubai-bound-biman-bangladesh-flight-at-chattogram-airport> Last visited, 3 October 2024.

[84] 'CID: Biman Hijacker Used Plastic Toy Gun', *Dhaka Tribune*, available at <https://www.dhakatribune.com/bangladesh/nation/171306/cid-biman-hijacker-used-plastic-toy-gun> Last visited, 3 October 2024.

[85] 'Biman Hijacking: More Questions than Answers', *Dhaka Tribune*, available at <https://www.dhakatribune.com/bangladesh/nation/169756/biman-hijacking-more-questions-than-answers> Last visited, 3 October 2024.

[86] Ibid.

[87] 'Airport Security amid Cargo Flight Ban', *The Financial Express*, available at <https://thefinancialexpress.com.bd/views/opinions/airport-security-amid-cargo-flight-ban> Last visited, 3 October 2024.

measures at Dhaka airport are not tightened."[88] Most of these countries are the largest destinations for Bangladesh's RMG products. These countries found the security protocols at HSIA as "inefficient, weak and obsolete".[89] The security concerns at HSIA include a dysfunctional and outdated radar system, which was installed in 1984, which creates delays and safety concerns, insufficient screening and scanning process, etc.[90] These inefficient, outdated and inefficient security protocols at HSIA affect Bangladesh's aviation reputation, especially with countries having stringent airport security policies themselves. These repercussions may have a serious impact on export industries, that is, RMG products.[91] These repercussions call for the urgent installation of modern security infrastructure at HSIA to meet international security standards.[92]

6 Conclusions

Ensuring robust security is essential for Bangladesh to compete in the global civil aviation industry and to be a regional hub of air communications. As an emerging economy, ensuring security in accordance with global standards is a must to avoid repercussions such as bans on direct flights from vital and important trading partners. A critical examination of the legislative framework of Bangladesh has shown that it acknowledges the country's obligations under international aviation law and bilateral agreements with trading partners like EU, USA, Australia, etc. However, the case study on the country's largest and main airport, Hazrat Shahjalal International Airport (HSIA), shows that there is a difference between written commitment both in international, bilateral and national instruments and real practices. Some states have expressed their concern over security protocols at the airport. Even some states' concerns were so serious that they imposed bans on direct flights from HSIA. These security concerns include unauthorised entry, inefficient scanning and screening, attempts to hijack the aircraft, etcetera. These incidents occurred primarily due to inefficiencies of security personnel, lack of modern technologies, and other lack of other resources. Bangladesh should invest in creating a robust safety and security environment at the airports, providing training to the security personnel, incorporating artificial intelligence and other modern technologies to ensure better security, and ensuring robust and continuous monitoring mechanisms.

---

[88] Staff Correspondent, 'US Also Worried over Dhaka Airport Security', *Prothomalo*, 15 January 2016, available at <https://en.prothomalo.com/bangladesh/US-also-worried-over-Dhaka-airport-security> Last visited, 3 October 2024.

[89] *Supra* note 92.

[90] *Id.*

[91] 'BGMEA President Calls for Steps to Lift Ban on Direct Air Cargo to UK', available at <https://www.bgmea.com.bd/index.php/page/BGMEA_President_calls_for_steps_to_lift_ban_on_direct_air_cargo_to_UK> Last visited, 3 October 2024.

[92] '[Withdrawn] Bangladesh Airport Update', *GOV.UK*, 19 February 2018, available at <https://www.gov.uk/government/news/bangladesh-airport-update> Last visited, 3 October 2024.

Chapter 12
International Standards in Philippine Airport Development

Jessica Los Banos

Abstract The Philippines, with its high global connectivity index ranking and its major airport handling 45 million passengers in 2023, possesses substantial capability to ensure that its air transport ecosystem better facilitates travel and trade. Yet aerodrome governance in the country suffers from inertia and continues to be plagued by reactive decision-making and conventional operating strategies. This chapter proposes the enhanced integration of standards and recommended practices (SARPs) of the International Civil Aviation Organisation (ICAO) and other international aviation organisations to address institutional rigidities and regulatory inflexibility which hinder airport development in the country. Compliance with SARPs is effectively mandatory and crucial for both domestic and international air travel safety. Their inadequate implementation not only puts passengers at risk but also constrains the transport ecosystem's ability to catalyze regional economic activity. By rigorously internalizing and enforcing international standards in funding and procurement of airport projects, the Philippines may finally be able to unlock its long-delayed aviation potential and foster balanced regional economic development within the country.

Keywords Aviation safety plan · Civil Aviation Authority of the Philippines (CAAP) · Cost recovery · Global Air Navigation Plan (GANP) · Department of Transportation (DOTr) · RA 9497

I would like to thank Dr. Vivien Supangco, Dr. Erlinda Echanis, former Dean of the Virata School of Business (VSB), University of the Philippines (Diliman), Lawrence Velasco, former Project Development Director, Philippine Public-Private Partnership Center and VSB Assistant Professor of Accounting and Finance, Jillian Jay Feliciano and Marco Bienvenido Amora of the UP College of Law, and Maita A. for their invaluable insights and research assistance.

J. Los Banos (✉)
Faculty of Law, Universitas Pelita Harapan, Tangerang, Indonesia
e-mail: jessica.losbanos@uph.edu

© The Author(s), under exclusive license to Springer Nature Singapore Pte Ltd. 2025
S. Bhat B. (ed.), *Aerodrome Governance in Asia*,
https://doi.org/10.1007/978-981-96-7568-5_12

1 Introduction

Over the last fifty years, the governance of airports has increasingly come under the purview of the International Civil Aviation Organisation (ICAO). As an attached agency of the United Nations, among the aims of the ICAO are to promote the orderly development of the global aviation industry and achieve uniformity in the safety practices of the parties to the 1944 Chicago Convention (the Convention) through regulations harmonisation.[1] The organisation ensures global consistency in safety and security through the implementation of the Global Aviation Safety Plan (GASP), the Global Air Navigation Plan (GANP), and the Global Aviation Security Plan (GASeP). These frameworks support ICAO's strategic vision of an integrated network and ensure that member States' respective national plans, policies and practices are congruent with international standards. Planning and implementation regional groups (PIRGs) are integral to this effort, facilitating regional coordination to address local needs while ensuring adherence to global aviation objectives.

While the ICAO does not function as a global regulator[2] due to an inherent lack of direct enforcement power and jurisdiction over breaches of international aviation law,[3] it wields significant influence over aerodrome operations around the world. Given their pivotal role in air connectivity, the ICAO has progressively encouraged airports to harmonize their governance practices with the obligations of their home States under the Convention, its 19 Annexes and 6 procedures for air navigation services (PANS),[4] which have been translated into more than 12,000 standards and recommended practices (SARPs).[5] SARPs secure the highest practicable

---

[1] International Civil Aviation Organisation (ICAO), Doc 7300, *Chicago Convention on International Civil Aviation*, 2006, (9th edn.).

[2] Adam Disimine, 'The role of the ICAO in maintaining safe skies', 2021, available at <https://www.publicinternationallawandpolicygroup.org/lawyering-justice-blog/2021/8/23/the-critical-role-of-the-icao-in-maintaining-safe-skies> Last visited, 1 July 2024.

[3] Enforcement under international law remains vested in the States themselves. The Philippines was subjected to enforcement measures by the US and the EU which suspended entry of Filipino airlines in 2008 and 2010 respectively due to safety concerns. See 2013–2021 Update to FAA Historical Chronology: Civil Aviation and the Federal Government, 1926–1996, (Washington, DC: Federal Aviation Administration, 1998), available at <https://www.faa.gov/sites/faa.gov/files/2022-01/2013_2021_chronology.pdf>, Last visited, 10 June 2024; and Commission Regulation (EU) No. 273/2010 of 30 March 2010 amending Regulation (EC) No 474/2006 establishing the list of air carriers subject of an operating ban within the Community, p. L84-33, available at <https://eur-lex.europa.eu/LexUriServ/LexUriServ.do?uri=OJ:L:2010:084:0025:0049:EN:PDF> Last visited, 10 June 2024.

[4] PANS do not have the same status as the Convention's Annexes. States are not obliged to report differences in case of failure to adopt or implement them. ICAO, 'Note on the Notification of Differences and Form of Notification with respect to Language Provisions', Annexes 1, 6, 10 and 11, available at <https://www.icao.int/safety/fsix/Documents/lp/note.En.pdf> Last visited, 7 July 2024.

[5] ICAO, 'How ICAO develops standards', available at <https://www.icao.int/about-icao/AirNavigationCommission/Pages/how-icao-develops-standards.aspx#:~:text=The%20establishment%20and%20maintenance%20of,of%20ICAO's%20mission%20and%20role> Last visited, 7 July 2024.

degree of uniformity in laws, regulations, standards, organisation, and procedures of contracting parties relating to air navigation and transportation pursuant to Article 37 of the Convention. Accordingly, the primarily horizontal relationship that States maintain at the international plane on the basis of sovereign equality has in part been transformed operationally into a vertical safety system administered by the ICAO through the Universal Safety Oversight Audit Programme (USOAP),[6] a mandatory assessment[7] of the fulfilment of obligations relating to the safety oversight of their air transport systems including airports.[8] The aim of the USOAP is not to assess the level of SARP implementation which is the role of the compliance checklist under Article 38 of the Convention but to determine whether a State is effectively and consistently implementing the critical elements of its safety oversight system. As SARPs compliance requires significant resources, airports are advised to conduct their operations in accordance with member States' obligations relating to their economic regulation under Article 15 in relation to Article 68 of the Convention.[9]

For the Philippines, which is heavily dependent on air transportation for the movement of people and goods, it is imperative that the Civil Aviation Authority of the Philippines (CAAP) and four other autonomous airport operators[10] engage in governance practices that are consistent with the SARPs.[11] This synchronisation is essential not only for international aviation law compliance but, more importantly, for optimizing the social and developmental impacts of the country's airports.[12] While the ICAO has issued a comprehensive array of documents, manuals and guidance materials for this purpose, faithful implementation of SARPs can be administratively taxing and cumbersome for developing countries like the Philippines. Nonetheless, since the standards and recommended practices derive from industry best practices

---

[6] ICAO, 'Frequently Asked Questions', available at <https://www.icao.int/safety/CMAForum/Pages/FAQ.aspx> Last visited, 5 August 2024.

[7] The USOAP became mandatory as of the 33rd Session of the ICAO Assembly held on 22 September–5 October 2001 although violations and non-compliance of the SARPs remain to be resolved under dispute settlement rules applicable between the disputing parties. ICAO, Doc 9735 AN/960, '*Universal Safety Oversight Audit Programme Continuous Monitoring Manual'*, 2011 (3rd edn.) pp. 2–1.

[8] See generally ICAO, International Standards and Recommended Practices, *Annex 14 to the Convention on Civil Aviation, Aerodromes, Vol. 1, Aerodrome Design and Operations*, 2022 (9th edn).

[9] ICAO, Doc 9562, *Airport Economics Manual*, 2013 (3rd edn.), p. v.

[10] Manila International Airport Authority (Executive Order No. 903/1983), Clark International Airport Corporation (Executive Order No. 192/1994), Mactan Cebu International Airport Authority (Republic Act No. 6958/1990) and the Davao International Airport Authority (Republic Act No. 11457/2019).

[11] Mainstream institutional theory posits that SARPs adoption can be voluntary, normative, mimetic or coercive. See generally, P.J. DiMaggio, 'The Iron Cage Revisited: Institutional Isomorphism and Collective Rationality in Organizational Fields', *American Sociological Review*, Vol. 48, No. 2, 1983, pp. 147–160.

[12] Air Transport Action Group (ATAG), 'The Economic and Social Benefits of Air Transport', available at <https://www.icao.int/meetings/wrdss2011/documents/jointworkshop2005/atag_socialbenefitsairtransport.pdf> Last visited, 15 July 2024.

and are meticulously detailed, they explicitly guide adoption,[13] which in turn depends to a large extent on political will, resource prioritisation, and effective implementation by the parties. Technical assistance is also available such as the Korean government's development of the SARPS Management and Implementation System (SMIS), a web-based system designed for use by civil aviation authorities to assist in the processing of ICAO State letters and managing compliance with SARPs. A number of countries, including the Philippines, are reported to have acquired the system.[14]

The Philippines has consistently scored above the global mean in its USOAP audits. In 2022, it achieved a perfect effective implementation (EI) rating of 100% in the legislation audit (LEG) area which only a few countries like Singapore have achieved. The country also obtained satisfactory ratings in the civil aviation organisation (ORG), personnel licensing and training (PEL), aircraft operations (OPS), airworthiness of aircraft (AIR), and aircraft accident and incident investigation (AIG) audit areas. However, its EI of SARPs relating to aerodromes and ground aids (AGA) and air navigation services (ANS) are 20 percentage points below average.[15] Countries which obtain below average AGA EI ratings, such as the Philippines, are those that have not established aerodrome certification requirements and formal surveillance systems, failed to certify their airports, or lack qualified aerodrome technical staff with the appropriate mix of technical disciplines to cover all aspects of aerodrome certification, including processes for addressing deficiencies within a reasonable time.[16] The Philippines' unsatisfactory performance does not only indicate substantial operational and technical deficiencies in the country's safety oversight obligations in these audit areas, but is also evidence of a more systemic underlying cause: the sluggish development of its air navigation network.

The 2022 USOAP audit findings raise a more fundamental question for the Philippines: Why, despite its high global connectivity index ranking,[17] the largest airport

[13] Diffusion theory posits that the process of adoption occurs as new ideas, products, standards, practices, and philosophies are accepted, beginning with a few adapters and increasing thereafter as benefits are realized. See generally, Everett M. Rogers, *Diffusion of Innovations*, (New York: The Free Press, 1983).

[14] ICAO, 'Electric Aviation Safety Tool, SARPS Management and Implementation System', available at <https://www.icao.int/APAC/Meetings/2019%20COSCAPSEA%20SEARAST20/14.2.pdf> and <http://www.kocahelp.go.kr/helpDesk/getDisseminateMap.do> Last visited, 30 June 2024.

[15] The Philippine AGA and ANS EI ratings are 45.87 and 45.28 percent respectively. Assuming all the USOAP CMA 2020 Protocol Questions on Aerodromes and Ground Aids have equal weight, the country scored a satisfactory rating in only 65 of 143 and 55 of 122 indicators respectively. ICAO, 'Safety Audit Results: USOAP Interactive Viewer', available at <https://www.icao.int/safety/Pages/USOAP-Results.aspx> Last visited, 10 September 2024.

[16] ICAO, 'Report on Universal Safety Oversight Audit Programme Continuous Monitoring Approach Results', 2019–2021, pp. 38–39, available at <https://www.icao.int/safety/CMAForum/Documents/USOAP_REPORT_2019-2021.pdf> Last visited, 20 August 2024.

[17] OAG, 'Top 50 Airport Mega Hubs', available at <https://www.oag.com/megahub-airports-2023#top-megahubs-region> Last visited, 30 June 2024.

handling 45 million passengers in 2023,[18] and strong administrative capability to translate SARPs into domestic regulations, has the country's airport development potential been so severely constrained? The answer becomes clear when one observes the annual budget hearings of the Department of Transportation (DOTr) before the House of Representatives, where lawmakers question the perennial lack of funding and delayed procurement of airport projects.[19] There is indeed widespread consensus that the country's aerodrome governance and development are highly bureaucratic,[20] suffer from inertia,[21] and are plagued by reactive decision-making and conventional operating strategies. Accordingly, the IATA has urged the national government to take action on more than 20 airport development proposals from various bodies and administrations, noting that the number of travellers passing through the Philippines' main gateways is expected to rise to 140 million by 2035.[22] To date, only 5 of the country's 9 international airports committed to the Asia Pacific Regional Air Navigation Plan (RANP)[23] have been permanently certified while the remaining airports are either undergoing or require master planning and modernisation. Furthermore, missed opportunities for the airport network to support a more balanced regional development are evident, as the economic contribution of the country's 17 regions has remained stagnant and dominated by the greater capital region[24] despite the extensive network of 39 out of 85 listed airports that are commercially operating across 12 area centers connecting the country's three main islands.

---

[18] MIAA, 'NAIA sets all-time flight record in 2023; passenger volume recovers to 95% of pre-pandemic', available at <https://www.miaa.gov.ph/index.php/announcements/press-releases/naia-sets-all-time-flight-record-in-2023-passenger-volume-recovers-to-95-of-pre-pandemic> Last visited, 15 July 2024.

[19] Philippine House of Representatives, Committee on Appropriations, 'Budget Brief/Hearings of the FY 2025 Proposed Budget (DOTR) Part2', available at <https://www.youtube.com/watch?v=Ys4JwNEHfjg> Last visited, 10 September 2024.

[20] Melvin Gascon & Tyrone Piad, 'Marcos to Naia rehab group: Fix airport woes', 2024, available at <https://newsinfo.inquirer.net/1920265/marcos-to-naia-rehab-group-fix-airport-woes> Last visited, 25 July 2024.

[21] CAPA, 'Philippine government outlines five-year development plan to reassess airport infrastructure needs', available at <https://centreforaviation.com/analysis/reports/philippine-government-outlines-five-year-development-plan-to-reasses-airport-infrastructure-needs-635100> Last visited, 20 July 2024.

[22] PPP Center, 'IATA to PH gov't: Act on airport proposals now', available at <https://ppp.gov.ph/in_the_news/iata-to-ph-govt-act-on-airport-proposals-now/> Last visited, 20 July 2024.

[23] APAC ANP, Volume I Part II (AOP) Amendment Nos. APAC-I 23/20 and 23/22, January 2024, p. II-10.

[24] A comparative analysis of the Gross Regional Domestic Products (GDRP) for the period 2013–2023 using data from the Philippine Statistics Authority conducted by the author showed that while there was significant regional growth ranging from a low of 87% (Cordillera Administrative Region) to 153% (Davao Region), the percentage share of each region remained relatively constant. The GDRPs of the National Capital Region(NCR), Region IVA-Calabarzon and Region III-Central Luzon were the largest at 31.14%, 14.13% and 10.90% respectively while the rest of the regions' GDRPs were stagnant at 1.5–6.49% of total GDP. See also, Edo Andriesse, 'Regional Disparities in the Philippines: Structural Drivers and Policy Considerations', *Erdkunde*, Vol. 71, Issue 2, 2017, pp. 97–110.

This chapter aims primarily to contribute to the sparse literature and understanding of the Philippine airport development framework and proposes that the timely integration of SARPs can facilitate the orderly growth of the country's airport network. Proactive and early adoption of standards by the CAAP is essential to enable individuals and organisations within the air transportation ecosystem to accumulate foundational knowledge and capability to facilitate smoother transitions to future updates as new SARPs are often built on previous ones, thereby avoiding inertia and rigidities from complexities of delayed adaptations. Section II advocates for the methodical implementation of recommended practices on airport economics by dual function civil aviation authorities as the failure of proper revenue attribution hampers financial planning for airport development. The next two sections examine the country's bureaucratic infrastructure acquisition process and insufficient advanced master planning capability and suggest the conferral of strategic autonomy to the CAAP to significantly improve the funding and procurement of airport projects. The chapter concludes with the recommendation that cohering airport development practices with global standards requires Philippine regulators to move beyond traditional public utility regulation. Instead, they should adopt a business model that promotes common interests while recognizing the integral role of domestic airports within the broader global aviation network operationally overseen by the ICAO.

2 Fund Planning Through Proper Accounting of Airport Revenues and External Financing Sources

Air transport infrastructure is essential for economic growth. Airports provide adequate capacity and connectivity where they are needed the most to diffuse economic development into regions beyond those hosting the country's main hubs. In an archipelagic country like the Philippines, where air transportation is the most expedient way to connect, strategic airport infrastructure planning is central to fully leverage its direct, indirect, and catalytic effects on regional economic development. According to Fu et al., there exists a positive relationship between airport activities and regional economic well-being. Their empirical findings indicate that a 1% increase in scheduled airline seat capacity led to a 0.38% increase in per capita regional GDP in New Zealand.[25] This study serves as a significant benchmark for Philippine policymakers because, like New Zealand, the country is also

[25] Xiaowen Fu, Kan Tsui, Breno Sampaio, & David Tan, 'Do Airport Activities affect regional economies? Regional Analysis of New Zealand's Airport System', *Regional Studies*, Pre-Published Version, Taylor and Francis, pp. 1–27 at pp. 14 and 15, 2020, <https://jyx.jyu.fi/bitstream/handle/123456789/48933/1/regional%20airports%20and%20regional%20growth%20mukkala%20tervo%20revised%20version.pdf> Last visited, 30 July 2024.; See also Mukkala, K., & Tervo, H., Air Transportation and Regional Growth: Which Way Does the Causality Run?, *Environment and Planning A: Economy and Space*, Vol. 45, Vol. 6, 2013, pp. 1508–1520.

an archipelago that relies heavily on tourism[26] and lacks substantial manufacturing industries in many of its regions.[27] Indeed, the ICAO and other aviation organisations have time and again emphasized that well-planned airport networks directly facilitate people and cargo movement between islands boosting local economies through trade and tourism. Indirectly, efficient airport operations support local businesses such as hotels, restaurants, and retail outlets, inducing broader economic impacts. Additionally, catalytic effects lead to improved airport infrastructure which attracts investment, foster new industries, and drives regional development beyond immediate economic gains.[28]

New airport constructions and existing airport expansions in developing economies require substantial funding and support from governments. The ICAO is cognizant that securing the necessary resources for this purpose is challenging due to competing public expenditures.[29] As this was observed to be a common concern for airports in developing economies in the 1980s, the ICAO in 1991 issued the first draft of the Airport Economics Manual[30] to guide States in dispensing with their obligations to provide airport and air navigation services and facilities regardless of the organisational structure under which they are operated, whether public or private. The airport economics recommendations lay down "practical guidance to States, airport managing and operating entities and regulatory authorities, to assist in the efficient management of airports and in implementing ICAO's Policies on charges for Airports and Air Navigation Services (Doc 9082)".[31] While in the form of non-binding protocols, they address responsibilities of States under Articles 15, 28 and 68 of the Convention in relation to the core aspects of airport operations throughout its life cycle from determining levels of airport charges to ownership, control and governance issues, financial management, landside business development, and the financing of airport infrastructure.[32]

Indisputably planning for sourcing funds for airport projects remains a continuing operational concern for operators. Being engaged in the provision of inherently commercial activities, they are expected to be self-financing entities,[33] which

[26] PNA, 'DOT plan to transform PH into tourism powerhouse in 5 years', available at <https://www.pna.gov.ph/articles/1197497> Last visited, 15 July 2024.

[27] Bangko Sentral ng Pilipinas, 'Regional Economic Development in the Philippines 2022 (RREDP)', pp. i-45 at v., available at <https://www.bsp.gov.ph/Media_And_Research/Report%20on%20Regional%20Economic%20Developments/REDP_2022.pdf> Last visited, 20 July 2024.

[28] IATA, 'The air transport sector makes a major contribution to the Philippines' economy', available at <https://www.iata.org/en/iata-repository/publications/economic-reports/philippines--value-of-aviation/> Last visited, 15 June 2024.

[29] ICAO, 'A39-15: Consolidated statement of continuing ICAO policies in the air transport field', Resolutions adopted by the Assembly, (2016, Provisional edn.), p. 84, available at <a39_res_prov_en.pdf (icao.int)> Last visited, 30 July 2024.

[30] *Supra* note 9, at pp. 1–3.

[31] *Id.*, at para. 1, p. v.

[32] *Id.*, at para. 4, p. v.

[33] ICAO, 2000 CEANS, 'ANSConf-WP/15 16/2/00 ITEMS 3, 4, 5', available at <https://www.icao.int/Meetings/ansconf2000/Documents/wp15e.pdf> Last visited,10 July 2024.

imply that growth plans must be funded primarily from operations. As such, a number of flexible and efficient funding options are recommended by the ICAO to enable airports to raise their capital expenditure requirements including privatisation, public–private partnerships,[34] and charging airport users for services rendered to them.[35] According to the organisation, all States are fully within their rights to recover all costs relating to or associated with the provision of airport and air navigation services and facilities.[36] The twin principles of "user pays" and "full cost recovery" emphasize burden sharing in maintaining and developing airports.[37] The "user pays principle" mandates that those who benefit from airport services; such as airlines, passengers, commercial establishments, and other users must bear the costs associated with those services, while the "full cost recovery principle" requires that charges levied on them cover the total costs of providing services, including both direct operational costs and necessary investments in infrastructure.[38] Accordingly, States are encouraged to establish regulatory frameworks that ensure charges reflect the actual cost of providing these services, with mechanisms for regular review, including adjustment by the ICAO pursuant to Article 15 of the Convention.[39]

While the recommended practices on airport economics suggest a wide array of funding options, their implementation in practice poses a unique challenge for dual role civil aviation authorities, such as the CAAP, which function as both regulators and operators of airports. Unless, elaborate accounting and bookkeeping systems are in place, dual-role authorities face difficulties in distinguishing and attributing operational costs and revenues from airport activities from those generated in the conduct of regulatory functions.[40] This role dichotomy can create conflicts of interest,

[34] In September 2019, San Miguel Aerocity Inc. (SMAI) signed a concession agreement with the DOTr to develop, construct, operate, and maintain the New Manila International Airport (NMIA) in Bulacan. Thereafter, the Philippine Congress enacted Republic Act No. 11506 granting SMAI a 50-year concession to operate the NMIA. SMAI, New Manila International Airport (NMIA), available at <https://www.sanmiguel.com.ph/page/san-miguel-aerocity-inc> Last visited 10 July 2024.

[35] A41-WP/2281 EC/18 2/8/22, Assembly-41st Session Economic Commission, 'Agenda Item 36: Economics of Airports and Air Navigation Services—Policy In support of ICAO's Airport Economics Panel', (Presented by Airports Council International (ACI)), p. 2, available at <https://aci.aero/wp-content/uploads/2022/08/wp_228_en.pdf> Last visited, 7 July 2024.

[36] *Supra* note 33, at pp. 1–2.

[37] *Id.*, at pp. 2–4.

[38] *Id.*, at pp. 1–4.

[39] Article 15 of the Convention states:

"Every airport in a contracting State which is open to public use by its national aircraft shall likewise, subject to the provisions of Article 68, be open under uniform conditions to the aircraft of all the other contracting States. The like uniform conditions shall apply to the use, by aircraft of every contracting State, of all air navigation facilities, including radio and meteorological services, which may be provided for public use for the safety and expedition of air navigation. Any charges that may be imposed or permitted to be imposed by a Contracting State for the use of such airports and air navigation facilities by the aircraft of any other Contracting State shall not be higher."

[40] *Supra* note 33, at pp. 2–3.

complicate the accurate allocation of costs and even lead to regulatory capture,[41] as the same body overseeing the regulatory framework is also a participant in the very industry it governs. A quick review of the trial balance items maintained by the CAAP as of 2023[42] indicates that it may have engaged in the expedient comingling of revenues from both regulatory and operational activities, which prevents it from recovering full cost from the users of its airports and engaging in effective strategies to improve profitability. As an autonomous unit attached to the DOTr, since the CAAP cannot directly secure budgetary allocation for personnel, maintenance, and operating expenses through the regular appropriations process, it must necessarily rely on operating revenues from landing charges, terminal fees and royalties to finance its regulatory activities.[43] This dependence on airport revenues to perform its public functions is evident from its need to seek funding support from the DOTr for airport infrastructure year after year. To complicate the situation, the CAAP has not implemented the option of imposing additional airport charges and levies to raise revenues for airport development and has been unable to adjust terminal fees in the last two decades.[44] It also failed to exploit the landside business of its airports fully. It can therefore be reasonably assumed that the authority does not routinely engage in the practice of programming its profits and depreciation for infrastructure development planning. The last two airport projects financed through public–private partnership were also facilitated instead by the DOTr.[45]

More importantly, the CAAP has not asserted its right to directly access remittances from the MIAA, the operator of the Ninoy Aquino International Airport, since 1983. During the 13-year period from 2010 to 2022, the MIAA has remitted the sum of P15.369 billion to the Philippine government.[46] Executive Order No. 903, as amended by Executive Order No. 298 (1987)[47] expressly mandates that

---

[41] Regulatory capture is defined as the process through which special interests affect state intervention in any of its forms. See generally Ernesto Dal Bo., 'Regulatory Capture: A Review', *Oxford Review of Economic Policy*, Vol. 22, No. 2, 2006, pp. 203–25 at p. 1.

[42] CAAP, '2023 Trial Balance', available at <https://caap.gov.ph/wp-content/uploads/2023/12/Trial-Balance-as-of-March-2023.pdf> Last visited, 15 May 2024.

[43] An Act Creating the Civil Aviation Authority of the Philippines, Authorizing the Appropriation of Funds Therefor, and for Other Purposes, Republic Act No. 9497, 2008, Sections 3(eee), (fff) and (ggg).

[44] There have been suggestions over the years to increase boarding fees to generate enough revenue to pay back the real value of construction costs of the NAIA. See for example, Louis Berger International, Inc., Feasibility Study and Master Planning, Draft Final Report for the Republic of the Philippines Department of Transportation and Communications and Coordinating Council of the Philippine Assistance Program Cagayan De Oro- Iligan Airport Volume II-Masterplan, p. 2, available at <https://pdf.usaid.gov/pdf_docs/PNABT381.pdf> Last visited, 15 July 2024.

[45] House of Representatives, Committee on Appropriations, 'Budget Briefing of the FY 2025 Proposed Budget (DOTr)', available at <https://www.youtube.com/live/HA5kr0-f0lM> Last visited, 30 August 2024.

[46] MIAA, 2015 Annual Report, p. 54, available at <https://www.miaa.gov.ph/images/stories/TransparencySeal2019/II/MIAA-AR-2015.pdf> Last visited, 10 July 2024.

[47] Section 11. Contribution to the General Fund for the Maintenance and Operation of other Airports.

these remittances should be used for the maintenance and operation of other international and domestic airports in the country. The CAAP's continuing reliance on the DOTr and the Philippine Congress for funding support can be partly attributed to Section 29, Article VI of the 1987 Constitution which prohibits the withdrawal of money from the National Treasury unless authorized by law. However, even if the MIAA remittances fell under this prohibition, the lawmakers themselves could have easily amended existing laws to create a Special Fund for Airport Development by effectively earmarking them for multiyear and continuing airport projects without the need for general appropriations, subject only to appropriate oversight by the DOTr and the Department of Budget and Management (DBM). Furthermore, despite ongoing budget constraints, the authority has not requested an executive or legislative exemption from RA No. 7656, which mandates all GOCCs to remit 50% of their annual net earnings to the national government—funds that should not have been remitted in the first place, as they should have been allocated for routine maintenance and operations expenditures as part of its airports' normal operations.

The CAAP's funding shortfalls underscore the pressing need for similarly situated civil aviation authorities to rigorously implement the ICAO's recommended practices on the economic regulation of airports. Effectively identifying internal and external revenue sources is critical for infrastructure planning. Delayed adoption of these practices can have serious consequences, as demonstrated by the CAAP's infrastructure situation. The airports managed by the authority have fallen behind not only in upgrading facilities but also in improving passenger services due to funding shortages resulting from regulatory design failures. These shortcomings have hindered their ability to manage growing air traffic and facilitate the diffusion of development to less developed regions of the country that rely heavily on tourism and trade.

3 Master Planning is Key to Rationalizing New Airport Development and Maintenance Projects

Implementing SARPs on airport economic governance may advance the Philippines' framework for funding airport projects, but it is also necessary to further identify institutional constraints on airport infrastructure development in the country. Achieving a 100% EI rating for legislation through the adoption of SARPs into domestic regulations, circulars, memoranda, and manuals does not automatically translate into effective implementation in practice without putting in place appropriate structural arrangements for this purpose. Effective policy implementation requires a suitable organizational framework that enhances absorptive capacity to

Within thirty (30) days after the close of each quarter, twenty percentum (20%) of the gross operating income, excluding payments for utilities of tenants and concessionaires and terminal fee collections, shall be remitted to the General Fund in the National Treasury to be used for the maintenance and operation of other international and domestic airports in the country.

identify, assimilate, and apply knowledge and resources for successful execution.[48] Despite the CAAP's highly qualified legal department and its extensive experience with the domestication of international law, including active participation in the ICAO since 1947, the Philippines has been unable to translate its accumulated knowledge into the requisite institutional design and structure for contemporizing airport development. It also only signed a Management Services Agreement (MSA) with the ICAO on 17 October 2023 which would have allowed the authority to receive assistance from the ICAO's Capacity Development and Implementation Bureau for improving strategic and compliance outcomes in relation to aviation safety, capacity and efficiency, security and facilitation, environmental protection, and economic development.[49] As a consequence, the country is yet to develop a coherent regime for growing its airport infrastructure that better conforms with the SARPs and meets the country's air transport needs efficiently.

In 2008, when the ICAO Conference on the Economics of Airports and Air Navigation Services (CEANS)[50] was underway, the country renewed its commitment to develop capacity to manage its airports by enacting Republic Act No. 9497 (RA 9497), which transferred the technical and operational regulation of the air transport industry from the Air Transportation Office to the CAAP.[51] RA 9497 established a simple airport development and maintenance system vested in an independent and autonomous government-owned-and-controlled corporation (GOCC). Under the law, the Board of Directors was granted explicit authority to develop new airports, while the Director General was assigned the responsibility for maintaining the airports operated by the authority.[52] However, the law does not clarify whether this development power is exclusive to the Board. Consequently, the DOTr concurrently performs this function despite the express delegation of this authority to the CAAP.

To support this developmental role, the CAAP was given fiscal autonomy, the authority to set levies and charges, and broad corporate powers.[53] However, missing from the law were two key elements for exercising the authority's development power: airport master planning and project procurement procedures. This omission is particularly notable since the ICAO had long released its recommendations on the need for airport master plans as early as the 1960s.[54] As the organisational structure

48 See generally Fritz Sager & Anat Gofen, 'The polity of implementation: Organizational and institutional arrangements in policy implementation', *Governance*, Vol. 35, No. 2, 2022, pp. 347–364.

49 CAAP, 'Philippines signs Management Service Agreement with ICAO', available at <https://caap.gov.ph/philippines-signs-management-service-agreement-with-icao/> Last visited, 15 September 2024.

50 ICAO, Doc 9908 CEANS, available at <https://www.icao.int/Meetings/ceans/Documents/Doc 9908_en.pdf> Last visited, 20 June 2024.

51 *Supra* note 43. See also the legislative history of RA 9497, available at <https://caap.gov.ph/his torical-background/> Last visited, 15 July 2024.

52 *Id.*, Sections 78 & 35(l).

53 *Id.*, Sections 15, 26 & 23.

54 Airport master plans guide the strategic direction of infrastructure development and provides methods for planning runway layouts, taxiways, aprons, passenger terminals, transport links,

of the CAAP was prescribed by RA 9497, the Board was unable to amply organize its operations and build human capital around this critical planning activity and instead of fostering organic capacity, the authority has relied heavily on official development assistance from aid agencies including the JICA, ADB, and the World Bank in the assessment and preparation of master plans for its major airports over the years. It was only in 2021 when the CAAP explicitly incorporated provisions on airport master planning into its Manual on Standards of Aerodromes, which became effective in November 2022.[55]

As for project procurement, due to the lack of explicit rules on airport development—since the DOTr merely copied and pasted the entirety of Section 78 into the law's implementing rules and regulations—the CAAP was consequently subjected to the general procurement rules that apply to all infrastructure projects. The DOTr failed to design an appropriate procurement process for this inherently *sui generis* industry, which is an integral part of the global air navigation network and is subject to ICAO safety monitoring, unlike road and rail systems that are only overseen by domestic regulators. As a consequence, the authority was unable to exercise its fiscal autonomy independently of DOTr control. This issue is evident in how both the CAAP and autonomous airport operators are compelled to seek funding support from the agency for capital requirements exceeding a certain threshold. For example, the airport manager at Francisco Bangoy International Airport in Davao City cited "budget constraints" as the primary reason for the limited capacity to enhance airport facilities. The airport's spending power is restricted to projects under PHP 5 million, necessitating collaboration with the DOTr.[56] This limitation may also explain why, despite the CAAP's annual procurement plans for new airport development and maintenance being consistently endorsed by the DOTr, NEDA and the Office of the President, proposed projects may not receive support in subsequent years and could be removed from the Public Investment Program (PIP).

A closer examination of the interactions between lawmakers and DOTr and CAAP officials during the 2024 appropriations hearings before the House of Representatives sheds light on this conundrum.[57] One lawmaker pointed out that the disbursement rates for obligated funds have been very low, with allocated funds for airport projects often reverting to the National Treasury since they were not used within the legally mandated prescription periods. For example, the Catbalogan Airport, which has been undergoing rehabilitation since the 1960s, was allocated PHP 2.6 billion for various improvements between 2019 and 2023. However, an additional PHP 750 million needed for completion was not included in the 2025 National Expenditure Program. The DOTr reported that additional funding requests from the Department of Budget

---

parking, and cargo areas. Without such a plan, capacity expansion will not be based on realistic air traffic growth projections that meet community or regional needs. Doc 9184/AN 902, Part 1 Master Planning, Airport Planning Manual, pp. 1–1.

[55] CAAP, 'Manual of Standards for Aerodromes', pp. 1–8.

[56] Sunstar, 'Caap-Davao addresses public concerns, bares budget challenges', available at <https://www.sunstar.com.ph/davao/caap-davao-addresses-public-concerns-bares-budget-challenges> Last visited, 30 May 2024.

[57] See *supra* note 19.

and Management (DBM) were denied. The DBM representative explained that due to tight fiscal space, the government can only release funds to projects that are implementation-ready and listed in the PIP, TRIP, and IFP and that in fact most aviation projects for which funds were requested were not approved for inclusion in the 2025 infrastructure priority program. Airport projects typically have long lead times, making it important that their rationale and economic relevance are supported by solid evidence through comprehensive master planning and traffic growth forecasts and studies. For instance, Catbalogan Airport may have been deprioritized due to an analysis indicating that the Samar province already has two competing airports within a 100-km range. Master planning could have identified that expanding Calbayog Airport might have better served the entire province of Samar based on the city's population, tourism and economic profile.

Airport master planning is indeed central to successful airport operations as can be seen in the cases of Singapore and Indonesia which have consistently obtained USOAP EI ratings above global averages. In marked contrast to the practice of the CAAP, the Civil Aviation Authority of Singapore's (CAAS) airport project funding and procurement processes are characterized by a degree of leniency and flexibility. The law creating the CAAS has established a regime anchored on master planning and prescribed practical and comprehensive guidelines and specifications for identifying new airport locations, expanding existing airports in line with the approved master plans and ensuring compliance with growth plans by airport licensees.[58] It also distinguishes clearly between maintenance and major development projects,[59] and expressly exempts airport licensees from government procurement rules.[60] Similarly, Indonesia employs a less rigid approach to airport development. It has adopted ICAO's recommendation on the separation of regulatory functions from airport management and construction operations, delegating these responsibilities to two public corporations that also independently own and operate subsidiaries that provide regular logistics, engineering, and property maintenance services to airports across the country.[61]

Moving forward, the CAAP must enhance its capacity for strategic airport master planning to better integrate new development and maintenance projects into the country's national air navigation plan in the same manner that its ASEAN counterparts have done. A well-developed master plan offers a long-term framework for aligning infrastructure investments with regional needs and economic objectives.

---

[58] Section 47(2), Civil Aviation Authority of Singapore Act 2009, available at <https://sso.agc.gov.sg/Act/CAASA2009> Last visited, 19 November 2024.

[59] *Id.* at Section 49.

[60] To avoid doubt, nothing in this Act entitles the Government, Minister or Authority to issue any directions, or to impose any licence condition or other requirement, to control or regulate the procurement by an airport licensee or exempt airport operator of goods or service, or a combination of goods and service, by any contractual means, such as purchase or lease, rental or hire purchase, with or without an option to buy the goods or service or combination of goods or service, *Id.*, at Section 97.

[61] PT Angkasa Pura I, Annual Report, p.25, available at <https://injourneyairports.id/investor/annual-report> Last visited, 19 July 2025.

Effective airport master planning also helps to prioritize development projects based on sound and realistic market and traffic growth and capacity assumptions. To achieve this, the CAAP needs to establish a structured and informed approach to airport development, ensuring that planning is systematic, resource allocation is judicious, and implementation is methodical.

4 Consolidating Transport Infrastructure Potential Through Strategic Autonomy

In recognition of the deficiencies in its airport development framework, the Philippines has identified an urgent need to improve its airports and integrate them more effectively into the national transportation ecosystem. In 2020, the NEDA introduced the National Transport Policy which reaffirmed the country's commitment to seamless connectivity among various transport modes and infrastructure. This latest policy, which serves to guide the implementation of the Philippine Development Plan for the period 2023–2028, calls for the enhanced integration of the intermodal logistics network to improve the handling of passenger and cargo movements in the country.[62] The NEDA clarified that national government resources will be primarily allocated to facilities classified as "national", such as airports serving as international and regional gateways.[63] Exceptions to this rule apply only to projects participating in established convergence programs.[64] Collaboration and resource sharing between national and local governments will therefore be required for the rest of the country's domestic airport development programs.[65] However, a closer examination of this new policy shows that it is not materially different from existing policies on funding and procurement of airport projects, and may therefore, have minimal impact on achieving intermodal connectivity.

Likewise, current efforts in the Philippine Congress to transfer operations of airports in the country to a Philippine Airport Authority (PAA) focus primarily on administrative and organisational aspects, such as the composition and responsibilities of the new authority's Board of Directors, rather than on articulating an operational policy for the new operator that is agile and responsive to effective compliance with international obligations under the Convention and implementation of the SARPs. In fact, the proposed bills, House Bill No. 2234 and Senate Bill No. 1073,

---

[62] NEDA, 'National Transport Policy and its Implementing Rules and Regulations', p. 12, available at <https://neda.gov.ph/wp-content/uploads/2020/02/NTP-IRR-Final.pdf> Last visited, 15 August 2024.

[63] *Id.*, at p. 20.

[64] In 2020, the DOTr and the Department of Tourism (DOT) signed a memorandum of agreement on the Institutionalized Leveraging of Infrastructure Program for Airport Development (iLIPAD) that aims to synchronize efforts to boost airport and route development programs. PNA, 'DOT, DOTr sign pact to boost airport, route development programs', 2020, available at <https://www.pna.gov.ph/articles/1090321> Last visited, 5 August 2024.

[65] *Supra* note 62, at p. 22.

merely mirror RA 9497's existing framework and do not also sufficiently address the need for clear delineation of procurement powers between the proposed PAA and the DOTr nor specify the extent of the latter's oversight over the former.

Since the power to develop new airports and maintain existing infrastructure has been expressly delegated to the CAAP, the Philippine government must confer on the authority the much-needed strategic and operational autonomy in matters relating to funding and procurement. This independence will enable the authority to develop the necessary organisational competences, enhance its human capital and technical capacity, and improve decision-making processes. It will also reduce administrative burdens and boost operational efficiency, allowing the CAAP to manage infrastructure projects with greater flexibility and responsiveness. This will, however, require the various transport regulators and stakeholders, particularly the DOTr, NEDA, and the Office of the President, to design and prescribe the nature, content and limits of such autonomy, which can be articulated in a corresponding executive order to be issued by the president or in a law amending RA 9497. The CAAP's ongoing challenges in managing multiple stakeholders and rigid funding and project procurement processes highlight the need for a more streamlined and efficient operational system for airport development. Current efforts by the Philippine government fail to sufficiently resolve issues of regulatory overlap and governance inefficiencies. In contrast, giving the CAAP strategic autonomy is a more pragmatic and strategic solution to manage ongoing and future airport projects more efficiently and in line with the SARPs. This approach also will equip the authority with power to deal with regulatory and administrative constraints for a more robust air transport infrastructure that meets national, regional and global expectations.

5 Conclusion

Airports are highly integrated into the global aviation network and are fundamentally different from rail or road infrastructure, which are primarily under national jurisdiction. Accordingly, Philippine transport regulators must move beyond traditional public utility regulation and establish an airport development regime that is designed for continuing compliance with the safety and operational oversight by the ICAO. Even if the aviation transport system of the country is fundamentally safe, there is a strong case for the timely adoption of international aviation standards. Currently, the country's rigid airport infrastructure funding and procurement processes, which are tailored to domestic sectors, are impeding the CAAP's efforts to develop new airports and modernize existing facilities. It is fundamentally flawed to require the CAAP and autonomous airport operators to remit their net earnings to the National Treasury as dividends, only for them to request those same funds back through the DOTr for airport development and maintenance via the cumbersome yearly general appropriations process before the Philippine Congress. A more nuanced understanding of the global aviation industry's unique operational framework is therefore essential at all levels of government. Specifically, the Philippine Congress and the DOTr must craft a regulatory framework that vests strategic autonomy in the CAAP to develop human capital, expertise, and technical capability to perform its airport development and maintenance function independently and without unnecessary interference from the other government agencies, except for appropriate oversight. This will require closer cooperation between the authority and its regulators to streamline funding and procurement procedures ensuring that airport projects are completed without unnecessary delays based on coherent airport master planning. This paradigm shift must underpin ongoing initiatives to hasten airport infrastructure development and harmonize governance policies and practices with international standards to enable the Philippines to better meet its airport infrastructure needs and support regional economic growth objectives.

Chapter 13
Airport Management in Vietnam: Ensuring Safety and Efficiency

Nguyen Thi Hong Yen and Nguyen Toan Thang

Abstract Airport management in Vietnam is a complex and multifaceted endeavour characterised by the need to balance safety imperatives with operational efficiency in a rapidly growing aviation sector. This comprehensive study examines the various strategies and challenges involved in ensuring the safety and efficiency of airports in Vietnam. It explores vital factors influencing airport management practices in Vietnam by drawing upon multiple sources, including academic literature, industry reports, regulatory documents, and international instruments. These factors include national regulatory frameworks and international standards, especially the Chicago Convention of 1944 and its Annexes, safety management systems, technological advancements, and infrastructure development. Through a comprehensive analysis of these factors, the study aims to provide insights into the current state of airport management in Vietnam and identify opportunities for improvement, thereby reassuring the reader about the validity and reliability of the findings.

Keywords Airport authority · Aviation industry · Aviation safety · Adopted Air Traffic Flow Management (ATFM) · Civil Aviation Authority of Vietnam (CAAV) · Law on civil aviation · Safety performance · Vietnam Air Traffic Management Corporation (VATM)

1 Introduction

The management of airports in Vietnam has undergone remarkable changes over the past century, influenced by historical events, socio-economic shifts, and the country's integration into the global economy. Over the past 68 years, Vietnam's airport management has experienced significant transformations, evolving from its colonial beginnings to its current status as a rapidly growing aviation hub in Southeast Asia. Airports play a crucial role in the Vietnam Civil Aviation industry, overseeing

N. T. H. Yen (✉) · N. T. Thang
Hanoi Law University (HLU), Hanoi, Vietnam

© The Author(s), under exclusive license to Springer Nature Singapore Pte Ltd. 2025

S. Bhat B. (ed.), *Aerodrome Governance in Asia*,
https://doi.org/10.1007/978-981-96-7568-5_13

airport infrastructure and the passenger and cargo check-in process before and after flights. They are integral to the safe and efficient operation of air transport services.[1]

On 15 January 1956, a significant milestone was marked as the Prime Minister issued Decree No. 666-TTg, leading to the establishment of the Civil Aviation Department, and this pivotal moment laid the groundwork for the birth, growth, and sustainable development of Vietnam's Civil Aviation. Following the country's unification, there was a surge in demand for air travel between the regions, propelling civil aviation into an essential economic and technical sector. Recognising this, on 11 February 1976, the Prime Minister issued Decision No. 28/CP, setting up the General Department of Civil Aviation under the Government Council. To facilitate Vietnam Civil Aviation's rapid integration with international civil aviation, Vietnam acceded to the Convention on International Civil Aviation, signed in Chicago, and became a member of the International Civil Aviation Organization (ICAO) on 12 April 1980. The General Department of Civil Aviation of Vietnam is dedicated to developing airports to achieve its objectives. In 1982, Noi Bai International Airport Terminal and Guest House A of Tan Son Nhat International Airport were proudly inaugurated.[2]

In a period marked by a focus on innovation and a keen economic mindset, the General Department of Civil Aviation proposed to the Council of Ministers to introduce a mechanism for business and investment autonomy to capitalise on all available resources and swiftly seize market opportunities within the evolving economy. As a result, on July 30, 1992, the Council of Ministers issued Decision No. 242/HDBT, leading to the establishment of the Civil Aviation Authority of Vietnam (CAAV) under the Ministry of Transport and Post. The CAAV, as the state management agency of civil aviation, was granted legal status, a seal, and a budget and was authorised to open an account at the State Treasury. This pivotal decision signified the Vietnam Aviation industry's transition from centralised to independent accounting, heralding a new era of essential and transformative changes.[3]

Throughout its 68-year history, the Vietnamese aviation industry has continually adapted to meet its evolving transportation demands and support its journey towards industrialisation and modernisation amidst regional and global economic integration. Presently, Vietnam boasts a network of 22 airports, encompassing 15

---

[1] 'LịchsửhìnhthànhvàpháttriểncủaTổngcông ty quản lý bay Việt Nam/History of formation and development of Vietnam Air Traffic Management Corporation', available at, https://vatm.vn/lich-su-hinh-thanh-va-phat-trien-cua-tong-cong-ty-quan-ly-bay-viet-nam-phan-i-s729.html. Last visited, 1 August 2024.

[2] Civil Aviation Authority of Vietnam, 'Lịch Sử Hình Thành và Phát Triển Ngành Hàng Không Dân Dụng Việt Nam/History of formation and development of Vietnam Civil Aviation Industry', available at, https://caa.gov.vn/gioi-thieu/lich-su-hinh-thanh-va-phat-trien-nganh-hang-khong-dan-dung-viet-nam-20240326154159236.htm. Last visited, 01 August 2024.

[3] *Id.*

domestic and seven international facilities. Airport management has undergone positive transformations, enhancing national airport and airport network capacities.[4] This growth has placed considerable pressure on the country's airport infrastructure and management practices, necessitating a careful balance between ensuring safety and maintaining operational efficiency. This study seeks to explore the strategies and challenges inherent in managing Vietnam's airports, with a particular focus on how these elements contribute to the overall performance of the aviation sector. The study explores vital factors influencing airport management practices in Vietnam, including national regulatory frameworks and international standards, especially the Chicago Convention of 1944 and its Annexes, safety management systems, technological advancements, infrastructure development, and human resource management. Through a comprehensive analysis of these factors, the study aims to provide insights into the current state of airport management in Vietnam and identify opportunities for improvement.

2 Regulatory Frameworks

Vietnamese legal regulations for airport management are comprehensive and cover various aspects of airport operations, safety, security, environmental protection, and infrastructure development. These regulations are shaped by national laws, decrees, circulars, and international agreements to which Vietnam is a party.

As a member of the global aviation community, Vietnam adheres to international rules and standards set by various international organisations. Currently, Vietnam has signed 69 bilateral aviation agreements, joined 28 multilateral international treaties on civil aviation, actively participated in building the ASEAN unified aviation market (ASAM), negotiated and constructed multilateral air transport agreements towards liberalisation between ASEAN and partner countries such as China, EU, Japan, Korea, New Zealand. Vietnam Supports Laos and Cambodia in aviation safety supervision and promotes cooperation with countries with strengths in aviation, such as France, the Netherlands, Japan, and the United States, through technical cooperation agreements. In particular, in 2014, Vietnam became a member of the Convention on International Interests in Mobile Equipment and the Protocol on Matters Specific to Aircraft Equipment (Convention, Cape Town Protocol 2001). In 2018, it became a member of the Montreal Convention for the Unification of Certain Rules for International Carriage by Air (Montreal Convention 1999). These frameworks ensure that Vietnamese airports operate in line with global best practices for safety, security, and efficiency.[5]

[4] 'Trình Chínhphủhồsơđềnghịxâydựng Luật Hàngkhôngdândụngsửađổi/Submit to the Government the proposal to develop the revised Law on Civil Aviation', available at, https://tapchigiaothong.vn/trinh-chinh-phu-ho-so-de-nghi-xay-dung-luat-hang-khong-dan-dung-sua-doi-183240103131757389.htm. Last visited, 01 August 2024.

[5] Bộ Giao thôngVậntải/Ministry of Transport, 'Báo Cáo TổngKếtThiHànhLuậtHàngKhôngDânDụng Việt Nam/Report on the implementation of the Law on Civil Aviation of Vietnam', 21 December

The Chicago Convention of 1944 is the foundation of global civil aviation regulation. As a signatory to this convention, Vietnam must adhere to the standards and practices outlined in its 19 Annexes. These Annexes cover various aspects of civil aviation, including safety, security, environmental protection, and air traffic management. Compliance with these standards is crucial for Vietnam's airports to maintain international recognition and ensure safe operations, particularly through compliance with the following ICAO annexes:

- Annex 9 (Facilitation) aims to streamline and simplify border-crossing formalities while maintaining security and compliance with relevant laws. The goal is to ensure efficient and expeditious processing of passengers, cargo, and mail, enhancing safety and convenience at international airports.[6]
- Annex 14 (Aerodromes): Governs airport design and operational safety. It focuses on standards and recommended practices for aerodromes.[7]
- Annex 19 (Safety Management Systems): Provides a framework for airports to manage aviation safety systematically. CAAV ensures that Vietnamese airports meet ICAO standards, and Vietnam participates in ICAO audits to improve airport safety and operational practices continuously.[8]

Vietnam's regulatory framework for airport management is primarily governed by Vietnam's Law on Civil Aviation. This important law, enacted by the National Assembly on 26 December 1991, provides the essential legal foundation for overseeing civil aviation activities across all economic sectors. Furthermore, during the 7th session, 9th tenure, on 20 April 1995, the National Assembly passed amendments and additions to the Law on Civil Aviation, which addressed various aspects such as state management of civil aviation, flight management, airport management and operation, as well as aviation security and safety. On 22 June 2006, the amended Law on Civil Aviation was passed by the National Assembly and officially took effect from 1 January 2007. The Law amending and supplementing a number of articles of the Law on Civil Aviation was passed by the 13th National Assembly at the 8th session in 2014. It took effect on 1 July 2015 (hereinafter referred to as The Law on Civil Aviation 2006). The State Management Agency on Aviation has issued legal documents and appropriate policies to regulate air transport. The aviation industry has been proactive and flexible in international integration towards liberalisation, making an essential contribution to the development of the aviation market, especially the State's policy of allowing expansion for economic sectors to participate in the air transport business, encouraging and ensuring the rights of foreign airlines to operate to/from Vietnam.

2022, available at, https://datafiles.chinhphu.vn/cpp/files/duthaovbpl/bao-cao-tong-ket-luat-hkdd.docx. Last visited, 15 July 2024.

[6] ICAO, Chicago Convention 1944, Annex 9, available at, https://cil.nus.edu.sg/wp-content/uploads/2019/02/1944-Convention-on-International-Civil-Aviation-Annex-1-to-18.pdf. Last visited, 18 November 2024.

[7] *Id,* Annex 14.

[8] *Id*, Annex 19.

Implementing the Law on Civil Aviation has seen the comprehensive development of detailed regulations and implementation instructions by the Government, the Ministry of Transport (MOT), and relevant ministries and branches. By 2023, a series of documents guiding the implementation of the Law on Civil Aviation have been released, including 01 Ordinance, 12 Government Decrees, 02 Prime Minister Decisions, and 31 Circulars under the authority of the Ministers. Notably, Decree No. 05/2021/ND-CP, dated January 25, 2021, of the Government on the management and exploitation of airports has been amended and supplemented by Decree No. 20/2024/ND-CP, dated 23 February 2024.[9]

Vietnam has made remarkable strides in implementing the Law on Civil Aviation over 16 years. The timely issuance of detailed legal documents has provided clear guidance for compliance. Efforts to disseminate and promote awareness of the Law and associated regulations have been consistently and effectively pursued, leading to increased adherence among aviation agencies, organisations, and individuals. The Law has laid a solid legal foundation for establishing a management and supervision system following ICAO standards, significantly enhancing aviation safety. Comprehensive improvements in flight operations management, particularly in airport infrastructure development, have been a focal point. Notably, the completion of significant projects, such as the new Phu Quoc International Airport and the expansion of terminals at Noi Bai, Tan Son Nhat, and Da Nang International Airports, have effectively met the escalating demands of the air transport sector and have contributed to the socio-economic progress of the region.[10]

3 Entities Managing and Participating in Airport Operation

Civil aviation activities in Vietnam are carefully coordinated and managed by the Ministry of Transport and other government agencies. These activities are designed to respect Vietnam's independence, sovereignty, unity, and territorial integrity while ensuring aviation safety and security. The goal is to effectively harness the potential of aviation to support the country's socio-economic development. That involves

[9] Bộ Giao thông vận tải/ Ministry of Transport, 'Văn bảnhợpnhấtNghịđịnhvềquảnlý, khaitháccảnghàngkhông, sân bay/Consolidated text of the Decree on management and operation of airports and aerodromes' (11/VBHN-BGTVT 2024), 30 Mách 2024, Available at, https://mt.gov.vn/vn/tin-tuc/91932/ban-hanh-van-ban-hop-nhat-ve-quan-ly--khai-thac-cang-hang-khong--san-bay.aspx. Last visited, 18 November 2024.

[10] Viện chiếnlượcvàPháttriển GTVT/Institute of Transport Strategy and Development, 'Bộ GTVT tổngkết, đánhgiáthihànhLuậtHàngkhôngdândụng Việt Nam nhằmxâydựngbáocáo, trìnhsửađổiLuật/The Ministry of Transport summarizes and evaluates the implementation of the Law on Civil Aviation of Vietnam in order to prepare a report and submit amendments to the Law', 21 December 2022, available at, https://localhost:44325//news-detail/bo-gtvt-tong-ket-danh-gia-thi-hanh-luat-hang-khong-dan-dung-viet-nam-nham-xay-dung-bao-cao-trinh-sua-doi-luat-1-10427.html. Last visited, 11 August 2024.

maintaining a seamless and efficient chain of operations at airports while prioritising service quality, healthy competition, and creating a conducive environment for civil aviation activities. Additionally, the development of the airport system is aligned with national transport and socio-economic development plans, international civil aviation trends, and the growing demand for air transport in Vietnam. All airport infrastructures are designed and operated following international standards and legal provisions to ensure safety and efficiency.[11]

CAAV is entrusted with the implementation of the duties and powers of the Aviation Authority. As stipulated in Article 9 of the Law on Civil Aviation and specified by Decree No. 66/2015/ND-CP of the Government dated 12 August 2015, CAAV has established a comprehensive aviation safety monitoring system that conforms to international standards. This system enables CAAV to directly oversee and command the response to a wide range of aviation safety and security threats, including aviation incidents, acts of terrorism, illegal interference, and urgent situations. In addition, CAAV is empowered to take emergency measures to safeguard aviation security and safety, such as suspending flights and operations of aircraft, equipment, and aviation personnel. Furthermore, CAAV is responsible for managing the use of airspace, establishing air routes, developing flight methods, and providing flight assurance services to the international community. These services are intricately linked with the management and protection of national airspace.[12]

Aviation authorities are empowered to designate supervisors tasked with upholding aviation safety, security, and service quality by the standards outlined by the Minister of Transport (Point d, Clause 2a, Article 9 of the Law on Civil Aviation). As stipulated by ICAO, a proficient team is responsible for carrying out aviation safety supervision based on the criteria set forth in Document (Doc) 9734 (Part A). It constitutes one of the elements that ICAO scrutinises and assesses during evaluations of aviation safety supervision capacity and adherence to the Annexes of the 1944 Chicago Convention. In Vietnam, the regulatory framework for civil aviation mandates that supervisors must possess the requisite experience, qualifications, and skills and be officially appointed by Vietnamese aviation authorities to fulfil their supervisory role.[13]

---

[11] Văn phòng Quốc hội/Ofice of the National Parliament,'Văn bảnhợpnhấtLuậtHàngkhôngdândụng Việt Nam/Consolidated text of the Law on Civil Aviation of Vietnam' (03/VBHN-VPQH, 2023), Art. 5, available at, https://thuvienphapluat.vn/van-ban/Giao-thong-Van-tai/Van-ban-hop-nhat-03-VBHN-VPQH-2023-Luat-Hang-khong-dan-dung-Viet-Nam-588949.aspx. Last visited, 18 November 2024; Bộ Giao thông vận tải/ Ministry of Transport, 'Văn bảnhợpnhấtNghịđịnhvềquảnlý, khaitháccảnghàngkhông, sân bay/Consolidated text of the Decree on management and operation of airports and aerodromes' (11/VBHN-BGTVT 2024), 30 March 2024, Art. 4, available at, https://mt.gov.vn/vn/tin-tuc/91932/ban-hanh-van-ban-hop-nhat-ve-quan-ly--khai-thac-cang-hang-khong--san-bay.aspx. Last visited, 18 November 2024.

[12] Chính Phủ/Vietnamese Government, 'Nghịđịnh Quy địnhvềNhàchứctráchhàngkhông/Decree on Regulations on Aviation Authorities', 2015 (66/2015/NĐ-CP), available at, https://vanban.chinhphu.vn/default.aspx?pageid=27160&docid=180939. Last visited, 18 November 2024.

[13] Bộ Giao thôngVậntải/Ministry of Transport, 'Báo Cáo TổngKếtThiHànhLuậtHàngKhôngDânDụng Việt Nam/Report on the implementation of the Law on Civil Aviation of Vietnam', 21 December

In aviation law, CAAV has been granted the authority to actively oversee the transfer of aviation personnel to ensure safety in civil aviation operations. Furthermore, the authority is tasked with proactively training aviation safety supervisors across various domains, focusing on those overseeing aircraft and aircraft operations. The ultimate aim is to have at least 50% of full-time flight supervisors meeting international safety standards by 2025 and to raise this figure to over 75% by 2030. That will bolster the capacity to oversee flight safety in line with global benchmarks, thus opening doors for airlines to gain unrestricted access to the North American and European markets, recognised for their stringent aircraft operation safety standards.[14]

The Law on Civil Aviation outlines the Airport Authority's responsibilities, including the management of civil aviation and the authority to oversee compliance with aviation laws at airports. The Airport Authority has recently demonstrated its effectiveness in fulfilling these responsibilities. It is entrusted with managing airport land for infrastructure development and supervising construction activities based on approved plans. Additionally, the Airport Authority ensures compliance with airport planning and development plans, aviation safety standards, aviation security, public order, and environmental protection at airports. Moreover, it oversees airport technical equipment, cargo transportation, and flight operations services. In emergencies, incidents, or aircraft accidents, the Airport Authority is well-prepared and collaborates with airport enterprises to take necessary measures, including the authority to close the airport temporarily. Furthermore, the Airport Authority is empowered to address law violations, suspend construction and renovation activities that violate airport planning, suspend flights, request aircraft to land, and temporarily detain aircraft. It also has the authority to execute aircraft arrest warrants and suspend the activities of flight crew members who do not meet aviation safety and security requirements.[15]

Individuals and organisations involved in activities related to civil aviation at airports, such as airport operators and aviation enterprises, are under the regulatory oversight of the aviation authority. Airport enterprises, which are specialised business entities, are responsible for the management and operation of airports. They must obtain an airport business license from the Ministry of Transport to operate their activities.[16] An airport operator refers to an organisation responsible for directly managing and operating airport infrastructure and essential services, excluding those related to flight operations. Specialised flight operations assurance companies oversee these

2022, available at, https://datafiles.chinhphu.vn/cpp/files/duthaovbpl/bao-cao-tong-ket-luat-hkdd.docx. Last visited, 15 July 2024.

[14] *Id.*

[15] Văn phòng Quốc hội/Ofice of the National Parliament,'Văn bản hợp nhất Luật Hàng không dân dụng Việt Nam/Consolidated text of the Law on Civil Aviation of Vietnam' (03/VBHN-VPQH, 2023), Arts. 59–61, available at, https://thuvienphapluat.vn/van-ban/Giao-thong-Van-tai/Van-ban-hop-nhat-03-VBHN-VPQH-2023-Luat-Hang-khong-dan-dung-Viet-Nam-588949.aspx. Last visited, 18 November 2024.

[16] *Id.*, Arts. 62–64.

flight operations, and CAAV has granted an airport operation certificate.[17] The legal framework for civil aviation in Vietnam addresses the rights and obligations of airport enterprises and the specific responsibilities of airport operators. However, there is a lack of clarity in defining the relationship between these two entities within the country's legal system. Therefore, it is essential to provide more detailed guidelines to clearly outline the management objectives and the autonomy of legal entities for both airport enterprises and operators. That should include a clear definition of the role of airport operators in line with ICAO regulations and a comprehensive understanding of the relationship dynamics between airport operators and airport enterprises.

Article 64 of the Law on Civil Aviation states that establishing an airport enterprise is mandated to oversee the operations of a specific airport. This includes providing various services such as aviation security, safety, and other public services in compliance with Clause 3, Article 64. The airport enterprise is both obligated and authorised to directly provide these services or enter into franchise agreements as per the requirements specified in Clause 1, Article 66 of the Law. It is important to note that the legal responsibility for these services lies with the airport enterprise and not with external service providers. However, the current process of granting licenses for aviation services, which involves the airport enterprise engaging in a franchise agreement after an aviation service provider receives a permit, does not fully reflect the role of the airport enterprise.

The Law on Civil Aviation delves into the range of services offered by airport enterprises and operators. It defines aviation services in Article 11 as those directly tied to aircraft, air transport, and flight operations. Articles 65 and 66 broaden this definition to encompass all aviation services provided at airports without the limitations set in Article 11. However, there is a lack of clarity on how the State recognises and manages aviation services outside airports, such as long-term air warehouse services and in-town check-in procedures. Furthermore, there is uncertainty regarding the interplay between the Airport Business License, the Aviation Service Provision License of the airport operator, and the airport enterprise. Clause 4, Article 65 specifies the Government's responsibility to determine the list of aviation services, adding additional complexity to the regulatory landscape.[18]

---

[17] Bộ Giao thông vận tải/ Ministry of Transport, 'Văn bảnhợpnhấtNghịđịnhvềquảnlý, khaitháccảnghàngkhông, sân bay/Consolidated text of the Decree on management and operation of airports and aerodromes' (11/VBHN-BGTVT 2024), 30 March 2024, Arts. 3,6, available at, https://mt.gov.vn/vn/tin-tuc/91932/ban-hanh-van-ban-hop-nhat-ve-quan-ly--khai-thac-cang-hang-khong--san-bay.aspx. Last visited, 18 November 2024.

[18] Bộ Giao thôngVậntải/Ministry of Transport, 'Báo Cáo TổngKếtThiHànhLuậtHàngKhôngDânDụng Việt Nam/Report on the implementation of the Law on Civil Aviation of Vietnam', 21 December 2022, Art. 33, available at, https://datafiles.chinhphu.vn/cpp/files/duthaovbpl/bao-cao-tong-ket-luat-hkdd.docx. Last visited, 15 July 2024.

4 Ensuring Airport Management and Operation Activities

The effective management and operations of airports play a crucial role in upholding the safety, efficiency, security, and sustainability of aviation. To accomplish this, airports must diligently oversee various operational and management activities that align with national regulations and international standards, including those established by ICAO.

4.1 Safety Management Systems

Safety work is of utmost importance in the aviation industry. It requires unique characteristics that are specific to aviation. Therefore, establishing a safety management system is significant in ensuring safe and effective airport management. Safety Management Systems (SMS) are foundational in modern airport management, offering a structured approach to managing safety risks in aviation operations. That includes organisational structure, delineation of responsibilities, formulation of policies and procedures, and adherence to regulations.[19]

In Vietnam, the adoption of SMS in airports is mandated by national regulations and guidelines set by ICAO. All operators and aviation service providers must implement SMS to ensure compliance with the standards outlined in Annex 19 and the guidance provided in Doc 9859 on safety management. According to Clause 1, Article 68 of Circular No. 29/2021/TT-BGTVT issued by the Ministry of Transport on 30 November 2021, SMS is structured based on the framework announced by ICAO, encompassing four key components: safety policy and objectives, safety risk management, safety assurance, and safety promotion. These components apply to organisations engaged in civil aviation activities at airports in Vietnam.[20]

The safety policy and objectives ensure that the organisation is fully committed to managing safety effectively. That includes the organisation's clear commitment to safety, defining safety responsibilities and holding individuals accountable for safety. Additionally, the policy covers the coordination of emergency planning, the documentation of the safety management system, and the provision of resources to implement the safety policy. It also outlines the procedures for reporting safety issues, specifies unacceptable behaviours related to the organisation's aviation operations, and guides cases where disciplinary action is inappropriate.[21]

---

[19] Michaela Kešeľová & *et.al.*, 'Safety Management System in Aviation: Comparative Analysis of Safety Management System Approaches in V4 Countries', 2021, Management Systems in Production Engineering, p. 208 & 209.

[20] Bộ Giao thông vận tải/Msnistry of Transport, 'Thông tưhướngdẫnquảnlýkhaitháccảnghàngkhôngsân bay/Circular guiding management and operation of airports and aerodromes (29/2021/TT-BGTVT), 30 November 2021, available at, https://thuvienphapluat.vn/van-ban/Giao-thong-Van-tai/Thong-tu-29-2021-TT-BGTVT-huong-dan-quan-ly-khai-thac-cang-hang-khong-san-bay-496788.aspx. Last visited, 18 November 2024.

[21] *Id.*, Art. 70 para 1.

The practical implementation of a robust safety policy is paramount for meeting the stringent requirements set forth by the Vietnamese aviation authorities and adhering to the recommended practices of ICAO. This policy ensures full compliance with the regulations of the Vietnamese aviation authorities and strives to uphold the highest safety standards within the aviation industry. Within the safety policy, the organisation engaged in airport civil aviation activities clearly delineates each employee's accountability and safety responsibilities. That includes providing necessary resources to uphold the safety policy and fostering a work environment characterised by trust and a strong sense of responsibility. Additionally, the policy ensures the regular and effective maintenance of safety management practices to uphold the highest levels of safety.[22]

In the realm of aviation operations, the process of defining safety objectives holds paramount importance in ensuring the successful execution of the safety management system. Organisations engaged in civil aviation activities at airports must establish safety objectives as a fundamental framework for assessing and evaluating safety performance. This practice is a visible demonstration of the organisation's unwavering commitment to upholding and constantly enhancing the effectiveness of the safety management system. Furthermore, it is essential to subject safety objectives to periodic review, thereby guaranteeing their sustained relevance and suitability within the organisational context.[23] Organisations such as the Vietnam Air Traffic Management Corporation (VATM) carefully establish safety objectives for each operational phase in the context of Vietnam's civil aviation activities at airports. These objectives serve as comprehensive safety guidelines that encompass all facets of the organisation's activities. Additionally, these organisations wholeheartedly demonstrate their dedication to maintaining a safety management system, ensuring they effectively meet the established safety objectives.

Organisations engaged in civil aviation activities at airports, such as VATM, strive to establish and nurture a safety culture that integrates the unique values of individuals and the organisation. An individual's safety culture encompasses their behaviours, thoughts, and actions about safety issues. In contrast, an organisation's safety culture is reflected in its approach to and implementation of safety-related procedures and regulations. The safety culture comprises five fundamental elements:

- Culture of voluntary reporting: This is an environment where individuals can be trusted to report safety issues without fear of reprimand voluntarily. Safety informants must be confident that their information and reports will be received and acted upon appropriately.

[22] Triet Minh Huynh, Gyuseung Kim & Hun-Koo Ha, 'Comparative analysis of efficiency for major Southeast Asia airports: A two-stage approach', *Journal of Air Transport Management*, Vol. 89, 2020.

[23] Bộ Giao thông vận tải/Msnistry of Transport, 'Thông tưhướngdẫnquảnlýkhaitháccảnghàngkhôngsân bay/Circular guiding management and oparation of airports and aerodromes (29/2021/TT-BGTVT), 30 November 2021, Art. 70, para 2, available at, https://thuvienphapluat.vn/van-ban/Giao-thong-Van-tai/Thong-tu-29-2021-TT-BGTVT-huong-dan-quan-ly-khai-thac-cang-hang-khong-san-bay-496788.aspx. Last visited, 18 November 2024.

- Reporting culture: The organisation will collect and analyse relevant safety data and actively disseminate safety information to individuals.
- Culture of flexibility: The organisation's employees are adaptable, flexible in all situations, and proactive in reporting hazards.
- Learning Culture: Individuals can learn from their mistakes and seek to correct them. Employees are encouraged to learn and apply their skills and knowledge to improve the organisation's safety. Employees are informed and updated about safety issues, the consequences of incidents and lessons learned.
- Non-punitive culture: It refers to a safety culture where errors and potentially unsafe actions are considered without penalty if they are careless or unintentional and the risk is acceptable. However, intentional violations or careless actions with unacceptable risks will be punished according to regulations.[24]

Safety risk management is a crucial process that involves identifying potential hazards, assessing the associated safety risks, and taking steps to reduce these risks to the lowest acceptable level. This is done in accordance with the regulations and standards set by Vietnamese aviation authorities and international guidelines. The primary objective of safety risk management is to allocate resources in a balanced manner to address all identified safety risks and ensure that they are controlled and reduced effectively. It is crucial in balancing production and protection, which is essential in the overall safety management process. By implementing risk management practices, organisations can enhance safety across various facets of their operations, including service provision, maintenance, and the utilisation of modern and advanced technical systems. The safety risk management process encompasses several vital steps, including hazard identification, risk assessment, and risk mitigation. This involves classifying hazards, recording and monitoring them, conducting thorough analysis and evaluation, proposing and selecting appropriate risk reduction measures and actions, and providing feedback on the identified hazards. Overall, safety risk management is a comprehensive approach to ensure the safety and well-being of all individuals involved in aviation operations.[25]

Safety assurance is a critical component of SMS to ensure the continuous, appropriate, and effective management of safety risks. That involves regularly monitoring aviation operations and the operating environment to identify any changes that could lead to hazards or compromise the effectiveness of safety risk control measures. These changes could encompass deteriorating equipment performance, evolving operating procedures and conditions, or fluctuations in human capacity. Organisations engaged in civil aviation activities at airports are responsible for monitoring and evaluating

---

[24] Vietnam Air Traffic Management Corporation, 'Quyết định về việc phê duyệt Tài Liệu HệThống Quản Lý an Toàn (SMS)/Decision of approval of Safety Management System (SMS) Documentation', available at, https://www.vnaic.vn/images/stories/vnaic.vn/Van_hoa_ATHK/Thang_72014/03_5146-SMSM%20VATM%20V2.pdf. Last visited, 15 August 2024.

[25] Bộ Giao thông vận tải/Msnistry of Transport, 'Thông tưhướngdẫnquảnlýkhaitháccảnghàngkhôngsân bay/Circular guiding management and oparation of airports and aerodromes (29/2021/TT-BGTVT), 30 November 2021, Art. 71, available at, https://thuvienphapluat.vn/van-ban/Giao-thong-Van-tai/Thong-tu-29-2021-TT-BGTVT-huong-dan-quan-ly-khai-thac-cang-hang-khong-san-bay-496788.aspx. Last visited, 18 November 2024.

safety performance. They achieve this by developing and maintaining measures to verify and validate the organisation's safety performance and confirming the effectiveness of safety risk control measures. This process involves comparing safety indicators and targets within the safety management system to facilitate attaining safety objectives. Furthermore, organisations must establish and uphold a process for identifying changes that could impact the safety risks associated with their aviation products and services. They must also identify and manage safety risks resulting from such changes. In addition, organisations should continuously monitor and assess the effectiveness of safety management system processes to uphold and enhance the system's effectiveness over time.[26]

A comprehensive safety assurance process is in place to ensure safety within the SMS system of VATM. This process includes monitoring and evaluating safety performance, managing changes, and continually enhancing the SMS. Monitoring and measuring safety performance involves reviewing the Corporation's performance indicators focusing on safety goals. That encompasses safety reporting, safety performance assessment, safety inspection, supervision, safety survey, and internal verification. During operations, any changes introduced can create new hazards that may impact the effectiveness of existing safety risk mitigation methods. These changes can arise from internal sources, such as alterations in management structure, introduction of new equipment, or implementation of new strategies, as well as from external factors, such as changes in security regulations and requirements. Before implementing any changes, a rigorous change management process is applied to ensure safe implementation and reduce safety risks to an acceptable level. The Corporation's change management process is a structured approach consisting of four essential steps: change identification, change assessment, change approval, and change implementation. This comprehensive process considers various factors, including the criticality of the system and operations, the system's stability and operating environment, and past performance. The primary objective is continually enhancing the SMS to improve operational efficiency and meet evolving safety management requirements amidst changing conditions involving people, equipment, and the operating environment. The principle of safety assurance is based on a continuous improvement cycle, encompassing the control of safety implementation, adherence to regulations, regular assessments, and system upgrades. Additionally, VATM's SMS improvement process is an ongoing cycle that involves five fundamental steps: requirement identification, planning, implementation of improvement, inspection, assessment, and subsequent action.[27]

It is crucial for organisations to establish a comprehensive safety training program to ensure the safety of civilian aviation activities at airports. This program ensures that all employees have the necessary skills and knowledge to effectively carry

[26] *Id.*, Art. 72.

[27] Vietnam Air Traffic Management Corporation, 'Quyết định về việc phê duyệt Tài Liệu HệThống Quản Lý an Toàn (SMS)/Decision of approval of Safety Management System (SMS) Documentation', available at, https://www.vnaic.vn/images/stories/vnaic.vn/Van_hoa_ATHK/Thang_72014/03_5146-SMSM%20VATM%20V2.pdf. Last visited, 15 August 2024.

out safety management tasks. Moreover, organisations must implement a robust communication method and share safety-related information with all employees. That includes disseminating crucial safety updates, explaining the measures taken to enhance safety, and outlining the ongoing development and refinement of safety procedures. Cultivating a solid safety culture within the organisation is pivotal in meeting the stringent requirements set forth by ICAO and CAAV about SMS.[28]

The Civil Aviation Authority of Vietnam (CAAV) has taken steps to streamline document preparation and implement safety management systems at airports. These guidelines are designed to ensure that all procedures align with national laws and adhere to the standards and guidelines set by ICAO. They focus on meticulously preparing documents and establishing thorough safety management systems for airport operations[29]and infrastructure projects within the national airport system.[30] Implementing SMS is a mandatory requirement for organisations involved in airport operations and aviation services. As stated in Article 68 of Circular No. 29/2021/TT-BGTVT, these organisations encompass airport and airport operators, as well as other aviation service providers such as those offering passenger terminal operation services, terminal and cargo warehouse operation services, aviation fuel supply services, ground technical and commercial services, aviation catering services, and repair and maintenance services for aviation vehicles and equipment (Clause 2). CAAV and the Airport Authority are responsible for inspecting and supervising the implementation of the airport safety management system (Clause 6).

The aviation industry at airports is managed by various entities, all of which must adhere to SMS per the standards established by ICAO. ICAO emphasises the importance of a country's safety oversight capacity in ensuring adequate safety assurance. ICAO initiated the Universal Safety Oversight Audit Programme (USOAP) in January 1999 to evaluate this. The USOAP aims to assess whether countries effectively implement safety oversight systems, comply with ICAO standards and recommended practices, issue accurate documents and regulations, and allocate adequate

[28] Bộ Giao thông vận tải/Msnistry of Transport, 'Thông tưhướngdẫnquảnlýkhaitháccảnghàngkhôngsân bay/Circular guiding management and oparation of airports and aerodromes (29/2021/TT-BGTVT), 30 November 2021, Art. 73, available at, https://thuvienphapluat.vn/van-ban/Giao-thong-Van-tai/Thong-tu-29-2021-TT-BGTVT-huong-dan-quan-ly-khai-thac-cang-hang-khong-san-bay-496788.aspx. Last visited, 18 November 2024; Vietnam Air Traffic Management Corporation, 'Quyết định về việc phê duyệt Tài Liệu HệThống Quản Lý an Toàn (SMS)/Decision of approval of Safety Management System (SMS) Documentation', available at, https://www.vnaic.vn/images/stories/vnaic.vn/Van_hoa_ATHK/Thang_72014/03_5146-SMSM%20VATM%20V2.pdf. Last visited, 15 August 2024; Vietnam Airlines, 'Đào tạoHệthốngquảnlý an toàn (SMS) và Văn hóa an toànchocánbộchủchốtcủa VACS/Safety Management System SMS) and Safety Culture Training for VACS Key Staff',3 October 2023, available at, https://spirit.vietnamairlines.com/nang-tam-vna/dao-tao-he-thong-quan-ly-an-toan-sms-va-van-hoa-an-toan-cho-can-bo-chu-chot-cua-vacs.html. Last visited, 10 September 2024.

[29] CAAV, 'HướngDẫnLập Tài Liệu vàThiếtLậpHệThống Quản Lý an ToànCảngHàngKhông, Sân Bay/Guidance on Documenting and Establishing an Airport Safety Management System', available at, https://caa.gov.vn/tai-lieu-huong-dan-an-ninh-an-toan/huong-dan-lap-tai-lieu-va-thiet-lap-he-thong-quan-ly-an-toan-cang-hang-khong-san-bay-20160614143014402.htm. Last visited, 10 September 2024.

[30] *Id.*

resources for services. In May 2024, the USOAP Global Aviation Safety Inspection Team conducted a comprehensive assessment of the safety assurance capacity of the entire Vietnamese aviation industry.

According to the 2016 assessment results, Vietnam's aviation industry achieved an average Effective Implementation Index (EI) score of 65.56% for ensuring safety. However, the AGA field in Vietnam only scored 54.95%, placing it among the countries with AGA field scores lower than 60% in the Asia–Pacific region. That highlights the need for further improvements to ensure safety within Vietnam's aviation industry.[31] In 2024, the ICAO Aviation Safety Inspection Team released the assessment results, revealing that the Vietnamese aviation industry achieved significant progress in safety assurance work. The industry's efficiency index (EI) reached an impressive 78.14%, showing a notable increase of 12.58% compared to the 2016 assessment results. Notably, the airport and aerodrome operations (AGA) sector achieved an outstanding score of 83.85%, reflecting a substantial 28.9% improvement from the 2016 assessment. These results position Vietnam among the countries with a safety assurance efficiency index (EI) higher than the Asia–Pacific region's average of 65.31% and the global average of 68.81%. Notably, Vietnam's AGA sector outperformed with an efficiency performance index (EI) 23.12% higher than the average of countries in the Asia–Pacific region and 23.85% higher than the global average.[32]

SMS frameworks include identifying and mitigating safety risks, establishing performance indicators, and continuously monitoring and improving safety practices. However, the effective implementation of SMS requires regulatory compliance and a strong safety culture among all stakeholders, including airport management, airlines, and ground handling services.

---

[31] International Civil Aviation Organisation (ICAO), 'Safety Audit Results: USOAP Interactive Viewer', available at, https://www.icao.int/safety/Pages/USOAP-Results.aspx. Last visited, 8 September 2024.

[32] CAAV, 'Công TácĐảm Bảo an ToànHàngKhông 6 ThángĐầuNămvà Phương HướngThựcHiệnNhiệmvụ 6 ThángCuốiNăm 2024/Aviation Safety Assurance Work in the first 6 months of the year and Direction for Implementing Tasks in the last 6 months of 2024',22 July 2024, available at, https://caa.gov.vn/an-ninh-an-toan/cong-tac-dam-bao-an-toan-hang-khong-6-thang-dau-nam-va-phuong-huong-thuc-hien-nhiem-vu-6-thang-cuoi-nam-2024-20240722104307643.htm. Last visited, 8 September 2024; Phan Trang, 'Việt Nam đạtđiểmsốấntượngtrongthanhsát an toànhàngkhôngcủa ICAO/Vietnam scores impressively in ICAO aviation safety inspection',2024,*Government Electronic Newspaper*, available at, https://baochinhphu.vn/viet-nam-dat-diem-so-an-tuong-trong-thanh-sat-an-toan-hang-khong-cua-icao-102240917173422004.htm. Last visited, 11 September 2024.

4.2 Technological Advancements and Infrastructure Development

4.2.1 Role of Technology in Enhancing Safety and Efficiency

In Vietnam, the aviation sector leverages cutting-edge scientific and technological advancements to meet and exceed stringent international standards, enhancing operational efficiency and ensuring top-notch safety. Technological products such as airport lighting systems, automatic dependent surveillance systems (ADS-B), and air traffic message processing systems (AMHS) are employed. Moreover, adopting an automatic air traffic management system (ATM), integrated flight plan and flight data processing system, air traffic message processing system (AMHS), and 3D technology SIM systems for training and education significantly elevate the efficiency and quality of flight operations. In addition, global reservation systems (Galileo, Amadeus), passenger check-in systems (Sabres), pre-flight passenger information systems (APIS), and CUTE (Common Use Terminal Equipment) passenger check-in systems have played pivotal roles in enhancing service quality and streamlining travel for passengers. Notably, Vietnam has recently achieved significant milestones through the strategic application of technology in airport management.[33]

In the realm of automation and intelligent systems, Vietnam's airports, including critical hubs like Tan Son Nhat, Noi Bai International Airports, Da Nang, Phu Quoc, and Cam Ranh, have implemented cutting-edge technologies to enhance the passenger experience. Automated check-in kiosks and e-gates have been introduced to streamline the check-in and boarding processes, significantly reducing manual intervention and wait times. The Autogate system utilises facial recognition, passport scanning, and electronic chip reading to identify passengers accurately during immigration procedures. Notably, the Autogate system is seamlessly integrated with a comprehensive database of passport samples from countries worldwide, allowing it to read passports under international standards, such as ICAO. That means that upon completion of immigration procedures, the system rapidly cross-references the data with the database, enabling verified users to proceed with their flight swiftly. The implementation of the Autogate system at the airport offers a multitude of advantages. That includes facilitating administrative procedure reform, streamlining immigration processes, and significantly reducing the time required for immigration procedures for individuals and tourists. Furthermore, it alleviates congestion at the airport during immigration processes while enabling the comprehensive storage of information to support statistical analysis and state management. Additionally, the system conserves human resources by aiding inspectors and expediting passport issuance for travellers

---

[33] Bộ Giao thông Vận tải/Ministry of Transport, 'Báo Cáo Tổng Kết Thi Hành Luật Hàng Không Dân Dụng Việt Nam/Report on the implementation of the Law on Civil Aviation of Vietnam', 21 December 2022, available at, https://datafiles.chinhphu.vn/cpp/files/duthaovbpl/bao-cao-tong-ket-luat-hkdd.docx. Last visited, 15 July 2024.

while fortifying security measures and effectively preventing the falsification of immigration documents.[34]

Automated baggage handling systems are becoming more common, increasing efficiency and reducing lost luggage. These systems use advanced scanners and tracking technologies like RFID (Radio Frequency Identification) to monitor baggage in real time. Some airports have introduced intelligent parking management systems that help drivers locate available parking spots through mobile apps, reducing congestion and improving traffic flow within the airport. Some major airports, such as Tan Son Nhat and Noi Bai International Airports, apply the Airport Collaborative Decision Making (A-CDM) model to help aircraft take off and land faster and more on time. Previously, due to overload and separate operations of units, current procedures could not optimise operational efficiency, leading to many cases of departure order disruption, with aircraft departing only following the first come, first served method, resulting in many aircraft having to queue up for takeoff and landing.[35]

Technological advancements in Air Traffic Management (ATM) systems in Vietnam's airports have been instrumental in improving operational efficiency, ensuring flight safety, and managing the increasing demand for air traffic. Automatic Dependent Surveillance-Broadcast (ADS-B) technology allows aircraft to automatically transmit real time data about their position, altitude, and speed to ground stations. This enhances situational awareness for air traffic controllers, improving the accuracy of aircraft tracking. ADS-B has been deployed in Vietnam, especially in remote or offshore areas where traditional radar coverage is limited, increasing surveillance capabilities and reducing risks in air traffic management. Global Navigation Satellite System (GNSS) is replacing traditional ground-based navigation systems. It provides precise, real-time positioning for aircraft, improving navigation accuracy, especially in challenging weather conditions or limited visibility. This technology enhances route optimisation, allowing aircraft to follow more direct flight paths, saving fuel, reducing flight times, and lowering emissions. Vietnam has also adopted Air Traffic Flow Management (ATFM) systems to regulate air traffic flow efficiently. These systems analyse air traffic data to predict demand and manage capacity in real-time, helping to optimise the use of airspace and airport facilities.

---

[34] Khanh Linh & Anh Tu, 'CậncảnhhệthốngxuấtnhậpcảnhtựđộnghiệnđạiAutogatetạisân bay Tân Sơn Nhất/Modern automatic immigration system Autogate at Tan Son Nhat airport', *Labor Newspaper*, 4 August 2023, available at, https://laodong.vn/photo/can-canh-he-thong-xuat-nhap-canh-tu-dong-hien-dai-autogate-tai-san-bay-tan-son-nhat-1225066.ldo. Last visited, 15 August 2024; Thanh Dat & Son Bach, 'Cậncảnhhệthốngxuất, nhậpcảnhtựđộngtạisân bay Nội Bài/Automatic immigration system at Noi Bai airport', *People's Electronic Newspaper*, 23 December 2023, available at, https://nhandan.vn/post-788939.html. Last visited, 15 August 2024.

[35] Phan Trang, 'Chínhthứcápdụngcôngnghệ A-DCM tạisân bay Nội Bài/Implementing A-DCM technology at Noi Bai airport', *Government Electronic Newspaper*, 31 January 2024, available at, https://baochinhphu.vn/chinh-thuc-ap-dung-cong-nghe-a-dcm-tai-san-bay-noi-bai-102240131130619261.htm. Last visited, 11 August 2024; Tam Linh, 'Môhìnhgiúptăngtỷlệ bay đúnggiờchínhthứckhaithác tại Tân Sơn Nhất/Model to increase on-time flight rate officially launched at Tan Son Nhat', *Dan Tri Electronic Newspaper*, 31 January 2024, available at, https://dantri.com.vn/xa-hoi/mo-hinh-giup-tang-ty-le-bay-dung-gio-chinh-thuc-khai-thac-tai-tan-son-nhat-20240130161802154.htm. Last visited, 12 August 2024.

ATFM reduces congestion, minimises delays, and ensures air traffic moves smoothly during peak travel times, improving airport and airspace utilisation.

Controller-Pilot Data Link Communications (CPDLC) is a data-based communication system that enables air traffic controllers and pilots to exchange messages digitally rather than via traditional voice radio. This reduces radio congestion and improves the accuracy of communication, especially in busy airspaces. CPDLC is increasingly used in Vietnam to enhance communication reliability and reduce misunderstandings between pilots and air traffic controllers. Safety systems such as the Traffic Collision Avoidance System (TCAS) and Ground Proximity Warning System (GPWS) are integrated into Vietnam's ATM systems to prevent mid-air collisions and ground accidents. These systems, combined with advanced ATM technologies, ensure that aircraft maintain safe distances from one another, both in the air and during landing and takeoff, contributing to safer flight operations. Vietnam is utilising advanced simulation technologies to train air traffic controllers. These systems recreate real-world air traffic scenarios, enabling controllers to practice handling complex situations, such as high traffic volumes or emergencies. Continuous training through simulation enhances controllers' skills and prepares them for real life challenges in managing air traffic efficiently.[36]

The aviation industry is currently undergoing a digital transformation in line with the Prime Minister's guidelines outlined in Decision No. 794/QD-TTg dated June 3, 2020. This transformation involves the development of digital infrastructure and platforms through various initiatives. These initiatives include implementing CASORT software to provide and manage comprehensive information on aircraft and pilots, establishing a database system for vehicles, air vehicle operators, and aviation traffic infrastructure, and creating a specialised aviation database system for effective state management. Furthermore, activities such as managing private flights, aviation security, and coordinating take-off/landing times of airlines and airports are now being carried out through a secure and reliable software system.

4.2.2 Infrastructure Development

Infrastructure development is critical to addressing many of Vietnam's airports' capacity constraints. Major airports such as Tan Son Nhat International Airport and Noi Bai International Airport have undergone significant expansions and upgrades to accommodate the growing number of passengers and flights. However, infrastructure development must be carefully planned and executed to avoid disruptions to ongoing operations and to ensure that new facilities meet the highest safety and efficiency standards. Public–private partnerships (PPPs) have been explored to finance these projects, bringing together government resources and private sector expertise.

[36] Ha Anh, 'Pháttriểnhệthốngcảnghàngkhôngtheohướngđồngbộ, hiệnđại/Developing the airport system in a synchronous and modern direction', *Finance Journal*, 2023, available at, https://tapchitaichinh.vn/phat-trien-he-thong-cang-hang-khong-theo-huong-dong-bo-hien-dai.html. Last visited, 12 September 2024.

The strategic planning and development of airport and seaport infrastructure are essential factors that drive economic growth and the progress of the civil aviation sector. These plans encompass establishing, adjusting, and enhancing infrastructure to ensure timely upgrades and investments in airport construction. This is done to meet the growing demand for air transport while also considering the critical aspects of national defence and security, ensuring that all types of military aircraft can utilise the infrastructure of airports and seaports across the country. In 1997, the Prime Minister approved planning No. 911/1997/QD-TTg to develop a comprehensive national airport system comprising 34 major airports and 18 service airports. In 2009, the Prime Minister issued Decision No. 21/QD-TTg, which approved a comprehensive plan for the development of aviation transport up to 2020 and provided a long-term orientation towards 2030. This decision was a significant step in shaping the future of aviation in Vietnam. Subsequently, in 2018, the Prime Minister issued Decision No. 236/QD-TTg, which approved the adjustment of the aviation transport development plan, aiming to establish a system of 23 airports by 2020 and 28 airports by 2030. The government is currently reviewing and updating airport planning at a scale of 1/2000, a significant effort to ensure the efficient operation of the nationwide airport network system. This strategic planning is crucial in meeting the growing transportation demands of various localities and the entire country, contributing to the remarkable growth of Vietnam's aviation market, which has now become the world's second-fastest-growing.[37]

Over the last decade (2010–2020), Vietnam has seen a substantial influx of investment in its airport infrastructure. The total investment capital for airport projects during this period amounted to about 113.558 trillion VND. This investment was utilised to develop the aviation infrastructure system for 22 airports, comprising ten international airports (Noi Bai, Van Don, Cat Bi, Vinh, Phu Bai, Da Nang, Cam Ranh, Tan Son Nhat, Can Tho, Phu Quoc) and 12 domestic airports (Dien Bien, Tho Xuan, Dong Hoi, Chu Lai, Pleiku, Phu Cat, Tuy Hoa, Buon Ma Thuot, Lien Khuong, Rach Gia, Ca Mau, Con Dao). These airports and airfields have been invested in, constructed, renovated, and upgraded according to a planned strategy to enhance operational capacity, ensure security and safety, and meet national defence and security requirements. Of the 22 airports in Vietnam, Van Don International Airport is the only one operated under a public–private partnership model with a BOT contract.[38]

The Long Thanh International Airport in the Dong Nai Province near Ho Chi Minh City is Vietnam's most ambitious infrastructure endeavour. Projections indicate that it will become a pivotal regional aviation hub upon completion. The comprehensive project is estimated to cost around $16 billion and will be executed in several phases. Phase 1, slated for conclusion by 2025, aims to accommodate 25 million passengers

[37] Tri Dung, 'Tiếptụchoànthiệnmạnglướicảnghàngkhônghiệnđại, đồngbộ/Continue to complete the modern and synchronous airport network',*Vietnam Financial Times*, 2024, available at, https://thoibaotaichinhvietnam.vn/tiep-tuc-hoan-thien-mang-luoi-cang-hang-khong-hien-dai-dong-bo-151421-151421.html. Last visited, 10 September 2024.

[38] Thao Ngan, 'Ưutiênđầutưchohạtầngcảnghàngkhông/Priority investment in airport infrastructure', *Mekong ASEAN*, 2024, available at, https://mekongasean.vn/uu-tien-dau-tu-cho-ha-tang-cang-hang-khong-31288.html. Last visited, 11 September 2024.

annually. Upon full realisation, the Long Thanh International Airport will be able to cater to up to 100 million passengers each year, thereby alleviating congestion at Tan Son Nhat International Airport and establishing itself as a prominent international flight hub. Furthermore, Vietnam is actively enhancing its existing airports. Notably, Noi Bai International Airport, northern Vietnam's primary air travel hub, is undergoing substantial expansion efforts, including constructing a third terminal (T3) and extending its runways to bolster its flight-handling capabilities. By 2030, the airport will handle around 50 million passengers annually. Tan Son Nhat International Airport (Ho Chi Minh City) is one of the busiest airports in Southeast Asia. It is expanding with a new terminal (T3), increasing its capacity to handle up to 50 million passengers annually. Additional projects include runway upgrades and the construction of new taxiways to reduce congestion. As the gateway to central Vietnam, Da Nang International Airport is undergoing upgrades to meet the rising demand for both domestic and international flights. Expanding passenger terminals and runway improvements will boost its capacity to serve 20 million passengers annually.

Regional Airports have been developed. Van Don International Airport (Quang Ninh) is Vietnam's first privately developed airport, operated by Sun Group. Van Don serves the Ha Long Bay region and is a gateway for international tourists. The airport is designed with a capacity of 2.5 million passengers annually and is expected to expand further as regional tourism grows. Phu Quoc International Airport (Phu Quoc Island) has become a significant hub for tourism. It was developed to handle up to 10 million passengers annually, meeting the growing demand from international travellers. The island's strategic location makes the airport crucial for boosting tourism and economic development in the region. Cam Ranh International Airport (Khanh Hoa Province) serves Nha Trang, a popular beach destination. Cam Ranh has seen significant upgrades, including the addition of a new terminal, allowing it to accommodate over 8 million passengers per year, with further expansions planned.

The significant investment in airport infrastructure has led to substantial upgrades and expansions in various airports across Vietnam. Notable projects include the construction of the new Phu Quoc International Airport, the expansion of the Can Tho International Airport, and the enhancements of terminals and airport areas at Noi Bai, Tan Son Nhat, and Da Nang international airports. Civil aviation projects in Tuy Hoa, Phu Cat, and Cat Bi have been initiated. These developments, encompassing 22 airports, are aligned with modern and synchronised approaches, catering to the growing air transport industry while positively impacting local economic and social development. Additionally, they facilitate regional and international connectivity, propelling Vietnam towards becoming a high-income developed country.[39]

---

[39] Thu Huong, 'Quy hoạchpháttriểncảnghàngkhông Việt Nam: Tạođộnglựcpháttriểnkinhtế - xãhộiđịaphươngvàcảnước/Vietnam Airport Development Planning: Creating momentum for local and national socio-economic development', *Numbers & Facts Magazine*, 2023, available at, http://consosukien.vn/quy-hoach-phat-trien-cang-hang-khong-viet-nam-tao-dong-luc-phat-trien-kinh-te-xa-hoi-dia-phuong-va-c.htm. Last visited, 18 August 2024.

5 Shortcomings, Challenges and Recommendations

5.1 Shortcomings and Challenges

5.1.1 Challenges in Performing the Tasks of the State Aviation Management Agency

The current functions of the airport authority involve overseeing and managing airport operations, but several factors hinder its effectiveness. These include limited resources, organisational constraints, and enforcement mechanisms. The authority faces challenges related to staffing, particularly the lack of a specialised inspection organisation, which complicates the execution of public service activities. Furthermore, the staff's lower-than-average income compared to other industry units hampers the formation of aviation safety supervisory teams in line with ICAO requirements. It is imperative to explore and implement mechanisms to enhance its capacity and effectiveness to bolster the airport authority's role.[40]

Section 2a, Article 9 of the Law on Civil Aviation of Vietnam discusses the role of the supervisor and the standards the Minister of Transport sets. However, the law does not clearly define the legal status of supervisor or explain their role in the State management agency's inspection, examination, and supervision tasks. It has been observed that supervisors from the civil servant team of the Aviation Authority are well-suited for the supervisory function. However, implementing this is challenging due to job position restrictions outlined in Decree No. 111/2022/ND-CP, as well as the high cost of training and maintaining the quality of the supervisory team. Although Decree No. 66/2015/ND-CP and Decision No. 51/2016/QD-TTg of the Prime Minister allow the Vietnam Aviation Authority to hire flight safety supervisors and qualified flight safety supervisors through labour contracts using a unique financial mechanism, conflicts regarding the power and independence of the supervisor persist. This individual performs inspection and supervision functions on behalf of the Aviation Authority. Therefore, it is necessary to study the issue of supervisors in the Vietnam Aviation Law to address shortcomings and ensure compliance with international regulations.[41]

[40] Hoai Nga, 'ChứcNăng, Nhiệmvụ, CơCấuCụcHàngKhông Việt Nam/Functions, Tasks and Structure of the Civil Aviation Authority of Vietnam', *State Organization Journal*, 2015, available at, https://tcnn.vn/news/detail/18391/Chuc-nang-nhiem-vu-co-cau-Cuc-Hang-khong-Viet-Nam.html. Last visited, 18 August 2024.

[41] Tue Van, 'Đềxuấtmởrộngđốitượnggiámsátviên an toàn bay/Proposal to expand the scope of flight safety supervisors', *Government e-magazine*, 2024, available at, https://baochinhphu.vn/de-xuat-mo-rong-doi-tuong-giam-sat-vien-an-toan-linh-vuc-quan-ly-hoat-dong-bay-102240227170435308.htm. Last visited, 11 September 2024.

5.1.2 Challenges in SMS Implementation

The fundamental principle of civil aviation operations centres around the critical task of ensuring aviation safety. However, the current state of aviation operations reveals a growing complexity in the global aviation transport system, necessitating close coordination between civil aviation operations, aircraft safety, and the safety of airport and seaport operations. That has led to a concerted effort by countries worldwide to refine a proactive strategy focused on implementing the National Safety Program. This strategy aims to enhance the sustainability and stability of the components that constitute a system aimed at mitigating safety risks, ultimately fortifying the country's capacity for monitoring aviation safety.[42]

Annex 19 of the Chicago Convention on the Improvement of Safety Management Capacity requires restructuring the safety regulations based on existing principles to ensure that Annex 19 is implemented more effectively. The necessary additional contents currently include:

- Enhance the provisions of the National Civil Aviation Safety Program (SSP), which integrates 08 essential elements (CEs) of the National Safety Oversight System (1. Basic aviation laws and regulations; 2. Specific operational regulations; 3. Safety systems and functions; 4. Qualified technical personnel; 5. Technical guidance tools and provision of critical safety information; 6. Licensing, certification, authorisation and approval responsibilities; 7. Oversight responsibilities; 8. Addressing safety issues).
- Enhance Safety Management System (SMS) regulations to ensure effective implementation, including extending SMS applications to engine design and manufacturing organisations.

The content has been revised in the supplementary legal documents and operational guidelines of the Aviation Authority. Despite these adjustments, it is essential that these documents fully adhere to the regulations outlined in the Chicago Convention and the national safety framework. Consequently, there is a need to conduct a comprehensive review of aviation safety management regulations and make necessary additions to ensure they are thorough. That is crucial for establishing a robust national aviation safety monitoring capability.[43]

[42] Anh Tu, 'Kếhoạchhiệnthựchoáquyhoạchsân bay toànquốc/Plan to realize national airport planning', *VnEconomy Magazine*, 2024, available at, https://vneconomy.vn/ke-hoach-hien-thuc-hoa-quy-hoach-san-bay-toan-quoc.htm. Last visited, 14 September 2024.

[43] Bộ Giao thôngVậntải/Ministry of Transport, 'Báo Cáo TổngKếtThiHànhLuậtHàngKhôngDânDụng Việt Nam/Report on the implementation of the Law on Civil Aviation of Vietnam', 21 December 2022, available at, https://datafiles.chinhphu.vn/cpp/files/duthaovbpl/bao-cao-tong-ket-luat-hkdd.docx. Last visited, 15 July 2024.

5.1.3 Challenges in Infrastructure Development

The airport and airfield planning process in Vietnam is being carried out per Article 56 of the Law on Civil Aviation, Decree No. 05/2021/ND-CP, and the legal framework for planning. However, challenges have arisen due to inconsistencies in the classification of specialised technical planning between the Law on Civil Aviation and the Law on Planning, particularly in the terminology used. For example, while Clause 2, Article 56 of the Law on Civil Aviation refers to detailed planning of airports and airfields, Sect. 18 of Appendix II of the Law on Planning refers to planning of airports and airfields. This discrepancy implies that, if implemented according to the Law on Planning, airport and airfield planning may be conducted for the entire facility without the detailed planning required by the Law on Civil Aviation for each specific area within the airport and airfield. Therefore, the planning regulations in the Law on Civil Aviation need to be defined and adjusted to ensure accuracy and consistency in both terminology and content of implementation responsibilities.[44]

The investment in constructing airports is subject to the regulations outlined in the laws governing investment and construction. The Ministry of Transport is responsible for overseeing and managing the investment in construction, maintenance, and repair and ensuring the necessary conditions for the operation of airports. However, challenges have arisen in the execution process due to uncertainties surrounding the authority responsible for approving investment policies for construction projects and works. The Investment Law only designates the Prime Minister and the Provincial People's Committee as the two levels of authority to approve investment policies. In contrast, the Ministry of Transport is tasked with planning and developing airports. That has led to confusion regarding the entity responsible for approving investment policies for constructing items and works in airports.[45]

The government oversees and maintains essential infrastructure such as runways, taxiways, and airport facilities, which require significant investment and ongoing upkeep. Currently, the government has delegated the management and maintenance of these assets to private enterprises by the Law on Public Asset Management (Article 99) and Decree No. 44/2018/ND-CP (Clause 1, Article 27). However, there have been challenges in efficiently allocating resources to address the increasing demands for upgrades, repairs, and expansions, especially as the frequency and capacity of runways and taxiways grow. At the same time, the government's budget remains constrained by procedural and financial limitations.

---

[44] Tue Van, 'CầnthiếtxâydựngdựthảoLuậtHàngkhôngdândụng Việt Nam (sửađổi)/The necessity of drafting the Law on Civil Aviation of Vietnam (amended)', *Government e-magazine*, 2023, available at, https://baochinhphu.vn/can-thiet-xay-dung-du-thao-luat-hang-khong-dan-dung-viet-nam-sua-doi-102230609150930382.htm. Last visited, 18 August 2024.

[45] Thu Ha & Ngoc Bich, 'ĐầuTưHệThốngCảngHàngKhông Liên Hoàn, ĐồngBộ/Investing in a Complete and Synchronous Airport System', *Nhan Dan Magazine*, 2024, available at, https://special.nhandan.vn/phat-trien-he-thong-cang-hang-khong/. Last visited, 11 September 2024.

5.2 Recommendations

5.2.1 Legal Improvement: Amending the Law on Civil Aviation

Vietnam's aviation sector has experienced significant advancements over the past two decades, particularly in developing air transport and airport infrastructure. However, the legal framework governing civil aviation has evolved at a pace different from the rapid growth of the socio-economy and the practical demands of aviation management. While the Law on Civil Aviation of Vietnam and its associated regulations implemented since 2006 have generally ensured compliance with international standards, the system has not been promptly updated to incorporate ICAO's recent revisions, supplements, and practical recommendations introduced since 2016. The following areas require attention and review: specialised state management of civil aviation, the team of supervisors of the Aviation Authority, investment in airport construction, and the issuance of airport exploitation certificates. It is essential to revise the regulations on airport enterprises and airport operators to ensure that the rights and obligations of the involved parties are clearly defined and consistent with practical implementation. Additionally, the concepts of aviation services and aviation services at airports need to be reassessed to ensure clarity, consistency, and practical management, especially about the development of services at long-distance air warehouses, city airports (city air terminals), and in-town check-in procedures, to meet the evolving needs of the economy.[46]

The proposed amendment to the Law on Civil Aviation of Vietnam seeks to realign its objectives with the 2013 Constitution and to institutionalise the State's policy for developing civil aviation. It aims to ensure that the law aligns with the Chicago Convention and other international treaties on civil aviation, to which Vietnam is a signatory. The draft Law on Civil Aviation aims to build upon the current law, enhance its strengths, and address any outdated or obstructive provisions that may hinder the development of the civil aviation sector. It also seeks to draw from the experiences of other countries with conditions similar to Vietnam's to develop civil aviation further. Additionally, the amendment aims to promote the development of civil aviation through market mechanisms, create a fair, competitive environment for enterprises, and attract non-state resources to invest in aviation businesses. That is intended to reduce the burden on the State budget and develop a modern, safe, and efficient airport system per the strategy and planning approved by the Prime Minister.[47]

---

[46] Tue Van, 'CầnthiếtxâydựngdựthảoLuậtHàngkhôngdândụng Việt Nam (sửađổi)/The necessity of drafting the Law on Civil Aviation of Vietnam (amended)', *Government e-magazine*, 2023, available at, https://baochinhphu.vn/can-thiet-xay-dung-du-thao-luat-hang-khong-dan-dung-viet-nam-sua-doi-102230609150930382.htm. Last visited, 18 August 2024.

[47] Thien Thanh, 'LuậtHàngkhôngdândụng Việt Nam sửađổi: Khai tháchiệuquảtiềmnăngvềhàngkhôngdândụngphụcvụpháttriểnkinhtế - xãhội/Amended Law on Civil Aviation of Vietnam: Effectively exploiting the potential of civil aviation to serve socio-economic development', *Vietnam Law Newspaper Online*, 22 August 2023, available at, https://baophapluat.vn/post-485356.html. Last visited, 1 September 2024.

5.2.2 Enhancing Regulatory Compliance and Oversight

Enhancing regulatory compliance and oversight is necessary to ensure that Vietnam's airports continue to meet international safety and efficiency standards. This could involve establishing more robust monitoring mechanisms, periodic audits, and performance-based regulations incentivising continuous improvement. Additionally, greater coordination between the CAAV and other stakeholders, such as airlines and airport operators, can help align efforts to achieve standard safety and efficiency goals.[48]

It is essential to emphasise the pivotal role of the Airport Authority in managing the state's aviation operations. That involves closely monitoring and supervising the enforcement of aviation safety regulations. Revising the Civil Aviation Law to bolster the Airport Authority's ability to conduct thorough inspections and adequate supervision is necessary. These revisions will provide a clear framework for the airport authority's structure, functions, and responsibilities and outline its rights and obligations in overseeing civil aviation operations.

The amended Law on Civil Aviation aims to ensure enough resources for supervisors. If the specialised management agency has enough civil servants to carry out the task, the Aviation Authority will appoint the supervisor. However, if there is a shortage of civil servants, the Aviation Authority will appoint, employ, or assign supervisors who are enterprise employees and have the necessary capacity to perform the task. It is crucial to establish a rigorous management mechanism to prevent conflicts of interest between the supervised entity and the authorised supervisor and between the employee's role in the enterprise and their role as a supervisor when authorised by the state agency.[49]

CAAV has released a series of Aviation Safety Regulations, which includes the initial regulations from 2011 and subsequent amendments and supplements in 2016, 2017, 2018, 2020, 2022, and 2023. The authority has completed a draft for the 2024 amendments and supplements and seeks input from relevant units to ensure alignment with the latest international standards and best practices in aviation operations.[50]

---

[48] Pham Dong, 'Đềcaocôngtáckiểmtra, giámsáttronglĩnhvực an ninhhàngkhông/Promote inspection and supervision in the field of aviation safety', *Labor newspaper*, 22 February 2023, available at, https://laodong.vn/thoi-su/de-cao-cong-tac-kiem-tra-giam-sat-trong-linh-vuc-an-ninh-hang-khong-1150667.ldo. Last visited, 5 September 2024.

[49] Le Huu Viet, 'Nhân Lực GiámSát Viên HàngKhôngMớiĐápỨng 62%/Aviation Supervisor Staff Meets 62%', *Pioneer Magazine*, 2024, available at < https://tienphong.vn/nhan-luc-giam-sat-vien-hang-khong-moi-dap-ung-62-post1603648.tpo > Last visited, 4 September 2024.

[50] CAAV, 'Bộ Quy Chế an ToànHàngKhông/Aviation Safety Regulations', available at, https://caa.gov.vn/tai-lieu-quy-pham-phap-luat-an-toan-bay/bo-quy-che-an-toan-hang-khong---vietnam-aviation-regulations--20160728010010028.htm. Last visited, 12 September 2024.

5.2.3 Aviation Safety Management

The focus is on improving the sustainability and stability of the aviation system components to minimise safety risks and enhance the effectiveness of national aviation safety monitoring to comply with Annex 19 of the Chicago Convention. It is crucial to introduce specific regulations on system safety management in Vietnam's Civil Aviation Law to align with ICAO's eight critical elements of the national aviation safety monitoring system. Additionally, there is a need to research managing vehicles that operate regularly in restricted areas of airports and airfields to enhance the safety of civil aviation activities. That involves regulating regular airport and airfield operations, conducting inspections, and establishing detailed technical documentation for vehicle management, inspection, and monitoring.

We must prioritise enhancing aviation safety at enterprises by intensifying efforts to promote and educate people on safety procedures and regulations. It is crucial to closely monitor and investigate safety concerns and ensure strict enforcement of sanctions for any non-compliance that directly impacts flight safety. Furthermore, we should bolster inspection and supervision to maintain a well-coordinated operational system. It is essential to thoroughly evaluate the system and the process of addressing safety issues within airlines and disseminate safety lessons to all individuals in the system. Additionally, there is a need to establish research teams at various levels to propose specific regulations, procedures, and solutions for operating in dangerous weather conditions at airports. These teams should also be able to issue warnings or suspend operations when hazardous weather conditions are present.[51]

5.2.4 Leveraging Technology for Future Growth

As Vietnam's aviation sector continues to expand, it becomes increasingly important to harness the power of technology to manage the growing complexity of airport operations. Potential advancements could involve the implementation of artificial intelligence (AI) and machine learning algorithms to predict maintenance needs, utilising big data analytics to streamline airport processes and integrating the Internet of Things (IoT) for real-time monitoring and control of airport facilities. These technological innovations have the potential to significantly enhance both safety and efficiency, thereby ensuring that Vietnam's airports remain competitive in the

[51] CAAV, 'Công TácĐảm Bảo an ToànHàngKhông 6 ThángĐầuNămvà Phương HướngThựcHiệnNhiệmvụ 6 ThángCuốiNăm 2024/Aviation Safety Assurance Work in the first 6 months of the year and Direction for Implementing Tasks in the last 6 months of 2024', 22 July 2024, available at, https://caa.gov.vn/an-ninh-an-toan/cong-tac-dam-bao-an-toan-hang-khong-6-thang-dau-nam-va-phuong-huong-thuc-hien-nhiem-vu-6-thang-cuoi-nam-2024-20240722104307643.htm. Last visited, 8 September 2024; Phan Trang, 'Việt Nam đạtđiểmsốấntượngtrongthanhsát an toànhàngkhôngcủa ICAO/Vietnam scores impressively in ICAO aviation safety inspection', 2024, *Government Electronic Newspaper*, available at, https://baochinhphu.vn/viet-nam-dat-diem-so-an-tuong-trong-thanh-sat-an-toan-hang-khong-cua-icao-102240917173422004.htm. Last visited, 11 September 2024.

global aviation market. To proactively embrace the demands of Industry 4.0 and the ongoing digital transformation in state management activities, it is imperative to revise and supplement regulations about the application of science and technology in the management and advancement of the civil aviation sector, as well as rules related to digital transformation to meet the criteria outlined in Decision No. 749/QD-TTg concerning national digital transformation. That will enable Vietnam to participate actively in the Fourth Industrial Revolution.[52]

5.2.5 Planning and Investing in a Synchronous and Integrated Airport

The growth of the civil aviation industry is heavily dependent on thorough planning. It is crucial to establish harmony between the laws governing civil aviation and the Law on Planning to create a cohesive legal foundation for airport planning. Furthermore, it is essential to clearly define the scope of the comprehensive planning for developing the national airport system, focusing solely on planning its development and excluding specialised airports. With airports planned within a 100 km radius, nearly 96% of Vietnam's population has access to airports, surpassing the global average of 75%. The airport network is designed based on a hub-and-spoke structure model while incorporating the point-to-point model to meet market demand and facilitate domestic and international connections.[53]

It is crucial to diversify investment resources and modernise infrastructure systems and equipment to ensure the safety and efficiency of airport operations. That will enable airports to meet security requirements, maintain airspace sovereignty, and comply with ICAO roadmaps, requirements, and standards. Additionally, establishing logistics centres at airports with a transport demand exceeding 250 thousand tons per year is essential. These logistics centres will ensure appropriate warehouse conditions and facilitate the connection of different types of transport to handle the movement of goods at airports effectively. Furthermore, constructing aircraft maintenance and repair centres at airports in need is of utmost importance. Priority should be given to creating these centres at large airports with excellent infrastructure conditions and international routes.[54]

[52] N. Huyen, 'ChuyểnĐổiSốGắnVớiNhiệmvụPhátTriểnBềnVữngTạiMộtSốCảngHàngKhông/Digital Transformation Associated with Sustainable Development Tasks at Some Airports', *Vietnamnet Magazine*, 2023, available at, https://vietnamnet.vn/chuyen-doi-so-tai-mot-so-cang-hang-khong-2190751.html. Last visited, 3 September 2024.

[53] Thu Ha & Ngoc Bich, 'ĐầuTưHệThốngCảngHàngKhông Liên Hoàn, ĐồngBộ/Investing in a Complete and Synchronous Airport System',*Nhan Dan Magazine*, 2024, available at, https://special.nhandan.vn/phat-trien-he-thong-cang-hang-khong/. Last visited, 11 September 2024.

[54] Tri Dung, 'Đadạnghóanguồnlựcđầutưxâydựngkếtcấuhạtầnggiaothông/Diversify investment resources for building airport infrastructure', *Vietnam Financial Times*, 2022, available at, https://thoibaotaichinhvietnam.vn/da-dang-hoa-nguon-luc-dau-tu-xay-dung-ket-cau-ha-tang-giao-thong-101977.html. Last visited,12 September 2024.

Implementing these recommendations can enhance Vietnam's airport management system, ensuring it meets safety and efficiency benchmarks while preparing for future passenger and cargo traffic growth.

6 Conclusion

The efficient and safe operation of airports in Vietnam is paramount for the country's aviation sector to adhere to global safety and productivity standards. The existing regulatory frameworks provide a solid foundation for overseeing airport operations, but there is a pressing need for more flexible and forward-thinking policies. As technology advances and the aviation industry becomes more intricate, regulations must adapt to these changes. It is crucial to maintain alignment between Vietnam's regulatory framework and international standards to enhance safety, streamline operations, and support sustainable growth in airport management.

The efficient and safe management of airport operations relies on clearly defined and enforceable rights and obligations for all parties involved. Operators, service providers, and government bodies must comprehensively understand their roles and responsibilities to ensure the seamless functioning of airport activities. That includes adhering to stringent safety protocols, environmental regulations, and operational standards to guarantee the highest level of safety and efficiency. Furthermore, fostering transparent communication and collaboration between public and private entities is vital for establishing a robust and adaptable airport system that can effectively meet the needs of all stakeholders.

To ensure effective management and operational activities, Vietnam must prioritise continuous investments in modernising its infrastructure, such as runways, terminals, and air traffic control systems. Upgrading technologies, including radar systems and communication tools, is also crucial. Expanding the workforce's capabilities through training programs and skill development initiatives will also be essential. Streamlining processes, such as baggage handling and security checks, and improving coordination between key stakeholders, such as airlines, airport authorities, and government agencies, will lead to more efficient operations, reduced delays, and enhanced service quality for passengers. However, the current pace of expansion and modernisation has highlighted several areas for improvement and challenges. These include outdated infrastructure in some regional airports, congestion at major hubs and insufficient safety measures that require immediate attention to ensure sustainable growth and development within the aviation sector.

It is imperative to update regulations to foster innovation, strengthen safety and security protocols, foster collaboration between entities, and embrace sustainable practices. By addressing these critical areas, Vietnam can guarantee its airports' efficient and secure operation, solidifying the country's position as a competitive hub in the global aviation industry. Forward-looking investments in infrastructure, regulatory reform, and stakeholder engagement are crucial to surmounting existing barriers and ensuring the enduring success of airport management in Vietnam.

Chapter 14
An Evaluation of the Public Private Partnership Model in the Governance of Indian Airports

Anuradha Roy Chowdhury

Abstract India has been an enthusiastic supporter of the Public Private Partnership (PPP) model in recent years and numerous infrastructure projects have been conducted through this model. Being the third largest aviation market in the world has put significant pressure on the development of Indian airports and the PPP model has been adopted in many airport projects, both greenfield and brownfield. Since the use of the PPP model to develop the Greenfield Cochin International Airport in 1994, there are now 14 operational PPP airports in India. More PPP airport projects are planned as per the National Monetisation Pipeline, which states that 25 airports currently operated by the Airports Authority of India are earmarked for leasing between 2022 and 2025.In light of this, it becomes crucial to evaluate the operations and governance of these long-term projects. The importance of the analysis is compounded by the fact that in the financial year 2022–2023, only 3 of these PPP airports made a profit. Many other PPP airports made significant losses and some airport PPP projects have failed to materialise. Here, the author considers some of the differences between various PPP airports in India, both profit and loss making and highlights the potential governance concerns that arise and potential ways to resolve them. These include prior resolution of land allocation issues, a fair and transparent tendering process and the appropriate designing of PPP contracts with sufficient flexibility, clarity of scope and dispute resolution mechanisms.

Keywords Airports Authority of India (AAI) · Bangalore International Airport Limited (BIAL) · GMR-Fraport · Greenfield airport · Indira Gandhi International Airport (IGIA) · Kempegowda International Airport in Bengaluru (KIA) · National Infrastructure Pipeline (NIP)

A. Roy Chowdhury (✉)
The West Bengal National University of Juridical Sciences, Kolkata, India
e-mail: anuradharoychowdhury@nujs.edu

© The Author(s), under exclusive license to Springer Nature Singapore Pte Ltd. 2025

S. Bhat B. (ed.), *Aerodrome Governance in Asia*,
https://doi.org/10.1007/978-981-96-7568-5_14

1 Introduction

As economies grow, so do their infrastructure needs. Often, governments are unable to keep up with the requisite demand for infrastructure or are unable to finance the required infrastructure projects from the public budget. This has led to the search for 'innovative financing techniques that will allow important projects to move forward without the political downside of increasing taxes or fees.'[1] In that respect, governments often seek help from the private sector, hoping to capitalise on the efficiency gains and deeper pockets that private players can provide. However, governments (and the governed) may not be keen to allow the private sector to take complete responsibility over infrastructure projects This is because there is often some political and social sensitivity and anxiety in relation to the private sector operating on projects that may be linked to providing basic needs to the public. This hesitation has led to the popularity of the Public Private Partnership (PPP) model.

The PPP model has been highlighted as a modern revolution of governance[2] as it allows a unique structure where both the private and public sectors are involved. There exists no canonical or universal definition of the PPP. This may well be intentional since it offers a flexibility that allows many formations within its ambit. However, many definitions abound of the PPP and these render the PPP as an 'agreement between at least a private entity and a public authority for the joint management of one or more activities in the satisfaction of a public interest.'[3] Similar definitions are used by International Organisations. For instance, the World Bank views the PPP as 'a long-term contract between a private party and a government entity, for providing a public asset or service, in which the private party bears significant risk and management responsibility, and remuneration is linked to performance.'[4] The International Monetary Fund (IMF) on the other hand takes a much broader view and describes public private partnerships as 'arrangements where the private sector supplies infrastructure assets and services that traditionally have been provided by the government'.[5]

A more detailed description emerges from the Indian government which defines a PPP as.

> a form of fixed-term contractual arrangement between a public entity on one side and a private entity on the other, for the provision of public assets and/or public services, through

---

[1] Jeffrey N. Buxbaum & Iris N. Ortiz, 'Protecting the Public Interest: The Role of Long-Term Concession Agreements for Providing Transportation Infrastructure', *The Keston Institute for Public Finance and Infrastructure Policy Research Paper Series Index, Research Paper* 07–02 – June 2007, p. 3, available at, https://worldcat.org/digitalarchive/content/cdm266301.cdmhost.com/CBT/p266401coll4/0000069133/20070618-trans-concession-agreements.pdf. Last visited, 18 August 2024.

[2] Sara Valaguzza & Eduardo Parisi, *Public Private Partnerships: Governing Common Interests*, (Edward Elgar Publishing Ltd, 2020) p. 2.

[3] *Id.*, at 115.

[4] World Bank, *Public–Private Partnerships: Reference Guide Version 3*, (World Bank, Washington, 2017) p. 1.

[5] International Monetary Fund, Fiscal Affairs Department, *Public-Private Partnerships*, (IMF, 2004) p.4.

investments being made and/or management being undertaken by the private entity, may or may not require payment of fee by users, for a specified period of time, where there is well defined allocation of risk between the private entity and the public entity and the private entity's performance is contractually obligated to conform (or are benchmarked) to specified and pre-determined performance standards.[6]

PPP projects tend to have significant differences from either entirely commercial projects or traditional procurement projects as they are funded by private investors, tend to be medium to long term projects, typically greater than 20 years and with shared risk allocation with a greater burden of risk on the private sector. These projects may be of several types- they can range from the simplest form, design-build, to more complex transactions, including design-build-finance-operate (DBFO) or long-term leases/concession agreements.[7] The various models of PPP involve some collaboration between the government and the private sector, but the extent of involvement, financial liability and risk may differ based on the type of agreement.

PPP projects have significant benefits that can be tapped into, since they allow the public sector to attract private capital, transfer some risk to the private sector and also benefit from the efficiency gains and access to technology that the private sector has. It also encourages competition in the tendering process. In a sense, the PPP is a long-term solution to the provision of public infrastructure where problems such as poor construction quality and inadequate maintenance abound. The PPP model addresses this since in most PPP projects the private sector recoups their investment at a later stage and thus both maintenance and construction costs are included and a priority for the private partner.

Considering these advantages, it is unsurprising that the PPP model has been 'strongly endorsed by international organisations including the United Nations, the Organisation for Economic Cooperation and Development (OECD), the International Monetary Fund (IMF), the United Nations Educational, Scientific and Cultural Organisation (UNESCO) and the United Nations Commission on International Trade Law (UNCITRAL) (to name just a few) as a means to achieve globally significant goals.'[8] Alongside this, due to the complexity, international organisations have strongly promoted good practices and confidence and capacity building in the public sector[9] in relation to PPPs. There has also been a push towards the development of international guidelines and principles on the operation of PPPs by the OECD, the World Bank, the IMF and UNCITRAL.[10]

---

[6] 'Glossary of Terms- Public Private Partnership', *Public Private Partnership in India*, available at, https://www.pppinindia.gov.in/glossary. Last visited, 25 August 2024.

[7] *Supra* note 1, at 4.

[8] *Supra* note 2, at 30 & 31.

[9] *Id.*, at 48.

[10] See Organization for Economic Cooperation and Development, Recommendation of the Council on Principlesfor Public Governance of Public Private Partnerships,OECD/LEGAL/03932, (2024);UNCITRAL Model Legislative Provisions onPrivately Financed Infrastructure Projects, (2004).

PPPs have also been globally used in developing both brownfield and Greenfield airports. Article 79 of the Chicago Convention[11] expressly permits the use of PPPs in airports.[12] The World Bank data highlights that between 1900 and 2023, 52 countries have private participation in the airport sector, with 207 Projects reaching financial closure with total investment of $ 129,502 million US dollars.[13] Of these, 15 Projects representing 4.77% of total investment were cancelled or under distress.[14]

2 PPP Airports in India

India has wholeheartedly subscribed to the PPP model. In recent years, there has been a significant surge in PPI investments. The Indian government has made a concentrated effort towards attracting private investors to invest in infrastructure projects in India, through the National Infrastructure Pipeline (NIP) and National Monetisation Pipeline (NMP).[15] The NIP was launched in 2019 by the government with an intention to attract investment in social and economic infrastructure projects over a 5-year period. This was to operate in tandem with the NMP, launched in 2021, to create new sources of revenue for the government and its entities by unlocking the economic value of unutilised or underutilised public assets, and using private sector investment to create new infrastructure. The Indian Government has established the Private Investment Unit as part of the Infrastructure Finance Secretariat in the Department of Economic Affairs. This Private Investment Unit is responsible for policy-level matters concerning PPPs and also gives clearances through the Public Private Partnership Appraisal Committee as well as Government funding schemes relating to the same. However, despite the creation of a government department, there is no specific regulation or law that governs all PPPs in India. Like many other jurisdictions, the PPP agreement is subject to contract law and the Special Purpose Vehicle that is created for the PPP is governed by company law. This is alongside any sectoral laws and rules that may exist.

India now has a significant number of PPPs with a significant amount of investment- the World Bank data highlights that 297,412 million US dollars have been

[11] International Convention on International Civil Aviation (Chicago Convention), (1994) 15 U.N.T.S. 295.

[12] Article 79 states that a 'State may participate in joint operating organizations or in pooling arrangements, either through its government or through an airline company or companies designated by its government. The companies may, at the sole discretion of the State concerned, be state-owned or partly state-owned or privately owned'.

[13] World Bank- Infrastructure Finance, PPPs and Guarantees, 'Sector Snapshots- Airport', available at, https://ppi.worldbank.org/en/snapshots/sector/airports. Last visited, 25 August 2024.

[14] *Id.*

[15] World Bank, 'Private Participation in Infrastructure- Annual Report', 2022, p. 14, available at, https://ppi.worldbank.org/content/dam/PPI/documents/PPI-2022-Annual-Report.pdf. Last Visited, 9 November 2024.

invested in PPP projects with 1,182 projects reaching financial closure.[16] However, the data also shows that 35 projects representing 4.97% of total investment were projects cancelled or under distress.[17] This is more than the average of distressed projects in South Asia which stands at 3.29% as per the data published by the World Bank.[18]

As a part of the growth of investment in infrastructure, investments in airports have also been a significant agenda of the Indian government. This investment becomes even more crucial if we consider the fact that India now has the third largest domestic aviation market globally, second only to the United States of America and China.[19] The number of seats in domestic sectors is growing at a rate of 6.9% making it the fastest growing domestic aviation market in the world.[20] Due to this increased air traffic, there is an urgent need for capacity augmentation at the existing airports or development of new airports near existing airports.[21]

In this context it is unsurprising that the Indian government has looked at alternative financing methods of meeting their aerodrome requirements. The appeal of the PPP model in providing infrastructure for airports is undeniable. It allows financing from external sources but recognises that due to the public utility nature of the industry as well as national security concerns, the government would wish to retain a stake in the airport. This was recognised by the Indian Government in the Airport Infrastructure Policy of 1997 which cited that due to the unavailability of public funds, private participation would be important in the development of airport infrastructure.[22] Airports in India are governed by the Airports Authority of India (AAI) which was established by the Airports Authority Act (AAA) 1994. It is also pertinent to observe that India has ratified and is bound to the international standards imposed

---

[16] World Bank- Infrastructure Finance, PPPs and Guarantees, 'Country Snapshots- India', available at, https://ppi.worldbank.org/en/snapshots/country/india. Last visited, 25 August 2024.

[17] *Id.*

[18] World Bank- Infrastructure Finance, PPPs and Guarantees, 'Region Snapshots- South Asia', available at, https://ppi.worldbank.org/en/snapshots/region/south-asia. Last visited, 25 August 2024.

[19] 'India becomes world's third-largest domestic aviation market', *News on Air*, 28 June 2024, available at, https://www.newsonair.gov.in/india-becomes-worlds-third-largest-domestic-aviation-market/. Last visited, 18 August 2024.

[20] *Id.*

[21] CRISIL Infrastructure Advisory and NITI Aayog (Government of India), 'New Approaches to PPP Focusing on the Airport Sector-Final Report', May 2019, pp. 14, available at, https://www.niti.gov.in/sites/default/files/2023-03/New%20Approaches%20to%20PPP%20focusing%20on%20the%20Airport%20Sector.pdf. Last visited, 19 August 2024.

[22] Sairam Bhat, 'A Sectoral Analysis of Public Private Partnership', in Sairam Bhat (ed.), *Public Private Partnership in India- A Sectoral Analysis,* (Bengaluru: National Printing Press, 2018) pp. 1–35 at p. 14.

by the Chicago Convention[23] as well as the International Civil Aviation Organisation (ICAO) Standards and Recommended Practices (SARPs) adoption that regulate international air transport.[24]

PPP in airports is permitted in India. The Constitution of India places the provision, regulation and organisation of aerodromes within the Union List[25] which means that Parliament has exclusive power to make laws in respect of aerodrome requirements.[26] In that regard, the Government has passed many laws in relation to aerodrome requirements. The Aircraft Rules, 1937 state that a license for an aerodrome can only be granted to a citizen of India; a company or body corporate that is registered and having its principal place of business in India as well as meeting the equity holding criteria specified by the central government; the central government or state government or company controlled by said governments or a registered society.[27] A 2003 amendment to the AAA 1994 introduces the concept of a private airport which permits airports to be owned, managed and controlled by any person or agency other than the AAI or any State Government, or any person or agency jointly with the AAI or any State Government or both where the share of such person or agency in the assets of the private airport is more than fifty per cent.[28] This paves the way for PPPs being established as a mode of building and operating airports in India.

To further encourage private players into aerodrome infrastructure, the National Civil Aviation Policy 2016 highlights that the Ministry of Civil Aviation (MoCA) will endeavour to provide regulatory certainty by coordinating with various stakeholders, by trying to ensure that future airport projects in India are cost effective with no compromise on safety, security and efficiency and will explore ways to unlock restrictions on the use of land allocated for commercial use of airport.[29] Other regulations are also geared towards permitting private investment into airports. For instance, to allow foreign investment in airports, foreign direct investment of 100% under the automatic route is permitted for Greenfield and brownfield airports.[30]

The World Bank's data on India's private participation in infrastructure highlights that 16 projects in the Airport sector were reaching financial completion in

---

[23] *Supra* note 11.

[24] Press Information Bureau, Cabinet Press Release, 22February 2023, available at, https://www.pib.gov.in/PressReleasePage.aspx?PRID=1901256. Last visited, 19 August 2024.

[25] The Constitution of India, 1950, Seventh Schedule, List 1, Entry 29.

[26] *Id.*, Art. 246 (1).

[27] The Aircraft Rules, 1937, Rule 79.

[28] Airports Authority of India (Amendment) Act, 2003, No. 43 of 2003 (7 September 2003), Sec. 2(nn).

[29] Ministry of Civil Aviation (Government of India), National Civil Aviation Policy, 2016, available at, https://www.aai.aero/sites/default/files/basic_page_files/Final_NCAP_2016_15-06-2016-3%20%281%29.pdf. Last visited, 20 August 2024.

[30] Ministry of Commerce and Industry, Consolidated FDI Policy, 15 October 2020, available at, https://dpiit.gov.in/sites/default/files/FDI-PolicyCircular-2020-29October2020.pdf. Last visited, 20 August 2024.

2023 representing a value of 14,687 million US dollars.[31] There are currently 14 PPP airports in India. These are the airports in Cochin, Bangalore, Hyderabad, Kannur, Delhi, Mumbai, Ahmedabad, Lucknow, Mangalore, Jaipur, Guwahati, Thiruvananthapuram, Durgapur and Mopa.[32] Yet, out of these PPP airports, only 3 airports (Cochin, Bangalore and Hyderabad) made profit in the financial year 2022–2023 (and only 1 airport (Cochin)) made a profit in the financial year 2021–2022.[33] This is also replicated in the generally dismal profitability of airports in India- of the 125 non-PPP airports in India, 93 also made a loss in the financial year 2022–2023 (25.6%).[34]

A number of proposed PPP projects for airports have also failed to take off. For instance, 3 proposed projects in Karnataka- the Shimoga, Bijapur and Kalaburagi airport PPP projects did not materialise. The Bijapur airport failed to materialise as the private agency which had received the contract to implement it, demanded an additional 1,000 acres of land, which the government viewed as a breach of the Memorandum of Understanding[35] after which the government decided to abandon the PPP model. The Shimoga airport had been awarded to a consortium led by Maytas Infra Ltd, NCC Infrastructure Holdings Ltd (NCC), and VIE India Project Development and Holdings on 15 November 2007 on a Build Operate Transfer (BOT) basis which was for 30 years with an option to extend for another 30 years.[36] In order to facilitate the PPP, a special purpose vehicle, Shivamogga Airport Developers Private Limited (SDAPL) was created where the shareholding pattern of Maytas Infra Ltd, NCC and VIE was 37 per cent, 37 per cent and 26 per cent, respectively.[37] The project development agreement was signed on 21 December 2008 between this special purpose vehicle and with the Infrastructure Development Department (IDD) of the Government of Karnataka. There was a change in the project shareholding after which another supplementary development agreement, was signed in 2010and Regional Airport-Holdings International Limited acquired 22% of the company.[38] However, this project too was shelved in 2015 by the Government which decided to annul the land allotment for the airport on grounds like "indifference and infighting" among

[31] World Bank- Infrastructure Finance, PPPs and Guarantees, 'Country Snapshots- India', available at, https://ppi.worldbank.org/en/snapshots/country/india. Last visited, 9 November 2024.

[32] Press Information Bureau, Ministry of Civil Aviation Press Release, 4 December 2023, available at, https;//pib.gov.in/PressReleaseIframePage.aspx?PRID = 1,982,289. Last visited, 19 August 2024.

[33] *Id.*

[34] *Id.*

[35] Firoz Rozindar, 'Greenfield airport project in Bijapurhits a roadblock', *The Hindu*, 5 July 2012, available at, https://www.thehindu.com/todays-paper/tp-national/greenfield-airport-project-in-bijapur-hits-a-roadblock/article3604298.ece. Last visited, 12 August 2024.

[36] Manohar Yadavatti, 'Shivamoga Airport: A much delayed, derailed project has a safe landing', *Organiser*, 6 March 2023, available at, https://organiser.org/2023/03/06/163961/bharat/shivamoga-airport-a-much-delayed-derailed-project-has-a-safe-landing/. Last visited, 12 August 2024.

[37] *Id.*

[38] *Id.*

the promoters- no construction had happened till then.[39] This failed PPP, however, has a happy ending as ultimately the project was completed by the government and the airport opened for business in 2023.

A similar situation occurred in case of the Kalaburagi Airport. This airport project had commenced in 2007 on PPP mode by Gulbarga Airport Developers Limited [GADL a consortium of Maytas Infra Ltd, NCC Infra Holdings & VIE India]. However, the contract was terminated as GADL could not complete the work, following which the state government has taken up the project.[40] The Government backed out of the PPP due to significant delays caused by serious disputes in relation to financial mismanagement between the shareholders of the project.[41]

This highlights some of the issues that PPP projects in the aerodrome industry face. This idea will be revisited, highlighting the governance issues that are faced by such projects and how these can be resolved. However, the next section looks at two PPP airports operating in India- one which is profit making and one that is loss making, to help identify the key stresspoints for PPP governance in India.

3 Case Studies

This Section looks at two PPP airports in India- the Kempegowda International Airport in Bengaluru (KIA) and the Indira Gandhi International Airport in New Delhi (IGIA). The choice to look into these two airports is based on the fact that as per the data published by the MoCA, in 2022–2023 KIA made a profit of INR 528.31 crore and IGIA made a loss of INR 284.86.[42] Based on this, the case studies highlight some of the factors that may be responsible for a more profitable (and thereby successful) PPP airport project and some of the factors that may lead to problems in the future. The case studies are also used to highlight certain pressure points in PPP projects that need to be addressed at any earlier stage for these projects to operate smoothly, making a profit and being fully compliant with international obligations like the Chicago Convention.

---

[39] *Id.*

[40] Editor, 'Karnataka government signs MoU with AAI for development of Kalaburagi airport', *The New Indian Express*, 24 August 2019, available at, https://www.newindianexpress.com/states/karnataka/2019/Aug/24/karnataka-government-signs-mou-with-aai-for-development-of-kalaburagi-airport-2023771.html. Last visited, 18 August 2024.

[41] Editor, 'Airport projects in four cities in limbo as promoters back out', *Deccan Herald*, 19 June 2013, available at, https://www.deccanherald.com/content/339636/airport-projects-four-cities-limbo.html. Last visited, 19 August 2024.

[42] Press Information Bureau, Ministry of Civil Aviation Press Release, 4 December 2023, available at, https;//pib.gov.in/PressReleaseIframePage.aspx?PRID = 1,982,289. Last visited, 19 August 2024.

3.1 Kempegowda International Airport, Bengaluru

The KIA is an international airport that operates in Bengaluru which is the Capital of the State of Karnataka. The Airport is located 40 km outside the city and is spread over 4000 acres of land.[43] It is the third-busiest airport in India, after the airports in Delhi and Mumbai, with annual passenger traffic of 37,528,533 in 2023–2024.[44] The airport commenced operations in May 2008.

The KIA was developed under the Build Own Operate Transfer (BOOT) Model. Under this model, the developer designs and builds a complete project or a facility at little or no cost to the government, owns and operates the facility as a business for a specified period, after which transfers it to the government at a previously agreed-upon or market-price.[45] This project was first proposed to be completed with a consortium comprising the Tata Group, Raytheon and Singapore's Changi Airports Authority with the Memorandum of Understanding (MOU) signed in 1995but was later shelved due to delays in clearance.[46] This project was ultimately awarded to an international consortium in October 2001 who had participated in the tender process. A special purpose vehicle called Bangalore International Airport Limited (BIAL) was created and the concession agreement between the Government of India and BIAL was signed in July 2004.

At the time of the signing of the agreement a private consortium held a 74% stake in BIAL which consisted of the following private promoters: Siemens Project Ventures 40%, Flughafen Zurich AG Ltd 17% and L&T 17%.[47] However this shareholding has changed since then, although the 74% private stake remains. These changes happened after certain lock in stipulations that were present in the original shareholder agreement.[48] The remaining 26% are owned by State promoters; AAI

---

[43] 'Kempegowda International Airport, Bengaluru, India', *Airport Technology*, 7 June 2023, available at, https://www.airport-technology.com/projects/kempegowda-international-airport-bangalore/?cf-view. Last visited, 20 August 2024.

[44] 'Top 10 Busiest Airports in India', *Forbes India*, 16 July 2024, available at, https://www.forbesindia.com/article/explainers/busiest-airports-india/93641/1. Last visited, 20 August 2024.

[45] 'Glossary of Terms- BOOT', *Public Private Partnerships in India*, available at, https://www.pppinindia.gov.in/glossary. Last visited, 20 August 2024.

[46] Stephen David, 'Grounded by Politics', *India Today*, 31 January 1997, available at, https://web.archive.org/web/20160403153833/; http://indiatoday.intoday.in/story/wranglings-between-the-centre-and-karnataka-puts-proposed-devanahalli-airport-in-limbo/1/276255.html. Last visited, 19 August 2024.

[47] Concession Agreement for the Development, Construction, Operation and Maintenance of the Bangalore International Airport between Ministry of Civil Aviation, Government of India and Bangalore International Airport Limited,5 July 2004, available at, https://www.civilaviation.gov.in/sites/default/files/2023-02/moca_000743.pdf. Last visited, 19 August 2024, Clause 6.1.2.

[48] Shareholder Agreement between Karnataka State Industrial Investment and Development Corporation Limited, Airports Authority of India, Siemens Project Ventures GmbH, Flughagen Zuerich AG, Larsen & Toubro Limited, Bangalore International Airport Limited in respect of the Greenfield Bangalore International Airport Project, 23 January 2002, available at, https://ksiidc.karnataka.gov.in/storage/pdf-files/Projects/Share-holder-agreement-min.pdf. Last visited, 20 August 2024, Clause 7.7.

as well as the Karnataka State Industrial Investment & Development Corporation Limited (KSIIDC) each hold each 13%.[49]

The concession period for this project is of thirty years, with an option to extend it for another thirty years. The concession agreement states that the Indian government grants BIAL the exclusive right and privilege to carry out the development, design, financing, construction, commissioning, maintenance, operation and management of the Airport, excluding any reserved activities.[50] While the profits of the airport are to be retained by BIAL, a concession fee of 4 per cent of the gross revenue is to be paid annually by BIAL to the government of India.[51]

The initial estimated cost of KIA was initially Rs. 1,410 crores.[52] However, this figure was based on the fact that the project was initiated when traffic growth was comparatively low. As traffic growth increased, AAI increased the capacity of the airport, leading to an increase in the project scope and therefore the cost increased, with a final cost of Rs. 2470 crores.[53] Financing for this project was heavily skewed towards debt, with a debt-equity ratio of 70:30 with a significant amount of financing from commercial and development banks.[54] This is also apparent from the equity commitment in BIAL where the commitment of the private players was Rs. 207.2 crores and the government commitment was Rs. 72.8 crore.[55]

The construction of the project started on 2 July 2005, after the financial closure. The concession agreement stated that the construction would have to be completed within 33 months of financial closure and would otherwise attract penalties,[56] and BIAL managed to complete the project within that time frame. It is interesting to compare this with the significantly longer 73 months that it took from conceptualisation of the project to the signing of the land lease deed.[57] In this context it is unsurprising that the financial closure for BIAL was completed soon after the signing of the land lease agreement as the lenders did not wish to shoulder the risk involved in land acquisition and refused to make any financial commitment till it was over.[58]

---

[49] ICAO, 'Public Private Partnerships- Case Study- India', July 2015, p. 3, available at, https://www.icao.int/sustainability/PPP%20Case%20Studies/PPP_Airport_India.pdf. Last visited, 19 August 2024.

[50] *Supra* note 47, Clause 3.1.1.

[51] *Id.*, Clause 3.3.1.

[52] The Secretariat for the Committee on Infrastructure, *Report of the Task Force- Financing Plan for Airports*, July 2006, p. 6.

[53] Press Information Bureau, Ministry of Civil Aviation Press Release, 11November 2022, available at, https://pib.gov.in/PressReleaseIframePage.aspx?PRID=1875214. Last visited, 19 August 2024.

[54] Alok Gupta & Smita Agrawal, 'Greenfield Airport Development in India: A Case Study of Bangalore International Airport', 2013, available at, http://vslir.iima.ac.in:8080/jspui/bitstream/11718/11494/1/CMS-PP-217-Greenfield_Airport_Development_in_India-151-Gupta_b.pdf. Last visited, 20 August 2024.

[55] *Supra* note 48, Schedule 3.

[56] *Supra* note 47, Clause 7.5.

[57] *Supra* note 54, at 13.

[58] *Id.*

This highlights one of the issues that is discussed in detail later- that land acquisition delays are one of the greatest problems facing PPP projects in India.

KIA commenced its operations on 24 May 2008. As per the agreement, BIAL is primarily responsible for the provision of services at the Airport and shall work to improve the facilities, standards and services at the Airport.[59] It is the responsibility of BIAL to ensure that the airport is performing according to the standards laid out in the International Air Transport Association (IATA) Global Airport Monitor service standards.[60] The cost that has been incurred in the development of the airport is to be recovered through the collection of charges levied upon airline operators, passengers and other users and these maybe in the form of Landing, Housing and Parking charges, Passenger Service Fees or User Development Fee.[61] Construction on the second phase of the KIA project that included the development of one more terminal and another runway commenced in 2018. It was built at the cost of Rs 5,000 crore and became operational from 15 January 2023.[62]

As mentioned earlier, in the financial year 2022- 2023, KIA made a significant profit and was the most profitable of the PPP airports in India.[63] This was despite the fact that it had made significant losses in the two previous financial years, although that can be attributed to the COVID-19 pandemic to some extent. The KIA project highlights many positive attributes, such as the use of expert agencies with equity stakes in the project. For instance, L&T had an equity stake but also were responsible for the construction aspects of the project. Bringing in such experts as equity partners was done to 'bring about ownership sense among partners to achieve highest level of efficiency and commitment.'[64] This is reflected in the fact that project was completed within the timeframe due to the efficiency of the construction partners. It is also positive that the Concession Agreement has certain flexibility for the equity partners to be able to depart while maintaining an exit barrier for some time to ensure that the disruption of partners leaving does not affect the project. Moreover, the international standard imposed for maintaining service levels is one way of ensuring that BIAL is operating the airport to the highest of standards, which is important as it is essentially providing a public service.

However, despite profitability and the timely completion of the project, certain concerns about the project are worth noting. An inordinate amount of time was taken before construction on the project could begin. The first hurdle was the significant amount of time for selection of a concessionaire which took 32 months from the day of signing of the MoU this is almost equal to the time taken for the construction

---

[59] *Supra* note 47, Clause 9.1.

[60] *Id.*, Clause 9.2.

[61] *Id.*, Schedule 6.

[62] Editor, 'Bengaluru airport's Terminal 2 to begin domestic operations on January 15', *Indian Express*, 11 January 2023, available at, https://indianexpress.com/article/cities/bangalore/bengaluru-airport-terminal-2-begin-domestic-operations-on-january-15-8373826/. Last visited, 21 August 2024.

[63] *Supra* note 42.

[64] *Supra* note 54, at 16.

of the airport.[65] The land acquisition process was also extremely long, which is surprising considering the fact that the public agency KSIIDC was also an equity partner to the project. This delay in clearance also led to the first big delay to the project since its initial conception when the Tata led consortium exited the project because of delays in 1998.[66] Another matter of substantial concern was the budget-as mentioned earlier, the project was completed at a significantly higher cost than that which was estimated. One of the reasons for this is that the costs could not be determined at the outset because of the significant expected delays from the long bidding and uncertain land acquisition process.[67] Another reason was that the ambit of the contract was changed with the government increasing the ambit of the project due to increasing air traffic.

There were various problems that dogged the project, one was the controversy due to its location at Devanahalli, which is 40 km outside the city. There had been a significant public reaction to the location. There were also financial implications of the location on the government, which had to bear costs associated with access to the airport from the main city by developing roads and other transport facilities[68] as well as on BIAL which may have lost revenue due to passengers choosing not to fly out of KIA due to the travelling distance. Another controversy arose in relation to the closure of the original Bengaluru airport, the old Hindustan Aeronautics Laboratories Airport (HAL). A public outcry began demanding that this airport remained open due to poor connectivity to the new airport, distance from the city and insufficient capacity to cater to current and future demand amongst others.[69] However, the wording of the Concession Agreement made it clear that when KIA became effective, HAL would no longer be used for commercial passenger traffic and this was given effect.[70]

It is also interesting and perhaps unsurprising to note that as soon as the minimum lock in period for equity participation were complete, some of the foreign partners chose to exit from BIAL. While this may serve as an indicator of lack of confidence it also means that KIA was deprived at the outset from the expertise of the foreign participants which could have increased efficiency.[71] Thus, despite the profits the KIA project demonstrates certain concerns for PPP governance.

[65] *Id.*, at 18.

[66] Kalpana Gopalan, 'Pain Without Gain?: Land Assembly and Acquisition for Infrastructure Mega Projects: The Indian Experience with the Bangalore International Airport', *Dharana*, Vol. 6, No.2, 2012, pp. 3–45 at p.10.

[67] *Supra* note 54, at 18.

[68] *Supra* note 54, at 19.

[69] *Supra* note 66, at 22.

[70] *Id.*, at 29.

[71] *Supra* note 54, at 19.

3.2 Indira Gandhi International Airport, New Delhi

The IGIA is an international airport located in the city of New Delhi. The airport, spread over an area of 5,106 acres is situated in Palam, Delhi, 16 km from New Delhi city centre.[72] It is the busiest airport in India with annual passenger traffic of 73,673,708 in 2023–2024[73] and is the tenth busiest airport in the world.[74] The IGIA, which opened in 1962, was managed by the AAI. In June 2003, the AAI board approved a modernisation proposal and on 11 September 2003, the National Democratic Alliance government approved a proposal permitting private investment (including foreign direct investment) of up to 74% in order to modernise the Mumbai and Delhi Airports.[75] These projects were to operate as a joint venture with the creation of a Joint Venture Company (JVC) with 74 per cent equity owned by a private consortium and 26 per cent of the AAI. This JVC would be given a long-term lease of 30 years extendable to another 30 years of operations in the airport.

The bidding process for both the Delhi and Mumbai airports was to be conducted simultaneously. Stage 1 of the bidding process began with an invitation to register expressions of interest for acquisition of 74 percent of the JVC was issued on February 2004 with the last date of submission in June 2004. This process was to be used by the AAI to shortlist the prospective qualified bidders, on the basis of pre-decided evaluation criteria. Stage 2 of the process would involve the preparation and lodging of full, legally binding bids by these qualified bidders which would be lodged by August 2004. Stage 2 was to involve several steps with all documentation, confidentiality deeds, presentations, site visits and discussions with regulatory authorities. It had been intended that AAI would finalise the transactions soon after the bids were lodged and that this process would be completed by September 2004.[76] It was also specified that although the same bidder could bid for both airports, if the same bidder proved to be highest bidder for both airports, the highest bidder would be declared as the successful bidder for the airport where the margin between the highest offer and

---

[72] 'Overview- Indira Gandhi International Airport', *JSW Steel*, available at, https://www.jsw.in/groups/indira-gandhi-international-airport#:~:text=Gandhi%20International%20Airport-,Overview,from%20New%20Delhi's%20city%20centre. Last visited, 20 August 2024.

[73] 'Top 10 Busiest Airports in India', *Forbes India*, 16 July 2024, available at, https://www.forbesindia.com/article/explainers/busiest-airports-india/93641/1. Last visited, 20 August 2024.

[74] Vasudha Mukherjee, 'Delhi's airport among top 10 busiest airports in the world: Full list here', *Business Standard*, 31 May 2024, available at, https://www.business-standard.com/industry/news/delhi-s-airport-among-top-10-busiest-airports-in-the-world-full-list-here-124053101148_1.html. Last visited, 20 August 2024.

[75] Ila Halai, 'Indira Gandhi International-Delhi Airport', *IJ Global*, 3 February 2009, available at, https://www.ijglobal.com/articles/49548/indira-gandhi-international-delhi-airport. Last visited, 21 August 2024.

[76] Rekha Jain, G Raghuram & Rachna Gangwar, 'Airport Privatization in India: Lessons from the Bidding Process in Delhi and Mumbai', *Indian Institute of Management Working Paper No. 2007–05-01*, May 2007, available at, https://www.iima.ac.in/sites/default/files/rnpfiles/15501336412007-05-01.pdf. Last visited, 15 August 2024, p. 26.

the second best offer was the most.[77] However, the difficulties and delays started at the bidding phase itself. The transaction documents were finalised only by 30 August 2005 and were issued to 8 bidders with the extended bid date of September 2005. Ultimately 5 consortia bid for Delhi airport and 6 for Mumbai airport.[78]

The Evaluation Process was to consist of 4 phases. The first phase was the assessment of mandatory requirement, failing which the bidder would be removed. The second phase was the assessment of financial commitment such as the debt-to-equity commitment and offers not meeting these would also be excluded. The remaining offers would be judged in the third technical phase based on the management capability, commitment and value and development capability and value. Only the offers which met the technical pre-qualification criteria of both with 80 percent would be able to proceed to phase 4 where the bidder with the highest financial consideration would be selected as the successful bidder.[79]

Based on these criteria, the Evaluation Committee announced that the two short listed consortia who had qualified by receiving more than 80% on the technical grounds were the Reliance-ASA and GMR-Fraport.[80] This evaluation was then reviewed by an independent eight member Government Review Committee which was of the opinion that a majority of the evaluation criteria were necessarily subjective in nature and therefore, it would be difficult to allocate a purely objective marking across all bidders but there was no apparent indication of bias or prejudice for or against any individual bidder.[81] This report also went to an Inter-Ministerial Group for consideration but no consensus was reached. The final decision was then left to the Empowered Group of Ministers headed by Pranab Mukherjee, which referred the issue to a Committee of Secretaries headed by the Cabinet Secretary who, in turn, appointed a sub-committee headed by E Sreedharan.[82] This committee found certain technical flaws in the technical evaluation process and highlighted that a liberal attitude was shown by the Evaluation Committee to Reliance-ASA Consortium and on reassessment the marks received by the Consortium was less than 80 per cent.[83] On that basis the Reliance-ASA bid was disqualified and the GMR-Fraport consortium was the only one that qualified as having more than 80 percent on technical grounds based on the revised yardsticks.

Finally, on 31 January 2006, it was announced that GMR-Fraport was the only technically qualified bidder for both airports. Since there was only one technically

---

[77] *Id.*, at 5.

[78] *Id.*, at 8.

[79] *Id.*, at 40.

[80] Paranjoy Guha Thakurta & Ranabir Majumdar, 'How the Airport Bids were Evaluated', *Rediff.com*, 30 December 2005, available at, https://www.rediff.com/money/2005/dec/30paran.htm. Last visited, 16 August 2024.

[81] Paranjoy Guha Thakurta & Ranabir Majumdar, 'India's Airport Upgrade Takes a New Turn', *Rediff.com*, 29 December 2005, available at, https://www.rediff.com/money/2005/dec/29spec1.htm. Last visited, 20 August 2024.

[82] Editor, 'New Committee for Airports' Revamp', *Rediff.com*, 29 December 2005, available at, https://in.rediff.com/money/2005/dec/29airport.htm. Last visited, 20 August 2024.

[83] *Supra* note 76, at 15.

qualified bidder, the financial bids of the top four bidders would be opened. GMR-Fraport were given the choice of selecting the airport, subject to matching the highest financial bid. It was decided that the other airport, would be awarded to the highest financial bidder. This was done in lieu of another bidding process, which would have taken significant time, especially when the government was keen to complete the airports before the Commonwealth Games to be held in 2010. GMR-Fraport chose Delhi airport and matched the highest financial bid of Reliance ASA of 45.99 percent.[84] After this, the Mumbai airport was awarded to GVK-ACSA.

To bring this into effect, in March 2006, a Special Purpose Vehicle, Delhi International Airport Private Limited (DIAL) was formed for the project in Delhi Airport. The shareholding of DIAL was determined at 26 percent shareholding by the AAI and 74 percent shareholding of private participants (GMR Infrastructure Ltd at 31.10 per cent, GMR Energy Ltd at 10 per cent, GCL Investments Pvt. Ltd. at 9 per cent, Fraport AG Frankfurt Airport Services Worldwide at 10 per cent and Malaysia Airports (Mauritius) Private Limited at 10 per cent and Indian Development Fund at 3.90 per cent).[85] In April 2006, an Operations Management and Development (OMDA) was signed between AAI and DIAL. The OMDA states that DIAL will undertake the functions of operation, maintenance, development, design, construction, upgradation, modernisation, finance and management of the Airport and at all times keep the Airport in good repair and operating condition.[86] The agreement allows for a transitional period of 3 months[87] and a further period of 3 years of operational support from AAI.[88] The OMDA also requires that DIAL shall prepare a Master Plan for the Airport setting out the proposed development for the entire Airport, planned over a 20 year time horizon.[89] Apart from this, international standards will also be imposed on IGIA- from two years the airport must achieve and thereafter maintain throughout the Term ISO9001: 2000 certification for all facilities relating to Aeronautical Services[90] and must maintain both service quality standards as per the relevant ICAO Annexes and Documents[91] both in an objective set of criteria[92] and subjective quality standards of a rating of 3.75 or higher in the IATA/ACI AETRA

[84] *Id.*, at 17.

[85] Shareholders Agreement by and between Airports Authority of India and Delhi International Airport Pvt. Ltd. and GMR Infrastructure Ltd. and GMR Energy Ltd. and GVL Investments Pvt. Ltd and Fraport AG Frankfurt Airport Services Worldwide and Malaysia Airports (Mauritius) Private Limited and India Development Fund, available at, https://www.civilaviation.gov.in/sites/default/files/2023-07/moca_000973.pdf. Last visited, 19 August 2024, Clause 3.2.

[86] Operation, Management and Development Agreement between Airports Authority of India and Delhi International Airport Private Limited for Delhi Airport, 4 April 2006, available at, https://www.civilaviation.gov.in/sites/default/files/2023-07/moca_000971.pdf. Last viewed, 20 August 2024, Clause 2.1.1.

[87] *Id.*, Clause 5.2.

[88] *Id.*, Clause 6.1.

[89] *Id.*, Clause 8.3.1.

[90] *Id.*, Clause 9.1.1.

[91] *Id.*, Schedule 2.

[92] *Id.*, Schedule 3.

passenger survey.[93] As mentioned earlier, DIAL shall pay to the AAI an annual fee of 45.99 per cent of the projected revenue of the airport[94] as well as the upfront payment of 150 crore rupees[95] and to recoup this, it shall be free to fix the charges for non-aeronautical services, subject to the provisions of the existing contracts and other agreements.[96]

However, while the formalities were being proceeded with between DIAL and the AAI, another issue was brewing. Displeased by the results of the bid, the losing bidder, Reliance Airport Developers Private Limited, filed a writ petition under Article 226 of the Constitution in Delhi High Court on 2 February 2006 alleging that an arbitrary and discriminatory decision-making process was adopted for awarding the contract. The division bench dismissed the petition on the grounds that the Empowered Group of Ministers had absolute discretion in the matter of choosing the methods used for decision-making. An appeal to the Supreme Court was also dismissed for the same grounds.[97]

Since DIAL took over the operations of IGIA on 3 May 2006, several strides have been made. As per the first masterplan in September 2008, the airport inaugurated a 4,430 m (14,530 ft) runway.[98] DIAL also built and commenced operations at Terminal 3 in 2010, before the Commonwealth Games, completing the first phase of development. This terminal was completed within 37 months, making IGIA capable of handling 62 million passengers per annum.[99] On 17August 2024, DIAL announced the opening and operationalisation of the new Terminal 1 which was developed as part of the Phase 3A expansion project that it undertook from 2019.[100] The expansion work was carried out as per the Master Plan 2016 as Delhi Airport witnessed a massive surge in air traffic movements and passenger numbers that had far exceeded the projections. The airport has also won many awards and amongst others has been lauded with being the first Carbon Neutral Airport in the Asia Pacific Region and is the first airport globally to have ISO 50001 certified Energy Management System.[101]

However, despite accolades, IGIA cannot be counted as a complete success story. As discussed earlier, the figures show that the airport is making a significant loss.

---

[93] *Id.*, Clause 9.1.3.

[94] *Id.*, Clause 11.1.2.1.

[95] *Id.*, Clause 11.1.1.

[96] *Id.*, Clause 12.2.

[97] *Reliance Airport Developers Pvt. Ltd v. Airports Authority of India and Others (2006)* 10 SCC 1.

[98] Gaurav Choudhury, 'New runway by 2008, new terminal by 2010', *Hindustan Times*, 8 November 2006, available at, https://www.hindustantimes.com/india/new-runway-by-2008-new-terminal-by-2010/story-K8rZJgWVNhPUZCmoO6XU7L.html. Last visited, 25 August 2024.

[99] 'Delhi International Airport Limited', *Delhi Airport*, available at, https://www.newdelhiairport.in/corporate/our-company. Last visited, 25 August 2024.

[100] 'GMR-run Delhi Airport's New State-of-the-Art Terminal 1 to Become Operational from August 17', *Airports Council International- Asia Pacific & Middle East*, 14 August 2024, available at, https://www.aci-asiapac.aero/media-centre/news/gmr-run-delhi-airport-s-new-state-of-the-art-terminal-1-to-become-operational-from-august-17th. Last visited, 25 August 2024.

[101] *Supra* note 99.

One of the reasons behind this may be the fact that the GMR consortium had to match the financial bid that had been provided by Reliance which compelled them to share a significantly greater amount of the profits with AAI than they had bid (or planned) for. This could raise concerns about the extent to which the project was financially sustainable for GMR which may be reflected in the profitability of the airport. This leads on to one of the biggest problems of this project which emerged right at the outset- the bidding process and the metrics. The metrics of the bidding seem rushed with additional corrections to the technical bids being necessary. As outlined, there were also criticism about transparency and subjectivity in the process, and the sheer number of committees as well their constitution can also be challenged. The lack of clear metrics contributed to time delays as well as concerns that the process was politically motivated. Many have also questioned the rush to complete terminal 3 before the Commonwealth Games at huge expense.[102] There was a 40 percent increase in expenditure as compared to projected expenditure, which DIAL claimed was due to the scope of the project being changed. AERA allowed DIAL to collect a higher development fee to make up this deficit of Rs. 1230 Crore,[103] leading to the Supreme Court citing that such a fee was unreasonable.[104] This later led to a removal of these development fees pending a review. A recent fatal roof collapse to a portion of the airport constructed in 2009 (after the commencement of the Brownfield project), has also brought DIAL's operations under scrutiny, compelling it to forma technical committee to investigate the incident.[105] Many of the problems that IGIA faces can be attributed to various governance issues that are faced by airports developed and operating through the PPP model.

4 Governance Issues in PPP Airports

PPP projects in general have many issues and challenges associated with them. PPPs for airports, which are critical to countries, trigger not only social, political and economic concerns but also security ones. Airports thus are subject to many levels of scrutiny at both a domestic and international level through the use of various standards such as the Chicago Convention Requirements for aerodromes. Many of these issues or pressure points for airport PPP projects in India are discussed here.

---

[102] Jason Burke & Aashish Jethra, '£2 Bn Delhi Airport Terminal Signals a New India, says PM', *The Guardian*, 4 July 2010, available at, https://www.theguardian.com/world/2010/jul/04/delhi-india-airport-terminal. Last visited, 25 August 2024.

[103] Airports Economic Regulatory Authority of India, 'Review of Levy of Development Fee at Indira Gandhi International Airport', New Delhi, 12 December 2012, *Consultation Paper 32/2012–13*, p. 5.

[104] *Consumer Online Foundation* v. *Union of India & Ors.* (2011) AIR SCW 2815.

[105] Ashish Srivastava, 'DIAL forms technical committee to probe roof collapse at Terminal 1', *The New Indian Express*, 28 June 2024, available at, https://www.newindianexpress.com/cities/delhi/2024/Jun/28/dial-forms-technical-committee-to-probe-roof-collapse-at-terminal-1. Last visited, 25 August 2024.

One significant hurdle for Greenfield airport projects is the land acquisition or allocation process. The Convention clearly states that land needed for airport facilities will require that the State shall provide the land itself retaining the title if it wishes, or facilitate the use of the land on just and reasonable terms and in accordance with the laws of the State concerned.[106] The case study of KIA highlighted that the project faced significant delays before commencing due to land allocation issues. The Navi Mumbai airport also was delayed substantially due to land allocation issues.[107] It is imperative that for projects to operate within a particular time line, land allocation issues are dealt with swiftly and at the outset by the public partner who is best equipped to handle it. Land allocation can also have a significant disincentivising impact on private partners who may be unwilling to undertake the risk.

The case studies also highlight that timeline issues often arise due to change in the scope of the contract. For instance, in both the airports discussed here, changes were made to the scope of the contract which led to additional costs and a longer time. One key factor to keep in mind to ensure that PPPs are conducted properly is that at the contracting phase, the PPP contract must be drafted in a manner that the terms of the contract are clear and well understood which gives bidders clarity on the requirements of the project and satisfies them that the public partner is credible and well organised.[108] Another way to deal with the changing needs that a PPP project may face is to frame contracts with some flexibility so that a change in scope can fall within its remit. This may reduce the likelihood of infighting and projects being shelved. Only if the contract is clear will it be possible for the participants to the PPP to assess the risks attached to the project and understand the allocation of the risks. Appropriate risk allocation to the partner best equipped to handle it is critical to the success of PPP project. This is especially true in the case of airports, since investing in airports has a very high capital cost, investors and operators require a level of comfort in terms of adequate risk allocation.[109]

This high capital cost will only be undertaken by private partners if they believe that the project is commercially viable. This will mean that investors will invest only if they can ensure that the revenues earned from the project are adequate to cover capital costs and operations and maintenance costs.[110] As we have seen, in the case of airports, this will be gained from a component of profit share as well as tariffs that are imposed. Because tariffs are imposed on all travellers, as in the case of IGIA, higher tariffs may cause significant public distress and complaints leading to revision of tariffs. But if costs escalate, what other choice may a private partner have? Both the airports discussed here overran costs. The key here is to factor for cost overruns and

---

[106] *Supra* note 11, at Art. 72.

[107] *Supra* note 21, at 24.

[108] Infrastructure Finance Secretariat, Department of Economic Affairs, Ministry of Finance, Government of India, *Reference Guide for PPP Project Appraisal*, June 2023, available at, https://www.pppinindia.gov.in/report/Book%20Reference%20Guide%20for%20PPP%20%20Project%20Appraisal%20_June%2016_1687005378.pdf. Last visited, 29 August 2024, p. 22.

[109] *Supra* note 21, at 14.

[110] *Supra* note 108, at 29.

to limit changes in scope and delay which lead to added costs. The use of Viability Gap Funding to pay back contractors when costs are too high is also another solution whereby the costs are not passed-off directly to consumers in tariffs. Another pitfall for airport PPPs may be the length of time for which these are awarded- both KIA and IGIA were for 30 years with the possibility of extending for another 30 years. Due to the very high initial capital outlay, private participants may be deterred by this term and wish for an initial longer contract. This has been taken into account by the Indian government and recent PPP projects for India have been longer than 40 years with a scope of extending for another 20 years.[111]

The cost of a private participant may also be significantly affected by the lack of clarity in the tendering process. As seen in the case of IGIA, GMR which won the bid had matched the highest financial bid, which involved a significantly larger profit share going to AAI. Usually when a bid is made, the private player will give careful consideration to place the bid based on what they believe is financially viable for them. Taking on a significantly less profit share at a later stage may signal trouble in the future. One of the key objectives of ensuring that the tendering process is fair and effective is complete unambiguity in bid parameter and bid evaluation criteria.[112] Confusions in the bidding process and changing parameters in the technical component of the assessment lead to repeated assessment by different government committees which can contribute to delays. These confusions can also be used in a manner that leaves the government open towards accusations of favouritism and manipulation of the bidding process.

PPPs have an intense political component to them- since they are used to provide services that are usually within the public sector's remit, they touch upon the social and political sensitivities of the population. Since profits can be made by the private sector, there are possible concerns of corruption to further aggravate the anxieties of the public. For instance, the fact that seven airports in India are managed by Adani enterprises has been a source of grievance to the opposition party.[113] Moreover concerns arise regarding the ramifications of changes to the ruling political party on these long term projects. In the case of KIA, there was a change in the government from the time the project began to when it was inaugurated, leading to greater delays due to the policy shifts.[114] Such political changes and shifts may also serve as a significant risk that may deter private investors, especially foreign investors.

The public nature of the PPP means that that PPP contracting processes cannot simply be delegated to third parties and public responsibility be avoided,[115] the PPP

[111] *Supra* note 21, at 38.

[112] *Supra* note 108, at 32.

[113] Editor, 'How many tempos did it take to hand over airports to Adani?: Rahul Gandhi', *The Wire*, 14 May 2024, available at, https://thewire.in/politics/rahul-gandhi-tempo-adani-airport-modi/?mid_related_new. Last visited, 30 August 2024.

[114] *Supra* note 66, at 38.

[115] Sudhir Krishnaswamy, 'Airport Privatisation Case: Public Law and Public Sector Reform', *Economic and Political Weekly*, Vol. 41, No. 40, Oct. 7–13, 2006, pp. 4239–4241 at p. 4240.

process needs to be audited as does the project itself. There is a continuing responsibility on the public sector to ensure that the PPPs are operating according to the contracts. This means that any international standards that are binding on Indian airports must be followed by these PPP airports. This would necessarily include that the requirements in Annex 14 of the Chicago Convention in relation to Aerodrome Design and Operation must be maintained.[116] The recent fall of the roof in IGIA must be taken very seriously in the context of these requirements. It is thus essential that there is complete transparency in communication channels and full disclosure is made to the public and the public sector. Additionally, there must be proper procedure for constant and vigilant monitoring of the private partners performance with penalties being enforced if necessary. Moreover, there must be clear dispute resolution mechanisms in place so as to ensure that the parties can enforce the contract.

It also must be considered that the nature of the PPP contract for the airport, whether it is a Greenfield or Brownfield airport also brings important considerations into play. Brownfield airports tend to be a more lucrative opportunity for private participants due to a lower initial capital outlay. Thus, they may be subject to greater political manipulations during the tendering process. Moreover, Greenfield airports are likely to suffer from significant land allocation issues at the outset, leading to them being considered more expensive and riskier projects. However, since Greenfield projects essentially allow greater freedom to the private sector, there may be efficiency gains from such projects leading to greater long-term profits. Ultimately, the PPP is a delicate balancing exercise between the public and private sectors- the allocation of risk, the cost and the profits must be distributed in a manner that capitalises on the greatest benefit to both.

5 Conclusion

Increased air traffic and demand have made it imperative to expand airports in India and the PPP model has become a popular choice. However, not many of these PPP airports have been profitable. The Bangalore and Delhi airports serve as models to highlight some of the many issues that PPPs in Indian airports face. It is essential that these issues are resolved by enhancing clarity in the PPP contract as well as improvements in processes like land allocation and tendering. Only if these issues are resolved, can the Indian public avail of the significant efficiency benefits of the PPP model.

[116] International Civil Aviation Organisation, *Annex 14 to the Convention on International Civil Aviation, Volume I: Aerodrome Design and Operations*, (9th edn.), July 2022.

Chapter 15
Legal Nature and Challenges of a 'Seasonal International Airport': A Study of the Bhopal Airport

Barsha Sinha

Abstract In 2010, the Ministry of Civil Aviation of India suddenly converted the Bhopal airport into a "seasonal" international airport to facilitate Hajj travellers. While the basic function and operational character may look very similar in all airports and in India, aerodrome licencing requirements are also very similar for all airports, there are certain additional safety and security requirements for an international airport. The reasons behind it are primarily two-fold. First, the magnitude of daily operations is considerably greater in the case of an international airport, and secondly, the cross-border movements of cargo and passengers must be strictly regulated to control transnational offences. Bhopal, being a seasonal international airport, may face certain legal challenges in terms of regulatory or environmental compliances, cross-border legal issues, complexities regarding insurance liability, security breaches or violation of customs law. Besides the legal challenges, in such airports, the infrastructure may not be adequate for handling such huge air traffic during seasonal operations and will eventually generate safety threats. Such infrastructural challenges may include the understaffed Air Traffic Control, runway safety mechanism, inadequate visual aid facilities, passenger amenities, etc. Therefore, an airport should never have such a confusing status, and it can only be either an international or a domestic one.

Keywords Accidents and incidents · Airport Authority of India (AAI) · Air Traffic Control (ATC) · Electrical vehicles (EVs) · Noise pollution · Poor connectivity · Workforce

---

B. Sinha (✉)
The West, Bengal National University of Juridical Sciences, Kolkata, India
e-mail: barshapg21826@nujs.edu

NALSAR University of Law, Hyderabad, India

The Centre for Aviation and Space Laws (CASL), WBNUJS, Kolkata, India

© The Author(s), under exclusive license to Springer Nature Singapore Pte Ltd. 2025

S. Bhat B. (ed.), *Aerodrome Governance in Asia*,
https://doi.org/10.1007/978-981-96-7568-5_15

1 Introduction

The Raja Bhoj Airport at Bhopal has a peculiar status, straddling the line between a domestic and an international airport. It operates a few seasonal international flights and has a temporary set-up for customs and immigration formalities for these seasonal flights. The Bhopal Airport has been in the news for its infamous status of being a seasonal international airport, which is unique. In Madhya Pradesh, it is the largest airport in terms of area and the second busiest in terms of passenger and aircraft movements.[1] Bhopal is a significant city in central India, not only as the capital of Madhya Pradesh but also due to several other factors. However, residents of Bhopal and the surrounding areas have consistently voiced concerns about the poor domestic and almost non-existent international air connectivity at the airport. Despite its huge potential, including its proximity to national parks and UNESCO World Heritage Sites like Sanchi, Bhimbetka, and Bhojpur, the airport's development has been hindered by a lack of administrative support at various levels. This neglect by the state government could negatively impact the capital region both commercially and economically. The Airport is located in very close proximity to the city, however, in a less crowded area. Hence, the obstacles to possible expansion near the Airport are comparatively fewer, indicating ample scope for its further development. Considering its advantageous location in the central part of India, a Maintenance, Repair and Overhaul (MRO) facility is planned to be constructed here.[2]

A well-connected airport is crucial not only for daily travel but also for boosting the tourism industry. Unfortunately, due to inadequate flight operations and high operating costs, Bhopal Airport reported a loss of Rs. 47.19 crore in Financial Year (FY) 2022–23.[3] Moreover, the confusing operational status of this airport has led to several governance-related challenges. Madhya Pradesh is a large state, and with only one designated international airport in Indore, which also has limited connectivity, there is significant potential to develop Bhopal Airport with state-of-the-art facilities. It is high time that the international status must be rendered officially.

[1] 'Airport Information: Bhopal Airport,' *Air India*, available at, https://www.airindia.com/in/en/travel-information/airport-information/bhopal.html. Last visited, 12 July 2024.

[2] Amit Mishra, 'Madhya Pradesh: Raja Bhoj Airport in Bhopal All Set To Be Hub For Aircraft Maintenance,' *Swarajya*, 8 October 2022, available at, https://swarajyamag.com/infrastructure/madhya-pradesh-raja-bhoj-airport-in-bhopal-all-set-to-be-hub-for-aircraft-maintenance#:~:text=Bhopal%20Airport%20is%20all%20set%20to%20become%20the,sqm%20at%20an%20investment%20of%20Rs%2030%20crore. Last visited, 12 July 2024.

[3] '25 AAI airports earmarked for leasing between 2022 and 2025 as per National Monetisation Pipeline,' *Press Information Bureau- MoCA*, available at, https://pib.gov.in/PressReleseDetailm.aspx?PRID=1982289. Last visited, 3 May 2024.

2 Infrastructural Developments

Over time, there have been several infrastructural developments at Bhopal Airport. In 2010, the runway was extended to 2,744 m to accommodate larger aircraft.[4] Following this, the airport was designated as a "seasonal" international airport. The first international flight was a Hajj charter to Jeddah, operated by Saudi Airlines, on 23 October 2010.[5] Since then, the airport has facilitated several such flights for Hajj travellers. Temporary facilities for customs and immigration were established to support these international flights. However, the concept of a "seasonal" international airport does not align with international legal frameworks or national aviation regulations, highlighting the need for proper attention and resolution.

On June 28, 2011, Bhopal Airport inaugurated a new integrated terminal building covering 26,936 square meters. The facility features14 check-in counters, 10 immigration counters, four aerobridges, 6 X-ray machines, 22 customs counters, an eatery, and retail outlets. It was constructed for Rs. 1.35 billion, with 400 acres of land provided by the state government, and officiated by Civil Aviation Minister Vayalar Ravi.[6]

In 2013, Bhopal Airport made significant strides by becoming the first airport in Madhya Pradesh to utilise solar power for its operations. A 100-kilowatt solar power plant was commissioned in June 2013, with plans for a future expansion to a 2-megawatt capacity.[7] Furthermore, a 17-acre site near the airport has been designated for a new air cargo hub.[8] The old terminal building was repurposed into a cargo complex to bolster cargo operations, and the new cargo terminal commenced operations in February 2020, though its growth was hampered by the lockdown.[9]

---

[4] 'Direct Haj flight from Bhopal', *Hindustan Times*, 6 January 2014, available at, https://web.archive.org/web/20140106182955/; http://www.hindustantimes.com/india-news/direct-haj-flight-from-bhopal/article1-552532.aspx. Last visited, 23 June 2024.

[5] 'First direct flight from Bhopal to Jeddah from tomorrow,' *The Times of India*, 21 October 2010, available at, https://timesofindia.indiatimes.com/india/First-direct-flight-from-Bhopal-to-Jeddah-from-tomorrow/articleshow/6785546.cms. Last visited, 26 December 2023.

[6] 'Inauguration of NITB Bhopal,' *Airport Authority of India Press Release*, 28 June 2011, available at, https://www.aai.aero/sites/default/files/press_aai_bhopal_28Jun_2011.pdf. Last visited, 11 July 2024.

[7] Yogendra Pratap Singh, 'Raja Bhoj Airport all set to use solar energy', *Hindustan Times*, 20 June 2013, available at, https://www.hindustantimes.com/bhopal/raja-bhoj-airport-all-set-to-use-solar-energy/story-muzwpRi53ZC3cIDO3K5MwL.html#:~:text=Raja%20Bhoj%20Airport%20is%20all%20set%20to%20become,save%20electricity%20cost%20and%20utilise%20renewable%20energy%20sources. Last visited, 11 July 2024.

[8] 'Bhopal to get air cargo services within a month', *The Free Press Journal*, 3 August 2019, available at, https://www.freepressjournal.in/bhopal/bhopal-to-get-air-cargo-services-within-a-month. Last visited, 26 December 2023.

[9] Ramendra Singh, 'Newly Built Cargo Terminal at Raja Bhoj Airport Faces Lockdown Blues,' *The Times of India*, 12 April 2020, available at, https://timesofindia.indiatimes.com/city/bhopal/newly-built-cargo-terminal-at-raja-bhoj-airport-faces-lockdown-blues/articleshow/75105566.cms. Last visited, 5 May 2024.

The efforts to grant Raja Bhoj Airport international status began several years ago. In November 2019, a joint team from the Ministry of Home Affairs and the Ministry of Civil Aviation conducted a review of the airport's facilities to assess readiness for international operations, including immigration procedures. The team found the airport well-prepared to become an immigration checkpost.[10] However, the official international status was not fully established until the end of December 2023, when the Ministry of Home Affairs officially declared Raja Bhoj Airport as an immigration checkpost.[11]

Looking ahead, Bhopal Airport plans to upgrade its Instrument Landing System (ILS) to CAT II for improved safety in low visibility and adverse weather conditions. The Airport Authority of India has already begun the land acquisition for this upgrade. Additionally, new runway edge lights have been installed and successfully tested for better visibility during night-time operations.[12] This year, the Airport Authority of India (AAI) has completed the finalisation of the airport's master plan, which encompasses three phases of extensive infrastructural upgrades, including the extension of runways to a length of 4000 m, reaching the ultimate capacity of the airport, and the acquisition of an additional 65 acres of land. All these significant developments are scheduled for completion by the year 2047.[13] Most recently, the Airport Authority of India urged airlines to initiate international flights from Bhopal's Raja Bhoj Airport to destinations including Abu Dhabi, Doha, Kuala Lumpur, and Bangkok. Airport Director Ramjee Awasthi stated that this initiative aims to enhance connectivity, stimulate tourism, and foster economic growth in the region, ultimately benefiting travellers and the local economy.[14]

---

[10] 'Immigration facility at Raja Bhoj Airport very soon', *The Times of India*, 7 November 2019, available at, https://timesofindia.indiatimes.com/city/bhopal/immigration-facility-at-raja-bhoj-airport-soon/articleshow/71946236.cms. Last visited, 26 December 2023.

[11] 'Bhopal's Raja Bhoj International Airport granted Immigration Check Post status, here's what it means', *Financial Express*, 22 December 2023, available at, https://www.financialexpress.com/business/airlines-aviation-bhopals-raja-bhoj-international-airport-granted-immigration-check-post-status-heres-what-it-means-3345627/. Last visited, 5 May 2024.

[12] 'Scaling up: Bhopal's Raja Bhoj airport set to get advanced landing system tech', *The Times of India*, 20 March 2023, available at, https://timesofindia.indiatimes.com/city/bhopal/scaling-up-bhopals-raja-bhoj-airport-set-to-get-advanced-landing-system-tech/articleshow/98789838.cms. Last visited, 27 December 2023.

[13] Ramendra Singh, 'Raja Bhoj airport master plan final, development in 3 phases by 2047', *The Times of India*, 6 August 2024, available at, https://timesofindia.indiatimes.com/city/bhopal/raja-bhoj-airport-masterplan-for-development-in-3-phases-by-2047/articleshow/112301153.cms. Last visited, 22 August 2024.

[14] 'AAI asks airlines to start international operations from Bhopal Airport', *The Economic Times*, 6 August 2024, available at, https://travel.economictimes.indiatimes.com/news/aviation/domestic/aai-asks-airlines-to-start-international-operations-from-bhopal-airport-/112282354#:~:text=The%20Airport%20Authority%20of%20India%20%28AAI%29%20has%20ramped,to%20Abu%20Dhabi%2C%20Doha%2C%20Kuala%20Lumpur%20and%20Bangkok. Last visited, 22 August 2024.

3 Licensing of Domestic Vis-A-Vis International Airports

A domestic airport operates flights within the territory of a country, and on the other hand, the international airport operates flights across the borders. Therefore, the only significant difference between the two lies in the presence or absence of customs and immigration authorities, which regulate the cross-border movement of passengers and cargo. Ideally, there should be no difference in terms of safety requirements or other technical aspects, considering the inherently risky nature of air transport. However, domestic airports are typically smaller and have all the basic amenities and facilities. On the contrary, passenger traffic is much higher in international airports, and the aircraft used for international air travel are comparatively bigger in size and complex in nature. The international airports are usually larger and must have all the world-class amenities to enhance the consumer experience. Not only that, they must also comply with all the safety standards laid down by national and international regulators.

From an aerodrome governance perspective, there are key differences largely because of the distinct operational nature of these airports. The most significant factor in aerodrome governance is the licensing procedure. In India, licensing is a mandatory requirement for operating an international airport as well as a domestic airport. The licensing of an international airport requires compliance with international standards, which includes adherence to International Civil Aviation Organization (ICAO) Annex 14 requirements for airport design, operations, safety, security, and environmental management. The second and most significant criterion is ensuring the availability of customs, immigration, and quarantine (CIQ) facilities that comply with Indian regulations and international standards. The international airports must also secure bilateral air services agreements between India and other countries to operate international flights. Another key factor in granting licenses is compliance with security standards. Licensing requires adherence to aviation security regulations issued by the Bureau of Civil Aviation Security (BCAS) and other relevant authorities. Other than these, the international airports must also accommodate international airlines by offering competitive incentives, airport facilities, and services. They must offer passenger services and amenities to meet the needs of international travellers, including check-in facilities, lounges, immigration counters, and retail outlets.

Licensing a domestic airport in India entails a comprehensive process that begins with ensuring compliance with national regulations issued by the Directorate General of Civil Aviation (DGCA) and other relevant authorities. This regulatory adherence is crucial for the airport to operate within the legal framework of domestic aviation. Additionally, the airport must establish agreements with domestic airlines, outlining terms of service, operational details, and route networks. Safety and security are paramount, requiring the implementation of Safety Management Systems (SMS) and security protocols that align with Indian aviation standards. Beyond regulatory and safety measures, the licensing process also involves strategic collaboration with domestic airlines to enhance connectivity, expand route networks, and attract passengers. To support these goals, airports often offer competitive incentives to airlines, fostering growth in domestic air travel. Unlike international airports, the infrastructural requirements for domestic airports are generally simpler, reflecting the specific needs and scale of domestic operations. Together, these elements form the foundation of the licensing process, ensuring that domestic airports can effectively serve the needs of passengers and airlines while maintaining high standards of safety, security, and operational efficiency.

4 Operational Nature of Bhopal Airport as Recognised by the AAI

The Bhopal Airport is listed as a domestic airport, and the list is available on the official website of AAI.[15] Therefore, this airport is not recognised by the Appropriate Authority as an international airport. An Indian airport not listed in a gazette may encounter several significant challenges, including a lack of official recognition, which impedes access to funding, resources, and support. Regulatory compliance might be compromised, affecting safety, security, and environmental standards. The airport could struggle with limited services, such as customs and immigration facilities, impacting its ability to handle international flights. Without a gazette listing, the airport may miss out on government funding, face operational difficulties, and encounter legal challenges related to land ownership or environmental concerns. Connectivity issues may arise, limiting its integration with other airports and airlines. Additionally, security risks, challenges in attracting airlines, and potential damage to its reputation and credibility could further hinder its development and operations. Overall, being listed in the gazette is crucial for an airport to gain official recognition, ensure regulatory compliance, and secure the necessary resources and support.

The overall infrastructure of Bhopal airport is good, and the significance of its location has also been discussed earlier in this chapter. However, the international operational status is still not confirmed, and the last international operations were carried out in 2011 for Hajj travellers.[16] Even at the domestic level, it has very poor connectivity because the airlines do not find the operations profitable here.[17] There is potential demand for more connectivity with other major cities and famous tourist destinations within the country. Not only that, because of its non-recognition as an

[15] 'List of Airports', *Airport Authority of India*, available at, https://www.aai.aero/sites/default/files/basic_page_files/list%20of%20airport%20bilingual.pdf. Last visited, 24 August 2024.

[16] Ramendra Singh, 'Only in Name? Bhopal Airport far from International Status', *The Times of India*, 4 August 2022, available at, https://timesofindia.indiatimes.com/city/bhopal/only-in-name-bhopal-airport-far-from-international-status/articleshow/93334405.cms. Last visited, 21 August 2024.

[17] Ramendra Singh, 'Connectivity still a major issue at Bhopal airport', *The Times of India*, 4 August 2022, available at, https://timesofindia.indiatimes.com/city/bhopal/connectivity-still-major-issue-at-bhopal-airport/articleshow/93334465.cms. Last visited, 21 August 2024.

international airport during its seasonal operations, it operates international flights only to one destination. At the recent ISSF World Cup held at the MP Shooting Academy, the absence of international flights was highlighted as a major issue. Despite the sports department's commendable efforts in creating world-class final ranges, players and coaches expressed concern that the lack of international flight options could present a significant challenge for future visits to the state capital.[18] The other potential challenges that may be encountered by a seasonal international airport like Bhopal have been discussed in the next point.

5 Challenges of a Seasonal International Airport

If the operational nature of an airport is not specified, it may encounter various operational as well as governance-related challenges. Ensuring compliance with aviation regulations framed by both national and international aviation authorities is crucial for licensing both international and domestic airports. But as discussed earlier, domestic airports must primarily comply with the national rules and regulations formulated for airport governance, while on the other hand, international airports are bound to implement all safety standards along with all the rules and regulations set by the ICAO. As a member of the ICAO, which establishes global standards and regulations for aviation safety, security, and environmental sustainability, India is obligated to align its aviation regulations with these international standards and recommended practices.

The Directorate General of Civil Aviation (DGCA) works closely with ICAO to ensure compliance through regular safety audits of airlines and airports, thereby placing significant emphasis on adhering to international obligations within the regulatory framework of India's aviation industry.[19] Although Article 38 stipulates that if a State is unable to fully comply with any international standards or procedures, or to bring its regulations or practices into complete alignment with an amended international standard or procedure, or if it considers it necessary to adopt regulations or practices that differ in any respect from those set by an international standard, it must immediately notify ICAO.[20] However, the main problem in this regard is that reports of deviation are very few in number, and the national aviation regulators are

[18] Ramendra Singh, 'No international flights, poor connectivity to Delhi and Mumbai hurdles for Bhopal's world sporting venue dream', *The Times of India*, 28 March 2023, available at, https://timesofindia.indiatimes.com/city/bhopal/no-intl-flights-poor-connectivity-to-delhi-mum-hurdles-for-bhopals-world-sporting-venue-dream/articleshow/99048436.cms. Last visited, 21 August 2024.

[19] Vidhyth Narain Selvam, 'Flying High: Navigating the Legal Challenges in India's Rapidly Expanding Aviation Industry', *International Journal of Advanced Legal Research*, Vol. 4, Issue 1, available at, https://ijalr.in/volume-4-issue-1/flying-high-navigating-the-legal-challenges-in-indias-rapidly-expanding-aviation-industry-vidhyth-narain-selvam/, Last visited, 23 August 2024.

[20] Convention on International Civil Aviation, Doc 7300, Chicago Convention, (entered into force on 4 April 1947), Art. 38.

often reluctant to share the actual status of the implementation of ICAO standards or information about any such deviations. The actual scenario in this regard was well perceived by a team of researchers from the National University of Juridical Sciences, Kolkata and Maharashtra National Law University, Mumbai, two of the most prime Indian educational institutes, while surveying various Indian airports as a part of their academic project. Therefore, the current safety framework in Indian airports is questionable, and when the operational status is confusing, the situation may become even worse.

5.1 Coordination Problem

A significant issue pointed out by the airport administration of Bhopal Airport is the pervasive issue of miscommunication and lack of coordination among the different national aviation regulators, such as the Airports Authority of India, DGCA, and the Bureau of Civil Aviation Security. Considering the current 'seasonal' operational nature of the Bhopal Airport, there arises a question of which safety standards should be made applicable. Are the standards set by the ICAO or the national regulators? Already, there exists so much inconsistency regarding the proper implementation of international safety standards formulated by ICAO. Furthermore, the lack of coordination among national regulators may have a serious impact on operational safety. The confusing status of Bhopal airport is making things worse.

5.2 Functioning of Air Traffic Control

An extremely serious challenge that is encountered by the Bhopal airport is related to the functioning of Air Traffic Control (ATC). The Universal Safety Oversight Audit Programme (USOAP) under the ICAO Continuous Monitoring Approach was conducted in India from 9 to 16 November 2022.When the report was published, it clearly pointed out several safety priorities, among which air proximity incidents, miscommunication between ATC and aircraft crew, failure of ATC, and communication error, which are of practical significance when analysing the trend of air accidents and incidents.[21] The numerical data for each safety concern has been given, and preventive measures like safety oversight, training and educating technical personnel, compliance with international standards and procedures, establishment of the regulatory framework at the domestic level and many other things were planned.

---

[21] 'India jumps to 55th place in ICAO's aviation safety oversight ranking: DGCA', *The Economic Times*, 10 February 2023, available at, https://economictimes.indiatimes.com/industry/transportation/airlines-/-aviation/india-jumps-to-55th-place-in-icaos-aviation-safety-oversight-ranking-dgca/articleshow/97801587.cms. Last visited, 28 July 2023.

In addition to discussing various aspects of aviation safety, the document also addresses emerging threats, including improper communication or miscommunication between ATC and pilots, which has been identified as a significant factor contributing to air accidents and incidents. It proposes potential solutions to mitigate these risks.[22] Now, this threat can multiply in international airports if the ATC personnel are not well-versed in foreign languages because linguistic barriers are one of the biggest factors contributing to miscommunication that ultimately leads to accidents.[23] The consequences of ineffective communication in aviation can be both life-threatening and drastic, as communication misunderstandings are frequently cited as contributing factors to aviation accidents and incidents. Thus, the risk associated with inadequate communication is relatively high, influenced by various factors such as language barriers, non-standardized phraseology, ambiguous communication, regional differences, and premature communication, all of which collectively contribute to the likelihood of communication errors during flight operations.[24]

One more crucial factor may also arise that could adversely impact the effective functioning of the ATC while handling additional international air traffic during seasonal operations. The ATC in the Indian aviation sector is severely under-staffed. According to a newspaper report of 2022, the sanctioned strength of Air Traffic Control Officers (ATCOs) in the country is 3,901, against which only 3,162 personnel are employed. This means there exists a shortage of 19%, and the shortage is only increasing with time.[25] The scarcity of ATCOs may have an adverse impact on the global position of India, create hindrances to passenger safety and may also attract negative remarks from global regulators such as ICAO.[26] Facing an urgent need for more air traffic controllers due to the rapid growth in airports and slow recruitment rates, the Airports Authority of India (AAI) has recently urged the aviation safety regulator to amend the rules on duty hours to enable shorter rest periods. This is aimed to adhere to the Director General of Civil Aviation's guidelines on "watch duty limitations and rest requirements." The AAI will also need a 40% increase in its current workforce of 3,162 personnel for 2022, a 60% increase for 2023, reaching a

---

[22] 'National Aviation Safety Plan 2018–2022',*DGCA*, (II ed.) 30 August 2018, p. 3.

[23] 'What are the Common Causes of Plane Crashes,' *Wilson Kehoe Winingham*, 21 December 2023, available at, https://www.wkw.com/aviation-accidents/faqs/what-are-the-common-causes-of-aviation-accidents/. Last visited, 12 February 2024.

[24] Omar Alharasees, Abeer Jazzar & Utku Kale, 'Misunderstandings in Aviation Communication', *International Symposium on Electric Aircraft and Autonomous Systems*, 2021, pp. 131–138, at p. 131.

[25] Jagriti Chandra, 'Air Traffic Controllers overworked, understaffed', *The Hindu*, 4 February 2022, available at, https://www.thehindu.com/news/national/overworked-air-traffic-controllers-put-air-safety-at-risk/article38372218.ece. Last visited, 31 July 2024.

[26] 'Ensuring adequate number of air traffic controllers as air traffic grows: Government', *The Times of India*, 25 October 2022, available at, https://timesofindia.indiatimes.com/india/ensuring-adequate-number-of-air-traffic-controllers-as-air-traffic-grows-government/articleshow/104690118.cms. Last visited, 23 July 2024.

total of 5,131 controllers, and a 70% increase for 2024, amounting to 5,428 officers, as stated by a government official during an interview for an esteemed newspaper.[27]

An airport like Bhopal Airport, which operates seasonal international flights, may not have experienced and trained ATC personnel who can efficiently handle additional air traffic due to seasonal international flights. It may also lack the linguistic expertise essential for effective communication with the crew members. Deploying a seasonal workforce in times of need is neither financially nor practically a viable solution and it has its own drawbacks, which will be discussed later in this Chapter. Therefore, the effective functioning of the ATC at a seasonal international airport is questionable, and this raises the question of whether the Bhopal Airport is well equipped to handle a larger magnitude of air traffic during seasonal international operations. In addition to this, whether the current radar technology or the communication and navigation system can facilitate international operation and ensure operational safety is also doubtful. The number of accidents and incidents induced by various human factors is considerably high world-wide[28] and if we talk about Indian aviation industry then the data available on the Aircraft Accident Investigation Bureau clearly shows that one of the most common cause is failure of ATC.[29] Unfortunately, this issue has remained unnoticed for a long time, and various safety recommendations have only been issued after the actual occurrence of an accident or incident.

5.3 *Environmental Standards*

Compliance with environmental standards is the next concern at a seasonal international airport. This includes noise pollution management, waste management, energy efficiency measures, and conservation efforts to protect local ecosystems. International airports have much higher air traffic than domestic airports, and the aircraft involved in international air transport are also larger. Therefore, some additional measures are required to protect the environment from any type of damage due to flight operations. The most common and significant measure in this regard is noise reduction techniques because noise pollution is one of the most obvious effects of

[27] Jagriti Chandra, 'Shortage of air traffic controllers widen', *The Hindu*, 26 July 2022, available at, https://www.thehindu.com/news/national/shortage-of-air-traffic-controllers-widens/article65675057.ece. Last visited, 22 July 2024.

[28] Graham Wild, 'A review of human factors causations in commercial air transport accidents and incidents: From to 2000–2016, *Research Gate*, Vol. 99, 2018, available at, https://www.researchgate.net/publication/324575974_A_review_of_human_factors_causations_in_commercial_air_transport_accidents_and_incidents_From_to_2000-2016. Last visited, 18 January 2024.

[29] 'Safety Data', *Aircraft Accident Investigation Bureau*, available at, https://aaib.gov.in/Accidenetstatistics.html. Last visited, 18 January 2024.

aviation operations that elicit adverse community reactions.[30] Major international airports like the Mumbai Airport[31] and the Delhi Airport[32] have these infrastructures in place. In 2017, a 24-h-long research was conducted at the Bhopal Airport, and samples were collected for noise pollution at four different locations.[33]These samples were analysed, and the study showed that at three monitoring stations, noise levels were below the permissible limits. However, in the apron area, for a short time, noise pollution was above the permissible limits, and this was caused mainly by operational activities such as flight movements in the apron area.[34] According to recent newspaper reports, Bhopal Airport has introduced significant infrastructural upgrades to enhance passenger experience and the airport is all set to start international operations with increased connectivity at both the domestic as well as international levels.[35] But the airport is yet to take any effective steps for combating noise pollution resulting from aviation operations.

The second most common environmental concern under Environmental Sustainability Management is the popularisation of the use of alternative energy resources to meet the significant energy demands of an airport regularly. The government and its various agencies have taken many significant steps to promote environment friendly measures in the aviation industry, mainly to minimise its harmful impact on the earth. In 2022, the Ministry of Civil Aviation (MoCA) initiated efforts to achieve carbon neutrality and net-zero carbon emissions at airports nationwide. This included organising knowledge-sharing sessions to standardise carbon accounting and reporting and advising airport operators to monitor and reduce emissions in a phased manner.[36] The Bhopal Airport has been awarded the 'level-2' (Reduction) Airport Carbon Accreditation in 2023 for its proactive measures in mapping and cutting down CO2

[30] 'Reducing Aircraft Noise-Overview', *ICAO Secretariat*, Chapter 2, (2016) p. 27, available at, https://www.icao.int/environmental-protection/Documents/EnvironmentalReports/2016/ENVReport2016_pg27-29.pdf. Last visited, 23 July 2024.

[31] 'Noise Desk installed at Mumbai airport to reduce sound levels', *Indian Express*, 18 July 2019, available at, https://indianexpress.com/article/cities/mumbai/noise-desk-installed-at-mumbai-airport-to-reduce-sound-levels-2920228/. Last visited, 23 July 2024.

[32] Nikita Prasad, 'Cheer for Delhiites near airport! IGI airport installs sound barriers to curb noise pollution', *Financial Express*, 4 June 2019, available at, https://www.financialexpress.com/business/airlines-aviation-cheer-for-delhiites-near-airport-igi-airport-installs-sound-barriers-to-curb-noise-pollution-1597734/. Last visited, 23 July 2024.

[33] Virag Bohare & Pankaj Jain, 'Analysis of Air, Water and Noise of International Airport, Bhopal', *International Journal of Scientific Research in Science, Engineering and Technology*, Vol. 3, Issue 6, 2017, pp. 779–786, at p. 779.

[34] *Id.*, at 786.

[35] Ramendra Singh, 'Major Upgrades on Cards to Improve Travel Experience', *The Times of India*, 28 July 2024, available at, https://timesofindia.indiatimes.com/city/bhopal/bhopal-airport-upgrades-for-enhanced-travel-experience/articleshow/112072069.cms. Last visited, 23 August 2024.

[36] 'Government is making all efforts to promote the use of green energy at airports', *Press Information Bureau, MoCA, Govt. of India*, 21 March 2022, available at, https://pib.gov.in/Pressreleaseshare.aspx?PRID=1807630#:~:text=For%20encouraging%20green%20energy%20at%20the%20airports%2C%20the,generation%20and%20self-consumption%20of%20green%20and%20renewable%20energy. Last visited, 21 July 2024.

emissions in alignment with the global airport industry's climate change efforts.[37] Additionally, the Airport Authority of India, in the same year, planned to introduce electrical vehicles (EVs) with other vehicles in a phased manner to reduce carbon emissions on the premises, and their target is to replace all the existing vehicles completely with EVs by 2024.[38] While this airport is doing quite well in this regard, if in future it is planning to become a fully operational international airport, then more proactive changes need to be made in terms of the use of solar power and other environment-friendly measures.

5.4 Workforce Management

Workforce management is also a vital issue in the aviation industry. The Indian aviation sector's earnings are profoundly affected by fluctuating demand and cyclical trends, where peak seasons with high passenger traffic and fierce competition may drive airlines to cut fares, squeezing profit margins. In contrast, off-peak times often see a struggle with empty seats and underutilised capacity, resulting in elevated per-passenger costs and reduced overall profitability.[39] To survive the pandemic, airports and airlines drastically reduced their workforce, with Oxford Economics reporting a loss of over 2.3 million jobs, representing a 21% decrease from pre-pandemic levels. However, this downsizing has led to a recruitment and retention crisis, exemplified by London's Heathrow Airport, one of the world's busiest, capping its daily passenger traffic at 100,000 travellers in October 2022 due to an inability to manage the demand caused by severe labour shortages.[40]

Therefore, it is evident that employee shortage is a problem in the aviation industry worldwide. In such an environment, things may get even more challenging for an airport with a seasonal nature in terms of international flight operations. As it is a well-established fact that international airports handle more traffic than domestic airports, there exists a requirement for an additional workforce that is well trained to handle such passengers. Suppose an airport operates seasonal international flights during a certain time of the year. In that case, they will have to rely upon a seasonal

[37] Ramendra Singh, 'Bhopal airport gets L-2 tag in carbon accreditation', *The Times of India*, 12 Sep 2023, available at, https://timesofindia.indiatimes.com/city/bhopal/bhopal-airport-gets-l-2-tag-in-carbon-accreditation/articleshow/103592571.cms. Last visited, 21 July 2024.

[38] 'Bhopal's Raja Bhoj Airport is all set to go green', *The Times of India*, 20 May 2023, available at, https://timesofindia.indiatimes.com/travel/travel-news/bhopals-raja-bhoj-airport-all-set-to-go-green/articleshow/100386037.cms. Last visited, 23 July 2023.

[39] 'Indian Aviation Industry: Potential and Challenges', *Avalon Consulting*, available at, https://www.consultavalon.com/our-blog/indian-aviation-industry-potential-challenges/. Last visited, 23 August 2024.

[40] 'Employee and skills shortages in the aviation industry: How can SWP help prevent and fight it?', *HR Forecast*, available at, https://hrforecast.com/employee-and-skills-shortages-in-the-aviation-industry-how-can-strategic-workforce-planning-prevent-and-fight-them/. Last visited, 21 June 2024.

workforce because the air traffic situation is not consistent around the year. Additionally, deploying an additional workforce imposes an additional financial burden on the government.

Now, there are some common challenges associated with the management of the seasonal workforce. Two major problems associated with this type of workforce are, firstly, the lack of expertise stemming from insufficient or inadequate training delivered within a short timeframe, and secondly, the fact that employees frequently do not receive all the employment-related benefits that the full-time or regular employees do, which consequently diminishes their commitment and dedication to their work.[41] While the engagement of seasonal employees may be very common in sectors like agriculture, tourism industry, retail business, and construction, the aviation sector needs extremely qualified, well-trained and highly committed employees because of its sensitive nature. Hiring a seasonal workforce can cause both safety and security threats to an aerodrome. An airport like Bhopal, which handles seasonal international flights, is bound to face various operational and governance-related challenges, including the complexities of adjusting staffing and resources to match fluctuating passenger numbers, navigating the intricacies of adhering to international regulatory standards, and effectively coordinating with both domestic and international partners to ensure smooth and efficient airport operations throughout the varying seasons.

5.5 *Infrastructural Issues*

Lastly, the overall infrastructure and amenities available for passengers at an international airport are also vital. The airport industry has evolved so much, and today, it is expected that an airport operating international flights and handling international passengers must have world-class facilities. There is an international body named Airport Council International (ACI) that actively promotes practices to enhance consumer experience. ACI serves as the global representative for airports, acting as a key advocate for the interests of its members at the global level.[42] It has a highly specialized structure and works in close partnership with government agencies, industry stakeholders, and regulators like ICAO to ensure that the collective needs of airports are addressed.[43] By fostering innovation and promoting best practices, it helps to ensure that the aviation industry evolves safely and efficiently. ACI has created an extensive set of guidelines, standards, and recommendations to support

---

[41] 'The Pros and Cons of Temporary vs. Seasonal Workers', *CPA Practice Advisor*, available at, https://www.cpapracticeadvisor.com/2019/11/20/the-pros-and-cons-of-temp-vs-seasonal-workers/35550/#:~:text=Take%20a%20look%20at%20a%20few%20hiring%20seasonal,workforce%20Cons%3A%20Less%20time%20for%20training%20Uncommitted%20employees. Last visited, 21 August 2024.

[42] 'What is ACI', *ACI World*, available at, https://airportscouncil.org/about/aci-world/. Last visited, 17 November 2024.

[43] *Id.*

its members in improving operations, safety, and customer service.[44] Furthermore, it has introduced numerous non-mandatory policies to guide the industry towards higher performance and greater sustainability. ACI operates through a range of programs and services. The Safety Enhancement Program (APEX) and the Airport Service Quality Awards (ASQ) are the two key initiatives in this regard, These initiatives are grounded in passenger satisfaction ratings that serve as the primary measure of success and performance.[45] On the other hand, the availability of basic facilities is considered adequate in the domestic airports and in India, there are many such small domestic airports.

So, if an airport operates as a seasonal international airport, then it is obvious that it might not have world-class amenities like other fully functional airports. Also, during seasonal flight operations, even the basic facilities and amenities might not be sufficient to facilitate the additional passenger traffic and may create dissatisfaction among the passengers. Bhopal is a very small airport with all the basic amenities, but when comparing it with other big Indian airports, the passengers found it inadequate and not up to the mark. The airport handles approximately 4000 passengers daily. Due to such low air traffic issues like check-in delays or mismanagement are not very prominent like other airports. Rather, the most common concerns raised by the passengers are flight cancellations, delays and poor connectivity.[46] As mentioned earlier in this Chapter, during the seasonal operations, the authority makes temporary arrangements for customs and immigration formalities to ensure security, but it is practically not possible to have other temporary amenities like restrooms, sitting arrangements, food and water, clean washrooms etc. for the passengers at specific times. The airport currently has all the basic amenities which are suitable for the current passenger traffic, but if they are planning to become a fully functional international airport, then some more development is needed. The most recent developments are an indication that the AAI is planning to make Bhopal an international airport.[47]

6 Conclusion

Although the fundamental operations of airports are largely similar, they function as crucial terminals where passengers board flights, necessitating strict adherence to safety and security protocols due to the inherent risks involved with air travel. Given

---

[44] 'ACI Programmes and Services', *ACI World*, available at, https://aci.aero/programs-and-services/asq/airport-customer-experience-accreditation/. Last visited, 17 November 2024.

[45] 'ASQ Awards and Recognitions', *ACI World*, available at, https://aci.aero/programs-and-services/asq/asq-awards-and-recognition/. Last visited, 21 August 2024.

[46] Ramendra Singh, 'Few Airlines, Fewer Flyers make Hit Air Connectivity of Bhopal', *The Times of India*, 10 January 2017, available at, https://timesofindia.indiatimes.com/city/bhopal/few-airlines-fewer-flyers-make-hit-citys-air-connectivity/articleshow/56429719.cms. Last visited, 21 August 2024.

[47] *Supra* note 32.

the potentially hazardous nature of aviation, comprehensive safety and security regulations have been developed and enforced by various regulatory bodies to oversee airport operations. These measures are designed to ensure that air travel remains one of the safest modes of transportation available. This high level of vigilance is maintained for both domestic and international airports, reflecting the global commitment to safeguarding passengers and airline staff. Beyond safety and security, airports also focus on enhancing the passenger experience, recognising their significant role in driving economic growth. Modern airports strive to offer improved amenities, efficient services, and a more pleasant travel experience, thereby contributing to their importance as vital economic and transportation hubs in contemporary society.

It is undeniable that there is a significant disparity between domestic and international airports, influenced by their operational scope and the volume of passenger traffic they handle. This distinction also extends to their economic and environmental impacts. To address the complexities associated with international airports, both global and domestic regulators have established additional safety and security requirements that these airports must meet. In contrast, many domestic airports in India continue to operate with relatively basic infrastructure, which can present challenges, as exemplified by the Bhopal Airport. Bhopal's situation is particularly problematic due to its lack of recognition as an international airport by the Airport Authority of India, which leads to a reluctance among airlines to operate from this location. The seasonal nature of Bhopal further complicates matters, affecting various aspects such as aerodrome governance, environmental impact assessment, adherence to safety and security standards, passenger experience, and connectivity. The absence of provisions for managing seasonal airports under both international regulations and Indian aviation laws exacerbates these challenges. Given the significant potential for Bhopal Airport to evolve into a major aviation hub and the evident demand for enhanced connectivity, it is crucial for the government to undertake necessary developments and grant international status to the airport.

Chapter 16
Tabletop Airport Administration: A Case Study of the Mangalore Airport

N. Harsha

Abstract The Mangalore Airport, situated in the coastal region of India, has long served as a crucial hub for airline operations. However, the 2010 Mangalore Airport accident thrust the unique challenges of tabletop airports in India into the spotlight. Under the management of the Airports Authority of India, a statutory body, this incident marked a turning point in the airport's history. Since October 2020, the airport has been under the control of a private entity, operating under a Public–Private Partnership (PPP) Model. This transition and the airport's tabletop status present two key aspects for analysis: compliance with a tabletop runway and change in facilitation services after the takeover by the private entity. Based on the two important aspects highlighted above, the first part of this Chapter unearths the challenges of tabletop airports, especially in the coastal region and the choice of technology adoption. The observations and recommendations made by the Accident Investigation Committee in their report on the Mangalore and Kozhikode airports highlight thematic issues of tabletop runway safety. These thematic issues of tabletop runway provide a factual matrix to evaluate the standards adopted by the airport. The second part focuses on the impact of the airport's operation under the PPP model. The passenger feedback will be sourced from platforms like Google reviews to identify the facilitation standards. This Chapter's thematic focus is on evaluating compliance, and the critical analysis aims to highlight the Mangalore Airport's challenges with Standards and Best Practices.

Keywords Air India Express · Engineered Material Arrestor System (EMAS) · Firefighting service · Good industry practice (GIP) · Green Airport · Kozhikode airport · Runway End Safety Area (RESA) · Surveillance inspection

N. Harsha (✉)
National Law School of India University, Bengaluru, India
e-mail: harshan@nls.ac.in

© The Author(s), under exclusive license to Springer Nature Singapore Pte Ltd. 2025
S. Bhat B. (ed.), *Aerodrome Governance in Asia*,
https://doi.org/10.1007/978-981-96-7568-5_16

1 Introduction

The Mangalore International Airport, situated in the coastal city of Mangaluru, Karnataka, India, has served as a vital link connecting the region with domestic and international destinations, particularly in the Middle East. Its distinctive tabletop configuration, perched atop a plateau with steep drops at both ends of the runway, presents substantial safety challenges. The 2010 Air India Express flight accident starkly underscored these challenges, drawing global attention to the perils associated with such airports.

In October 2020, the airport underwent a transition to private management under a Public–Private Partnership (PPP) model, heralding a new phase in its operational trajectory. This transition, combined with its tabletop runway, presents crucial aspects for examination. The paper scrutinises the airport's adherence to international safety standards, especially post-accident safety measures, and assesses the impact of privatisation on passenger services and operational efficacy. By focusing on both technical safety protocols and user experiences, this study strives to deliver a comprehensive evaluation of the Mangalore Airport's commitment to best practices in aviation safety and management.

2 Mangalore City and Airport

The city of Mangaluru or Mangalore, both used interchangeably across, has a long-drawn history. Mangalore is the anglicised word for Mangaluru. Post-independence, the name was changed from Mangalore to Mangaluru. According to the Scottish physician Francis Buchanan who visited Mangalore in 1801, Mangalore was a rich and prosperous port with flourishing trading activity.

There are two airports bearing the name Mangalore globally: the Mangalore Airport (ICAO: YMNG) located in Victoria, Australia, and the Mangalore International Airport (IATA: IXE, ICAO: VOML) located in the state of Karnataka, India. In this chapter, the focus is on the Mangalore International Airport (IATA: IXE, ICAO: VOML).

The Bajpe Aerodrome (now known as the Mangalore International Airport) operated its first flight on 25 December 1951, when Vonthibettu Prabhakar Hegde carried Pandit Jawaharlal Nehru, the First Prime Minister of India on a DC-3 (Dakota).[1] The word "Mangalore Airport" may resonate with one of two aspects: the 2010 accident and the airport's being on a tabletop. The Indian media has covered the challenges of tabletop airports on multiple occasions.

Mangaluru International Airport (MIA), formerly known as Mangalore Bajpe Airport, serves the port city of Mangaluru. It is served by most major Indian airlines

[1] 'First man who landed in Mangalore: Airport is fine', *Mangalore Today News Network*, (Mangalore edn.) 28 May 2024, available at <https://www.mangaloretoday.com/main/First-man-who-landed-in-Mangalore-Airport-is-fine-.html> Last visited, 16 June 2024.

and offers domestic and international services to destinations. Adani Airports took over the operation and management from the Airports Authority of India (AAI) on 30 October 2020 under a 50-year contract.[2] The Mangalore International Airport has seen an increase in passenger movement by 21% in the first Quarter of 2024–2025.[3] The Airport also commenced international cargo handling services.[4] Currently, 15 Indigo, 1 Air India, and 6 Air India Express flights are operated out of the Mangalore Airport.[5]

The Airport received level three Airport Customer Experience Accreditation from the Airports Council International (ACI).[6] In 2023, Green Airports Recognition 2023 recognised twelve airports in our regions for their outstanding achievements in mitigating the use of single-use plastic. ACI recognised Mangalore International Airport as Platinum for the Asia–Pacific and Middle East region in the category of fewer than 8 million passengers per annum for Single Use Plastic Free Airport.[7] Implementing the above project, MIA has reduced plastic waste from an average of 1238 kg per month in FY 22 to an average of 444 kg per month in FY 23, resulting in a reduction of 23.8 tons of CO_2.[8] In 2024, MIA participated in Green Airports Recognition Programme and has stated that it has implemented "Landscape Development Project" and as a part of this project, has developed 13,200 Ha of landscape area.[9]

[2] Centre for Aviation, *Profile of Mangaluru International Airport*, available at <https://centreforaviation.com/data/profiles/airports/mangaluru-international-airport-ixe> Last visited, 20 June 2024.

[3] Naina J. A., 'Mangaluru International Airport reports 21% increase in passenger traffic in Q1', *Deccan Herald*, 22 July 2024, available at <https://www.deccanherald.com/business/companies/mangaluru-international-airport-reports-21-increase-in-passenger-traffic-in-q1-3116520> Last visited, 27 July 2024.

[4] 'Mangaluru International Airport commences international cargo operations', *Airports Council International (ACI) Asia-Pacific and Middle East*, 5 July 2024, available at <https://www.aci-asiapac.aero/media-centre/news/mangaluru-international-airport-commences-international-cargo-operations> Last visited, 27 July 2024.

[5] 'Flight arrival information', *Adani Mangaluru Airport*, 4 August 2024, available at <https://www.adani.com/en/mangaluru-airport/flight-status> Last visited, 27 August 2024.

[6] 'Mangaluru International Airport receives level 3 ACI Customer Experience Accreditation', *Airports Council International (ACI) Asia-Pacific and Middle East,* 15 February 2024, available at <https://www.aci-asiapac.aero/media-centre/news/mangaluru-international-airport-receives-level-3-aci-customer-experience-accreditation> Last visited, 27 August 2024.

[7] 'Green Airports Recognition 2023: Single-Use Plastic Elimination', *Airports Council International (ACI) Asia–Pacific and Middle East*, available at <https://www.aci-asiapac.aero/advocacy/environment/green-airports-recognition> Last visited, 27 August 2024.

[8] 'Green Airports Recognition 2023: Single-Use Plastic Elimination', *Airports Council International ACI-Asia Pacific*, p. 21, available at <https://www.aci-asiapac.aero/f/library/4698/Green%20Airports%20Recognition%202023%20-%20Single%20Use%20Plastic%20Elimination%20Publication.pdf> Last visited, 27 August 2024.

[9] *Id.*, at 15.

3 Tabletop Airports

Skybrary provides the following description for the Tabletop runway[10]

> A tabletop runway is a runway that is located on the top of a plateau or hill with one or both ends adjacent to a steep precipice which drops into a deep gorge. This type of runway can create an optical illusion of being at the same level as the plains below, which requires a very precise visual approach by the pilot when autoland is not used or is not available.

The categorisation of tabletop runways/tabletop airports is not founded in law but is based on the position of the runway strip, which has a deep gorge at the end. In India, there are six tabletop runways: Mangalore Airport, Kozhikode Airport, Kannur Airport, Lingpui Airport, Pakyong Airport, and Shimla Airport. The tabletop airports are also recognised as critical airfields. Luca Zamparini and Joseph Szyliowicz argue that a completely safe aviation system is impossible, but proactive efforts can reduce the number of safety episodes.[11] The approach in the chapter is not about focusing on ensuring a foolproof safety system in place rather identifying the principles applicable to dangers associated with the tabletop runway through the example of the Mangaluru Airport.

4 Accidents and the Challenges of Compliance

The Mangaluru Airport had two events under consideration here along with that of the Kozhikode Airport. The central focus is that both Mangaluru and Kozhikode Airports are categorised as tabletop airports. We shall look into the incidents and analyse the findings and obligations identified.

4.1 The Mangaluru Airport

On 22 May 2010, a Boeing 737-800 aircraft (Flight IX-812) operated by Air India Express from Dubai to Mangalore met with an accident at Mangalore from a runway excursion. The report on the Accident identified direct causes and contributing factors. The recommendations to the Airport Operator, that is, AAI thirteen points,[12] including avoidance of downward slope in the Overshoot Area; frangible structures in

---

[10] 'Tabletop Runway', *Skybrary,* available at <https://skybrary.aero/articles/tabletop-runway> Last visited, 27 August 2024.

[11] Luca Zamparini & Joseph Szyliowicz, 'Aviation Safety', Anna Masutti & Pablo Mendes de Leon (eds.), *Elgar Concise Encyclopedia of Aviation Law*, (United Kingdom: Edward Elgar Publishing Limited, 2023) pp. 157–160.

[12] 'Report on Accident to Air India Express Boeing 737-800 Aircraft VT-AXV on 22nd May 2010 at Mangalore, Aircraft Accident Report, Mangalore, 31 October 2010, p. 122, available at <https://skybrary.aero/sites/default/files/bookshelf/1680.pdf> Last visited, 10 August 2024.

the Overshoot Areas; Maintenance of Runway End Safety Area (RESA); Engineered Material Arrestor System (EMAS) and Soft Ground Arrestor (SGA); Installation of Distance to Go Markers; Location of Air Traffic Controller (ATC); Approach Radar/ Area Radar Repeater in the ATC Tower; Preventing Erosion of Strip Width; Rescue Fire Fighting (RFF) Vehicles Based on Terrain; Obstruction removal.

Aircraft Accident Investigation Bureau, in accordance with Rule 8 (3) (h) of Aircraft (Investigation of Accidents and Incidents) Rules, 2017, forwards the recommendations made in investigation reports and safety studies to Directorate General of Civil Aviation (DGCA) and other regulatory authorities for their follow-up and to obtain compliance of the same.[13] Runway 24/06 has a declared distance of 2450 m. There were 60 m of Basic Strip and a RESA of 180 m. The Multi-Mode Secondary Surveillance Radar (MSSR) was unserviceable on 20 May 2010.[14] It continued to be unavailable on the day of the accident. Due to unserviceability, the aircraft was given descent at a shorter distance on Distance-Measuring equipment.[15]

On 20 June 2019, a Boeing 737-800 aircraft (Flight AXB 384) operated by Air India Express from Dubai to Mangalore met with a senior incident from a runway excursion at Mangalore. The report of the Serious Incident identified certain causes of the incident without any specific recommendations to the Airport Operator, that is, AAI. The Pilot in Command deliberately turned the aircraft to the right, exited the paved surface, and finally halted on the unpaved surface 80 m away from the runway edge.[16]

4.2 *Mangaluru Airport Inspections and Surveillance Reports*

The DGCA and the AAI team conducted an extensive aerodrome inspection from 31 July to 3 August 2007. During the inspection, several significant issues were identified. RESA was not maintained or graded. Additionally, obstacles were noted at the transitional surface of runway 24, posing potential safety hazards. The Fire Services also exhibited deficiencies, including a lack of rescue and firefighting training records, and no emergency exercises were observed to address aerodrome emergencies.

Furthermore, the AAI's Safety Audit Report dated 9 November 2009, highlighted the presence of coconut trees south of runway 24, which could pose a threat to aircraft

---

[13] Safety Recommendations, *Aircraft Accident Investigation Bureau,* available at <https://aaib.gov.in/safetyrecommendations.html> Last visited, 10 August 2024.

[14] *Supra* note 12, at 33.

[15] B738, Mangalore India, 2010, *Skybrary*, available at <https://skybrary.aero/accidents-and-incidents/b738-mangalore-india-2010> Last visited, 10 June 2024.

[16] 'Final Investigation Report on Serious Incident to M/S Air India Express Ltd. Boeing 737-800 Aircraft VT-AYA', *Aircraft Accident Investigation Bureau,* 30 June 2019, p. 8, available at <https://aaib.gov.in/Reports/2019/SeriousIncident/VT_AYA_at_Mangalore_on_30Jun19.pdf> Last visited, 10 June 2024.

safety. It also pointed out the absence of tabletop exercises for various contingencies, reflecting a gap in emergency preparedness.

Subsequent surveillance inspections revealed crucial information. The Aerodrome Standards Directorate, DGCA, inspected on 19 and 20 May, 2010, just two days before the accident occurred on 22 May2010. The inspection indicated that the RESA for runway 24 measured 180 × 90 m. However, AAI reduced RESA width to 175 m following the accident from 180 m, as stated in the Accident Report.[17]

A surveillance inspection checklist based on the examination carried out on 28 and 29 June 2012, mentioned that the RESA for runway 24 was 180 × 90 m, which indicates a consistent observation across multiple inspections and variations in the size of RESA. The inspection was carried out on 27 and 28 March 2012 by DGCA, and the point of EMAS and Soft Ground Arrestor Barrier is closed with the observation that the RESA created addressed the issue as per Para 5.3.22 of the ICAO Aerodrome Design Manual Part 1. However, the Off Airport mock drill was not conducted and the roads outside the perimeter wall were not wide enough, and it took 11 min for the Crash Fire Tenders to reach. The roads outside the perimeter wall were a major hurdle during the accident in 2010.

The Aviation Safety Audit Report was conducted by AAI[18] from 17 to 21 March 2015. It found that there were no adequate emergency roads in the aerodrome, and the gates were inaccessible to emergency vehicles. Further, it was observed that there was no mutual aid agreement between the City Fire Brigade or similar large-scale firefighting units such as Mangalore Refineries and Petroleum Limited. The observation on agreement/understanding might be valid, but this cannot be mutual aid unless there is a validation mechanism that the deployment of the Crash Fire Tenders outside the Airport will not reduce the category of protection at the Airport.

DGCA conducted a surveillance inspection from 9 to 12 October 2018, and it was observed that the RESA for runway 06 is 240 × 90 m and for runway 24, it is 240 × 90 m and that specialist rescue services, and firefighting equipment appropriate to the hazard were not available. The observation on the firefighting equipment is in reference to the water body, which is 1000 m from runway 06, and there were no specialist rescue services and appropriate equipment.

As per the latest information provided by DGCA,[19] the RESA for runway 06 is 92 m and was completed on 27 June 2022. Work is in progress for runway 24, and the provisional date of completion is 30 September 2024. The satellite fire station is yet to be completed for an emergency response beyond the boundary wall, and the arrangements with the local administration for support of fire services in case of exigencies are also pending.

[17] *Supra* note 12, at 36.

[18] RTI Requests No. AAICH/R/E/24/00063, dated 16 May 2024, (Information obtained through RTI from Mangalore Airport, AAI).

[19] *Id.*

4.3 The Kozhikode Airport

On 7 August 2020, a Boeing 737-800 aircraft (Flight AXB 1344) operated by Air India Express from Dubai to Kozhikode met with an accident at Kozhikode from a runway excursion. The report on the Accident identified direct causes and contributing factors.[20] The dissemination of information pertinent to administrative and policy decisions derived from the recommendations stipulated in the 2010 Mangalore Airport report is a pivotal function of the report. Additionally, the Kozhikode Airport report serves to appraise adherence to the recommendations outlined in the Mangalore Airport accident report. It has been observed that numerous recommendations specified in the Mangalore Airport accident report have remained unaddressed, despite the passage of a decade.

The three reports hold significant importance in assessing compliance and integrating standards in Aerodrome regulation and administration. The selection of focus areas in this analysis is based not on the significance or criticality of the technology/decision at the airport operation but rather on the availability of information from public sources. The primary objective here is to present an approach for analysing aviation issues in India without generalisation. Three aspects will be considered for analysis: firstly, the choice of technology and cost–benefit analysis; secondly, the implementation and administrative response; and thirdly, the principles under consideration are grounded in existing literature.

5 Compliance—After the Accident

5.1 Runway End Safety Area

As per the Concession Agreement on page 309 and 310 under Schedule U—the list of proposed works by Authority and the Concessionaire must submit the list of works that it shall complete, including the extension of RESA for 120 m.[21] The AAI can waive this RESA project of 120 m as per the Concession Agreement. AAI might be in a position to waive the mandated projects, but the clause appears to be out of place as AAI might not be in a place to waive the statutory requirements. It is also of concern

[20] 'Final Investigation Report Accident Involving M/S Air India Express B737-800 Aircraft VTon7 August', *Aircraft Accident Investigation Bureau*, August 2020, p. 201, available at <https://www.flightradar24.com/blog/wp-content/uploads/2021/09/Final-Report-VT-AXH.pdf> Last visited, 12 June 2024.

[21] 'Concession Agreement for Mangaluru International Airport between AAI and Adani Enterprises', *Airports Authority of India,* 14 February 2020, available at <https://www.aai.aero/sites/default/files/Concession-Agreement-Mangaluru-Airport.pdf, p. 309> Last visited, 10 June 2024.

that the RESA is where the majority of serious and fatal aircraft crashes occur.[22] As per the Response by DGCA to the RTI Application, RESA on Runway 06–24 (92 m) was completed on 27 June 2022 but the RESA on Runway 24 is expected to be completed by 30 September2024. As per news reports, the 2450 m runway was recarpeted in May 2023.[23]

Analysing and contrasting tabletop runway designs and technology implementations could yield valuable insights into optimal practices across diverse jurisdictions. Tabletop runways are ubiquitous globally. A few of these runways are identified for comparative evaluation, considering their specific standards, implemented technology, and any pertinent incidents or accidents.

The São Paulo/Congonhas–Deputado Freitas Nobre Airport (IATA: CGH, ICAO: SBSP) is a commercial airport serving São Paulo, Brazil. On 17 July 2007, Airbus A.320 TAM Flight 3054 was on a standard route from Porto Alegre (POA) to São Paulo-Congonhas (CGH). The aircraft departed from Porto Alegre and as it approached São Paulo, the weather was rainy and the runway was wet. The runway at São Paulo-Congonhas is at a higher elevation compared to the surrounding area. The aircraft likely became airborne, cleared the perimeter fence and a busy highway, and then collided with a concrete building, bursting into flames.[24] The Congonhas–Deputado Freitas Nobre Airport as per reports is the first South America's Engineered Material Arresting System (EMAS) being installed.[25] The work started in early 2021, and Brazil's Airport Authority, Infraero, paid the costs of BRL123 million (USD26 million).[26] As per reports, work was completed on 30 June 2022.[27]

The Vágar Airport, (IATA: FAE, ICAO: EKVG) stands as the sole airport serving the Faroe Islands. On 10 October 2006, during a routine approach and landing at Stord Airport Sørstokken, aircraft OY-CRG veered off the runway, careening down a steep slope. This incident resulted in significant damage to the aircraft, igniting

---

[22] Norman J. Ashford, Saleh Mumayiz, & Paul H. Wright, *Airport Engineering Planning, Design, and Development of 21st Century Airports*, Fourth edition, (New Jersey: John Wiley & Sons, Inc., 2011) p. 353.

[23] Naina J. A., 'Mangaluru International Airport recarpets 2.45-km-long runway', 31 May 2023, *Deccan Herald*, available at <https://www.deccanherald.com/india/karnataka/mangaluru-international-airport-recarpets-245-km-long-runway-1223562.html> Last visited, 10 June 2024.

[24] 'Final Report A – N° 67/CENIPA/2009', Aeronautical Accidents Investigation and Prevention Centre, PR-MBK, Airbus A-320, 17 July 2007 (RF A-67/CENIPA/2009), available at <https://asn.flightsafety.org/reports/2007/20070717_A320_PR-MBK.pdf> Last visited, 10 August 2024.

[25] 'Runway Safe's EMAS is getting attention in Brazil', *AviationPros*, 23 February 2022, available at <https://www.aviationpros.com/aoa/runway-management/press-release/21257878/runway-safes-emas-is-getting-attention-in-brazil> Last visited, 10 August 2024.

[26] 'Runway safety works at Congonhas Airport', *Legal One*, 1 January 2023, available at <https://www.legaloneglobal.com/deal/Runway-safety-works-at-Congonhas-Airport-1653294873157> Last visited, 10 August 2024.

[27] 'EMAS System works are completed at Congonhas Airport (SP)', *Aeroflap*, 30 June 2022, available at <https://www.aeroflap.com.br/en/emas-system-works-are-completed-at-congonhas-sp-airport/> Last visited, 20 August 2024.

an immediate and rapid spreading fire, which tragically led to four fatalities and six serious injuries, with insufficient time for full aircraft evacuation.[28]

The Telluride Regional Airport (IATA: TEX, ICAO: KTEX, FAA LID: TEX) has EMAS at the end of the runway instead of acquiring land for a full-length RESA. The cost of EMAS was much cheaper than the land acquisition cost for RESA.[29]

EMAS is installed on 121 runway ends at 71 airports in the United States of America, and EMAS has been able to arrest 21 aircraft and safely stopped overrunning aircraft carrying 430 crew and passengers aboard those flights.[30] The Federal Aviation Administration Advisory Circular AC 150/5220-22B—Engineered Materials Arresting Systems (EMAS) for Aircraft Overruns provides the mandates regarding the installation of EMAS.[31]

5.2 *Choice of Technology—A Cost–Benefit Analysis*

The decision-making process involving aviation safety and technology is complex, especially considering the ICAO mandate. This is evident in the challenges that States face when exercising their discretion in this area, such as choosing between the RESA and the EMAS. Some argue that not adhering to international standards is justified as it allows for greater sovereignty and administrative discretion. The comparison between RESA and EMAS has sparked significant interest, with the debate being brought before the Supreme Court of India and gaining attention in the media.[32] The state's freedom to choose between these two options is at the heart of the discussion. Nonetheless, the ICAO mandate clearly states that RESA is sufficient to ensure safety when meeting the mandatory dimensions.

Post Kozhikode air crash, Minister for Civil Aviation, Mr Puri said on Twitter:

---

[28] 'Report on Aircraft Accident on 10 October, 2006 at Stord Airport, Sørstokken (Enso) Norway Involving A Bae 146-200, Oy-Crg, Operated By Atlantic Airways', *Accident Investigation Board Norway*, available at <https://asn.flightsafety.org/reports/2006/20061010_B462_OY-CRG.pdf> Last visited, 20 August 2024.

[29] 'Master Plan Telluride Airport', *Telluride Airport*, available at <https://tellurideairport.com/airport-master-plan/> Last visited, 20 August 2024; 'Telluride Airport will close in April for runway replacement', *The Watch*, 26 January 2009, available at <https://www.telluridenews.com/the_watch/news/article_2612bc3a-e157-58c8-a2ed-ce09d96fbe36.html> Last visited, 20 August 2024.

[30] 'Engineered Material Arresting System (EMAS)', *Federal Aviation Administration*, 11 September 2023, available at <https://www.faa.gov/newsroom/engineered-material-arresting-system-emas-0> Last visited, 20 August 2024.

[31] 'AC 150/5220-22B—Engineered Materials Arresting Systems (EMAS) for Aircraft Overruns', *Federal Aviation Administration*, available at <https://www.faa.gov/documentLibrary/media/Advisory_Circular/AC_150_5220-22B.pdf> Last visited, 20 August 2024; Lakshmanan Ravi, 'Fundamentals of Airport Planning: Theory and Practice', (New York: Routledge, 2024) p. 95.

[32] Manu Kaushik, 'How an 85-year-old is taking on Aviation Ministry, DGCA for Calicut crash', *Business Today*, 22 September 2020, available at <https://www.businesstoday.in/industry/aviation/story/how-an-85-year-old-is-taking-on-aviation-ministry-dgca-for-calicut-crash-273608-2020-09-22> Last visited, 22 August 2024.

> Kozhikode airport is equipped with a Runway End Safety Area (RESA) as per ICAO guidelines on safety. Engineered Material Arrestor System (EMAS) provides safety benefit if less than standard RESA length is available or at Airports where RESA cannot be provided due to constraints. Both Airports Authority of India and industry regulator DGCA had evaluated the option to install EMAS at Kozhikode and Mangalore airports - tabletops where last two major aviation mishaps have taken place. But the idea was dropped considering the complexities of post-installation maintenance & issues related with immediate replacement of product[33]

On the day of the Mangalore and Kozhikode incidents, the atmosphere was marked by poor weather conditions. Under such circumstances, even a well-designed RESA may prove inadequate to handle an overrunning aircraft. This is primarily due to the saturated ground surface, which can become compromised, losing its ability to effectively bear the weight of the aircraft. The combination of these factors significantly heightened the risks associated with aircraft operations on that fateful day.[34]

The Supreme Court of India has been involved in deliberations regarding the selection of technology between EMAS and RESA.[35] As a result of the Court's directive, the Ministry of Civil Aviation (MoCA) was tasked with granting the petitioner an opportunity to present their case. A specialised committee comprising officials from the AAI, the DGCA, and the MoCA was constituted to facilitate this.

During the committee's proceedings, the petitioner was given a hearing to substantiate their position on the technology selection. The committee found that the petitioner was unable to provide compelling evidence regarding the technical specifications. Consequently, the committee arrived at the conclusion that it is the State's obligation to adhere to the International Civil Aviation Organization (ICAO) requirements. The committee found that adopting the Runway End Safety Area (RESA) has achieved compliance with these requirements. It is important to highlight that the committee comprised exclusively of Government members, lacking any input from the private sector or independent agencies. This limited participation may have affected the comprehensiveness and effectiveness of their decisions.

---

[33] Hardeep S. Puri, *X*, available at <https://x.com/HardeepSPuri/status/1292760422274105344> 10 August 2020, Last visited, 19 July 2024.

[34] Tony Kazda & Bob Caves, 'Runway Strips and Other Areas', Antonin Kazda & Robert E. Caves (eds.), *Airport Design and Operation*, Third edition, (United Kingdom: Emerald Group Publishing, 2015) p. 110.

[35] *Rajen Mehta* v. *Directorate General of Civil Aviation & Anr.,* Supreme Court of India, Writ Petition(s) (Civil) No(s). 998/2020, 31 October 2022.

5.3 Economics of RESA

According to recent reporting by a newspaper, the estimated cost for an Engineered Material Arresting System (EMAS) is INR 100 crores.[36] The significance of this cost lies not just in the initial implementation but also in the recurring expense of replacement following any runway overrun incidents. This becomes even more apparent when considering the compensation already disbursed to the families of the victims of the tragic incident at the Mangalore Airport. Air India's statement revealed that over Rs. 50 crores have been paid to settle claims for 62 victims and partially settle claims for 6 others.[37]

It has been projected that approximately Rs. 282.49 crores will need to be allocated as compensation for the victims or their families.[38] This estimation starkly contrasts the cost of INR 100 crores for EMAS. From a broader aviation ecosystem perspective, prioritising the financial prudence of adopting EMAS over questioning who will cover its expenses appears to be the prevailing approach. Notably, the case of the Kozhikode Airport stands out, as it underwent a Social Impact Assessment for land acquisition, resulting in a compensation of 2 crores.[39]

On the other hand, the estimated project cost for creating a Runway End Safety Area (RESA) amount to 484 crores.[40] When comparing the cost of building RESA with the compensation provided, it seems advantageous to consider implementing RESA. Examining the potential expense of EMAS alongside the replacement cost for each runway overrun suggests a compelling case for the adoption of RESA.

---

[36] Prince Mathews Thomas, 'Air India Express crash: This safety instrument could have prevented Kozhikode tragedy', 10 August 2020, *Money Control*, available at <https://www.moneycontrol.com/news/eye-on-india/videos/air-india-express-crash-this-safety-instrument-could-have-prevented-kozhikode-tragedy-5663341.html> Last visited, 22 August 2024.

[37] *National Aviation Company Of India Ltd* v. *S. Abdul Salam* (2011) WA.No. 1197 of 2011, Kerala High Court(Matter pending in appeal before the Hon'ble Supreme Court of India inC.A. No. 008128 - 008131/2018, registered on 7 August 2018, SLP(C) No. 009895 - 009898/2013, registered on 26 February 2013).

[38] 'Air India Express crash cost insurers highest-ever Rs 660 crore', *Business Today*, 29 October 2020, available at <https://www.businesstoday.in/industry/aviation/story/air-india-express-crash-costs-insurers-highest-ever-rs-660-crore-277028-2020-10-29> Last visited, 19 July 2024.

[39] 'Social Impact Assessment on Study of Land Acquisition for the Extension of RESA at Calicut International Airport', *Centre for Management Development*, Thiruvananthapuram, April 2023, available at <https://cmd.kerala.gov.in/wp-content/uploads/2023/04/Final-Construction-of-RESA-at-Calicut-International-Airport-Final-Report-English.pdf> Last visited, 19 July 2024.

[40] 'Calicut International Airport RESA renovation project', *Albatross Airport Database*, 21 June 2023, available at <https://airport-information.com/data/news/calicut-international-airport-resa-renovation-project-71868.html> Last visited, 19 July 2024.

6 Aerodrome Rescue and Fire Fighting Services: Challenges on a Tabletop Runway

Sandeepa Bhat while discussing the Search and Rescue Operations[41] highlights that the focus should be on technical capacity building in case of an overhaul of the legal regime governing search and rescue operations. The primary objective of a rescue and firefighting service is to safeguard lives in an aircraft accident or incident at, or in close proximity to, an aerodrome. The rescue and firefighting service aims to establish and preserve conditions conducive to survival, facilitate the egress of occupants, and rescue individuals requiring direct assistance in escaping. The rescue operations may necessitate utilising equipment and personnel beyond those primarily designated for rescue and firefighting activities.

The Airport Services Manual provides mandates regarding the Fire Station's location and an important categorisation. Firefighting services at Airports are categorised into primary and secondary requirements.[42] The primary requirement is to ensure that the capacity to deal with fire at the runway's end is comparatively important compared to dealing with structural fire incidents. The primary requirement is measured regarding response time from the fire station to the end of the runway. Further, the mandate is that a satellite fire station has to be created in case of the need to ensure that the response time can be achieved.

The Mangalore Aircraft Accident Report of 2010 observed that there are two types of RFF vehicles, and it was observed that both the vehicles cannot be used outside the periphery of the MIA due to the narrow and winding access roads.[43]

The most critical factors bearing on effective rescue in a survivable aircraft accident are:

a. the training received,
b. the effectiveness of the equipment, and
c. the speed with which personnel and equipment designated for rescue and firefighting purposes can be used.[44]

Crash Fire Tenders (CFT) have been imagined to have operation limits within the airport premises. However, this limited scope of operations has been expanded from the learnings of the Mangalore Airport incident of 2010. As per the Response by DGCA to the RTI application, the process to position one of the CFTs has been initiated to ensure timely response in case of need beyond the boundary walls.[45]

---

[41] Sandeepa Bhat B., 'Search and Rescue Operations', Anna Masutti & Pablo Mendes de Leon (eds.), *Elgar Concise Encyclopedia of Aviation Law*, (United Kingdom: Edward Elgar Publishing Limited, 2023) pp. 455–458.

[42] Airport Services Manual, Part 1, Rescue and Fire Fighting, International Civil Aviation Organization, (2014, 4th edn.), Doc 9137 – AN/898, p. 54, para 9.2.1.

[43] *Supra* note 12, at 124.

[44] *Supra* note, at 4, para 1.1.6.

[45] RTI Request No. DGOCA/R/E/24/00302, dated 14 June 2024, (Information obtained through RTI from DGCA).

In the Canadian context, discussing negligence in firefighting,[46] Spenser presents a brief list of judicial decisions highlighting the negligence of firefighting agencies and officers. He highlights through judicial decisions that negligence may arise from incorrect approach/plan,[47] faculty equipment,[48] indirect consequences of firefighting,[49] and contaminants from firefighting foam.[50] The analysis identifies the firefighting departments' responsibility in three pre-incident phases, during operations and post operations. Even though there are no comparable decisions that were identifiable in India except a few Insurance decisions of no direct relevance, it can be interpreted that the decisions of the Canadian Courts are able to provide guidance on corporate foresight and responsibility.

Further, Russel discusses firefighting responsibilities in the framework of Scottish UK Law[51] and the rescue doctrine[52] that provided a defence to the fire fighters however the same was not recognised by the Supreme Court of Indiana. Sandeepa Bhat while discussing the reimbursement of the cost of search and rescue operation suggests that this would ensure that there is no cost minimisation by the State or its agencies.[53] It is interesting to note that in both the Mangalore and Kozhikode accident the fault was identified as that of the pilot and thereby there was no legal obligation created on the Airport Operator.

[46] Spencer Putnam, 'Negligence in Firefighting in 2022', Cunningham Swan Lawyers, 6 September 2022, available at <https://cswan.com/negligence-in-firefighting-in-2022/> Last visited, 18 July 2024.

[47] *Schouten* v. *Rideau (Township)* (2009) ONCA 541 (CanLII); see also Spencer Putnam, 'Negligence in Firefighting in 2022', *Cunningham Swan Lawyers*, 6 September 2022, available at <https://cswan.com/negligence-in-firefighting-in-2022/> Last visited, 18 July 2024.

[48] *Léveillé c. Courses Stock-Car Drummond inc.* (2010) QCCA 1357 (CanLII); see also *id.*

[49] *Levesque* v. *Grand Falls (Town)* (2014) NBQB 266 (CanLII); see also *id.*

[50] *Egan* et al. v. *National Research Council of Canada* et al. (2021) ONSC 4561 (CanLII); see also *id.*

[51] Russell, E 2016, 'Revisiting the liability of fire services', *Scots Law Times*, Vol. 20, pp. 99–111.

[52] *Dolsen* v. *Veoride Inc.* (2024) Supreme Court Case No. 24S-CT-225, Supreme Court of Indiana; see also Curt Varone, 'Indiana Supreme Court Upholds Firefighter's Right to Sue Despite Firefighter's Rule', *Firelaw Blog*, 2 July 2024, available at <https://www.firelawblog.com/2024/07/02/indiana-supreme-court-upholds-firefighters-right-to-sue-despite-firefighters-rule/> Last visited, 20 July 2024.

[53] *Supra* note 41, at 469.

7 Responsibility

Ruwantissa, while analysing the responsibility of the pilots as determined by the courts has identified the three presumptions that will govern the pilot's responsibility.[54] Extending or rewriting the same three presumptions of the responsibility of the State through the Operator/Regulator would entail the following three presumptions:

i. Special skill and expertise of the regulator that presumed to be possessed
ii. Enhanced duty of care in view of special skill and expertise
iii. Magnitude of the damage to be caused in the eventuality of the breach of duty of care

There are a few cases in the Indian jurisdiction that will provide a basis to identify the duty of care. In the case of *Rabindra Nath Ghosal* v. *University of Calcutta and Others*,[55] The Supreme Court of India elucidated that when exercising the extraordinary power in writ cases, damages would not be awarded against public authorities merely due to the issuance of an order that exceeded their authority or due to inaction in the discharge of their duties unless there is substantiated evidence of malice or conscious abuse. In *Sanjeet Singh Kaila* v. *Union of India*,[56] the Delhi High Court, distinguishing the decision in *Rabindra Nath's* Case, determined that Hindustan Aeronautics Ltd. was considered negligent because of inadequate workmanship during the aircraft maintenance, which ultimately resulted in the aircraft crash and subsequent injury to the pilot. This determination was made by applying the principle of preponderance of probability.

*Geeta Jethani and Ors.*v. *Airport Authority of India and Ors*,[57] an accident took place due to faulty maintenance of escalators at the New Delhi Airport, and this caused the death of a 7-year-old. It was concluded that AAI lacked adequate service regarding maintenance, supervision, and sensitivity in handling the situation by its staff. During a routine inspection, the officials on duty found no defects in various electrical installations, including the escalator, which indicated that the checks were conducted casually. The National Consumer Disputes Redressal Commission (NCDRC) held that the Airport Operator was liable due to negligence on the part of the Airport Operator for the non-maintenance of the escalator.

Saroj Diksha & Ors. v. *International Airport Authority of India*,[58] the NCDRC recognised that there was an administrative lapse on the part of the Airport when adequate medical facilities and additional doctors were not available beyond the service of a single doctor with first aid. The commission recognised that the airport cannot be a specialised medical service provider like an intensive care unit. However,

[54] Ruwantissa Abeyratne, *Law and Regulation of Aerodromes*, (Canada: Springer, 2014) p. 86.

[55] AIR 2002 SC 3560.

[56] (2017) SCC Del. 8170.

[57] III (2004) CPJ 106 (NC).

[58] National Consumer Disputes Redressal Commission, New Delhi, First Appeal No. 167 of 2006, 1 February 2013.

the duty of Airports to have medical services beyond First Aid has increased in modern times with the footfall of passengers.

Mr. Kallol Basu v. *British Airway & Others*,[59] the NCDRC found the Airline negligent and liable for not providing medical support when the passenger was injured while disembarking the flight due to the unstable and dilapidated staircase. The NCDRC recognised the statutory responsibility of the Airline under the Carriage by Air Act, 1972 read along with the Consumer Protection Act, 1986 for the negligence exhibited by placing a defective staircase.

In *Paras Ram* v. *Ministry of Tourism & Civil Aviation*,[60] the NCDRC determined that the passenger is not entitled to additional compensation. The incident occurred during an emergency landing, where passengers were instructed to use the emergency exit, and the passenger sustained an injury while exiting. NCDRC recognised that the airline met its obligation to ensure the safety of its passengers, which takes precedence over providing protection against injuries sustained during evacuation.

In the context of the preponderance of probability principle, both the Airport Operator and the DGCA must ensure that tabletop runways are devoid of any negligent approaches when mandating and implementing best practices adopted elsewhere. The accident reports for Kozhikode and Mangalore underscore the necessity of addressing the RESA with the most effective solution. Although the findings of both accident reports attribute fault to the pilots, it is essential to acknowledge the contributory factors. The significant incident at the Mangalore Airport in 2019 accentuates the pressure on pilots. Instead of traversing the RESA, the pilot opted to steer the aircraft off the runway to the side embankment to avert an incident at the end of the tabletop runway.

Global Action Plan for the Prevention of Runway Excursions (GAPPRE) which is a joint coordinated effort of Eurocontrol and Flight Safety Foundation that prescribes recommendations.[61] Runway surroundings should be considered when designing or modifying strips or RESA. The local constraints against ICAO provisions and regional (for example, EASA) regulations must be considered to ensure relevant mitigation. The plan provides for two local ground considerations and an aircraft arresting system.

---

[59] State Consumer Disputes Redressal Commission, West Bengal, S.C. CASE NO.: SC/37/O/2006 decided on 27 May 2010.

[60] Complaint Case No. C-155/1998, State Consumer Disputes Redressal Commission, New Delhi, decided on 8 May 2007.

[61] 'Preventing runway excursions', *EuroControl*, available at <https://www.eurocontrol.int/news/preventing-runway-excursions-gappre> Last visited, 20 July 2024.

8 Runway Safety Programme—Global Runway Safety Action Plan

The International Civil Aviation Organization (ICAO) initiated the Global Runway Safety Action Plan (GRSAP) in 2017, collaborating with various partners to recommend actions for all stakeholders involved in runway safety. The goal of this initiative is to reduce the global rates of runway excursions and incursions.

The second edition of the Global Runway Safety Action Plan[62] recognises that Runway excursions can happen due to various weather and airport-related factors. Weather issues include thunderstorms, low visibility, crosswinds, tailwinds, wind shear, turbulence, heavy rain, lack of local knowledge, and insufficient training. Problems at the airport can also lead to mishaps. These include poor braking on slippery runways, mismanagement of ILS areas, navigation aids, visual aids, and control of ongoing work.

Specific details from the Accident Investigation Reports of the Mangalore and Kozhikode accidents highlight several contributing factors recognised in the GRSAP. These include challenging weather conditions such as crosswinds, tailwinds, and thunderstorms, as well as the presence of critical runways. These factors significantly contributed to the tragic outcomes of these accidents. This highlights that in addition to Standards and Recommended Practices (SARPs), those specified under the GRSAP play a pivotal role in ensuring runway safety.

9 DGCA: The Risk Manager

George Leloudas while discussing the concept of Courts as risk managers in a United States of America perspective highlights a pertinent point that it is impossible to eliminate risk mainly due to excessive cost however it is about the management of risks in a responsible manner that would strike a balance between safety and accidents.[63] Further, he contrasts in the United Kingdom perspective that the law imposes the following criteria in the scope and limits of duty of care: (a) foreseeability of damage; (b) sufficient proximate relationship between the parties; and (c) it must be fair, just and reasonable to impose such a duty.[64]

Expounding on the same and stretching the role of the Court of being risk managers to DGCA in the capacity that under the existing framework of laws in India, they are exercising the quasi -legislative functions along with quasi-judicial functions[65] are actively involved in risk allocation and risk determination. According to Ruwantissa, the Licensing Authority must carry out regular site inspections to ascertain

[62] Runway Safety Programme—Global Runway Safety Action Plan, International Civil Aviation Organisation, (February 2024, 2nd edn.) p. 6.

[63] George Leloudas, *Risk and Liability in Air Law*, (London: Informa Law, 2009) p. 37.

[64] *Id.*, at 39.

[65] The Aircraft Act 1934 along with rules and regulations made there under.

compliance with the standards. Thereby, DGCA, having the obligation, has carried out inspections on occasions.[66]

The DGCA has been engaged in a series of inspections to ensure safety and compliance; however, a troubling lack of enforcement measures has emerged as a significant issue. During the 2017 Surveillance Inspection,[67] several problems were identified, many of which remain unresolved and traced back to previous inspections conducted in 2007, 2012, 2014, 2015, and 2016.

It is important to acknowledge that some issues may take time to rectify due to the industry's financial constraints. However, the persistence of these unresolved problems for over a decade is particularly alarming, especially considering the context of a tabletop airport. This situation highlights the urgent need for effective action to address longstanding safety concerns that could jeopardise airport operations and passenger safety.

10 Public–Private Partnership

The basic principle of harmonisation and standardisation of regulations governing the operation of aerodromes will continue to be an obligation of the State in addition to its oversight functions when the operations are delegated to an operator.[68] Therefore, the regulations applicable to an operator such as Adani, which won the tender in February 2019 for six airports, cannot be granted concessions in compliance of the applicable laws.

The Concession Agreement states that Adani Enterprises shall always adhere to good industry practices.[69] Discussing Good Industry Practice (GIP) and Best Environmental Practice (BEP) in deep sea bed mining, Leonardus J. Gerbera and Renée L. Grogan identify that GIP reflects the process by which outcomes are achieved, and BEP establishes the process by which inputs are described, processes are determined with reference to specific triggers to ensure environmental protection at all times, and outputs are monitored.[70] Here, it is clear that Adani will have to establish clearly that they will have to put in place processes to achieve the Concession Agreement's outcomes. These policies shall establish and ensure that the GIP is achieved. One of the policies in place is the procurement policy.[71]

---

[66] *Supra* note 12.

[67] *Supra* note 18.

[68] *Supra* note 54, at 62.

[69] *Supra* note 21, at 30. (Art. 5, Clause 5.1.4.).

[70] Leonardus J. Gerbera & Renée L. Grogan, 'Challenges of Operationalising Good Industry Practice and Best Environmental Practice in Deep Seabed Mining Regulation', *Marine Policy,* Vol. 114, 2020, pp. 1–6 at p. 3.

[71] 'Procurement Policy', *Mangaluru International Airport*, available at <https://www.adani.com/-/media/Project/Adani/downloads/Procurement-Policy--IXE.pdf> Last visited, 10 July 2024. It provides the policy that there shall be competitive bidding, direct procurement and single source procurement.

Relying on GIP defined under New Zealand's Crown Minerals Act 1991 provides that the policies shall be technically competent and at a level of diligence and prudence reasonably and ordinarily exercised by experienced operators engaged in a similar activity and under similar circumstances. This approach seems to be the best available one in relation to GIP. Adani, under this mandate, will have to ensure that the performance is similar to that of any other private airport or airport under the PPP model.

There is a concern that airport privatisation might lead to the cutbacks in expansion programmes and reluctance to invest in infrastructure expansion[72] However, the advantages of privatisation outweigh the disadvantages, as it results in operational efficiency and aggressive non-aeronautical revenues being generated.[73]

11 Reviews on the Public Forum: Facility and Standards

Google reviews may be controversial as a source due to bias and individualised experience. Kiljae Lee and Chunyan Yu conducted a sentiment analysis and topic modelling using Google reviews. They found that ACI's extensive annual survey program on airport service quality and Google reviews are comparable to reliable estimates.[74] However, we must note that we all have inherent biases, and the same applies to Google reviews. The approach here is to use keywords as the review would be descriptive, and the users would have made an effort to mention the details rather than use ratings as metrics.

For comparison, the key words of a few airports are highlighted before proceeding to an analysis of the Mangalore Airport.

Airports	Number of reviews on google	Prominent keywords
Kempegowda International Airport, Bengaluru, India[75]	1,50,234	Bamboo, neet (read as neat), housekeeping, digiyatra, solar power, Idli, rainwater harvesting, South Indian food, Greenfield airport, and stray dogs

(continued)

[72] Ruwantissa Abeyratne, *Airport Business Law*, (Bloomington: Author House, 2009) p. 20.

[73] *Id*., at 21.

[74] Kiljae Lee & Chunyan Yu, 'Assessment of airport service quality: A complementary approach to measure perceived service quality based on Google reviews', *Journal of Air Transport Management*, Vol. 71, August 2018, pp. 28–44.

[75] Kempegowda International Airport, *Google Reviews*, available at <https://www.google.com/maps/place/Kempegowda+International+Airport/@13.1989142,77.7043177,17z/data=!4m8!3m7!1s0x3bae1cfe75446265:0x296c70e9a129418e!8m2!3d13.198909!4d77.7068926!9m1!1b1!16zL20vMGJmNm15?entry=ttu&g_ep=EgoyMDI0MDgyOC4wIKXMDSoASAFQAw%3D%3D> Last visited, 13 September 2024.

(continued)

Airports	Number of reviews on google	Prominent keywords
Biju Patnaik International Airport, Bhubaneswar, India[76]	19,179	Cooperative, mosquitoes, pigeons, smart city, chief minister, auto rickshaw, housekeeping, 5 March, 17 April and 1962
Singapore Changi Airport, Singapore[77]	50,663	Garden, waterfall, cinema, swimming pool, massage chairs, orchid, cactus, rainforest, koi, and city-state
Allama Iqbal International Airport, Lahore, Pakistan[78]	34,552	Cooperative, international standards, discipline, sops, bribe, mashallah, freight terminal, tuck shop, ring road, and poet

The references to these keywords may suggest a specific emphasis on either a negative or positive aspect or that the references could be related to historical contexts. It is also to be noted that there could be spelling mistakes.

There are 8,664 Google reviews for MIA,[79] and the following are the keywords that frequently appear on the website:

[76] Biju Patnaik International Airport, *Google Reviews*, available at <https://www.google.com/maps/place/Biju+Patnaik+International+Airport/@20.2504657,85.8119424,17z/data=!4m17!1m8!3m7!1s0x3a19a70f034c758d:0xda434edd567b3553!2sBiju+Patnaik+International+Airport!8m2!3d20.2506821!4d85.8145388!10e1!16zL20vMDdkM3Zk!3m7!1s0x3a19a70f034c758d:0xda434edd567b3553!8m2!3d20.2506821!4d85.8145388!9m1!1b1!16zL20vMDdkM3Zk?entry=ttu&g_ep=EgoyMDI0MDgyOC4wIKXMDSoASAFQAw%3D%3D> Last visited, 13 September 2024.

[77] Singapore Changi Airport, *Google Reviews*, available at <https://www.google.com/maps/place/Singapore+Changi+Airport/@1.3586094,103.9873687,17z/data=!3m1!5s0x31da17969b92192d:0x26b7e4dc37bb6d88!4m8!3m7!1s0x31da17d693d0cde3:0xd6d6dd5e414e4503!8m2!3d1.358604!4d103.9899436!9m1!1b1!16zL20vMDEydnN3?entry=ttu&g_ep=EgoyMDI0MDgyOC4wIKXMDSoASAFQAw%3D%3D> Last visited, 13 September 2024.

[78] Allama Iqbal International Airport, *Google Reviews*, available at <https://www.google.com/maps/place/Allama+Iqbal+International+Airport/@31.5203319,74.4077826,17z/data=!4m16!1m9!3m8!1s0x39190f7df22c3fe7:0x8dd7ffda40aa6b03!2sAllama+Iqbal+International+Airport!8m2!3d31.5203274!4d74.4103575!9m1!1b1!16zL20vMDIxNTFw!3m5!1s0x39190f7df22c3fe7:0x8dd7ffda40aa6b03!8m2!3d31.5203274!4d74.4103575!16zL20vMDIxNTFw?entry=ttu&g_ep=EgoyMDI0MDgyOC4wIKXMDSoASAFQAw%3D%3D> Last visited, 13 September 2024.

[79] Mangaluru International Airport, *Google Reviews*, available at <https://www.google.com/maps/place/Mangaluru+International+Airport/@12.9584251,74.8838258,15.88z/data=!4m8!3m7!1s0x3ba350d3616d95e9:0x46d57322d8165a30!8m2!3d12.9536624!4d74.8854022!9m1!1b1!16zL20vMGd4NGQx?entry=ttu&g_ep=EgoyMDI0MDgyOC4wIKXMDSoASAFQAw%3D%3D> Last visited, 13 September 2024.

Keywords	Number of reviews	Reference—Context
Prepaid	22	The availability of prepaid cab services for passengers. There is no alternative to prepaid cab services; however, Uber services are now available. There are also claims that the prepaid cab services are exorbitant in pricing
Cooperative	18	This is a highlight that staff and security personnel are identified and appreciated as being cooperative
Customs officer	15	The customs officers are found to be unreasonable, rude and harsh in their behaviour
Airport Authority	14	These comments highlight the need to call upon both AAI and Adani to streamline immigration, customs, and baggage screening. There are also complaints about parking fees and fare charges on taxis
Fare	14	Most of them are complaints regarding taxi fare being high
Hill	13	The majority are positive reviews that the airport is on top of a hill and that it is beautiful
Emigration	8	The immigration department's not being efficient is the main concern expressed by most of them
Privatised	7	Passengers are not able to distinguish between airport operators and services like customs and immigration. There is an appreciation of staff being there to help passengers as Adani took over the airport. However, there are also negative comments that infrastructure has not seen a real improvement
1951	6	Referring to the inaugural year of the airport
Looting	6	There are looting allegations against taxi services, parking services, and customs

The above effort highlights that Google reviews might provide the operator with the requisite information and passenger feedback on the airport's bottlenecks or pain points.

Cab services at the airport appear to be the major pain point, as they are expensive. The airport administration is not directly responsible for taxi operations. However, the bad impression formed from low-quality or poor-value taxi service impacts the airport's overall image.[80]

[80] Tony Kazda & Bob Caves, 'Landside Access', Antonin Kazda & Robert E. Caves (eds.), *Airport Design and Operation*, Third edition, (United Kingdom: Emerald Group Publishing, 2015) p. 354.

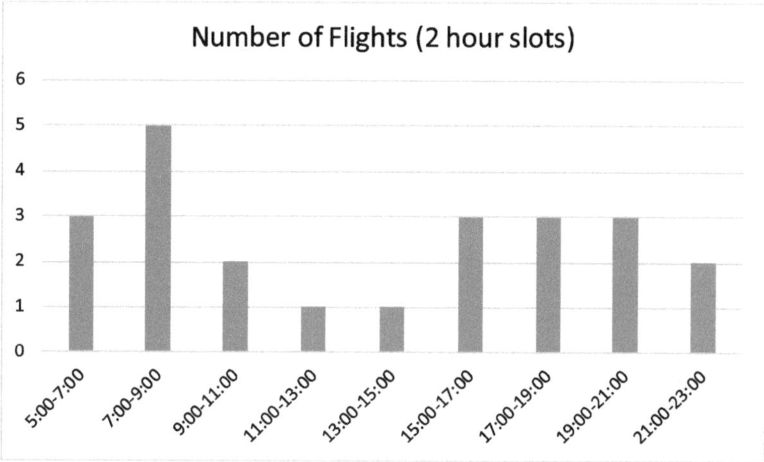

Source Mangalore International Airport, https://www.adani.com/en/mangaluru-airport—Flight Arrival Information collected on 4 August 2024

The passenger and user experience at the airport extends beyond the terminal building. The table above analyses the peak periods of movement. The data indicates that the highest demand occurs between 5:00 AM and 11:00 AM, as well as from 15:00 PM to 23:00 PM. As a result, passengers seeking taxi or cab services may have limited options outside of these peak times. Additionally, during peak hours, there is often less competition in pricing. Taxi and cab drivers may experience fluctuations in the number of passengers throughout the day, leading to potential shortages when two flights arrive closely together.[81] Improving the user experience on the city side could be achieved by ensuring adequate spacing between flight arrivals.

Airport users are expressing their concern regarding the bus service, which is available on the main road, which is situated around 1–1.5 km away from the Terminal, as per the information from Google reviews. Numerous individuals have voiced their concerns about the absence of a bus facility directly from the airport to the city, expressing a need for this service to be established. The concerns of the users regarding the availability of bus services, which is an essential mode of transport for staff, locals, and visitors,[82] need to be addressed to improve the user experience.

[81] *Id.*, at 354.

[82] *Id.*, at 355.

12 Conclusion

The Mangalore International Airport is confronted with unique operational challenges due to its strategic location and status as a tabletop airport. These challenges necessitate the implementation of advanced safety measures and efficient management techniques. The 2010 accident served as a stark reminder of the critical nature of stringent safety protocols, particularly for airports located in difficult terrains. While commendable progress has been achieved in terms of runway safety enhancements and adherence to global standards, the transition to private management under the Public–Private Partnership model presents both opportunities and challenges.

An evaluation of passenger feedback and operational changes after privatisation has revealed a varied outcome. While certain service aspects, particularly efficiency, have demonstrated improvement, others, such as taxi fares and customs procedures, continue to be sources of dispute. Moving ahead, the airport must strive to maintain a balance between safety compliance and enhancements in the passenger experience. The successful reduction of single-use plastics and the implementation of green initiatives at the Mangalore Airport are positive indicators of the new management's ability to institute global best practices.

In conclusion, the Mangalore International Airport's endeavours to align with international standards signify a dedication to safety and modernisation. However, there remains room for improvement in customer service and operational transparency. Ensuring continual adherence to safety regulations and enhancing passenger services will be pivotal to its future success as a pivotal hub in India's aviation network.

Chapter 17
Evaluating Compliance with International Standards and Best Practices at the Mumbai Airport

Adithya Variath

Abstract Chhatrapati Shivaji Maharaj International Airport (CSMIA), ranked 28th in the world and 14th in Asia in the fiscal year 2022 in terms of passenger traffic is one of the busiest airports located in the financial capital of India. It is the second busiest airport in India after Delhi. With the privatisation of Mumbai's CSMIA, the Indian airport industry saw a dramatic transformation in 2006. With the expansion of the new terminal, the economic value that the airport will hold in terms of trickling down economic benefits to the city and the financial growth opportunities will be immense. The International Civil Aviation Organisation (ICAO) has created a thorough set of Standards and Recommended Practices (SARPs) for airports in its Annex 14 to the Chicago Convention in order to guarantee the security, regularity, and effectiveness of international air navigation. The chapter attempts to provide an overview of 'International Standards' and 'Best Practices' at the CSMIA, specifically in the areas of 'Security Regulations', 'Passenger Service' and 'Sustainability'. The chapter evaluates Mumbai Airport's adherence to ICAO and IATA security protocols, including passenger screening, access controls, and threat detection. The second part of the chapter will focus on airport management along with global benchmarks for efficient processing, amenities, and overall traveller experience. The third part of the chapter delves into the initiatives to minimize environmental impact, optimize resource usage, and promote green operations. To achieve global net zero targets, the Mumbai airport will play a key role in accelerating renewable energy adoption, optimising resource consumption, and driving circular economy initiatives. The chapter is the outcome of an in-depth review of processes, and performance data against global benchmarks, feedback from airport management, airlines, regulatory authorities, and a first-hand assessment of operations, infrastructure, and passenger experience. The chapter also explores the issues associated with customs, human rights violations and the curious case of illegal wildlife trafficking that happens at the Mumbai Airport. The chapter provides a detailed understanding of Mumbai Airport's performance and compliance with global best practices. The chapter will also guide the airport's efforts to enhance security, passenger services, and sustainability and suggest mechanisms to

A. Variath (✉)
Jindal Global Law School, O.P. Jindal Global University, Sonipat, India
e-mail: adithya.variath@jgu.edu.in

© The Author(s), under exclusive license to Springer Nature Singapore Pte Ltd. 2025

S. Bhat B. (ed.), *Aerodrome Governance in Asia*,
https://doi.org/10.1007/978-981-96-7568-5_17

promote coordination with regulatory authorities for the successful implementation of the improvement initiatives.

Keywords Adani Group · Chhatrapati Shivaji Maharaj International Airport (CSMIA) · Chicago Convention · GVK Industries · Navi Mumbai Airport · Security regulations · Wildlife trafficking

1 Introduction

1.1 The Past

The British East India Company was encouraged to buy Bombay from the Portuguese in 1652 by the Surat Council of the British Empire.[1] The marriage treaty between Charles II of England and Catherine of Braganza, daughter of King John IV of Portugal, was signed on 11 May 1661, and as part of Catherine's dowry to Charles. It gave the British Empire control over Bombay and the North African city of Tangier. From facing the shivers during the Royal Indian Navy mutiny in 1946 to Dr Babasaheb Ambedkar drafting the Indian Constitution at Wayside Inn at Kalaghoda in 1948, Bombay (now Mumbai) has been politically an interesting city, full of stories that have played a crucial role in shaping modern India.[2] One can never ignore the role of Bombay's soft power and its role in globally popularising Indian arts, literature, movies and songs.[3] Today, the city is the financial backbone of India. Connectivity supports the city's position as the country's economic powerhouse and a global centre of power by acting as a vital entry point to India's financial centre. The Mumbai airport has also played a critical role in fostering the metropolitan growth of the city.

Using a Humber biplane, French pilot Monseigneur Piguet made the first commercial flight from Allahabad to Naini on 18 February 1911.[4] The flight covered around 10 miles and he carried 6500 mail packages. This is regarded as the start of Indian civil aviation as well as the first airmail service in history. In 1912, Indian State Air Services and Imperial Airways, UK, launched the first domestic flight route

[1] James Horsburgh, *Directions for Sailing to and from the East Indies, China, New Holland, Cape of Good Hope, and the Interjacent Ports: Compiled Chiefly from Original Journals at the East India House*, (Cambridge: Cambridge University Press, 2014) pp. 251–256 at p. 252.

[2] Adithya Variath, 'Locating Bombay in International Law: Answering Why, What & How', *Bombay Bulletin of International Law*, Vol. 1, 2023, p. 3.

[3] Douglas E. Haynes, 'Rethinking the Twentieth-Century History of Mumbai', *Modern Asian Studies*, Vol. 48, No. 5, 2014, pp. 1435–1449 at p. 1435; S. Patel, 'Bombay/Mumbai: Globalization, Inequalities, and Politics', in J. Gugler (ed.), *World Cities beyond the West: Globalization, Development and Inequality*, (Cambridge: Cambridge University Press, 2004) pp. 328–347 at p. 334.

[4] A.M. Hay, 'Transport Geography', *Progress in Geography*, Vol. 1, No. 2, 2016, pp. 313–318; A. P. Ellison, 'The Edwards Report and Civil Aviation in the 1970s', *The Aeronautical Journal*, Vol. 74, 2016, pp. 483–495 at p. 485.

between Karachi and Delhi.[5] Without receiving any support from the government, Tata Sons Ltd., the first airline in India, launched a regular airmail service between Karachi and Madras in 1915.[6] The Royal Air Force began offering frequent airmail service between Bombay and Karachi in 1919. In India, civil airport construction got underway in 1924 from Dum Dum in Calcutta, Bamrauli in Allahabad to Gilbert Hill in Bombay.[7]

Built-in 1930, the original airport in Bombay was known as RAF Santacruz.[8] Up until 1947, it was under British administration and used as a designated airstrip during World War II. The airport covered 610 acres and featured three runways at this time. Only a small portion of this construction, known as the Old Airport, remains today, standing south of runway 09/27. A few abandoned hangersof the Royal Air Force were turned into passenger terminals by the Director General of Civil Aviation for Civil Operations in 1946. Domestic traffic used one, whereas international traffic used the other. In its initial year of operation, it only dealt with six civilian aircraft every day.

Following the India-Pakistan partition, forty planes arrived at this airport. It prompted the Indian government to build new buildings with improved radio range, landing systems, and other features. Up until 1942, Mumbai's only airport was the Juhu Aerodrome. A transfer further inland became required due to operational limits imposed by its low-level location and its close proximity to the Arabian Sea coastline, which made it vulnerable during the monsoon season. In 1958, a new passenger terminal was also constructed. Following independence, the Ministry of Civil Aviation was in charge of the airport.

As the jumbo jet era began in the 1970s, Santacruz experienced a shortage of operating capacity despite multiple extensions. The Tata committee, which was established in 1967 to look into airport-related matters, had suggested building a new international terminal to accommodate traffic needs in the 1970s. Only domestic traffic was to be handled out of the Santa Cruz terminal. Constructing a new terminal building to handle international passenger traffic was planned by the International Airport Authority of India (IAAI), which was established in 1972 and was scheduled to be finished by 1981. Thus, at an anticipated cost of ₹ 110 million, work on the new international port in Sahar, northeast of Santacruz in Vile Parle, was started.

[5] '100 Years of Civil Aviation in India—Milestones', *Press Information Bureau*, available at <https://pib.gov.in/newsite/erelcontent.aspx?relid=69345> Last visited, 15 March 2024.

[6] Arunansh Goswami, 'The Maharajas of Indian Aviation—How three generations of Scindias pioneered air travel', *The Print*, available at <https://theprint.in/opinion/the-maharajas-of-indian-aviation-how-three-generations-of-scindias-pioneered-air-travel/1701073/> Last visited, 22 March 2024.

[7] See Iqbal Aashique Ahmed, 'Jodhpur and the Aeroplane: Aviation and Diplomacy in an Indian State 1924–1952', *The British Journal for the History of Science,* Vol. 57, No. 2, 2024, pp. 175–189 at p. 178; See also Jahnavi Phalkey, 'Flights of Freedom: German emigres, aeronautics and self-reliance in India', in Srinath Raghavan and Nandini Sundar (eds.), *A Functioning Anarchy: Essays for Ramachandra Guha*, (New Delhi: Allen Lane, 2021) pp. 251–270 at p. 251.

[8] *Supra* note 3, at 1437.

Although the Santacruz terminal was built to hold 600 people at a time, by the late 1970s, it was serving 1200 with 5 million domestic and international travellers arriving and exiting Santa Cruz airport in 1979–1980, compared to 3 million at the Delhi Airport. It was the most congested airport in the nation since the airlines were adding new services without increasing the available space at the terminal. Time magazine referred to the commotion at the terminal building as a 'black hole' in one of its issues as it was overcrowded and unsafe.[9] On 21 September 1979, a large fire destroyed the terminal building's International portion. In October of the same year, the Gulf Terminal, a temporary departure extension, went into operation while the terminal was being renovated.[10] The first phase of the new international terminal at Sahar took three years to complete, with construction starting in November 1977.

1.2 The Present

The airport underwent a complete renovation in 2003, and the management division was put out to bid. When the 2004 bidding opened, GVK Industries took the top spot and assumed management of the airport. Although the AAI board did not adopt a modernisation proposal until 2003, AAI has been exploring modernising Bombay Airport since 1996.[11] At that time, 38% of all aircraft movements in the nation were handled by Bombay and Delhi Airports, which also produced one-third of all AAI revenue. 13 million people used the Bombay airport during that period, with 60% of them being domestic travellers. Because it was handling twice as many aircraft movements per day as it was originally built for, the airport encountered extreme congestion for both passengers and aircraft.[12] After a decision by the Empowered Group of Ministers (EGoM) was made in January 2006, the bidding process for its renovation finally started in May 2004.[13] Delta Air Lines launched a direct route from Mumbai to New York in November 2006.[14] The government gave its approval

[9] Artur Araripe, 'MSK Productions releases Mumbai Airport for MSFS', *Threshold*, available at <https://www.thresholdx.net/news/mskmum> Last visited, 25 March 2024.

[10] 'Fire guts Bombay's Santa Cruz airport, family of three dies', *India Today*, available at <https://www.indiatoday.in/magazine/indiascope/story/19791015-fire-guts-bombay-santa-cruz-airport-family-of-three-dies-822405-2014-02-20> Last visited, at 10 March 2024.

[11] Rekha Jain, Raghuram G.,& Rachna Gangwar, 'Airport Privatization in India: Lessons from the Bidding Process in Delhi and Mumbai', *IIMA*, available at <http://vslir.iima.ac.in:8080/xmlui/bitstream/handle/11718/233/2007-05-01_RekhaJain.pdf?sequence=1&isAllowed=y> Last visited, 15 March 2024.

[12] See 'Steps Taken by Government of India to handle Air Space Congestion at Mumbai Airport', *Press Information Bureau*, available at <https://pib.gov.in/PressReleaseIframePage.aspx?PRID=2005825> Last visited, 25 March 2024.

[13] *Supra* note 11.

[14] 'Delta recommences Mumbai-New York flight', *Business Traveller*, available at <https://www.businesstraveller.com/business-travel/2019/12/26/delta-recommences-mumbai-new-york-flight/> Last visited, 20 March 2024.

in 2006 for the public–private partnership model to be used for the renovation and restructuring of the Brownfield airports in Delhi and Mumbai.[15]

GVK Industries Ltd. and the Airports Authority of India initiated a joint venture to take up this project. Since 2006, the airport's modernisation has been managed by a private enterprise. In 2014, the integrated terminal T2 was officially opened and commenced its operations. In 1999, Chhatrapati Shivaji, a renowned monarch and liberation warrior, was honoured with an airport named in his honour. The word 'Maharaja' was added to the title in 2018.The Mumbai Airport management contract was awarded to GVK Industries, Airports Company South Africa, and Bidvest. To carry out this assignment, the Airports Authority of India (26%) and the consortium (74%) established Mumbai International Airport Private Limited (MIAL) as a joint venture.[16] Since then, MIAL has renovated domestic terminals 1A and 1B, international terminals 2B and 2C, opened a brand-new domestic terminal 1C, and renovated Terminal T2. These modifications have improved the CSMIA's aesthetics, design, and passenger conveniences.

Along with these airside enhancement initiatives, MIAL also reconstructed both runways and commissioned new taxiways and aprons. MIAL and SITA, a leading provider of IT solutions for the aviation industry, signed a deal in February 2008 that made CSIA the first airport in India to install CUTE (Common Use Terminal Equipment) check-in systems and common-use self-service kiosks.

The Adani Group obtained GVK and Bidvest's shares in MIAL in February 2021 through its subsidiary Adani Enterprises, giving it a 74% controlling position. The airport is managed by Mumbai International Airport Limited (MIAL), a joint venture between the Airports Authority of India and Adani Enterprises, a division of the Adani Group. Mumbai International Airport Limited has been working diligently to make CSMIA an airport that offers its patrons the highest level of convenience and comfort possible.[17] In the fiscal year 2018–2019, 48.83 million travellers transit through CSMIA. However, the growth of the Mumbai Airport has also been subject to the supervision of ICAO norms and ICAO review. The airport has witnessed several complaints about the way the air traffic has been managed by the authorities. The cases of crashes, mismanagement, and flight cancellations have become a norm. According to recent data, "The Mumbai airport, with two intersecting runways, handles 950–1,000 flights a day and can handle 55 million passengers per annum."[18] Due to the inability to operate the two intersecting runways at the same time, only

---

[15] Mohan Phuyal, 'Understanding the Indian Way of Airport Privatization: Case of Indira Gandhi International Airport, Delhi', *Open Journal of Social Sciences*, Vol.11, No.6, 2023, pp. 237–254 at p. 245; P. Kriesler, 'Why Privatize Airports?', *The Economic and Labour Relations Review*, Vol. 7, No. 1, 1996, pp. 120–131 at p.120.

[16] 'CSMIA', *GVK*, available at <https://www.gvk.com/ourbusiness/airports/csiamumbai.aspx> Last visited, 10 March 2024.

[17] See *supra* note 3, at 1437.

[18] Anu Sharma, 'Better punctuality at Mumbai airport comes with higher fares too', *Mint*, available at <https://www.livemint.com/industry/better-punctuality-at-mumbai-airport-comes-with-higher-fares-too-11709114615206.html> Last visited, 15 April 2024.

one runway can handle a maximum of 46 aircraft movements per hour during high-intensity operations and 44 aircraft movements outside of that. It carried 44 million passengers in FY23, which was just a little less than the 46 million passengers it handled in FY20 before the pandemic.[19]

1.3 The Future

The COVID-19 pandemic disrupted the growth of Indian aviation. However, the sector has been on a recovery journey and is now growing quickly. In 2023, the country's passenger count increased by 26%, a growth that may continue in the following years.[20] Even more people were using Mumbai's airport, where a 37% increase in the first 11 months was recorded.[21] That explains the building of the new Navi Mumbai Airport, which is currently slated to open in March 2025, albeit with the disclaimer that it has a history of missing deadlines. The airport is expected to open in March 2025 and can handle 20 million people annually. If there is sufficient demand, that will increase to 90 million by 2032.[22] The entire makeover of the city depends on its success as well. Mumbai now has a population of 21 million and is expected to develop more in the coming years at the cost of gentrification. The city spend up to $30 billion in new infrastructure built in the coming years. It is expected that the $2.1 billion Navi Mumbai Airport by the Adani Group will further India's aviation goals and play a pivotal role in shaping the economy of the city.

1.4 Setting the Context

This chapter examines Mumbai Airport's governance structure in light of both national and international compliances, providing a thorough analysis of the airport's operations and performance. It examines the operational and regulatory guidelines that control the airport's operations and evaluates how well they comply with both Indian local aviation laws and international aviation regulations. The chapter addresses difficulties in complying with compliance standards and critically assesses

[19] *Id.*

[20] 'Global Outlook for Air Transport', *IATA*, available at <https://www.iata.org/economicsglobal-outlook-for-air-transport%E2%80%94december-2023%E2%80%94report/> Last visited, 25 March 2024.

[21] 'India Passenger Traffic Transitions to Growth', *Boeing*, available at <https://www.boeing.co.in/news/2023/india-passenger-traffic-transitions-to-growth> Last visited, 20 March 2024.

[22] 'Adani Group's $2.1 billion Navi Mumbai airport to boost India's aviation ambitions', *LiveMint*, available at <https://www.livemint.com/companies/adani-groups-2-1-billion-navi-mumbai-airport-to-boost-indias-aviation-ambitions-11710464789943.html> Last visited, 20 March 2024.

how well these governance structures work to guarantee the airport's operational sustainability, safety, and efficiency.

2 Governance Architecture and ICAO on Airport Governance

The economic value an international airport holds in terms of trickling down economic benefits to the diaspora and growth opportunities that it offers is immense. International civil aviation and the world economy both depend heavily on air travel and airport operations. As per data, air cargo transports over US $6 trillion worth of goods, accounting for approximately 35% of world trade by value."[23] It plays a critical role in boosting the global economy.[24] In this context, a comprehensive set of Standards and Recommended Practices (hereafter 'SARPs') has been developed by the International Civil Aviation Organisation (hereafter 'ICAO') to guarantee the efficiency, regularity, safety, and security of international civil aviation. The ultimate goal of these SARPs is to improve the safety and dependability of air travel globally by promoting uniformity in aviation practices, facilitating cooperation among member governments, and harmonising global aviation rules.

These standards cover ground equipment, procedures, and facilities, with the understanding that variations are only permitted to meet the various aircraft types that use the airports. First established on 29 May 1951, ICAO Annex 14 outlines the necessary specifications for aerodromes utilised in international civil aviation. Its institutional structure provides "information for planning, designing, and operating airports, and has been regularly amended and supplemented to keep up with advancements in aircraft technology and airport infrastructure."[25]

'Standards' and 'Recommendations' are the two degrees of duty and relevance in the jurisprudence of aviation compliance. To ensure the safety or regularity of international air navigation, standards are specifications for physical attributes, configuration, materials, performance, personnel, or procedures. Specifications for additional configuration, materials, performance, personnel, or processes are included in recommendations; acceptance of these recommendations is deemed preferable for reasons related to international air navigation economy, regularity, or safety. To promote their efficient use and to ensure the safety of intended aircraft operations, SARPs promote every effort to identify appropriate solutions. The appropriate maintenance of an

[23] 'Value of Air Cargo', *IATA*, available at <https://www.iata.org/en/programs/cargo/sustainability/benefits/> Last visited, 20 March 2024.

[24] N. Norman, 'Airport Development,' *The Journal of the Royal Aeronautical Society*, Vol. 37, No. 265, 1933, pp. 1–34 at p. 26.

[25] Convention on Civil Aviation, International Civil Aviation Organization (ICAO), (1994) 15 U.N.T.S. 295 (Chicago Convention), Annex 14.

aerodrome and its operating conditions is essential to the regularity and safety of air operations.[26]

While there is no specific Annex dedicated solely to airport governance, elements related to airport management and operations can be found throughout various Annexes. ICAO SARPs on Aerodrome Maintenance are contained in Chap. 10 of Annex 14, Volume I—Aerodrome Design and Operations. Additional recommendations are available in the Airport Services Manual, Part 9—Airport Maintenance Practices.[27] Annex 14 on Aerodromes primarily deals with standards and recommended practices for aerodrome design, operations, and safety. While it does not directly address governance, it does guide various aspects of airport infrastructure and operations that are relevant to governance. It addresses the provision of aerodrome services and facilities, which can include aspects of governance related to the management and operation of these services.

Aerodrome Maintenance covers requirements for aerodrome maintenance, which may involve governance considerations related to maintenance contracts, funding, and oversight. Annex 17 on Security focuses on standards and recommended practices for aviation security. While not directly related to governance, it addresses security measures at airports, which can have implications for airport management and operations. It also outlines the responsibilities of states in ensuring the implementation of security measures at airports within their jurisdiction, which may involve governance-related aspects such as regulatory oversight and coordination among relevant authorities. ICAO recommendations on Quality Control and Quality Assurance address the need for quality control and quality assurance measures in implementing security measures at airports. It may involve governance considerations related to oversight and accountability.[28] Annex 11 on Air Traffic Services focuses on air traffic services rather than airport governance and includes provisions related to airport operations and coordination with air traffic control, which can have governance implications.

The Operation, Management and Development Agreement between Airports Authority of India and Mumbai International Airport Private Limited for Mumbai Airport dated 04 April 2006 stated that the development standards and layout of aerodrome and provisions of essential facilitation shall be in accordance with "ICAO Annex 14—Aerodromes: Volume 1 Aerodrome Design and Operations—Fourth Edition, 2004"; "International Civil Aviation Organisation– International Standards and Recommended Practices, Aerodromes, Annex 14 to the Convention on International Civil Aviation", "Volume 1 Aerodrome Design and Operations –Fourth

[26] P. Dürner, B. Domres & R. Heinrich, 'Airports in Europe,' *Journal of the World Association for Emergency and Disaster Medicine*, Vol. 1, No. 2, 1985, pp. 130–132 at p.130.

[27] *Airport Services Manual—Part IX—Airport Maintenance Practices*, (Doc 9137P9), (ICAO, 1984).

[28] *Procedures for Air Navigation Services (PANS)—Aircraft Operations—Volume I Flight Procedures*, (Doc 8168), (ICAO, 2018).

Edition, 2004 and ICAO Aerodrome Design Manual (Doc 9157)"[29] However, there have been multiple instances wherein reports have pointed out inconsistencies.[30]

3 Security Regulations, Passenger Service, Sustainability and Other Aspects

3.1 Security Regulations

Aviation security culture in India grapples with a spectrum of challenges reflective of the dynamic global landscape. The unique geopolitical and socio-economic context of the country contributes to these complex issues. As India continues to play a pivotal role in global aviation, addressing these challenges requires a holistic and adaptive approach. Rapid advancements in technology bring both opportunities and challenges to aviation security. Integrating advanced technologies like artificial intelligence and biometrics becomes essential to stay ahead of the curve. With the increasing reliance on digital technologies in aviation operations, India confronts cybersecurity challenges. Ensuring the integrity of air traffic control systems, airline databases, and communication networks is imperative to prevent potential disruptions or unauthorized access. ICAO security regulations provide standards and recommended practices for ensuring aviation security worldwide. The Regional Safety Plan of the Regional Aviation Safety Group—Asia Pacific included Safety Enhancement Initiatives, and the DGCA released a five-year National Aviation Safety Plan (2018–2022) that aligns with the ICAO's Global Aviation Safety Plan.[31] The Federal Aviation Administration informed the Directorate General of Civil Aviation in 2023 that India satisfies the Chicago Convention's international standards for aviation safety oversight. The FAA International Aviation Safety Assessment Category 1 status was reconfirmed after the audit in November 2022, which greatly improved Indian global ranking.[32]

Mumbai Airport being a major international airport in India, adheres to ICAO security regulations to maintain safety and security standards. Security regulations

---

[29] 'Operation, Management and Development Agreement between Airports Authority of India and Mumbai International Airport Private Limited for Mumbai Airport', *Civil Aviation*, available at <https://www.civilaviation.gov.in/sites/default/files/2023-07/moca_000979.pdf> Last visited, 15 March 2024.

[30] 'Final Investigation Report on incident to M/s BH AIR Airbus', available at <http://164.100.60.133/accident/reports/incident/LZ-AOA.pdf> Last visited, 25 March 2024.

[31] 'National Aviation Safety Plan 2018–2022', *Directorate General of Civil Aviation*, available at <https://www.icao.int/safety/GASP/GASP%20Library/National%20aviation%20safety%20plans/India%20NASP%202018-2022.pdf> Last visited, 15 April 2024.

[32] 'India meets the international standards for aviation safety: US body FAA to DGCA', *Hindustan Times*, available at <https://www.hindustantimes.com/india-news/india-retains-faa-iasa-category-1-status-for-aviation-safety-oversight-allows-expansion-of-services-to-the-us-101681303744646.html> Last visited, 1 April 2024.

followed at Mumbai Airport include implementing strict access control measures to prevent unauthorized access to sensitive areas such as aircraft, baggage handling facilities, and other critical infrastructure.[33] The airport has heavily invested in conducting thorough screening of passengers and their baggage using advanced security screening equipment to detect prohibited items, weapons, explosives, and other threats. As per the empirical research conducted by the Centre for Research in Air and Space Laws, Maharashtra National Law University Mumbai as part of their joint research study with the Centre for Aviation and Space Laws of the National University of Juridical Sciences, Kolkata, it was noted that in the year 2022–2023, the airport also conducted comprehensive training for airport staff, security personnel, and airline employees on security procedures, threat recognition, and emergency response protocols.

Security checks for all individuals entering the airport premises, including passengers, employees, and visitors, to ensure that no unauthorized items or individuals are allowed access to restricted areas have been followed in both terminals. Mumbai airport has also put in resources for setting up advanced security technology such as CCTV cameras, biometric identification systems, and explosive detection systems to enhance security surveillance and threat detection capabilities. However, the Airport lacks stringent security measures for screening and inspecting cargo shipments to prevent the transportation of unauthorized or dangerous items through air cargo services.

3.2 Passenger Service[34]

Ground handling is a vital function at an airport. Ground handling is becoming increasingly recognised as a vital component of airport operations rather than merely a source of revenue since it helps increase efficiency at the airport. Because of this, it is wise to consider ground handling from a strategic rather than a financial standpoint. The goal of the National Civil Aviation Policy 2016 is to improve the aviation industry's sustainability, safety, and security by utilising technology and efficient

[33] 'India—eCTB on Aviations Security Culture obervance in India', *ICAO*, available at <https://www.icao.int/Security/Security-Culture/Presentations1/India%20-%20eCTB%20on%20Aviations%20Security%20Culture%20obervance%20in%20India.pdf> Last visited, 1 April 2024.

[34] As per the empirical research conducted by the Centre for Research in Air and Space Laws, Maharashtra National Law University Mumbai as part of their joint research study with the Centre for Aviation and Space Laws of the National University of Juridical Sciences, Kolkata, 2022–24. The editor of this volume and author of this chapter were part of this project.

monitoring.[35] To that end, the Government of India has created a framework for the ground handling service.[36]

When the project is finished, the new Navi Mumbai airport will be able to handle 60 million passengers annually.[37] The structure will have an H-shape, five stories, and 523,000 square meters of total space, including two concourses. With more than 350 check-in counters, 29 distant aircraft positions, and 78 contact airport positions, it will handle both domestic and international passenger traffic.[38] In the middle of the terminal building will be a three-story office complex. On the north and south faces of the terminal, there will be three curbs: two elevated and one at grade. Commercial vehicles will utilise the first-level curb, and arrivals and departures will use the second and third-level curbs, respectively.[39] A precise approach path indication and a CAT-I instrument landing system, with the option to upgrade to CAT-II, are among the visual landing aids that the airport plans to add.

3.3 Green Initiatives, Sustainability and Decarbonisation

The aviation industry in India has grown rapidly in the last several years, which has increased airport carbon emissions. The Ministry of Civil Aviation (MoCA) has implemented several measures aimed at encouraging environmentally friendly growth within the aviation industry and mitigating carbon emissions at airports. To lessen its influence on the environment and encourage sustainable development, Mumbai Airport has adopted several long-term sustainable practices. The airport wants to cut emissions and waste while minimising its carbon impact and conserving energy and water resources.

Initiatives are taken by MoCA to sensitise stakeholders to promote sustainable development in the aviation sector and reduce carbon emissions at airports. To raise awareness of climate change mitigation and standardise the Carbon Accounting and Reporting framework of Indian airports, MoCA arranged knowledge-sharing

---

[35] 'The National Civil Aviation Policy, 2016', available at <https://www.aai.aero/sites/default/files/basic_page_files/Final_NCAP_2016_15-06-2016-3%20%281%29.pdf> Last visited, 2 April 2024: "Provide safe, secure, affordable and sustainable air travel for passengers and air transportation of cargo with access to various parts of India and the world. Ensure safety, security and sustainability of aviation sector through the use of technology and effective monitoring.".

[36] Implementation of ground handling services at Indian airports, ICAO, available at <https://www.icao.int/Meetings/a40/Documents/WP/wp_381_en.pdf> Last visited, 4 April 2024.

[37] 'Navi Mumbai airport to be operational in March 2025', *The Hindu*, available at <https://www.thehindu.com/news/national/maharashtra/navi-mumbai-airport-to-be-operational-in-march-2025/article68399903.ece> Last visited, 13 July 2024.

[38] 'Navi Mumbai International Airport', available at <https://www.nmiairport.co.in/> Last visited, 4 April 2024.

[39] *Id.*

events.[40] MoCA recommended that all operators of Brownfield Airports and new Greenfield Airports strive for Carbon Neutrality and Net Zero, which includes, among other things, using 100% Green Energy and obtaining Airports Council International (ACI)/ISO 14064 Accreditation through empanelled verifiers. Adoption of carbon mitigation strategies and milestone-based carbon management plans were also recommended.[41]

Globally, the aviation industry is shifting towards decarbonisation and sustainability.[42]As discussed in the earlier part of this chapter, the Airport Authority of India was taken over by a business partnership known as MIAL in May 2006 and in April 2007, the Ministry of Environment and Forest (MoEF) authorised MIAL's expansion and modernisation of Mumbai Airport. The primary project components include constructing, expanding, and modernising passenger terminals, runways, aprons, and parking bays; additionally, establishing taxiways, parking garages, and other utility services, including state-of-the-art sewage treatment facilities. MIAL has also implemented the Environmental Management Standard ISO 14001:2015.[43]

A compliance management system at Mumbai Airport is used for legal registers, consent conditions, compliance registers, and compliance with all standards outlined in the multiple environmental clearances.[44] For every permission, records are regularly maintained under an environmental management system. These documents and records are reviewed every six months to make sure the terms are being adhered to.[45] CSMIA monitors and reports on a range of environmental indicators in addition to the continuous monitoring system. Furthermore, to conduct routine environmental sampling for storm water, wastewater quality, ambient noise levels, ambient air quality, emissions from DG sets, etc., MIAL has hired a laboratory that has been approved by the MoEF.[46] In compliance with the monitoring schedule, monthly environmental monitoring is carried out to confirm that the results adhere to the standards outlined in the permits and consents.

According to the Adani Group, environment management is an essential component of their airport governance framework. To satisfy environmental standards, they comply with all applicable laws and incorporate their approach with business

---

[40] 'Initiatives taken by MoCA to promote sustainable development in the aviation sector and reduce carbon emissions at airports', *PIB*, available at <https://pib.gov.in/PressReleasePage.aspx?PRID=1909435> Last visited, 22 March 2024.

[41] *Id.*

[42] Jae Woon Lee, Benoît Mayer & Joseph Wheeler, 'Aviation and Sustainable Development: Some Perspectives from the Asia–Pacific,' in Armand L.C. de Mestral, P. Paul Fitzgerald & Md. Tanveer Ahmad (eds.), *Sustainable Development, International Aviation, and Treaty Implementation*, (Cambridge: Cambridge University Press, 2018) pp. 133–153 at p. 140.

[43] 'Environment Management', *Chhatrapati Shivaji Maharaj International Airport*, available at <https://csmia.adaniairports.com/environment-management.aspx#:~:text=MIAL%20has%20also%20implemented%20Environmental,compliance%20management%20system%20at%20CSMIA.> Last visited, 20 April 2024.

[44] *Id.*

[45] *Id.*

[46] *Id.*

requirements. The airports are outfitted with authorised Environment Management Systems for efficient environmental performance monitoring. As part of its commitment to offering first-rate passenger facilities and limiting environmental impact, the strategy aims to optimise energy usage, support renewable energy sources, and preserve energy to minimise costs and carbon footprint.[47]The airports in Mumbai and Thiruvananthapuram have implemented ISO 50001:2018 Energy Management systems, with an emphasis on optimising resource utilisation. In the quest for net-zero emissions, Mumbai International Airport has set a noteworthy example by utilising only renewable energy sources, making it one of India's 100% sustainable airports.

Long-term investments in the aviation sector heavily depend on high-quality, sustainable infrastructure. The redesigned Mumbai Airport has shown to be exceptional and unique due to its superior architecture and infrastructure. Mumbai Airport has been steadily improving to become an airport that enthrals visitors with the greatest comfort and convenience available. The Mumbai Airport approaches sustainable infrastructure from a broad perspective, taking into account factors beyond just the technological and physical. These include attributes including usefulness, viability, transparency, efficiency, stability, integrity, governance, openness, resilience, and relationship to the Sustainable Development Goals (SDGs). They also include financial sustainability with contingent liabilities. As part of the ongoing effort to meet our energy consumption demands through non-conventional sources, Mumbai Airport is installing more solar rooftops to enhance our share of solar energy. It has around 4.6 MW of installed roof-top solar capacity.[48] Despite having limited area, Mumbai Airport has installed solar rooftops and uses them to generate roughly 5% of its total energy demand. It has a Carbon Management Plan and Carbon Roadmap to support the airport's endeavours to mitigate risks associated with climate change and to take advantage of opportunities to lessen its carbon footprint.[49] The airport is the first in India to introduce hybrid technology, which will allow aviation to become extremely efficient and low carbon in the future by running entirely on green energy starting in April 2022. Mumbai Airport is moving closer to 'Net Zero' emissions as a result of this sustainable project and other measures it is making to lessen its carbon impact.

---

[47] 'About Us', *Chhatrapati Shivaji Maharaj International Airport*, available at <https://csmia.adaniairports.com/about-us.aspx> Last visited, 10 April 2024.

[48] Environment Management', *Chhatrapati Shivaji Maharaj International Airport*, available at <https://csmia.adaniairports.com/environment-management.aspx#:~:text=MIAL%20has%20also%20implemented%20Environmental,compliance%20management%20system%20at%20CSMIA.> Last visited, 20 April 2024.

[49] *Id.*

4 Operational and Infrastructural Efficiency: From Congestion, Social Justice to Wildlife Management Concerns

4.1 Crisis of Congestion

After the travel restrictions were lifted following the pandemic, airports have seen a significant rise in air traffic and air space congestion. Mumbai Airport experiences excess capacity and congestion on its runways, which unintentionally causes air space congestion and forces planes to loiter over the city for up to 60 min at a time. Given that an aircraft uses 2000 kg of fuel per hour on average, prolonged circling times result in significant fuel waste for the aircraft. For example, during a 40-min flight, 1.7 kl of jet fuel (costing approximately Rs 1.8 Lakh) are wasted, while during a 60-min flight, 2.5 kl of jet fuel (costing approximately Rs 2.6 Lakhs) are wasted.[50] It has been reported that consumers will ultimately be responsible for paying for this increase in fuel costs. Additionally, this has a domino effect on how efficiently airports operate, resulting in longer wait times and excessive delays that negatively impact travellers as well as airlines.

The Airport Authority of India conducted an analysis to address this air space congestion and discovered that the amount of air traffic allowed per hour during the six hours of High-Intensity Runway Operations (HIRO, or from 0800 to 1100 and 1700 to 2000 h) was nearly equal to the amount of air traffic allowed per hour during the other eighteen hours of the day. Additionally, the operation of non-scheduled flights during peak hours exacerbates air traffic congestion due to the presence of transverse runways.

Even though Mumbai Airport is operating at full capacity, it was reported that the airport operator's excessive slot distribution with short time margins, airline non-adherence to the slots, and non-scheduled operations during peak hours were the main causes of the ongoing congestion.[51] To address this issue, the airport operator, which serves as both the airline's slot manager and provider of slots, had to have acted proactively to organise and control air traffic movements. However, since they had not started any such initiative, the Ministry of Civil Aviation had to take over. It is anticipated that Mumbai Airport will move right now to make sure that all airlines are adhering to the guidelines. To guarantee that travellers have a positive experience when using Mumbai Airport, the Indian government understands that it must intervene and strike a compromise between the interests of the airlines and the airport operators.

---

[50] 'Steps Taken by Government of India to handle Air Space Congestion at Mumbai Airport', *PIB*, available at <https://pib.gov.in/PressReleaseIframePage.aspx?PRID=2005825> Last visited, 14 February 2024.

[51] 'Steps Taken by Government of India to handle Air Space Congestion at Mumbai Airport', *PIB*, <https://pib.gov.in/PressReleaseIframePage.aspx?PRID=2005825> Last visited, 15 April 2024.

4.2 Wildlife Trafficking

The illicit trade of wild plants and animals, either as live or dead specimens or their parts, is known as "wildlife trafficking" and it has a devastating impact on economies, governance, biodiversity, and public health around the world.[52] It is a type of international organised crime that operates across borders and includes illicit wildlife gathering and smuggling, as well as poaching and capture of protected species. The World Wide Fund for Nature (WWF) estimates that wildlife trafficking, with an annual value of approximately £15 billion, is the fourth greatest type of international organised crime, behind drug smuggling, people trafficking, and counterfeiting.[53]

Despite being a signatory to the Convention on International Trade in Endangered Species of Wild Fauna and Flora (CITES), India is currently among the top 10 countries for wildlife trafficking by air and in the top 20 countries overall wildlife trafficking.[54] India's biodiversity makes it home to 8% of the world's species. However, India serves as both a source and a transit country for illicit wildlife and wildlife goods. Additionally, it is very challenging to track down illegal commodities after they have entered domestic markets. In addition, several additional issues have made the battle against the illicit wildlife trade more challenging.

In addition, the Ministry of Environment, Forests, and Climate Change Voluntary Disclosure Scheme has been abused by Indian smugglers of exotic wildlife in 2020. The program allowed Indians to declare the possession of exotic wild species without any documentation before 15 March 2021 to control the country's exploding exotic animal market, which began to flourish following the total prohibition on the trade in Indian species. The two main entry and exit points for international wildlife trafficking into and out of India are airports and the lengthy international border that runs across the Northeast. The 2018 Traffic Report *In Plane Sight* notes that cities in Northeast India, like Dimapur, Guwahati, and Imphal, are utilised as transit points for the trafficking of rhino horns, tiger parts, and pangolin scales, which is particularly prevalent along the Indo-Nepal and Indo-Myanmar-China borders. There is also a lot of avian and reptilian trafficking along the India-Bangladesh border. Most

---

[52] Amy Hinsley, et al., 'Trading species to extinction: evidence of extinction linked to the wildlife trade,' *Cambridge Prisms: Extinction*, Vol. 1, 2023, pp. 1–8 at p. 2; Radha Ivory, 'Corruption Gone Wild: Transnational Criminal Law and the International Trade in Endangered Species,' *AJIL Unbound*, Vol. 111, 2017, pp. 413–418 at p. 414; Justin Kurland, 'Wildlife Trafficking The Problem, Patterns, and a Promising Path Toward Prevention,' in Mangai Natarajan (ed), *International and Transnational Crime and Justice* (Cambridge: Cambridge University Press, 2019), pp. 55–60 at p. 59.

[53] 'Combatting Illegal Wildlife Trade in India', *WWF India*, available at <https://join.wwfindia.org/stop-illegal-wildlife-trade.php> Last visited, 14 April 2024.

[54] Anusha Krishnan, 'Why is India a major hub for wildlife trafficking?', *Mongabay*, available at <https://india.mongabay.com/2022/06/explainer-why-is-india-a-major-hub-for-wildlife-trafficking/> Last visited, 15 April 2024.

recently, the town of Jalpaiguri in the Dooars district of northern West Bengal grabbed headlines as a new transit hub for the trafficking of exotic birds and animals.[55]

The airports in Chennai and Mumbai are important hubs for the widespread trafficking of reptiles, particularly turtles and tortoises, into and out of India. The most traded reptile in the world, the Indian star tortoise, is mainly transported by air from trade hubs in Karnataka, Andhra Pradesh, Gujarat, and Tamil Nadu to Thailand, Singapore, and Malaysia. Reducing Opportunities for Unlawful Trade of Endangered Species (ROUTES) website seizure data reveals that approximately 11% of trafficking animals were in plane cargo and over 54% were in checked luggage.[56] Chennai, Kolkata, Mumbai, and Delhi are the main Indian cities where these types of airport seizures occur; reptile seizures are particularly common in Chennai airport.

India's legal system is slow and overworked, making it difficult to prosecute wildlife traffickers even with strong laws protecting wildlife. International syndicates are frequently involved in wildlife crime, making international coordination and collaboration necessary for a successful prosecution. This can be a difficult and time-consuming process. The issue of wildlife trafficking via airports is complex and calls for cooperation and coordination between law enforcement agencies, international organisations, and the Indian government. Mitigating this threat and preserving India's rich biodiversity for future generations requires bolstering airport security, tackling corruption, increasing public awareness, and fostering international cooperation.

Trafficking illegal wildlife through Mumbai airport is becoming a more common practice. Indian airports have seen the seizure of tiger skins, elephant tusks, pangolin scales, and Indian star tortoises, among other wildlife parts and derivatives. Air travel is more popular and efficient than ever, which makes it easier than ever for traffickers to use it to smuggle illicit wildlife products over international borders. The World Wildlife Report 2020 states that between 1999 and 2018, 6,000 different species of plants and animals were collected.[57] The discovery of alleged traffickers from 150 different nations demonstrates the global nature of the issue of wildlife crime. It has been reported that "India is among the top ten countries in terms of using the airline sector for wildlife trafficking, this is an unwanted accolade".[58]

Managing animal threats, which can endanger both aircraft safety and biodiversity, is a major concern for Mumbai Airport.[59] The airport needs to put in place a

---

[55] 'In Plane Sight: Wildlife Trafficking in the Air Transport Sector', *Traffic*, available at <https://www.traffic.org/publications/reports/in-plane-sight/> Last visited, 15 April 2024.

[56] 'Trafficking Data', *Reducing Opportunities for Unlawful Transport of Endangered Species*, available at <https://routespartnership.org/#:~:text=The%20USAID%20Reducing%20Opportunities%20for,to%20disrupt%20wildlife%20trafficking%20activities> Last visited, 15 March 2024.

[57] 'World Wildlife Crime Report 2020', *UNODC*, available at <https://www.unodc.org/documents/data-and-analysis/wildlife/2020/World_Wildlife_Report_2020_9July.pdf> Last visited, 15 April 2024.

[58] *Id.*

[59] 'New initiative combats wildlife trafficking in India's airports', *UNEP*, available at <https://www.unep.org/news-and-stories/story/new-initiative-combats-wildlife-trafficking-indias-airports> Last visited, 15 March 2024.

thorough wildlife management strategy that includes routine wildlife activity monitoring and assessment within and outside the airport perimeter to solve these problems. This could entail altering the ecosystem by getting rid of plants that draw birds and other wildlife, as well as using deterrent techniques like radar technology and bird scare devices to identify and lessen the likelihood of wildlife encounters. The airport should also collaborate closely with specialists in wildlife and the environment to make sure that these actions do not negatively affect nearby ecosystems. It is also critical to work in tandem with regional authorities and local communities to raise awareness and carry out long-term wildlife conservation plans. The Chicago Convention, in particular Annex 14 on Aerodromes, provides guidelines and best practices for the construction and maintenance of airports, including measures for managing animal hazards. In accordance with these regulations, airports must take action to reduce the hazards that wildlife poses to aircraft safety. For international airports like Mumbai, which have to coordinate their operations with international safety standards, adherence to these criteria is essential.

Apart from the Chicago Convention, safeguarding animals and ecosystems is emphasised in other environmental accords including the Convention on Biological Diversity 1992 and the Convention on Migratory Species 1979.[60] These agreements highlight how crucial it is to protect biodiversity while simultaneously resolving conflicts between people and wildlife. Mumbai Airport can create a more comprehensive strategy for managing wildlife by including these international commitments and striking a balance between the necessity for aircraft safety and environmental preservation. This strategy not only guarantees adherence to global norms but also establishes the airport as a conscientious participant in the worldwide endeavour to preserve wildlife and biodiversity.

4.3 *Human Rights Violations*

Human rights concerns are not specifically addressed by the Chicago Convention, which is mainly concerned with the security and regularity of international air travel. Nonetheless, its provisions have an impact on how airlines and airports function, which may affect human rights. The Chicago Convention on Facilitation, for example, has standards for border controls, customs, and immigration procedures in Annex 9. These standards can have an impact on human rights, especially when it comes to how passengers, refugees, and other people under airport authorities are treated. Human rights breaches involving specific Customs agents compelling travellers to undress and submit to body scanning without authorisation or court orders have been

---

[60] The Convention on Biological Diversity of 5 June 1992 (1760 U.N.T.S. 69); Michael Bowman, Peter Davies, & Catherine Redgwell, 'The Convention on the Conservation of Migratory Species,' in Michael Bowman, Peter Davies, & Catherine Redgwell (eds.), *Lyster's International Wildlife Law*, (Cambridge: Cambridge University Press, 2010) pp. 535–584 at p. 563.

documented by the CSMIA.[61] In 2024, the National Human Rights Commission of India sent a notice to the Directorate General of Civil Aviation over reports that an 80-year-old man died at the Mumbai airport after he was refused a wheelchair despite a prior request to an airline and forced to walk.[62] The Chicago Convention promotes treating everyone equally and humanely at airports, especially when it comes to immigration and customs processes. The Chicago Convention, although not specifically a human rights treaty, lays the groundwork for guaranteeing that international air travel is carried out in a way that upholds fundamental human dignity. To reduce human rights violations at airports like Mumbai, adherence to these principles, as well as national laws and international human rights treaties, is essential.

5 Conclusion

An evaluation of Mumbai Airport's compliance with international standards and best practices provides a comprehensive picture of the facility's security protocols, operational efficiency, and guest experience. The airport has done a fantastic job of bringing itself into compliance with international standards, but there are still certain sections that require maintenance and repair. Important elements include technological integration, environmental sustainability, infrastructure development, and stakeholder engagement greatly influence the airport's future course. Mumbai Airport's adherence to international standards and best practices will be essential to ensure its longevity, resilience, and competitiveness in the aviation industry. It is also important that the governance of Mumbai airport adapts to meet global trends and challenges. The airport must continue to be proactive, innovative, and sensitive to new requirements and opportunities if it is to retain its position as the premier entry point into India and a benchmark for excellence in the aviation industry.

---

61 'FPJ Investigation: Rampant Human Rights Violations at Mumbai Airport', *Free Press Journal*, available at <https://www.freepressjournal.in/mumbai/fpj-investigation-rampant-human-rights-violations-at-mumbai-airport#:~:text=Cases%20of%20violation%20of%20human,their%20consent%20or%20magistrate%20orders.> Last visited, 10 March 2024.

62 Press Release, 'NHRC takes suo motu cognizance of media reports on the death of an 80-year-old who had to walk due to non-availability of a wheelchair at the Mumbai airport', *National Human Rights Commission*, available at <https://nhrc.nic.in/media/press-release/nhrc-takes-suo-motu-cognizance-media-reports-death-80-year-old-who-had-walk-due> Last visited, 20 February 2024.

Index

© The Editor(s) (if applicable) and The Author(s), under exclusive license to Springer Nature Singapore Pte Ltd. 2025
S. Bhat B. (ed.), *Aerodrome Governance in Asia*,
https://doi.org/10.1007/978-981-96-7568-5

MIX
Papier aus verantwortungsvollen Quellen
Paper from responsible sources
FSC® C105338

If you have any concerns about our products,
you can contact us on
ProductSafety@springernature.com

In case Publisher is established outside the EU,
the EU authorized representative is:
Springer Nature Customer Service Center GmbH
Europaplatz 3, 69115 Heidelberg, Germany

Printed by Libri Plureos GmbH
in Hamburg, Germany